This book would not have been possible without the help and cooperation of each of the Wildlife Trusts it features. We would also like to say a big thank you to Jules Acton, Adam Cormack and Phillip Precey for their input and expertise.

Additional thanks go to Caroline Grogan, Steven Morris and Natalia Reddy for their invaluable assistance sourcing images and content.

For a full list of photo credits, please see page 294.

Contents

Foreword

by Chris Packham

I can set my trusty alarm clock and wake with the comforting knowledge that on any given Sunday I can visit a fabulous selection of Wildlife Trust reserves and enjoy amazing encounters with wildlife.

I know a spot where frog orchids will bloom, where glow-worms will twinkle, where nightingales sing and badgers snuffle. I am further excited that in my short life I have only had the pleasure of visiting a fraction of these reserves and that there are lots more of these wonderful refuges where the creatures and plants which stir us so much are safely conserved with the utmost care. They are out there on all of our doorsteps just waiting to be explored, and it's a rich legacy that we, the current crop of naturalists, walkers and picnickers, have inherited. Thus we are indebted to the forethought and often not inconsiderable endeavours of past generations of dedicated nature lovers...

But there is a problem. As I travel to these little jewels in our landscape I journey through huge tracts of green but not so pleasant land. It's 'countryside' as we know it, but it's not full of life by any means, and our precious reserves can be like tiny islands lost in the sea of our 'manscape' – as such they are, for all their beauty and our concern, definitely imperilled. Well, the time has come to redress this and the Trusts are already beginning some exciting and imaginative work.

You see, we are no longer solely concerned with wrapping up these little utopias and trying to keep them as they are, or were – we are now beginning to integrate them into a new joined-up Living Landscape so that all the flora and fauna in these invaluable arks can spread out, mix and successfully colonise new areas. And it's not only about the wildlife: in an intelligent and ground breaking series of projects we are renovating the countryside for people too. This will, I believe, be essential to the future of conservation in the UK. The economies of whole communities will benefit sustainably from the schemes, and opportunities for recreation, relaxation and healthier lifestyles will develop in tandem with greater security for our wildlife. And it's not just a rural objective – the same principals are being applied in urban areas too, even in the hearts of our largest cities, and it's here that the benefits could be the richest of all. We urgently need to engage this 'new' population with nature. We need to develop ownership of what can be very rich communities of species so that more people grow up with an affinity with nature and a real desire to preserve it, and to achieve this they need to meet it and learn to love it!

So set your alarms and go and enjoy this incredible selection of reserves and share in our optimism that not only will their future be secure but that they will be some of the key building blocks to a new wild UK. Don't forget your sandwiches, and make sure you dress up warmly (so my mum still keeps telling me!).

chunk!

How to use this book

This is more than just a guidebook. It is a companion to your discovery of the wealth of extraordinary nature that the UK has to offer. It has been compiled by rangers and wardens, Trust members and day visitors: in short, anyone who has been enthralled by nature at Wildlife Trust reserves up and down the country. We hope their enthusiasm will help fuel your own.

The book contains detailed maps and public transport instructions to help you access the reserves with greater ease and, hopefully, impact less on the fragile nature they protect. It also includes detailed information on facilities and access. A full list of the icons can be found on the right.

Unless otherwise stated the reserves are open all year during daylight hours. Most reserves are free to enter, but where this isn't the case, details of entry fees are included. If in doubt, please call the reserve warden or the Trust headquarters before you set out.

Finally, although every effort has been made to ensure accuracy in *Wildlife Walks*, reserves are living places, and may change. You may discover that a hide has been built since the book went to print, or that an access road has altered its name.

Perhaps you would like to tell us why a particular reserve appealed to you. Please let us know, and if we incorporate your comments in the next edition, we will send you a free copy. *Wildlife Walks* is not just about nature reserves, it is about the people who run them, visit them, and enjoy our natural wonders. Please send your comments, with name and address, to: *Wildlife Walks*, Think Publishing, The Pall Mall Deposit, 124-128 Barlby Road, London W10 6BL, or email editorial@thinkpublishing.co.uk.

ICONS / SYMBOLS

- P Parking
- WC WC
- Disabled facilities (only limited where indicated)
- Information/visitor centre
- Cafe/restaurant
- Shop
- Picnic area
- Hides
- Information boards
- Events/guided walks
- Family days/Wildlife Watch group
- Cycle hire
- Dogs on leads

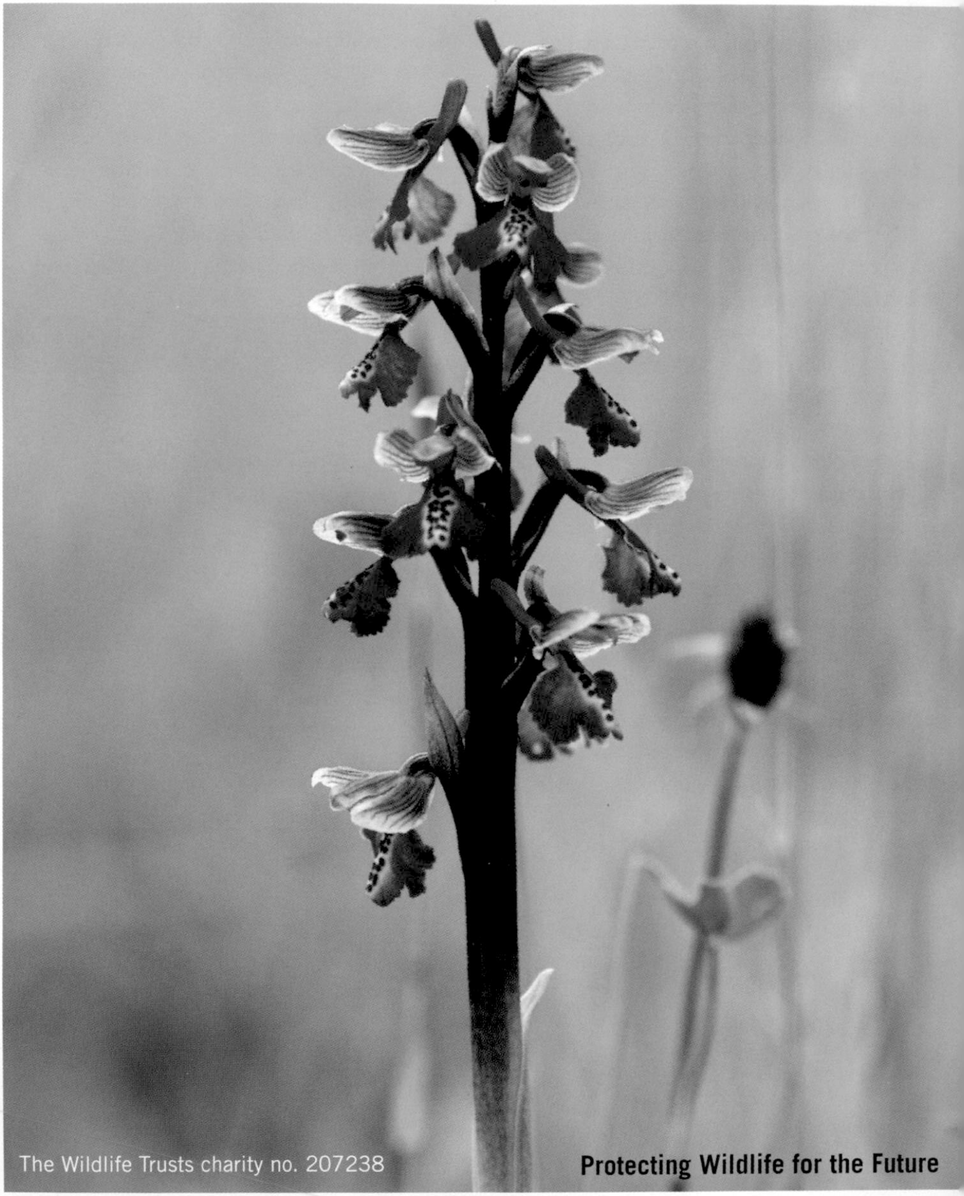

Green-winged orchid - Paul Lane

About The Wildlife Trusts

by Stephanie Hilborne

The Wildlife Trusts are all about people taking action for wildlife in their own local patch. Vitally, this is happening across the whole of the UK.

We have nearly 800,000 members and are the largest voluntary organisation championing and protecting the full range of the UK's habitats and species, whether they be in the countryside, in cities or at sea.

There are 47 Wildlife Trusts across the UK, as well as the Isle of Man and Alderney. The first Trust was formed in the 1920s and there was complete coverage across the UK by the mid-1960s. Each Trust has a unique knowledge of its own unique area: understanding not only the ecology, but the culture of the areas it covers and the people who live nearby, many of whom have devoted their lives to

THE WILDLIFE TRUSTS

The Wildlife Trusts manage 2,282 reserves covering over 93,409 hectares

Each year there are four million visits to Wildlife Trust reserves, and visitor and education centres

Volunteers give 6-7,000 days per year to support the work of The Wildlife Trusts

700,000 people take part in Wildlife Trust events, walks and talks each year

4,000 people take part in The Wildlife Trusts wildlife identification training schemes per year

The Wildlife Trusts hold 13,500 events per year

The Wildlife Trusts engage with 125,300 students through visits to schools, youth groups and colleges per year. They work with 5,600 schools as part of long-term projects, advising on greening their grounds

There are 150,000 members of Wildlife Watch

The Wildlife Trusts review around 94,000 planning applications per year

The Wildlife Trusts advise 5,900 landowners per year on wildlife-friendly land management

Protecting **Wildlife** for the Future
www.wildlifetrusts.org

nurturing the wildlife in their reserves.

It isn't only adult members and volunteers who are so dedicated to caring for reserves near their homes. Of our members 150,000 belong to our junior branch, Wildlife Watch. Many of them are involved in looking after local green spaces, learning about the plants and creatures there as well as enjoying activities from pond-dipping to fungi hunting.

Why is this all so important? Because the UK's wildlife is innately valuable and also because it is vital for our own well-being.

Wildlife is beautiful and diverse and its complexity recounts the story of millions of years of evolution. We, in turn, are very much a part of the ecosystem, and a healthy environment, rich in wildlife, is extremely important to us.

And wildlife in the UK needs the support of people now more than ever. The threats our flora and fauna face in the 21st century mean we have to redouble our efforts. Loss of habitat, development, intensive farming, overexploitation of the sea – all these things put the survival of vulnerable species at risk, and the added impact of a changing climate means they are under more pressure than ever before.

To adapt to such threats, the UK's wildlife will need to move along 'climate corridors' through town and country. Wildlife has adapted before, after the last Ice Age, but this time the change is faster and now there are so many obstacles: cities, motorways and expanses of hostile countryside.

But there are plenty of reasons to be optimistic about the future. The Wildlife Trusts have a strategy for both the land and the marine environment – A Living Landscape and Living Seas – and that is to restore those environments on a scale large enough to give wildlife room to manoeuvre and thrive.

Nature reserves are key to this: wildlife-rich areas from which both plants and animals can recolonise the wider landscape. The 2,250-plus Wildlife Trusts nature reserves in the UK cover more than 90,000 hectares of land and it is due to the forethought and care of the people behind The Wildlife Trusts movement that we have these strongholds, which are vital for a future rich in wildlife for everyone and to give us all renewed hope for the future.

STEPHANIE HILBORNE,
CHIEF EXECUTIVE, THE WILDLIFE TRUSTS

The Countryside Code

- **Be safe, plan ahead and follow any signs**

Even when going out locally, it's best to get the latest information about where and when you can go. For example, your rights to go on some areas of open land may be restricted while work is carried out for safety reasons, or during breeding seasons. Follow advice and local signs, and be prepared for the unexpected.

- **Leave gates and property as you find them**

Please respect the working life of the countryside, as our actions can affect people's livelihoods, our heritage, and the safety and welfare of animals and ourselves.

- **Protect plants and animals and take your litter home**

We have a responsibility to protect our countryside now and for future generations, so make sure you don't harm animals, birds, plants or trees.

- **Keep dogs under close control**

The countryside is a great place to exercise dogs, but it's every owner's duty to make sure their dog is not a danger or nuisance to farm animals, wildlife or other people.

- **Consider other people**

Showing consideration and respect for other people makes the countryside a pleasant environment for everyone – at home, at work and at leisure.

For more information visit:
www.countrysideaccess.gov.uk

Volunteers

The Wildlife Trusts need you

In 2008-09 around 39,000 people gave their time and energy to The Wildlife Trusts, which is the largest UK voluntary organisation dedicated to conserving the full range of the UK's habitats and species. The numbers are impressive, but there is always room for more, particularly as Trusts tackle new issues – either 'out there' managing areas for wildlife and people or in the day-to-day technicalities of the running of our businesses.

Chair of The Wildlife Trusts Michael Allen says: 'Volunteers are The Wildlife Trusts. The passion and commitment of volunteers for their local environment is vital to our effectiveness. The enthusiasm, expertise and specialist knowledge that so many volunteers contribute is our life blood.'

It's not always about scrub-bashing or dry stone-walling. Volunteers of all ages and backgrounds are involved at every level and in every corner of our work: supporting communications work, developing IT systems, promoting campaigns, working with children, providing legal advice and much more.

Martin Palmer found he had more time on his hands as his children grew older so visited the Devon Wildlife Trust website to seek a volunteering opportunity.

'The volunteer "database designer" caught my attention and I have been part of a small project team making this area of work easier and more efficient. We are aiming to lower costs and to release officer and volunteer time for other tasks as well as improving data quality. It's gratifying to be using my IT skills for the benefit, albeit indirectly, of wildlife and it's something I can do that fits in with my domestic circumstances. Ideal really!'

Across the UK, the day-to-day management of our reserves is largely in the hands of committed volunteers. **Gemma Burrows**, from Nottinghamshire, started volunteering to gain some hands-on experience after finishing her degree. 'I have learned more about practical conservation and habitat management than I did during my three years at university,' she says. 'Each site has its own unique charm and natural beauty, and it is a privilege to be part of the management of the reserves. You can look over the site at the end of the day, see what the team has achieved and feel proud that you have actually made a difference.'

The chance to learn new skills attracts a huge range of people. **Jane Ashworth** was looking to change her career and gain

practical skills when she signed up for three days a week for six months with Wiltshire Wildlife Trust.

'I found the promise that "no two days will be the same" very appealing, and that is exactly how it has proved to be! I've had a fantastic time getting out onto reserves I didn't know existed and getting stuck in at grassroots level in enhancing the biodiversity for both wildlife and people. In the last six months I've gained valuable conservation skills – hedgelaying, coppicing, boardwalk maintenance, scrub clearance and so on – while simultaneously working and having fun with a wonderful group of volunteers of all ages and from all walks of life. I'd recommend getting involved in outdoor conservation tasks with the Thursday or Sunday groups to anyone. I was new to the county and didn't know the area – people made me feel welcome and part of the group straight away.

'I start a new key volunteer role next week based in Devizes. I will be one of four Biodiversity Action Plan volunteers, working two days a week for four months, updating the Wiltshire and Swindon Biodiversity Action Plan websites and recording biodiversity data onto the BAP database. I will have the opportunity to get involved with external partner organisations and attend local and regional meetings. All change!'

Sue Holmes has been volunteering at Norton Wildlife Watch (NWW) Group for 20 years. 'The enthusiasm which started the group has endured. So what has kept the ball rolling so long? First and foremost, it has to be

the members, and by my reckoning NWW has kept over 250 children between four and 16 occupied over the 20 years. They've come from a dozen different schools and varied backgrounds, both urban and rural. Some stay with us for eight or nine years – what loyalty! Yes, we play games, yes, we have fun, but there is a serious purpose to everything we do. My Watch leader role is about getting alongside the young people and supporting their ideas, helping them to see a wider perspective while keeping feet firmly on the ground. It is a privilege to work with them in their leisure time. After all, they choose to come. With the ever-pressing need to get the environmental message across, and to educate and inform the public and society at large, I am inspired by the way young people engaging with policy makers can make that all-important difference. Our motivation concerns the future of our planet no less, and that's a big agenda! When asked to describe Watch in a nutshell for the 2008 calendar we have produced for our 20th-birthday year, a 13-year-old member said: "We make a local difference with a global impact…and it's fun!".'

The Wildlife Trusts have thousands of active volunteers who can vouch for the fact that volunteering not only benefits their chosen cause, but provides a warm glow, too – both literally and metaphorically.

To find out about opportunities to volunteer with your Wildlife Trust visit www.wildlifetrusts.org or call 01636 677711 for local contacts.

SOUTH WEST

From the rockpools in the coves of Cornwall to the tree-lined river valleys of Devon and the chalky grasslands of Wiltshire's Downs, the south-west corner of England is not only beautiful, but it's abundant with wildlife.

There are marine animals that can be spotted here that you are unlikely to see anywhere else in the country, such as turtles who feed in Cornish waters around August to October time.

Basking sharks are also summer visitors. Their large dorsal fins look pretty terrifying when seen on the sea's surface, but this huge creature only eats plankton and poses no danger to man. Some people have even been lucky enough to spot pilot whales off the coast of Devon.

On the seashore, the rockpools are a treasure trove for the wildlife explorer, revealing crabs, starfish, blennies, gobies and all manner of seaweeds and anemones.

On land, there is a rich diversity of habitats whether you want to walk through beautiful scenery or stay put in one place.

Many of the woodlands of Devon are ancient woodlands on steep hillsides that tumble down to crystal clear rivers and brooks. Walking among the old and gnarled trees is charming at any time of the year but, come springtime, when the forest floors bloom into colour with bluebells, wood anemones and primroses, it's a veritable delight. *Tarka the Otter* was set in Devon and there are otters living in many rivers and streams in the area. However, you'll be lucky to spot this shy and quiet animal. If you think you're getting close, look out for tracks and bubbles rising from the water.

The woodlands are also home to badgers, bats, dormice and owls, among others. Although these animals are nocturnal, many begin their night-time adventures around dusk.

Far easier to see, whatever your location, are the birds – and the south west has a huge selection. On the open moorland of Dartmoor there are golden plover, red grouse and skylarks, while the estuaries fill up in the winter time with migrating waders, ducks and geese. The Exe Estuary is well known as a spot where you can see them in their thousands.

Fields and hedgerows are also alive with birds, while the numerous hay meadows in the area are filled with flowers and butterflies throughout spring and early summer.

Whenever you visit the area, and wherever you go, you'll find yourself on the doorstep of a nature reserve, and you won't be disappointed with what you see.

Opposite: Bossiney Haven, Cornwall

NOT TO BE MISSED

- **BLAKEHILL FARM**

  A LEAF farm, a wildlife haven, one of the largest expanses of lowland neutral hay meadow in the UK and a slice of living history thanks to the role it played in World War II.

- **BROWNSEA ISLAND**

  Amongst the best venues in the South West for birdwatching thanks to the 1,000-plus birds who congregate here every year.

- **THE ISLES OF SCILLY**

  A unique gem of an archipelago that catches the Gulf Stream and boasts a unique diversity of plant, animal and birdlife. Also good for spotting whales and dolphins.

- **LOWER WOODS SSSI**

  One of England's largest ancient oak-ash woodlands with over 70 ancient woodland plant species to discover.

- **WEMBURY VMCA**

  Wembury's rocky shore is bursting with sea life. Look out for the porcelain crabs, squat lobsters and spiny starfish in its rockpools.

- **WESTHAY MOOR NNR**

  Somerset Wildlife Trust's pilot project for the Avalon Marshes, Westhay Moor is home to bitterns, otters and a winter roost of up to 10 million starlings.

Cornwall

About the Trust

Cornwall Wildlife Trust is a registered charity based in Truro, although they have nature reserves and volunteers throughout Cornwall. As well as organising a wide range of wildlife-related events and activities, they also support many wildlife and conservation specialist groups working on a variety of projects. Involving people in their work is essential to the future of nature conservation in Cornwall.

Cornwall Wildlife Trust ☎ 01872 273939
www.cornwallwildlifetrust.org.uk

Baker's Pit

Near St Ives
OS Map SW 481359; **Map Ref** A11

This is a former china clay extraction works with a standing engine house and settling tanks still intact and consists of lowland heath and open water. There are merlins and hen harriers in winter, white-throats in summer, and an excellent display of heathland flora in late summer. A network of paths with inclines crisscross the reserve, which can be muddy, especially in winter.

Five Acres

Near Truro
OS Map SW 793485; **Map Ref** A6

Demonstration wildlife garden created by the BBC *Ground Force* team, with mixed trees and ponds. Spring brings frantic bird activity, whereas summer brings out the damselflies and dragonflies, and butterflies are numerous around the flowering plants. Trust offices are open Monday to Friday, 8.30am to 4.30pm.

Kennall Vale

Near Falmouth
OS Map SW 753375; **Map Ref** A12

This reserve features woodland, a river, a quarry and old gunpowder works buildings. Breeding dippers, otters, stoats and Tunbridge filmy ferns may be seen. The tracks are muddy and uneven.

Maer Lake

Bude
OS Map SX 206076; **Map Ref** A1

Consisting of open water and marsh, Maer Lake has excellent birdlife and North American rarities in autumn. Golden plover, wigeon and curlew can be spotted. There is no visitor access, but there are excellent views from the adjacent elevated lane.

Penlee Battery

Rame Head
OS Map SX 436492; **Map Ref** A9

Penlee consists of grassland and scrub on a late-Victorian and Edwardian military installation. There are deer, bee orchids, bats and occasional rare birds during migration, as well as panoramic sea views. Its paths are fine all year round, but the site is only partially accessible to wheelchairs.

Ropehaven Cliffs

Near St Austell
OS Map SX 033489; **Map Ref** A8

These wooded, steep cliffs are home to colonies of fulmar and shag, and breeding peregrine, as well as bats. They are part of the South West Coast Path. The terrain is uneven and muddy, and steps are provided over steep sections.

Upton Towans SSSI

Near Gwithian
OS Map SW 780514; **Map Ref** A10

This is a large sand-dune complex on the site of a former explosives works. Flora and fauna includes pyramidal orchid, petalwort, silver-studded blue butterfly, bats and the solitary mining bee. Some paths are grassy and slippery with inclines.

Greena Moor

Near Week St Mary; **OS Map** SX 234963; **Map Ref** A2

ACCESS/CONDITIONS: There are pathways across the fields, but not the Culm grassland. Surfaces are uneven and can be very wet and muddy.
HOW TO GET THERE: Greena Moor is 1 mile south of the village of Week St Mary. From the A39, 5 miles south of Bude, take the turning for Week St Mary. In Week St Mary turn right towards Week Green, then fork right. Access to the reserve is via a path off to the left, after three-quarters of a mile. Park on the side of the road (room for two cars).
WALKING TIME: The reserve is 91 acres (37ha). A leisurely walk around the nature trail will take approximately 2 hours.

This is Cornwall's largest area of Culm grassland, preserved by a local farming family. There are fantastic floral displays in the summer with meadow thistle and whorled caraway. This damp, diverse grassland is alive with invertebrates including marsh fritillary and marbled white butterflies in summer. There are good numbers of snipe in winter due to its wet, sponge-like nature. Spring is when the flowers start to show, and in summer butterflies are on the wing among the wildflowers. In autumn and winter the site is very wet and good for waders including snipe. The site is jointly owned and managed with Plantlife.

Helman Tor

Near Bodmin; **OS Map** SX 062615; **Map Ref** A4

ACCESS/CONDITIONS: The Tor's Wilderness Trail has some small narrow lanes and sections of boardwalk. Paths can be wet and muddy in places with difficult terrain and some steep slopes. The Breney Common entrance is suitable for wheelchair access.
HOW TO GET THERE: Helman Tor is 2.5 miles from Bodmin towards Lanivet. Take the first left after passing under the A30 bridge. You can walk to Helman Tor along the Saints' Way. There are small car parks at Helman Tor and Breney Common, and limited parking at Red Moor.
WALKING TIME: The reserve is 536 acres (217ha). The Wilderness Trail, approximately 5 miles in length, takes 3 to 4 hours to walk.
30-MINUTE VISIT: Head straight to the top of Helman Tor where the reserve can be viewed from on high. On a clear day it is also possible to see both the north and south coasts from here.

A large wetland complex with a variety of habitats including dry and wet heathland, mire, sphagnum bog, wet woodland and open water. It is the Cornwall Wildlife Trust's largest inland nature reserve and a CGS with the remains of a Neolithic hill settlement. In the spring the dense areas of willow carr are alive with birdsong as willow tits, reed buntings, sedge and grasshopper warblers pair up and breed. When the warm days of summer arrive, the ponds swarm with dragonflies and damselflies and the grassland/heath brims with butterflies including the rare marsh fritillary. Sundews can be found in wet areas among sphagnum mosses. In autumn the heathland is at its best and ablaze with colour from the yellow gorse to the purple and pinks of the different heathers. The panoramic views from the top of Helman Tor can be stunning in the winter when the light is crisp and clear and it is not uncommon to find yourself looking down on a soaring raptor.

The Saints' Way passes through the reserve – this walk across Cornwall was once undertaken by cattle drovers from Ireland, then by pilgrims who built churches en route. A feeling of wilderness abounds as you pass through haunting wet willow woodland to wide open tracts of heath. As you reach the top of Helman Tor at the end of your visit, you given an illuminating perspective of the landscape below.

St George's Island

Near Looe; **OS Map** SX 257515; **Map Ref** A7

OPENING TIMES: The boat to the island runs from Easter to late summer when tide, weather and sea conditions allow. There is a boat fee plus a landing fee.

ACCESS/CONDITIONS: Paths around the island can be wet and slippery at times. The boat is not specifically equipped for wheelchair access and disembarks onto the beach or a small jetty with steep steps.

HOW TO GET THERE: The island boat leaves from East Looe steps, a chalkboard giving details of crossing times. The trip takes approximately 20 minutes. There are regular trains to Looe from Liskeard, 8 miles away; there are also local buses from Polperro, Liskeard and outlying villages to Looe.

WALKING TIME: The island is 22 acres (9ha) in size. The full circuit takes about 1 hour. Visits normally last 2 hours but can be longer depending on the tides.

A marine nature reserve with woodland, maritime grassland, cliffs, sand, shingle and a rocky reef, St George's Island is one of only a few inhabited islands off the Cornwall coast. On occasions you'll be escorted by a school of dolphins and watched off the boat by a grey seal. The islanders have become accustomed to the sea bringing them daily surprises, ranging from cannonballs to beached whales. The tide dictates how long you'll be able to stay, but we can guarantee a warm welcome and a glimpse of life on a Cornish island. In the spring the small woodland has a carpet of wild garlic and bluebells and the cool shade is a welcome resting spot on the trail around the island. Parts of the trail are closed in the spring and summer to protect nesting seabirds. The second largest breeding colony of great black-backed gulls in Cornwall can be found on the island. The cliffs are pink with swathes of thrift in the early summer and this is the time of year to see basking sharks feeding along the coast. In autumn and winter, gales batter the island and make sea-watching spectacular – although at this time of year the public can only watch from the mainland and think of the island's inhabitants, who are sometimes stranded for months.

WILDLIFE FACT: BROWN LONG-EARED BATS

Although the brown long-eared bat does have very long ears – about 5cm, the same length as its body – you can't always see them. The ears get tucked away under wings or rolled up like rams' horns, leaving just little pointy inner lobes visible. When they are up and in use, they are incredibly sensitive and the brown long-eared bat will often use hearing to locate its insect prey rather than use echo location.

Cabilla and Redrice Woods

Near Bodmin; **OS Map** SW 129652; **Map Ref** A3

ACCESS/CONDITIONS: There is good access throughout summer, but paths become wet and muddy in the winter. There is the occasional steep incline.
HOW TO GET THERE: Take the train to Bodmin Parkway and then walk to the reserve – approximately 10 minutes. By car, from the A38 east of Bodmin, take the turning towards Cardinham. Cross the bridge over the River Fowey and access is via the first track on the right.
WALKING TIME: The reserve is 190 acres (77ha) in size, and the full circuit takes an hour and a half at an easy pace.
30-MINUTE VISIT: From the entrance follow the main track for 500 metres, then left over the stile. Follow this track until it rejoins the main track and head right to return to the entrance.
A MEMBER SAYS: 'If you're a woodland enthusiast, look no further. It has everything – it's paradise on your doorstep.'

Among the largest ancient woodlands in Cornwall, Cabilla and Redrice Woods are undoubtedly a gem, an extensive area of mixed woodland with ancient oak and hazel coppice as well as river and wetland belts. The diverse habitats in this reserve encourage a variety of residents, and archaeological remains add interest. The wildlife on view incorporates all areas of interest for the naturalist from insect life to reptiles, birds and mammals. No two visits are the same and there is always something moving or making a noise to make you stop and investigate. Spring is by far the most colourful and spectacular time as wood anemones, bluebells and ramsons are in full blossom. Their bright colours and smells are a delight and a welcome sight after the bleak and grey wintry scene. Woodland birds such as pied flycatcher, nuthatch, treecreeper and woodpecker add a further sensory delight as they prepare for breeding and rearing young. In summer the woodland rides are teeming with butterfly life and on a calm dusky evening up to five species of bat can be seen hunting for prey. Visitors may be lucky to spot an otter or kingfisher along the river, or a rare blue ground beetle. Late autumn is a fungus bonanza and a treasure trove for the lichenologist with many rarities to be found. As winter sets in it's your last chance to see dormice (in the company of Trust staff) before hibernation.

DID YOU KNOW?

- **The adits that the bats occupy were mined for silver and lead in the 18th century.**
- **Parts of the wood have not changed for over 400 years and the network of paths are exactly the same as shown on the 1602 Lanhydrock map.**

Churchtown Farm CNR

Saltash; **OS Map** SX 417582 and SX 419575; **Map Ref** A5

ACCESS/CONDITIONS: Most of the path network is unsurfaced and becomes slippery when wet. Some areas are steep and uneven especially the track off Wearde Road.

HOW TO GET THERE: Churchtown Farm is on the outskirts of Saltash, behind St Stephens Church. A Little Blue Bus runs from Saltash centre to just outside the church. By car, from the A38 turn into Callington Road towards Burraton. Turn right into Church Road, then into St Stephens Road to the church. There is space for five cars at the entrance on Wearde Road but please do not block the road or entrances. If this space is full, park on the school road and walk down the hill.

WALKING TIME: The reserve is 150 acres (61ha) in size and the full circuit of 1.3 miles takes 2 hours at an easy pace.

30-MINUTE VISIT: Walk down the track from Wearde Road, over the railway bridge, turn left towards the beach, cut through the hedge opening onto the beach, turn right along the beach and cut back through the hedge into Point Field.

A MEMBER SAYS: 'I have walked this site for many years, and whatever the weather or time of year the atmosphere and ambience overwhelm me every time.'

Churchtown Farm CNR is situated within the Tamar Valley AONB with extensive views over the River Lynher, Antony Passage, Forder Creek, the River Tamar and beyond to Devonport and Plymouth. The majority of the reserve is farmland consisting of hay meadows and some arable fields, although there is also woodland, wetland, scrub, shoreline and mudflats, which are within the boundary of Plymouth Sound and Estuaries (cSAC), an extensive network of species-rich hedgerows and two disused quarries (designated CGS). In spring, the hedgerows are alive with birdsong and a plethora of wildflowers. Summer and autumn see the hay meadows in their full-colour glory, alive with butterflies, insect life, scurrying small mammals and flocks of seed-eating birds especially finches. The arrival of wading birds in winter is an unforgettable spectacle and the mudflats become crowded with oystercatchers, greenshank, redshank, egrets and the elegant avocet.

DID YOU KNOW?

- The large concrete blocks at Churchtown Farm were the anchors for barrage balloons that used to protect the area during World War II.
- The headland around some of the shore is composed of slates which contain tiny fossilised creatures called ostracods, which help geologists accurately date the rock.

Windmill Farm

Lizard; **OS Map** SW 694153; **Map Ref** A13

ACCESS/CONDITIONS: Generally level with some gentle slopes. It is on the whole dry in summer but in wet weather, particularly in the winter, the ground becomes waterlogged and wheelchair access is not feasible. There are some boardwalks. Cattle graze at certain times of the year so please shut gates after use.
HOW TO GET THERE: The reserve is 1 mile north of Lizard village. There is a regular bus service from Helston to Lizard. By car, take the A3083 from Helston to Lizard and turn right at the 'Wild Camping' sign (this is not a Trust sign). Follow the lane till you see the windmill.
WALKING TIME: The reserve is 185 acres (75ha) in size. The full circuit can be walked in 1 to 2 hours.
30-MINUTE VISIT: From the yard, head south towards the arable fields for birds or from the windmill, or walk west out onto the main heathland area for butterflies and Cornish heath.
A MEMBER SAYS: 'In spring, the hedgerows are alive with singing migrant birds; butterflies abound on a warm summer's day; in autumn the flowering heathers and gorse are just glorious; and in winter it's bleak and windswept, but moody and magnificent.'

Windmill Farm is within a Cornwall AONB and near a Heritage Coast, three County Wildlife sites, the Lizard cSAC, West Lizard SSSI and a SAM. Windmill Farm is still in its development stages – you could be the first to identify a rare dragonfly on the new pools, or a rare migrant wader on the scrape. If you don't get lucky, just sit on the pillbox by the windmill and enjoy the magnificent view across Predannick Downs to the sea. During spring and summer a range of birds breed, including grasshopper and willow warbler, reed bunting, skylark and house sparrow. Late spring and early summer also sees our important colony of the rare marsh fritillary butterfly. In autumn migrating warblers and finches are seen in the hedges and arable fields, while swallow and meadow pipit hunt over the hay stubbles. Migrating wheatears and whinchats rest on the hay bales. The heathland is a picture with the Cornish heath and western gorse in flower. Winter brings lapwing and golden plover. The wet heathlands and scrub are host to snipe and woodcock, and the screech of water rails can be heard.

DID YOU KNOW?

- In the 1820s the notorious 'Windmill Gang' of sheep rustlers used the windmill as a hideout.
- The reserve contains a Scheduled Ancient Monument (SAM) – the 17th century windmill – as well as Bronze Age barrows and World War II pillboxes.

Devon

About the Trust

Established as a registered charity in 1962, the Devon Wildlife Trust has over 37,000 members that help it to protect the county's wildlife for the future. Around 60 full-time staff, mainly based at Cricklepit Mill in Exeter, work in a range of areas to achieve its charitable aims. With nature reserves throughout the county, DWT is closely involved in land and marine management, surveying, policy formulation and education. Hundreds of people work on a voluntary basis, organising walks, talks and conservation projects, monitoring local wildlife and raising funds.

Devon Wildlife Trust ☎ 01392 279244
www.devonwildlifetrust.org

South West

Andrew's Wood

Near Kingsbridge
OS Map SX 714520; **Map Ref** B15

Andrew's Wood covers woods and grassland over a system of fields originally farmed by the villagers of Stanton. The ruins of this hamlet can still be found at the southern end of the reserve. Today the Trust manages the grassland areas by regular scrub clearance and cutting as well as by grazing with cattle and ponies. The clearings are great for butterflies and wildflowers. There are two circular trails. Wetter parts of the site feature boardwalks and bridges.

Ash Moor

Between Meeth and Petrockstow
OS Map SS 530089; **Map Ref** B7

What is now Ash Moor reserve had been earmarked as a potential burial site during the foot and mouth crisis. However, it was never used and now its Culm, woodland and open meadows teem with wildlife. Wood white butterflies have been found breeding on the site, and skylarks, grasshopper warbler and hobbies have been regularly seen hunting the many dragonflies on the reserve. Orchids, ragged robin, vetches and buttercups are abundant in the reserve. There is a boardwalk off the Tarka Trail, and leaflets with maps of the reserve are available.

Chudleigh Knighton Heath

Near Bovey Tracey
OS Map SX 838771; **Map Ref** B12

The heath was once part of a ball-clay works, but is now a thriving nature reserve. It is rare lowland heath which is kept in good condition through grazing. The site is known for its nightjars, dragonflies and great crested newts. There is a circular route around the site, though note that terrain is uneven. Leaflets with maps of the reserve are available.

Halwill Junction

Near Okehampton
OS Map SS 443002; **Map Ref** B8

This reserve is a small section of disused railway line and was purchased in 1990 by Devon Wildlife Trust. It is a mosaic of wet and dry grassland and scrub. The glades are excellent for butterflies and wildflowers. Look out for green woodpeckers, tits and warblers in the scrub. The wet areas have frogs, and the broad-bodied chaser (pictured above) and golden-ringed dragonflies.

Lady's Wood

Near South Brent
OS Map SX 688951; **Map Ref** B9

Lady's Wood was Devon Wildlife Trust's first ever nature reserve. This small woodland is a great example of a traditional hazel coppice and each year has an array of wildflowers. The breeding bird population is typical of mixed deciduous, coppiced woodland. Lady's Wood was noted for its breeding dormouse population. Grey squirrels and foxes are present in the wood A circular path runs around the site.

Marsland

Gooseham

OS Map SS 303077; **Map Ref** B2

Marsland is a very large reserve on the northern border of Devon and Cornwall. Extending several miles inland from a dramatic coastline, this inspiring site offers something for everyone. It is an exceptionally diverse nature reserve consisting largely of a wooded, steep-sided valley, along with coastal heath and grassland, meadows, woodland glades, bracken-covered slopes and small streams and ponds. At certain times of year it is rich in wildflowers and the woodlands are alive with birds. There is a huge variety of butterfly and dragonfly, as well as otters, seals and red deer. The reserve has quite rough terrain, is rocky in parts and can be muddy.

Meshaw Moor

Between South Molton and Witheridge

OS Map SS761185; **Map Ref** B5

Meshaw Moor consists largely of Culm grassland – a rare habitat typical of north Devon supporting a profusion of wildflowers and a small population of marsh fritillary butterflies. Parts of this reserve are very wet under foot and rough in the Culm fields where there are grass tussocks. The grassland areas can broadly be divided into two types. The wetter, acid Culm fields are typical of this habitat type, being dominated by purple moor grass and rushes, together with species such as tormentil, lousewort, heath spotted and southern marsh orchids, devil's bit scabious, meadow thistle and sneezewort. The drier neutral areas are typically dominated by sweet vernal grass together with a spectacular display of black knapweed during the first half of August. Other species include ox-eye daisy and yellow rattle.

North Devon VMCA

Between Combe Martin and Croyde

Map Ref B1

From the rare to the more common, the sea and shire of the North Devon VMCA is alive with life, from the common blenny and green shore crab to the rare Devonshire cup coral and summer visitors such as the basking shark. The VMCA spans a number of beaches and villages. The beaches are open all year round.

Rackenford and Knowstone Moors

Near Tiverton

OS Map SS 828211; **Map Ref** B4

The largest remaining area of Culm grassland in north Devon – a rare habitat once typical of the area. Here, you may find marsh and pearl boardered fritillary butterflies, typical Culm wildflowers such as bog asphodel and devil's bit scabious, and breeding curlews. The Two Moors Way long distance path runs through the area. The site is mostly muddy and wet with very few paths, though at Knowstone Moor the old road provides smooth dry access onto prime Culm grassland

Warleigh Point

Near Plymouth

OS Map SX 450608; **Map Ref** B14

Warleigh Point is one of the finest examples of coastal oak woods in Devon. Overlooking the Tamar/Tavy Estuary this site is good for spotting wildfowl and waders as well as an abundance of woodland birds. The mixture of mature woodland, scrub and coppice encourages a diversity of insect life. Speckled wood butterflies are numerous and an uncommon cricket, the short winged cone head, can be found on the reserve. A good number of woodland birds breed at Warleigh, including tawny owl, great spotted woodpecker and green woodpecker. There is also a large and active rookery, and good access to the point itself.

Bystock

Near Exmouth; **OS Map** SY 034844; **Map Ref** B10

ACCESS/CONDITIONS: An easy-access path leads onto the reserve with views over the reservoir. This track is suitable for pushchairs and wheelchairs. Paths across the rest of the reserve vary, as some are unsurfaced. An ideal place for the family to explore.
HOW TO GET THERE: Take the A376 from Exeter to Exmouth, then the B3179 through Woodbury. Take the first turning on the right as you leave the village, signed for Exmouth. At the end of this road turn right onto the B3180. Once you pass the turning for Exmouth (to the right) take the left turn a few hundred metres down the road. The reserve entrance is on the left by the reservoir.
WALKING TIME: The site is 67 acres (27ha). It takes 1 hour, possibly longer, to explore the wet and dry heath, the surrounding wooded areas and the wildflower meadow.
30-MINUTE VISIT: A short walk will allow a visit to the picturesque reservoir and the surrounding heath.

Bystock is part of a larger SSSI, the East Devon Pebblebed Heaths. It is home to an interesting mix of habitats: small deep pools provide a glimpse into another world as rare red damselflies flit over them; sphagnum moss and carnivorous sundew plants can be seen in the wet areas; and stonechats can be heard year round among the heathers. Wildflowers and butterflies are plentiful on the sunny slopes of the Bystock meadow and evidence of badgers and dormice can be seen in the woodland. Bystock is a great site for a visit at any time of year as the mix of habitats provides a wealth of wildlife interest. Visit in late spring to see the grassland teaming with butterflies. The pools and wet areas support important populations of dragonflies and damselflies and the heathland is at its most colourful in late summer when heather is in flower. This reserve provides stunning views across the heath and woodland during autumn. Birdlife is plentiful throughout the year.

Dunsdon NNR

Near Holsworthy; **OS Map** SS 295078; **Map Ref** B6

ACCESS/CONDITIONS: Wheelchair access to the Culm grassland viewing platform is via a 300-metre boardwalk. The rest of the reserve is very wet and boggy. Stout boots or wellingtons are a necessity.
HOW TO GET THERE: Buses X9 and 85 from Holsworthy. By car, take the A3072 from Holsworthy in the direction of Bude, then turn right to Pancrasweek. Turn right 1 mile past the church and follow the lane.
WALKING TIME: The site is 142 acres (58ha) of open reserve. Allow 2 hours to explore.
30-MINUTE VISIT: Walk through woodland on the boardwalk to the viewpoint overlooking the Culm grassland. Just beyond is a heronry. Go to the meadow to see wildflowers and butterflies.

This is one of few remaining Culm grassland sites in England and probably the best example in Devon. Visit in early summer to witness the marsh fritillary butterflies and to see vast quantities of wildflowers and orchids in the meadows. Raise your eyes to see buzzards soaring overhead and herons nesting in the tree tops. The reserve is a fairly bleak place in winter, very boggy and wet, but this is true for all Culm grassland. Visitors should see snipe and woodcock in reasonable numbers. If lucky short-eared owl and barn owl may also be seen. From mid-May through to June magnificent displays of butterfly, and heath spotted and southern marsh orchids abound. The delicately scented meadow thistle is everywhere and the grassland is a mass of colour. Hardy local north Devon cattle graze the extensive pastures. The reserve starts to get wetter in autumn. At the base leaves of the flowering devil's bit scabious, you may see a web of the larvae of the marsh fritillary butterfly.

Halsdon

Near Winkleigh; **OS Map** SS 555126; **Map Ref** B3

ACCESS/CONDITIONS: The track from the southern entrance is well surfaced with stone and suitable for wheelchairs and pushchairs as far as the river, although there is a moderate short slope in one or two places. Some of the woodland paths are steep, and may be wet and muddy. Access to some riverside areas is restricted – please contact the Devon Wildlife Trust for further information.

HOW TO GET THERE: Take the A377 from Exeter to Crediton onto Morchard Road, and then turn left onto the B3220. Five miles past Winkleigh, turn left to Dolton; drive through Dolton and turn right up Fore Street, down West Lane and right at the crossroads. The southern entrance to the reserve is on the left, or continue 1 mile and take the track to Ashwell car park. Parking is available at the Quarry (southern) entrance, or at the Ashwell entrance about 1 mile north. Follow the track to the car park.

WALKING TIME: Halsdon is a large site, 140 acre (77ha), with an extensive network of paths. A walk to the river and back will take about 30 minutes but a leisurely walk around the whole site and a visit to the hide is likely to take at least 4 hours.

30-MINUTE VISIT: From the lay-by parking area at the Quarry (southern) entrance to the river is about a 30-minute round trip. This will take you through woodland and alongside a stream, down to the river where you may see kingfishers or even an otter.

This magnificent reserve alongside the River Torridge includes a steep wooded valley side-edged with riverside pasture. A visit to the reserve is worthwhile at any time but spring and summer are undoubtedly the best. Woodland spring flowers include wood anemones, ramsons and bluebells, while nesting birds, including pied flycatchers and wood warblers, are present from May onwards. The new hide overlooks the Torridge which is famous for its otter population, kingfishers, dippers and sand martins seen here during July and August. White legged damselflies emerge with uncommon wavy St John's wort, which flowers in late summer. Halsdon is one of Devon Wildlife Trust's largest and most spectacular nature reserves. In addition to an abundance of wildlife the site offers beautiful riverside walks, magnificent views to Dartmoor and beyond and the opportunity to see where Tarka the Otter swam.

WILDLIFE FACT: MARSH FRITILLARY

With its orange and black markings that look like a leaded stained-glass window, the marsh fritillary is one of Britain's most attractive butterflies. Sadly, it is also one of Europe's most threatened, as loss of habitat causes rapidly declining numbers. Found at Dunsdon NNR and Rackenford and Knowstone Moors.

Bovey Heathfield LNR

Near Bovey Tracey; **OS Map** SX 824765; **Map Ref** B13

ACCESS/CONDITIONS: The main circular path rising to a view point has compact ground with some loose stones. An ideal site for a family visit.

HOW TO GET THERE: From the A38 take the A382 towards Bovey Tracey. At the traffic lights turn right, take the second left into Cavalier Road. Turn left into Dragoon Close. The gravel track on the right leads to the reserve. Parking is along the road side in Dragoon Close.

WALKING TIME: The site is 50 acres (23.5ha) in size. There are several paths through the heathland. To explore the reserve fully allow 1 hour.

30-MINUTE VISIT: A stroll to the view point overlooking Hay Tor on Dartmoor will take about half an hour.

A MEMBER SAYS: 'Bovey Heathfield Local Nature Reserve is a fantastic reminder of the lowland heaths that once covered this part of Devon.'

This rescued nature reserve is an important part of the Bovey Basin heaths. Three types of heather, bog myrtle, dragonflies and grayling butterflies, various insects including the bog-bush cricket, solitary bees, birds including stonechats, nightjars and Dartford warblers, slow worms, lizards and adders can be found here. It is home to many threatened heathland birds, butterflies and insects. Unlike upland moors, at lower altitudes heaths are hot, dry and humid; the highly acidic soils are thin and infertile. This is the key to the heath's special wildlife: it is so hostile that only a few specially adapted plants and animals can live here. In summer the heath is a purple jungle as the ling and bell heather flower. Bovey Heathfield is particularly important for insects and arachnids: it is home to up to 20 different dragonflies, numerous butterflies, half of the UK's 650 sorts of spiders and over 40 types of bees, ants and solitary wasps. Visit in autumn for the resident Dartford warblers, stonechats and roe deer. In spring, nightjars return to the heath from Africa to breed here. The rare earthwork found on site has been declared a Scheduled Ancient Monument (SAM).

DID YOU KNOW?

- Bovey Heathfield is home to over 60 notable, endangered and protected species.
- Each year a number of scrapes and ponds are excavated, creating important habitats for insects such as dragonflies. These have also attracted rare beetles.
- Bovey Heathfield still bares the scars of past neglect and the damaging activities of illegal off-roading, and may well take over a decade or more to recover fully.

Dunsford

Near Exeter; **OS Map** SX 805884; **Map Ref** B11

ACCESS/CONDITIONS: A footpath and bridleway run along the valley floor. The main track is flat and has a well-made stone surface. Access is possible by wheelchair from Steps Bridge.

HOW TO GET THERE: Dunsford is on the edge of Dartmoor, 7.5 miles west of Exeter. There are two entrances to the nature reserve: one at Steps Bridge, and the other not far from Clifford Bridge. Regular buses run between Moretonhampstead and Exeter past the Steps Bridge entrance. If coming by car, park in the Dartmoor National Park car park next to the Steps Bridge Tea Rooms.

WALKING TIME: The linear path that runs the length of the reserve will take between 2 to 2 and a half hours for a return walk. There are several small paths that go between the main track and river through the meadows, so any walk can be varied.

30-MINUTE VISIT: Choose any path for a linear walk or simply wander down to the picturesque river.

A MEMBER SAYS: 'A beautiful display of spring colour and a cacophony of birdsong – a real find.'

Dunsford is part of the Dartmoor National Park. Entering the reserve you get a sense of the power and size of nature, from the steep-sided valley's wooded slopes to the rare butterflies swooping over their food plants in the river meadows. In the background is the gentle, sparkling river during summer, which becomes a powerful, roaring one in winter. In spring, the glades are carpeted with yellow wild daffodils, and insects and butterflies such as the brimstone confirm that winter is over. The chorus of birdsong and the tropical sound of insects increase as the breeding season gets underway. Pied flycatchers nest in the oak woodlands, and rare fritillary butterflies such as the high brown and pearl bordered flit swiftly over the bracken. In autumn, the heather is coming to the end of its flowering period but is still covered with bees grabbing their last morsel of food. Butterflies such as the peacock are still around with latecomers looking for a mate before winter sets in. In winter, the River Teign cascades over the leat at Steps Bridge, which feeds a local mill. Despite the river being in full flow, this is a good time to spot otters.

DID YOU KNOW?

- The woodland on the slopes used to be coppiced (cut to ground level) for charcoal and timber.
- Look for otter spraints on the large rocks alongside the river – these look like small tarry deposits, but do not smell unpleasant if you are brave enough to sniff. Some people say they smell like jasmine tea.
- At the Clifford Bridge end of the reserve you can walk up the steep hillside to the heathland above the valley, getting a dramatic view of the River Teign and the countryside that surrounds this reserve.

Wembury VMCA

Near Plymouth; **OS Map** SX 518484; **Map Ref** B16

WALKING TIME: Wembury Marine Centre opens from the Easter weekend to the first weekend in October. Open 9am to 5pm weekdays (closed on Mondays) and 10am to 5pm weekends and school holidays. Wembury VMCA is open all year round.
ACCESS/CONDITIONS: There is wheelchair access to the visitor centre, which has a disabled toilet. There is a fairly steep slope and steps to beach, with no wheelchair access. The coast path level in most places but can get muddy.
HOW TO GET THERE: On foot, walk the South West Coast Path from Plymouth. Take the number 48 bus from Plymouth city centre. By car, take the A379 out of Plymouth towards Kingsbridge and at Elburton, turn off and follow signs to Wembury. Once in the village follow signs to the beach and St Werburgh's church.
WALKING TIME: The VMCA stretches for 4 miles along the coast, from Plymouth Sound to the Yealm Estuary. A full circuit is approximately an 8-mile round trip, although you would be backtracking on yourself, and would take about 4 to 5 hours. The walk to the top of the hill takes 2 to 3 hours.
30-MINUTE VISIT: Even a short stroll on the beach will yield all sorts of discoveries.
A MEMBER SAYS: 'The wealth of marine life waiting to be found in Wembury's rockpools is breathtaking.'

Wembury's rocky shore is bursting with life waiting to be discovered. In spring, the seaweeds start growing and creatures begin to reappear after the winter. Look out for berried (pregnant) crabs and adventurous starfish braving the cold. By the summer months, the rockpools are full of life and, if you have time, head out to the low tide mark and investigate the kelp forests. Turn over some rocks and you are guaranteed to find a plethora of edible and porcelain crabs, squat lobsters and, if you are lucky, spiny starfish. In the autumn there are still creatures to be found in the pools but you may have to go further to find them – the animals are beginning to move out to sea to survive the winter. By the winter there is less to see in the rockpools as creatures have retreated to deeper waters, but be patient and you will still see some of the hardier animals that have remained, such as shore crabs and blennies. The winter is a great time to see the wide variety of sea snails, limpets, winkles and dog whelks. Look out for birdlife all year round, especially the cirl buntings and peregrines in the spring and summer, and the coastal birds visiting over winter.

DID YOU KNOW?

- Wembury Voluntary Marine Conservation Area was founded in 1981 and was one of the first VMCAs in the country.
- The island you can see off Wembury Bay is Great Mewstone.
- Great Mewstone is owned by the National Trust and there is no public access because it is so important for nesting birds.

Glastonbury Tor, Somerset

Somerset

South West

About the Trust

Somerset Wildlife Trust has more than 20,000 members and around 80 nature reserves, and is dedicated to restoring our ecosystems by creating livi ng landscapes for wildlife and people – we must give our wildlife room to manoeuvre to avoid a collapse in biodiversity. The Trust helps wildlife adapt to climate change, encourages sustainable living and inspires people to create more green space.

Somerset Wildlife Trust ☎ 01823 652400
www.somersetwildlife.org

Bubwith Acres

Near Cheddar
OS Map ST 474538; **Map Ref** C9

This reserve is 47 acres (19ha) of limestone grassland and heath with bracken encroachment. Flowers recorded include St John's wort and betony. Butterflies such as dark green and small pearl-bordered fritillary can often be seen, as can linnets, kestrels and ravens. Note there are some steep slopes.

Great Breach Wood

Near Butleigh
OS Map ST 505325; **Map Ref** C15

A reserve of predominantly mature oak and ash with a rich scrub understorey. Plant species recorded include greater butterfly and early purple orchid. There are more than 600 species of fungus. Fauna includes tree pipits and woodcock. Paths can be muddy during wet weather.

Huish Moor

Near Chipstable
OS Map ST 034287; **Map Ref** C16

This moor is 30 acres (12ha) of unimproved grassland, mire communities and ancient woodland around the headwaters of the River Tone. There is a steep slope down to the site, which can be muddy.

Langford Heathfield

Near Langford Budville
OS Map ST 106227; **Map Ref** C18

A reserve of ancient, semi-natural ash and field maple woodland with bluebell, sanicle and twayblade. Ponds are home to breeding frogs, toads and palmate newts. Butterflies include the small pearl-bordered fritillary and green and brown hairstreaks. Birds that may be spotted include tree pipits and redstarts. Walking boots are recommended, and there is very limited wheelchair access.

Quants

Near Lowton
OS Map ST 188175; **Map Ref** C20

This reserve is a mosaic of relic heathy grassland and ancient and secondary woodland on a steep north-facing slope. There is a small dewpond, and flora that can be found here includes yellow archangel, sweet woodruff and yellow pimpernel. Fauna includes southern hawker dragonflies and silver-washed fritillary butterflies. Sparrowhawks, tree pipits and wood warblers are among the site's birdlife. There are some steep slopes and muddy paths.

Sutton's Ponds

Near Chilton Trinity
OS Map ST 295395; **Map Ref** C12

Sutton's Pond is 7 acres (3ha) of worked-out clay pit, now open water dominated by water lilies. Saucer bugs and water stick-insects have been recorded, as have many species of dragonfly and damselfly. Birdlife includes Cetti's warbler, long-tailed tits and great crested grebe. There are two simple viewing screens with wheelchair access.

Thurlbear Wood SSSI

Near Stoke St Mary
OS Map ST 274213; **Map Ref** C19

This SSSI is 40 acres (16ha) of ancient woodland of oak and ash standards, hazel and field maple coppice. Its wealth of wildlife includes dormice and nightingales. There are superb woodland flowers in spring. Note that paths can be muddy at times.

Catcott Reserves

Near Bridgwater; **OS Map** ST 400414 (Catcott Heath: ST 407411); **Map Ref** C14

ACCESS/CONDITIONS: In winter, the four meadows are very wet and unwalkable due to the softness of the peat and flooded lakes. Ladies Drove hide at the car park is suitable for wheelchair access.
HOW TO GET THERE: Catcott Lows is a mile north of Catcott village. Access to Catcott Heath is by foot east-south-east from ST 399 405 and 800 metres along the drove. Bus service 375 (Bridgwater to Wells) runs every day and stops in the village.
WALKING TIME: The 1- to 2-mile walk along droves, through meadows and carr woodland takes 1 hour.
30-MINUTE VISIT: Wildlife can be seen from the Ladies Drove hide at the car park in winter. Walk along the droves in summer.

In the winter, Catcott's fields are used by large numbers of lapwing, mallard, wigeon and important numbers of teal pintail and shoveler. The reserve should be visited for the closest views of over-wintering duck and hunting peregrines in the county. In spring, nationally important numbers of roosting spring passage whimbrel, as well as passage greenshank, ruff and black-tailed godwit are present. In the summer, quiet walks along the droves and through the carr woodland allow you to really appreciate the area. The field and ditch system provides an excellent habitat for numerous species of dragonfly and aquatic invertebrates. At Catcott Heath, purple moor grass, devil's bit scabious, marsh and meadow thistles are common, while a dense stand of bog myrtle has been maintained. A number of rare and threatened plants are cultivated on site, including great fen and saw sedge. Glastonbury Tor gives a fantastic backdrop to views from the main hide at Catcott Lows – one of the lowest points in the Brue Valley. It is a grazing marsh and an important site for wintering, spring passage and breeding bird interest, thanks to the flooded winter conditions and soft ground through early summer. The 127-acre (51ha) site forms part of the grazing meadows and ditch system at the western edge of the Avalon Marshes. Meanwhile, Catcott Heath is a further 34-acre (14ha) SSSI and split into several interesting areas.

Draycott Sleights

Near Cheddar; **OS Map** ST 485505; **Map Ref** C11

ACCESS/CONDITIONS: Draycott Sleights features steep slopes, with one moderately good path which has a gentle incline. The south-west facing scarp is at an altitude of 145 metres to 270 metres. The area is very exposed on higher ground.
HOW TO GET THERE: 2 miles south-west of Cheddar. By car, take the new road from Draycott on the A371. Park on the roadside.
WALKING TIME: 124-acre (50ha) reserve. A leisurely stroll takes 2 and a half hours.
30-MINUTE VISIT: Stroll through the main gate and along the track lined with beech trees to the dew pond for breathtaking views.

Draycott Sleights in the Mendip Hills AONB is located on the Mendip scarp with 90 acres (36ha) of unimproved to semi-improved calcareous grassland. It contains a diverse flora of over 200 species including more than 40 county notables. Skylarks are in song during spring and early summer and peregrines teach young to hunt. There's also a wide range of invertebrates, in particular the blue butterflies associated with limestone downland. It is a locally important site for butterflies and has fine views over the Somerset Levels including Glastonbury Tor, the Quantocks and beyond. June to August is the best time to visit for the butterflies; 34 have been recorded including marbled white and chalkhill blue. Spring and summer are also good for flowers with rockrose, marjoram and bird's-foot trefoil on the thinner soil, while on the deeper soils, ox-eye daisy, salad burnet and small scabious are found.

Black Rock

Near Cheddar; **OS Map** ST 483544; **Map Ref** C10

P

ACCESS/CONDITIONS: Care must be taken due to steep slopes and uneven surfaces. There is frequent flooding in winter or at times of high rainfall.
HOW TO GET THERE: Black Rock is at the head of the Cheddar Gorge, about 1.5 miles from Cheddar on the B3135 towards Priddy and Bath. For public transport and bus walks leaflet contact the Mendip Hills AONB (01761 462338).
WALKING TIME: 183-acre (74ha) reserve. The long trail of 1.5 miles takes about 1 and a half hours.
30-MINUTE VISIT: Take the short trail of 1 mile signposted by arrows.
A MEMBER SAYS: 'Black Rock offers something for everyone. Ideal for a Sunday afternoon stroll with the family or more strenuous walks following the longer trail on the top with spectacular views.'

If you are looking for a quiet, long and challenging walk in the ruggedly beautiful Mendip Hills, start from here. Most visitors take the flat stroll through the centre of the reserve, but the West Mendip Way will take you through other Wildlife Trust reserves and out on to the wild landscape of Mendip. The reserve, 183 acres (74ha) of limestone grassland, plantation, natural woodland and scree at the head of Cheddar Gorge, forms part of the Cheddar complex which is of national and European importance. Spring and summer are best for the botanical interest when the grassland is carpeted with flowers. The old drystone walls (and scree) of limestone are an interesting feature – one wall encountered near the car park is probably 200 years old. The exposed stone carries many lichens and ferns, including the uncommon limestone fern and the brittle bladder fern. There are butterflies to find – maybe the dark green fritillary in the sheltered glades on a sunny summer day – and at Black Rock Drove, the northern section is good for common and small blues together with their close relation the brown argus. The reserve is a stronghold for the nationally important common dormouse.

DID YOU KNOW?

- Many female blue butterflies are brownish in colour, but the closely related brown argus has no blue colour in either sex .
- The dormouse can sleep for up to half the year.

Netherclay Community Woodland

Near Taunton; **OS Map** ST 207252; **Map Ref** C17

ACCESS/CONDITIONS: Mainly flat and laid to grass with paths cut between the new trees. Parts of the reserve can get muddy during wet weather. Wheelchairs and pushchairs can visit much of the area. Take care near the river.
HOW TO GET THERE: Netherclay Community Woodland is on the north of Bishop's Hull in Taunton. Parking is made simple thanks to the Silk Mills park and ride across the road.
WALKING TIME: The site is 13.5 acres (5.5ha) and there is a figure-of-eight walk or a circular walk around the site that takes around 30 to 45 minutes. Part of the site is owned by Taunton Deane Borough Council who have erected some interesting wooden sculptures on their area.
30-MINUTE VISIT: A brisk walk around the site would take this amount of time.
A MEMBER SAYS: 'A wonderful stroll on level ground listening to the trickle of the river and an abundance of birdsong.'

This area of improved pasture land on the bank of the River Tone has been planted with native broad-leaved trees to create a new woodland. The site is an extension of the local council's existing plantation and was created with the help of volunteers. It was bought by Somerset Wildlife Trust in 2006 with financial support from Viridor Credits Environmental Company and Bishop's Hull Parish Council. Hedgerows lining the north and west boundaries have sections dominated by English elm. The northern hedge also features hawthorn, blackthorn, field maple, elder, common dogwood, pedunculate oak and one standard ash. The riverbank is mainly open but a number of mature standard trees occur, including several black poplars. The river supports a diverse fauna including a range of less common species such as otter, water shrew, kingfisher and dipper. Salmon and brown trout are known to migrate along this section of the river then spawn upstream. A pair of small ponds along the boundary provides a habitat for amphibians. Mice and voles are present, providing food for birds of prey including kestrels which have been seen hovering above the site.

DID YOU KNOW?

- As the trees grow they will slow the rate of rainwater run-off which reduces the flood risk downstream.
- The woodland also provides an attractive amenity for the local community, including local schools.

Westhay Moor NNR

Near Glastonbury; **OS Map** ST 457438; **Map Ref** C13

ACCESS/CONDITIONS: The water and wet peat are potentially dangerous – walk only on paths indicated on the leaflet map. The Dagg's Lane hides are suitable for wheelchair access.

HOW TO GET THERE: Westhay Moor NNR is alongside the minor road between Westhay village (on B315 Glastonbury to Wedmore) and Godney village. Bus service 668 (Street to Lower Langford) runs from Monday to Saturday and stops in Westhay village. There is a car park at the end of Dagg's Lane Drove. During busy times, such as winter, starlings roost so please park carefully, and with respect for local people. No coach access.

WALKING TIME: The full circuit takes 1 hour, but you could spend longer in the hides and viewing screens.

30-MINUTE VISIT: Head up Dagg's Lane Drove from the car park to the North Drain bridge for a view over the reserve and to hear Cetti's warblers.

A MEMBER SAYS: 'A dawn walk round the reserve just watching and listening is so relaxing – nature in Somerset at its best.'

This is the Somerset Wildlife Trust's pilot project for the Avalon Marshes, a scheme to create a nationally important nature conservation area on 3,500 acres (1,416ha) of derelict peat workings in the Brue Valley. This reserve started as a deep-drained hole in the ground, of no wildlife value, and is now so rich in wildlife that something of interest can be seen on every visit throughout the year. It offers bitterns, otters, peregrines, hobbies, warblers and a wealth of dragonflies and other wildlife at the appropriate time of year. It includes 30 acres (12ha) of lowland acid mire, the largest area of this habitat remaining in south-west England. Sphagnum mosses are spreading, as are sundews. Heather and cross-leaved heath are regenerating. The wildlife now using the reserve is impressive, with more than 100 species of bird recorded. In winter, there are good numbers of over-wintering duck on the lakes including goosander and merganser. Great crested grebes perform their dancing displays in spring. Cetti's warblers can be heard all the year round. Dragonflies are at their best in spring and summer. In autumn, the starling roost in the reedbeds can reach up to four million birds.

DID YOU KNOW?

- **Many raised bogs like Westhay Moor have been damaged by drainage for agriculture. You can help stop further damage to the remaining bogs by choosing to buy peat-free compost.**
- **Westhay Moor is the first NNR to be made from an old peat working.**
- **This is one of the most important sites in England for the liverwort *pallavicinia lyellii.***

Avon

About the Trust

Avon Wildlife Trust is an organisation on a mission. They've got a vision for the future, for the landscape and people around them, and they're committed to achieving it. They're focusing on four key themes of work which will bring that vision closer – of local landscapes richer in wildlife, delivering a better quality of life for all.

Avon Wildlife Trust ☎ 0117 9177270
www.avonwildlifetrust.org.uk

Clapton Moor

Near Clapton-in-Gordano
OS Map ST 458735; **Map Ref** C2

Clapton Moor is home to nationally scarce invertebrates such as hairy dragonfly and ruddy darter, and birdlife includes buzzards, peregrines, hobbies, breeding lapwings, redshank and snipe. Access is restricted to a path that leads to a hide, and care should be taken due to the potentially treacherous rhynes and wet grassland areas (a limited number of permits are available for access to the rest of the site). The Avon Cycleway passes the entrance and there are bus links from nearby major centres.

Dolebury Warren

Near Churchill
OS Map ST 455590; **Map Ref** C7;

At Dolebury Warren, you will hopefully see many butterflies, including the small blue and marbled white; adders, badgers, foxes and rabbits can also be spotted. Another feature of the reserve is the Iron Age hill-fort. There are paths and steps on the site, but going is strenuous in places and the warren is not suitable for wheelchairs or pushchairs.

Purn Hill SSSI

Near Bleadon
OS Map ST 3325737; **Map Ref** C8

Purn Hill is designated as an SSSI and is made up of limestone grassland and mixed scrub. Much of the grassland is of national importance and is only found here and on a few other sites on the south-facing slopes of the Mendips. It is home to three plants that are nationally rare and threatened – honewort, Somerset hairgrass and white rock-rose.

Tickenham Ridge SNCI

Near Tickenham
OS Map ST 446724; **Map Ref** C4

Access is restricted to events only at Tickenham Ridge SNCI, but the reserve is home to bluebell, dog's mercury, purple orchid, moschatel, autumn gentian and salad burnet. Silver-washed fritillary, brown argus, dingy and grizzled skipper butterflies can also be spotted.

Weston Big Wood

Near Portishead
OS Map ST 456750; **Map Ref** C1

Weston Big Wood is an ancient broadleaf woodland containing wood anemone, violets, bluebells and rare purple gromwell. Woodpeckers, nuthatches, tawny owls, bats and badgers can all be spotted. Paths can be muddy and steep-sided, and visitors must keep well away from the quarry sides.

Weston Moor

Near Weston-in-Gordano
OS Map ST 443739; **Map Ref** C3

Weston Moor is a large wild, untamed area with wet grassland, important for breeding waders and rare plants. During the spring and summer, the fields on the moor attract breeding lapwing, redshank and snipe. Little owl, linnet, reed bunting and skylark also breed in the area. Rhynes and wet grassland areas are potentially treacherous, and open access is restricted to fields north of Walton Brook. There are buses from nearby major centres, and parking is restricted.

Brown's Folly

Near Bath; **OS Map** ST 794660; **Map Ref** C5

ACCESS/CONDITIONS: Paths at Brown's Folly are muddy in winter, and extreme caution needs to be taken when approaching rock faces. Mines should not be entered under any circumstances.
HOW TO GET THERE: Badgerline buses 3 and 23 run from Bath bus station every 20 minutes to Dover's Park. By car, take the minor road from Bathford to Kingsdown, taking a steep right-hand turn to Monkton Farleigh. The nearest car park is near the brow of the hill on Prospect Place.
WALKING TIME: The full circuit takes 1 and a half to 2 hours.
30-MINUTE VISIT: Head towards the folly building for views over the valley.

This is a fascinating spot which combines natural beauty with an insight into the history of the building of Bath. The Folly itself is no longer owned by the Trust but by an organisation called the Folly Fellowship. The reserve stands high above the River Avon with commanding views towards Bath. It includes the remains of Bath stone quarries which provide a rich variety of wildlife habitats. Wild thyme, harebell and nine species of orchid, including the rare fly orchid can be found. Old mines provide a safe place for the threatened greater horseshoe bat, while the damp cliff faces support a variety of ferns, fungi and spiders. Some of the ancient woodland on the lower slopes is home to woodpeckers and unusual plants, like the Bath asparagus. To encourage the growth and spread of native trees, planted conifers have been removed. Invading scrub which threatens to shade out the grassland is being cleared.

WILDLIFE FACT: OWLS

That owls are creatures of the night is largely a myth. The short-eared owl is frequently seen hunting during the day, as is the barn owl. The little owl hunts at night and dusk, but is often seen sitting on telegraph poles during the day; the long eared owl is nocturnal and secretive but even that gets spotted in the day along the coasts when it is breeding in the winter time. The tawny owl is a nightbird and makes the most recognisable 'tu-whit tu-whoo' noise. Tawny owls nest in Weston Big Wood and on Folly Farm.

Pictured: Short-eared owl

Folly Farm

Near Bristol; **OS Map** ST 665708; **Map Ref** C5

P WC ♿ i

ACCESS/CONDITIONS: Access for All Trail through woodland is waymarked from car park. No dogs permitted.
HOW TO GET THERE: Buses 673, 674 and 675 Bristol to Bishop Sutton or bus 376 Bristol to Clutton. By car, take A368 towards Weston-super-Mare; just after the right turn to Chew Magna, Folly Farm is signposted on the left. Parking for disabled visitors next to farmhouse.
WALKING TIME: The full circuit walk takes approximately 2 hours. The woodland walk takes 1 and a half hours.
30-MINUTE VISIT: Take the Access for All Trail through the woods.
A MEMBER SAYS: 'Sunny or pouring with rain, it is an atmospheric site and as I stroll up the track I catch glimpses of the poetry and peace of nature, which is so rare in sites in this area.'

Folly Farm is a little piece of unspoilt English countryside, lying close to the Mendip Hills and offering impressive views over Chew Valley Lake. It has a peaceful atmosphere and is exceptionally rich in history and wildlife. In summer the meadows brim with flowers such as betony, ox-eye daisy and heath spotted orchid. In late summer, the meadows are covered by black knapweed and devil's-bit scabious. There are many butterflies, including ringlet, small tortoiseshell, gatekeeper and marbled white. The rare marsh fritillary has also been found here. Of the two woodlands, Dowlings Wood is largely ancient, being an old hazel coppice. In spring, the woodland floor is rich in flowers such as primrose, bluebell and early-purple orchid. Among the many birds that can be seen are nuthatch, buzzard and great spotted woodpecker. Tawny owls also nest and roost on the farm. Most of the fields are grazed by sheep. The SSSI is lightly grazed by cattle in the autumn to favour marsh fritillaries and other wildlife. The woods are selectively thinned and coppiced.

DID YOU KNOW?

- Folly Farm is one of the largest examples in England of a *ferme ornée* (ornamental farm), which provided a recreational pastoral landscape for the Strachey family at Sutton Court.
- Round Hill is an example of the 18th-century craze for planting beech trees on top of prominent hills.

Willsbridge Valley

Willsbridge; **OS Map** ST 665708; **Map Ref** D11

WC

OPENING TIMES: Facilities open April to September.
ACCESS/CONDITIONS: Most of valley, exhibition and WC are suitable for wheelchair access via Willsbridge Hill. An electric scooter is available for loan (0117 9326885).
HOW TO GET THERE: Bus 45 from Bristol to Long Beach Road or bus 332 from Willsbridge Hill. Take A431 Bristol to Bath road and turn into Long Beach Road. Park on left-hand side on Long Beach Road.
WALKING TIME: The full circuit takes about 1 hour.
30-MINUTE VISIT: The shorter version is known as the Heritage Trail and is fairly level. Brass waymarker plaques reflect the particular identity of various sites en route.
A MEMBER SAYS: 'The kids always love coming here, and being so close to the city it is an ideal place to escape the hustle and bustle without spending long getting there!'

Here on the edge of Bristol an oasis of wildlife survives among modern housing estates. This peaceful wooded valley is the home of Willsbridge Mill, the Wildlife Trust's Education and Countryside Centre, where you can discover the area's living links with its industrial past. The history of the valley makes an interesting addition to the wildlife on show, and there is a fascinating sculpture trail in the reserve. The woodlands are at their best in spring when they are full of bluebells, campions and the sounds of birdsong. The ponds are important homes for frogs, newts and dragonflies. Foxes and badgers live in the valley, and dippers and kingfishers can be seen feeding in the fast-flowing brook, which contains eel and bullhead, with evidence of otter and water vole. The wildlife garden has examples of how to make a household garden a better home for wildlife.

DID YOU KNOW?

- Catscliffe Wood in the Willsbridge Valley was once part of the great royal hunting grounds of Kingswood Forest.
- The powerful mill wheel was driven by water from the huge pond behind the mill. It burst its banks during the great floods of 1968.
- The valley was a hive of criminal activity in the 19th century. The notorious 'Cock Road Gang' robbed highway coaches, and deer poachers abounded.

Gloucestershire

About the Trust

Gloucestershire Wildlife Trust now safeguards and cares for over 70 nature reserves around the county, which covers around 2,500 acres of prime wildlife habitat. In these reserves you can see nature at its best, a place where wildlife is protected for its own sake, and this often means continuing the old-time practices which made them rich in wildlife in the first place.

Gloucestershire Wildlife Trust ☎ 01452 383333
www.gloucestershirewildlifetrust.co.uk

Badgeworth SSSI

Near Cheltenham
OS Map SO 910205; **Map Ref** D3

One of only two sites in the UK that support the rare adder's tongue spearwort. Boardwalk unsuitable for wheelchair access at present. Reserve leaflets on request. Open by permit only. Permits are available May to September. Open day held every year.

Chedworth

Near Cirencester
OS Map SP 048143; **Map Ref** D5

As you descend to the little River Coln, the magnificent panorama of Chedworth Woods unfolds before you. At the heart of these woods lies Chedworth nature reserve, an abandoned railway adjoining the famous Roman Villa. Geological features with good fossil-collecting resource in the screes. Dormice, fallow deer; greater butterfly orchid, autumn gentian and hairy violet. Woodcock, blackcap and wood warbler are among the bird visitors, while fallow deer, dormice, lizards and adders can also be seen from time to time. Access via a steep climb with steps. Reserve leaflets available.

Hobbs SSSI

Near Cinderford
OS Map SO 695195; **Map Ref** D2

Geological exposures from the Silurian period. A series of algal and coral reefs overlain by sinuous drapes of bedded limestone. Ancient woodland with primrose, sanicle, wild daffodil and a population of dormice. Footpath with steps leading to geological exposures.

Midger SSSI

Near Wotton-under-Edge
OS Map ST 794892; **Map Ref** D9

Ancient oak/ash woodland with fine understorey of hazel. Ancient woodland indicator plants include bluebell, herb Paris, wood anemone and spindle. The common dormouse and the bulin snail (*Ena montana*) are also present. Typical birds include the great spotted woodpecker, nuthatch, treecreeper and, near the stream, the grey wagtail. The moist habitat is ideal for fungi. Footpaths through wood, muddy in winter.

Siccaridge Wood

Near Daneway Banks
OS Map SO 935035; **Map Ref** D7

Ancient semi-natural woodland and disused canal. Bluebell, herb Paris, dog-violet and primrose in spring, lily-of-the-valley; nightingales; fungi. Reserve leaflets.

Three Groves Wood

Near Stroud
OS Map SO 912029; **Map Ref** D6

Little is known about the history of this wood, although it may once have been included within the bounds of Oakridge Common. It overlies oolitic limestone, which was extracted from a number of small quarries in the wood. The tree canopy is dominated by beech, with occasional ash and oak. In spring the woodland floor has a fine show of bluebell, woodruff, primrose and common dog-violet. Footpaths steep in places through the wood, muddy in winter.

Lancaut SSSI

Near Chepstow; **OS Map** ST 539966; **Map Ref** D8

ACCESS/CONDITIONS: A steep public footpath leads to the wood and the gorge bottom. Footpaths are uneven and can become very muddy. The Offa's Dyke LDP runs through part of the reserve.
HOW TO GET THERE: Train to Chepstow then bus. Small area for parking 200 metres from the entrance.
WALKING TIME: 60-acre (24ha) reserve. The full circuit takes 2 hours.
30-MINUTE VISIT: From the lay-by, walk a short way back down the road, turn right into the reserve and follow the circular walk round. Return to the B4228 to see the reserve and the Wye Valley from the famous Wintour's Leap.

Lancaut SSSI lies in one of the four most important woodland areas in Britain. Sixty acres (24ha) of the spectacular limestone Wye Gorge, with cliffs and disused quarries, woodland and saltmarsh. The cliff top offers breathtaking views of the Wye Gorge. The cliffs are home to peregrine falcons and ravens that nest on the rock faces. A wealth of wildflowers grows on the open rock faces, including hairy violet, lesser calamint, red valerian and shining cranesbill. In spring and summer, the woodland is marvellous, with oak, field maple and yew. But it also contains small-leaved lime and wild service tree, as well as many rare whitebeams, which are only found in ancient woodland. A luxuriant growth of ferns and a fine spring display of primrose, bluebell, dog-violet and wood anemone are seen in the wood. The saltmarsh flora includes sea aster, English scurvy grass and buck's-horn plantain. The winter months offer the best views of the dramatic cliffs comprising rocks from the Carboniferous period (354-290 million years ago).

WILDLIFE FACT: HEDGEHOGS

What everybody wants to know is: how do hedgehogs mate? Apart from very carefully, the answer is that the female completely flattens her back so that her 5,000 or so spines no longer stick upwards and then the male can mount her in safety. It normally takes him an hour or so of very loud grunting and snuffling to persuade her to mate and as one of their favourite habitats is gardens, it's a ritual that many Brits have overheard. Hedgehogs are usually a popular garden visitor as they eat slugs, snails and caterpillars and they have a healthy appetite, eating around 200g of food each night – one-fifth of their bodyweight. They also live in hedgerows and grassland where they dig out dens for shelter. They are nocturnal animals and hibernate between October and April, so the chances of seeing one on a country walk are limited.

Coombe Hill SSSI

Near Gloucester; **OS Map** SO 887272; **Map Ref** D1

OPENING TIMES: Open all year. The reserve is flooded November to March.
ACCESS/CONDITIONS: Flat terrain, but muddy in winter and spring.
HOW TO GET THERE: Bus from Gloucester, Cheltenham and Tewkesbury to Coombe Hill. Follow the lane off the A38 that runs alongside the Swan Inn. Small area for parking at the wharf end of the canal.
WALKING TIME: Disused canal 5-mile round trip takes 3 hours at an easy pace.
30-MINUTE VISIT: Follow the canal until the entrance to the meadows. Return via the opposite side of the canal.
A MEMBER SAYS: 'I was delighted to see both whooper and Bewick's swans on the scrapes as well as many teal and wigeon.'

A disused canal with a series of adjacent hay meadows, ditches and wet grassland within the River Severn floodplain, Coombe Hill is one of those reserves that has something for everyone. For the birdwatcher it is an absolute haven, with something to see throughout the year. A pleasant 2-mile walk along the old canal will offer visitors a chance to see wildflowers, butterflies, and perhaps even brown hares boxing in the meadows. During the winter months, the whole reserve is flooded providing excellent habitat for overwintering wildfowl, including large numbers of pintail, teal and wigeon. As the floodwater recedes in spring, the bare mud around the ditches and newly created shallow pools, called scrapes, provides foraging and nesting habitat for waders such as snipe. A number of clay bunds and sluices are now in place to help hold back the floodwater into early summer. The hay meadows at the north of the reserve are managed to create ideal habitat for curlew. As autumn approaches, redwing and fieldfare visit the hedgerows in large numbers. Restoration work currently underway includes re-profiling of ditches and the creation of scrapes.

DID YOU KNOW?

- **Although the reserve is flooded for much of the winter, harvest mice nests can still be found along the canal and ditch banks.**
- **The canal was built in 1796 and closed in 1876.**
- **More than 10 species of dragonfly and damselfly can be seen at the reserve.**

Greystones Farm

Near Cheltenham; **OS Map** SP 173209; **Map Ref** D4

ACCESS/CONDITIONS: Generally flat and easy walking, some paths are particularly muddy in winter.
HOW TO GET THERE: Buses to Bourton-on-the-Water from Cheltenham, Cirencester and Stow-on-the-Wold. By car, take Station Road from the A429 Fosse Way, into Bourton-on-the-Water, after the road bears right the large paying car park is on the right. Parking is best at the nearby garage on Station Road in Bourton-on-the-Water, approximately a 5-minute walk from the reserve.
WALKING TIME: Walks can be tailored to suit the individual, with anything from half an hour to a full circuit taking up to 1 and a half hours.
30-MINUTE VISIT: Head along the Oxfordshire Way to the river.
A MEMBER SAYS: 'On my visit to Greystones Farm I was thrilled to see a barn owl hunting over the fields at dusk, something I had not experienced before, it was an amazing sight.'

Greystones Farm is one of those magical places that can be visited many times and still yield surprises. An evening summer visit is a must when the barn owls are hunting for their supper over the meadows – an unforgettable sight. It lies on the edge of the busy tourist town of Bourton-on-the-Water, and the combination of traditional flower-rich hay meadows and clear Cotswold stream (which make up the SSSI), traditional farm buildings, SAM and grazed farmland combine to make a reserve rich in biological and cultural diversity. During the spring, the early wildflowers begin to appear, with cowslip and lady's-smock speckling the meadows, the thick hedgerows come alive with songbirds and the rustles of small mammals. Come the summer months, the meadows are alive with the sounds of insects feeding on nectar from the many wildflowers, including early and southern marsh orchids, ragged robin, meadow-rue and pepper saxifrage. The autumn months, after the hay has been taken, are a good time to spot the water voles feeding along the riverbanks. During the quieter winter months, some of the amazing old hedgerow trees can be examined at their best, and deer can frequently be seen grazing in the meadows.

DID YOU KNOW?

- The Iron Age hill-fort (Salmonsbury Camp) was occupied well over 2,000 years ago.
- More than 100 meadow plant species have been recorded in the SSSI meadows alone.
- One of the more unusual species to spot is the large black poplar which grows in a hedgerow near the river.

Lower Woods SSSI

Near Chipping Sodbury; **OS Map** ST 749885; **Map Ref** D10

ACCESS/CONDITIONS: Rides may be muddy throughout the year, some deep. Waterproof boots are advised. Stanley Loop Walk is mostly level and in a dry year, may be suitable for large-wheeled wheelchair access. All other routes are uneven, with steeper sections.
HOW TO GET THERE: 1.5 miles from Hawkesbury Upton and 1 mile from Wickwar along narrow lanes. Train to Yate (Bristol to Gloucester line). Buses 427, 621 and 627 run from Yate to Wotton via Wickwar (not Sunday) and 423 and 623 via Hawkesbury Upton (not Sunday). Walk to Lower Woods via footpaths. Park by the lodge leaving gateways clear.
WALKING TIME: 700-acre (284ha) reserve with a circumference of approximately 6.5 miles. The walk to the southern tip by the main trench is under 2 miles. Waymarked walks take 1 and a half to 2 and a half hours. Short cuts are possible.
30-MINUTE VISIT: Enjoy the red waymarked route, or walk through East Stanley Wood. Enter the gate directly opposite the sheds and keep turning first right to return to the car park.
A MEMBER SAYS: 'We work in offices and escape here as often as we can – it's the most relaxing place on the planet!'

Lower Woods SSSI is one of England's largest ancient oak-ash woodlands on heavy clay soils and a site of great biological diversity. The 23 woods, separated by ancient trenches and rides, were traditionally managed as coppice-with-standards, much of it grazed as wood commons. Significant habitats include the species-rich grassland on the Horton Great Trench, the picturesque Little Avon River and damp meadows. In early spring, violet, wood anemone, primrose, early-purple orchid and bluebell cover the woodland floor. By May, herb Paris and greater butterfly orchid emerge and the riverbanks are swathed in wild garlic. Young buzzards call and nightingales sing from dense blackthorn. In summer, dormice feed unseen. The mysterious adder's tongue fern emerges, and trenches are bright with yellow-rattle, devil's-bit scabious, common-spotted orchids and ragged robin. Last to appear, in deep shade, is the violet helleborine. Butterflies include white admiral and silver-washed fritillary. Autumn brings delicate autumn crocuses and a huge array of fungi. With winter, field maples turn brilliant yellow and the wild service trees, pink and gold. Highlights are bright green mosses, pink spindle berries and blue-black sloes.

Devotees continually return here, enchanted by the magical atmosphere, lush vegetation, exquisite wildflowers and antiquity. Some like to walk the maze of paths and rides, rarely encountering other people. Children love to explore and search for river life. Experts are excited about the diversity of wildlife. Novices marvel at buzzards and deer. Visit and discover its appeal for you!

DID YOU KNOW?

- **It has 71 ancient woodland plant species – the highest number recorded in the South West.**

Wiltshire

About the Trust

The Wiltshire Wildlife Trust's nature reserves provide a haven for wildlife and a place where people can experience the sights, sounds and smells of the natural world. Everyone is welcome to visit any of their nature reserves, on any day of the year, and they are all free of charge.

Wiltshire Wildlife Trust☎ 01380 725670
www.wiltshirewildlife.org

Blackmoor Copse – The Vaughan-Pickard Reserve

Near Salisbury
OS Map SU 233288; **Map Ref** E18

Parts of the wood are coppiced to maintain conditions for rare butterflies, including the pearl-bordered and silver-washed fritillary and purple emperor. Dormice and a pond with great crested newts. Primroses and violets are abundant.

Distillery Meadows

Near Minety
OS Map SU 032893; **Map Ref** E3

A sequence of wildflower hay meadows and pastures. Wood Ground has large numbers of green winged, heath and common-spotted orchids; Ten Acres has carpets of dyer's greenwood; Ring Ground goes purple with devil's-bit scabious; and Hill Ground purple and white with common knapweed and sneezewort.

High Clear Down

Near Aldbourne
OS Map SU 235765; **Map Ref** E5

A chalk downland slope grazed by cattle. The purplish trumpet of the early gentian can be seen in late May/early June. Abundant orchids such as the common-spotted, pyramidal, common rock-rose, fairy flax and squinancywort. Butterflies such as the green hairstreak, chalkhill blue and the Duke of Burgundy can be seen, along with moths such as the forester and wood tiger.

Jones's Mill – The Vera Jeans Nature Reserve

Near Pewsey
OS Map SU 168613; **Map Ref** E6

Extraordinary greater tussock sedge and giant horsetails in the wet woodland (alder carr). Ponds and wet grassland grazed by belted Galloway cattle. Snipe, scarlet tiger moths, bog pimpernel, southern marsh and common-spotted orchids, and the flag iris can all be seen at different times of year.

Landford Bog

Near Salisbury
OS Map SU259186; **Map Ref** E11

Lowland bog and wet heath on the edge of the New Forest. Home to the sundew, a carnivorous plant that wraps its tentacles around insects and slowly digests its prey. Also the raft spider, one of the UK's largest, cotton grass, purple moor-grass and bog asphodel.

Middleton Down SSSI

Near Salisbury
OS Map SU 043252; **Map Ref** E10

Two steep-sided combes linked by a larger valley. Slopes are full of plants such as early gentian, early-purple orchid, cowslips, autumn lady's-tresses and dwarf sedge. A wide range of butterflies include the rare Adonis blue, chalkhill blue, marbled white, grizzled and dingy skippers, and buzzards, sparrowhawks, skylarks, and glow-worms.

Ravensroost Wood

Near Minety
OS Map SU 023877; **Map Ref** E4

A remnant of the medieval Royal Hunting Forest of Braydon that is coppiced for wildlife. Tree cover is mostly oak and hazel, but two uncommon species are the small-leaved lime and the wild service tree. Bluebells, wood anemone, wood sorrel, sanicle, violet and primrose. Common-spotted, early-purple, and butterfly orchids. Butterflies such as the silver-washed fritillary and brown hairstreak, and birds such as the lesser white-throat, willow warblers, nuthatches and woodcock.

Blakehill Farm

Near Cricklade; **OS Map** SU 073923; **Map Ref** E2

P ♿ i

ACCESS/CONDITIONS: This level site has an extensive network of access routes and footpaths, which provide excellent all-year access for both wheelchair and pushchair users. Self closing, two-way gates provide easy access.

HOW TO GET THERE: From Swindon bus station, take either the 52/53, which will arrive at Crossroads, Malmesbury Road, Chelworth Upper Green. There is no cycle route but the country roads are reasonably flat. On the B4040, Malmesbury to Cricklade road. Travelling towards Cricklade, go through Minety and on towards the village of Leigh. The entrance to Blakehill Farm is on the right within Leigh, signposted from the B4040 by a brown tourist sign.

WALKING TIME: 580 acres (235ha). There are two waymarked trails, the 'Blue Walk', which is 1.7 miles, or a slightly shorter 'Red Walk' which is 1.4 miles. At a leisurely pace, a walk would take between 1 and a half to 2 and a half hours, depending on route.

30-MINUTE VISIT: The network of access routes provides flexibility for those visitors who want to find their own way around the reserve in their own time.

One of the largest expanses of lowland neutral hay meadow in the UK, and a slice of living history. Such meadows were once an everyday feature of the farmed landscape, but up to 98 per cent of them have been lost through the intensification of farming after the war. As a former RAF airfield, it used to reverberate to the sound of Dakotas delivering supplies to the battlefields of World War II Europe. Now you can hear the pure notes of the skylark and the ground is a rippling carpet of wildflowers. Rare plants such as the spiny restharrow and dyer's greenwood, once commonplace, almost vanished in the latter 20th century, but survived in patches here. You may see kestrels, wheatear, whinchat and stonechat. Butterflies include the small copper, meadow brown, and brown hairstreak and the six-spotted burnet moth. The reserve is also the base of the Trust's Northern Farming Enterprise. It is a LEAF (Linking Environment And Farming) Demonstration Farm, and aims to show that farming and wildlife can co-exist. It is grazed by the Trust's herd of belted Galloway, beef shorthorn, Aberdeen angus and Luing cattle. Mammals such as brown hare and roe deer can be seen all year round. Currently, the 300 acres (121ha) of the central plateau are cut for hay in July or August, after the skylarks have nested, and then grazed by cattle and sheep.

DID YOU KNOW?

- **After the war, Blakehill was used for many years as a listening station by the Ministry of Defence, and although some of the land was grazed, this was not intensive. This meant that very little artificial fertiliser had been used, allowing a rich variety of wildflowers to survive without competition from more vigorous grasses. The Trust is now carefully managing the land with the goal of restoring the entire site to wildflower-rich status within 15-20 years.**

Coombe Bissett SSSI

Near Salisbury; **OS Map** SU 112257; **Map Ref** E9

ACCESS/CONDITIONS: The reserve consists of different sections: flat valley floor and top, and steep downland slopes. Entrance is up a short hill. Access to reserve for wheelchair users is through small gate in car park. Key to gate is available on request from the Trust head office.
HOW TO GET THERE: From Salisbury bus station take the 'Wilts and Dorset' 184 or the 29 (302 on a Saturday). From Salisbury to Blandford road (A354) at Coombe Bissett, take turning to Homington. After 0.5 miles turn right into Pennings Drove.
WALKING TIME: 86 acres (35ha). To walk around the entire reserve would take about 1 and a half hours. Shorter circular walks varying in duration from 30 minutes to an hour are easily achievable.
30-MINUTE VISIT: Park on the verge of Pennings Drove, walk into the reserve by the main entrance, turn left and walk down the hill, past an information board and through a kissing gate to pick up the loop walk to the main entrance.

The views of the coombe and chalk downland are spectacular. In summer the downland is a blaze of wildflower colour, with butterflies and the sounds of grasshoppers and skylarks all around. The reserve bursts into life in spring, with cowslips lighting up the slopes. Sunny days in late April and May bring out the vivid green hairstreak butterfly, followed by the iridescent shades of the Adonis blue. In summer the slopes of the coombe are a blaze of colour and sound and the flowers include burnet saxifrage, burnt orchid and clustered bellflower. Also the common rock-rose, bird's-foot trefoil, kidney and horseshoe vetch. These are important food plants for bees and butterflies, including the chalkhill blue, brown argus, and dingy skipper. Autumn brings a stunning display of devil's-bit scabious, the blooms casting a purple haze over the furthest section of the downland, and yellow-hammers gather in the scrubby hedgerows. Cold winter mornings give a frosty glaze to the seed heads of the old-man's beard and the red berries of the hawthorn, and a soft piping sound heralds a flock of redwings passing through.

Langford Lakes

Near Wilton; **OS Map** SU 038369; **Map Ref** E7

ACCESS/CONDITIONS: Good flat access, including for wheelchairs, to buildings and hides via all-weather paths. There is unfenced deep water on site so children should be accompanied.
HOW TO GET THERE: 250 metres from National Cycle Network Route 24. Regular buses stop at Steeple Langford. Hourly bus (X4, X5, X6), Monday to Saturday, 7am to 6pm.
WALKING TIME: Birdwatchers could spend half a day here. A walk around the 1,000 metres of paths takes 1 to 1 and a half hours.
30-MINUTE VISIT: Sit in one of the hides and look out on to the lakes to see an ever-changing variety of birds, dragonflies and butterflies (depending on time of year).

This beautiful reserve consists of three lakes, which were former gravel pits, and a half-mile stretch of the internationally important chalk stream, the River Wylye. Look out for the kingfisher and the elusive water vole. Otters also regularly use the river and lakes. River restoration has improved the wetland habitats for many plants and animals, which are only found in chalk streams. Around the lakes, new islands have been created and marshes, ponds and wader scrapes have been excavated. The reed fringes are steadily increasing following reshaping of the shores, and numbers of breeding ducks and reed warblers are rising.

Langford offers opportunities to experience the migration of birds in spring and autumn, with the possibility of seeing waders, terns and osprey, as they stop over. Winter is the best time to experience a wildfowl spectacle, as many ducks, including tufted duck, pochard, gadwall, wigeon, teal and great crested grebe use the lakes as their wintering grounds. You may even catch a glimpse of one of the UK's most endangered birds, the bittern.

Lower Moor Farm

Near Malmesbury; **OS Map** SU 008936 **Map Ref** E1

ACCESS/CONDITIONS: All three bird hides have wheelchair facilities. The ground is flat.
HOW TO GET THERE: There is no cycle route but the reserve is situated on country roads with pleasant riding conditions. For information on the nearest bus routes phone the National Enquiry Line: 0870 6082608. By car, leave Oaksey in the direction of Somerford Keynes, cross the railway line and follow an S-bend. Immediately after the S-bend the entrance is on the right.
WALKING TIME: Lower Moor Farm is 96 acres (39ha) and a circular walk from the visitor centre past ponds, lakes and woodland takes 1 hour. You can easily spend half a day exploring the complex of reserves to enjoy the hay meadows and Swillbrook Lakes as well.
30-MINUTE VISIT: At the first bird hide, stop and enjoy the view of Cottage Lake. Move along the boardwalk to the grassy embankment separating Mallard Lake from the two smaller lakes and enjoy the vistas.

Lower Moor Farm is a wonderful waterscape of three lakes, two brooks, ponds and wetland scrapes linked together by ancient hedges, woodland and meadows. It forms the gateway to four neighbouring Wiltshire Wildlife Trust reserves, Clattinger Farm, Oaksey Moor Farm Meadow, Swillbrook Lakes and Sandpool, for which the Trust is currently fundraising. Combined, they form a sequence of habitats that provide year-round interest.

In spring you can see the delicate nodding heads of snake's head fritillary in Clattinger's meadows. In the early summer, these fields are a sea of wildflowers, including the southern marsh-orchid, and the nationally rare downy-fruited sedge, until July when the hay is cut. Also, migrant birds, such as hobbies and reed bunting, start to appear at Lower Moor Farm and Swillbrook. Swallows, swifts and both sand and housemartins duck and dive over the lakes in pursuit of insects. Kingfishers flash by and warblers and nightingales sing out from the lakeside scrub. Waterfowl, such as the great crested grebe, coot and mallard, nest around the lakes and the air brims with dragonflies, such as the downy emerald, and damselflies like the common blue. In winter the lakes are wintering grounds to large numbers of ducks, geese and swans, including teal, pochard and gadwall, grebes and the snipe with its extraordinary long bill.

DID YOU KNOW?

- The lakes were created by gravel extraction in the 1970s. The biggest is Mallard Lake, one of only two lakes in Wiltshire to be designated an SSSI.
- Three species of stonewort live in Lower Moor Farm's Mallard Lake, including the nationally scarce lesser bearded stonewort.
- The visitor centre, bird hides, paths and even an otter holt were built using sustainably-sourced timber or recycled waste materials.

Snake's head fritillary flowers in April and May

Dorset

About the Trust

The Dorset Wildlife Trust was founded in 1961 to protect the wildlife and natural habitats of the county. Its founders' efforts to conserve the unspoilt beauty of Dorset attracted wide-ranging support and the Trust has grown to become the largest voluntary conservation organisation in the county, with over 25,000 members.

Dorset Wildlife Trust
☎ 01305 264620
www.dorsetwildlife.co.uk

Bracketts Coppice

Between Halstock and Corscombe
OS Map ST 514074; **Map Ref** F11

Early-purple and greater butterfly orchids, wood anemone; silver-washed and marsh fritillaries; dipper, kingfisher; dormouse, bats. Undulating and steep in parts. Ground conditions can be difficult with gates and stiles.

Higher Hyde Heath

Between Bovington and Wareham
OS Map SY 851902; **Map Ref** F16

Emperor moths, large red damselfly; nightjars, water rail; sand lizard, smooth snake. Wheelchair access to hide and viewing area. Fairly level but wet for most of the year. Self-guided marked trail and reserve leaflet.

Lorton Meadows

Near Weymouth
OS Map SY 674826; **Map Ref** F14

Situated in a quiet valley running between Upwey and Littlemoor, with distant views of Weymouth Bay and the Isle of Portland. About half the reserve is scheduled as a SSSI, and the remains of a fine, formerly listed, traditional Dorset barn made from local limestone have been converted to a private dwelling and reserve information centre. Brown hare; black knapweed, bee orchid, corky-fruited water dropwort, grass vetchling; green-veined white, large skipper; stonechat, garden warbler. Undulating and heavy in wet winter conditions.

Sopley Common

Near Hurn
OS Map SZ 129971; **Map Ref** F18

Part of a heathland formed some 3,000 years ago, today agricultural improvement, afforestation and urban growth have left Sopley Common as a remnant of its former self, a much-valued example of a heathland habitat reduced and threatened throughout its limited European range. Sand lizard; green tiger, rare wood tiger beetles, raft spider; long-leaved sundew, cotton grass. Mainly fairly level and dry, but with wet areas and steep sloping scarp.

Upton Heath SSSI

Near Upton
OS Map SY 989951; **Map Ref** F17

Upton Heath is a little-known reserve in an urban setting, overlooking Poole Harbour, with views across to Corfe Castle and the Isle of Purbeck. It is a SSSI and proposed site Special Protection Area (European designation). Heath spotted orchid, bell heather, marsh gentian; Dartford warbler, stonechat; adder, sand lizard. Fairly level but wet.

Fontmell Down

Near Shaftesbury; **OS Map** ST 886187; **Map Ref** F7

ACCESS/CONDITIONS: Steep slopes.
HOW TO GET THERE: Nearest railway station Gillingham, 9 miles away. Local bus services Compton Abbas and Fontmell Magna (Monday to Saturday). Park in the National Trust car park immediately to the north of the reserve on B3081.
WALKING TIME: 148 acres (60ha). Allow 2 hours to see the major part of the reserve.
30-MINUTE VISIT: Walk the most northerly part of the reserve, known as 'The Curlews and Burys', for the best views. In spring and early summer, the abundance of orchids, as well as butterflies, in this area will be particularly rewarding.

Fontmell Down, just to the south of Shaftesbury, commands some of the most spectacular views across the Blackmore Vale in north Dorset. At an elevation of some 198 metres, this beautiful chalk escarpment offers a wealth of wildlife. In spring, there are stunning displays of chalk downland flowers, with many orchids, and a very broad range of butterflies, often including a number of rarities. Summer is the 'high' period for this chalk downland, when sightings of flower and butterfly species can be richly rewarding. Look out for chalk milkwort, lady's bedstraw, bird's-foot trefoil and early gentian; early-purple, bee, frog and pyramidal orchids; hay rattle, restharrow and small scabious. You may also see grizzled and dingy skippers: silver-washed and dark-green fritillary; comma, brimstone, green hairstreak and the occasional Duke of Burgundy.

History plays its part in this unspoilt tract of countryside. For example, there are traces of a Bronze Age field system and cross-ridge dykes on Fontmell Down.

Powerstock Common

Near Dorchester; **OS Map** SY 540973; **Map Ref** F13

ACCESS/CONDITIONS: Both waymarked trails are on level to gently sloping ground. Most of the walk is on forestry tracks or disused railway lines. Sections of these can get muddy. Plantation conifers are continuously being harvested and removed, so please take care.
HOW TO GET THERE: From the A35, follow signs to West Compton and then to Eggardon Hill.
WALKING TIME: 284-acre (115ha) reserve. Allow 2 hours to explore.
30-MINUTE VISIT: Follow the short waymarked walk.

Powerstock Common is a rare example of a historic landscape and the nearest one can get to 'wilderness' in West Dorset. There's a wonderful variety of wildlife and visitors will see evidence of man's vain attempts to tame the countryside in the remains of an old railway, a brick kiln and failed conifer plantations. A large reserve of 284 acres (115ha) with a mosaic of habitats, including a variety of grassland types, wet and dry woodland, ponds and streams. In the spring, birds are most evident, with chiffchaffs, willow warblers, white-throats, blackcaps, marsh tits, great spotted woodpeckers and ravens and buzzards overhead. Beneath the trees, bluebells, primrose, wood anemone, herb Paris and wild daffodil flower. Summer brings a splendid show of butterflies, including marsh fritillary and wood white. Grassland flowers such as devil's-bit scabious, meadow thistle, sneezewort, betony, common-spotted orchid and bee orchid can be found. The ponds support great crested newt and many dragonflies. In the autumn and winter, large mammals, such as roe and fallow deer, are frequently seen.

Tadnoll and Winfrith

Near Dorchester; **OS Map** SY 792873; **Map Ref** F15

ACCESS/CONDITIONS: Can be very wet in places during winter months. On Tadnoll, conditions of main paths/rides usually pretty good. Stay on paths, especially during summer months. The David Limb Trail at Winfrith (the main entrance track) is suitable for wheelchair access.
HOW TO GET THERE: From A352, Tadnoll entrance is along Redbridge Road, Winfrith Heath entrance is along Gatemore Road, less than 100 metres past the left turn signposted to Tadnoll. Limited parking on the verge at Tadnoll entrance. Park in a small lay-by by Winfrith entrance track.
WALKING TIME: 255-acre (103ha) reserve linked by footbridges to Tadnoll, creating a total area of around 400 acres (162ha). The full circuit of both takes 2 hours.
30-MINUTE VISIT: Stick to Tadnoll; stay on the main track towards Old Knowle Hill, then follow the walk through a copse of deciduous woodland.

Tadnoll and Winfrith make up nearly 400 acres (162ha) of mixed heathland habitats; dry, wet and humid heaths, bogs and pools, grazed flood meadows and a stream. Part of Thomas Hardy's 'Egdon Heath', the reserves are classified SSSI, SPA, SAC and Ramsar Site. You may catch a glimpse of a sand lizard basking in spring, or a smooth snake on the dry heath. Orchids start to show and summer migrants begin to arrive. The heathland and wet meadows are alive in summer with a multitude of insects, birds and flowers, such as orchids, knapweeds, small red damselflies, raft spider, silver-studded blue butterfly, nightjar, tree pipit and hobby. In autumn look out for marsh gentians, bog orchid, cotton grass, bog asphodels and autumn lady's tresses. In winter, the meadows are regularly flooded, attracting waders such as snipe. Merlin have been spotted and it is possible to see Dartford warblers, stonechat, meadow pipit, woodcock, fieldfare and redwing. Fine examples of all that is special among the plants and animals associated with heathland, with a combination of dry, breezy heights and molinia swamp/wet heath to provide interesting contrasts. There are also deep ditches, the Tadnoll stream and wet meadows, making this place truly diverse. The views from the tumuli on Old Knowle (Tadnoll) are fabulous, with dramatic cliffs comprising rocks from the Carboniferous period (354-290 million years ago).

WILDLIFE FACT: RED SQUIRRELS

Even when you know where to go to spot red squirrels, they are still difficult to see, as they tend to spend their time up in the treetops gnawing pine cones. Instead, look out for evidence of them, such as scratch marks on the bark of trees and large nests – or dreys – at the forks in trees. Look out also for the remnants of pine cones gnawed into the shape of an apple core. And red squirrels don't hibernate, they store up fungi to see them through winter, so look out for them all year in places in Cumbria, Scotland, the Isle of Wight and some areas of East Anglia.

Brownsea Island

Poole; **OS Map** SZ 028878; **Map Ref** F22

OPENING TIMES: Island: 10am to 5pm, mid-March to end of October; 10am to 6pm, July to August (afternoon guided tour only). Self-guided trail and tours (£2 adults, £1 children, Trust members free). High Hide is members only. In winter, there are 'Members Days' one day each month. Boat fee plus landing fee (National Trust members free).
ACCESS/CONDITIONS: One section of the trail has a steep path and not all of the trail is accessible to wheelchairs; the squirrel platform and alder carr boardwalk can be reached. The public hide has wheelchair facilities, the other hides have ramp access.
HOW TO GET THERE: Ferry from Poole Quay or Sandbanks (01202 669955/01202 666226). Train to Poole and Parkstone (Poole Quay is a 20-minute walk). Buses from Poole station travel to Sandbanks every hour (information: 01202 673555).
WALKING TIME: The well-marked self-guided trail takes anything up to 3 hours.
30-MINUTE VISIT: Go along the boardwalk and to the first hides for excellent views of the lagoon and its birds.
A MEMBER SAYS: 'It's like coming to another world, and only 10 minutes across the water.'

Brownsea's great variety of habitats offer a great day out for birdwatchers in the Poole area. The chance to watch at first hand the red squirrels and nesting gulls and terns incredibly close to the hides is a magical and relaxing experience. The island is owned by the National Trust, which leases the northern portion of 247 acres (100ha) to the Dorset Wildlife Trust. In summer, the lagoon is host to breeding sea birds, including black-headed gulls, sandwich and common terns. In a good year, there can be over 500 pairs of these birds combined. They can be seen in extreme close-up from the MacDonald Hide. Also nesting are oystercatcher, shelduck, mallard, teal and gadwall. In spring and autumn, the lagoon may play host to a variety of passage waders and wildfowl, including lingering avocets and black-tailed godwits, which are here in internationally important numbers in the winter. Curlew, sandpiper and little stint are regular visitors in autumn. The nature trail passes the reedbed where, with luck, water rail, water vole and a variety of dragonflies may be seen (including the nationally rare downy emerald and small red damselfly). On the lakes in summer there is a good chance of seeing little grebes and the herons and little egrets from the breeding colony.

DID YOU KNOW?

- At 1,000-plus birds, Brownsea Island hosts the UK's largest wintering flock of avocets.
- It is the first site in Britain where the little egret nested (1996) and hosted Britain's largest flock of spoonbills (2007).

Kingcombe Meadows

Near Toller Porcorum; **OS Map** SY 555992; **Map Ref** F12

ACCESS/CONDITIONS: Some parts have deep mud all year. Because of the terrain, this reserve may not be suitable for all disabilities. A ramp gives access to Pound Cottage. Keep out of dangerous swamps. Keep away from livestock.
HOW TO GET THERE: There is a train to Maiden Newton, 4 miles. By car, turn off the A356 to Toller Porcorum then on to Lower Kingcombe. Small car parks at Pound Cottage and Copse Close. No coaches. Large parties should make arrangements with the warden.
WALKING TIME: 289-acre (177ha) reserve. A full day is needed.
30-MINUTE VISIT: A nature trail is signposted with green arrows.
A MEMBER SAYS: 'The peace and quiet of the beautifully managed wildlife haven is unbelievable.'

The meadows, marshy ground, hedgerows and woodland around the hamlet of Lower Kingcombe are a legacy of farming carried out without the use of pesticides, artificial fertilisers or other modern agricultural practices. There are few areas in Dorset that compare with its distinctive patchwork of small fields, unimproved grasslands and thick ancient hedgerows. It is a large nature reserve of national importance managed as a working farm with suckler cows and sheep playing an important part in the annual grazing regime which preserves the various grassland habitats. To wander round Kingcombe is to get a glimpse of the past, reminiscent of Thomas Hardy's rural Dorset. The 'neutral' grassland meadows are of special importance, with great floral diversity, including the uncommon lady's mantle, corky-fruited water dropwort, pepper saxifrage and devil's-bit scabious. The marshy areas of these fields stand out with colourful flag iris, ragged robin and water forget-me-nots. Formerly a low-intensity farm, this reserve still uses traditional farming methods to achieve its conservation aims. A wide spectrum of geology allows a huge botanical diversity. In spring, cows are calving and the ewes are lambing – look out for otters, too. The lovely wildflower meadows are at their best in summer. Autumn sees mixed parties of tits and warblers along the hedges and woodland edges. Woodcocks occur in winter with ravens and buzzards being usually present.

DID YOU KNOW?

- **Kingcombe has a field boundary system and hedgerows which are centuries old.**
- **There are panoramic views from Kingcombe over Powerstock Vale to the sea at Lyme Bay.**

Purbeck MWR

Wareham; **OS Map** SY 909787; **Map Ref** F23

OPENING TIMES: Open all year. Kimmeridge Bay accessed via toll road (£1 per car, rising to £2 in summer). Marine centre: 10am to 5pm daily, Easter to September; weekends in winter.
ACCESS/CONDITIONS: The marine centre is suitable for disabled access. Steps down to Kimmeridge Bay from main car park make wheelchair access to the bay difficult.
HOW TO GET THERE: Signposted off A351 Wareham bypass, 7 miles from Wareham. Train to Wareham. Public transport infrequent. Pay-and-display parking for around 1,000 cars. Access via toll road.
WALKING TIME: Purbeck MWR covers about 6 miles of coast, with Kimmeridge Bay at its centre with about half a mile of rocky shore to explore.
30-MINUTE VISIT: The cliff-top car park has great views over Kimmeridge Bay and is a favoured spot for picnics, from where it is only a stone's throw down to the shore.
A MEMBER SAYS: 'I keep coming back to Kimmeridge to marvel at its fascinating geology and wonderful rockpools. And the new marine centre is a big asset – very interesting and informative.'

Kimmeridge Bay at the centre of Purbeck MWR is a great place to explore the life of the rocky shore. It is steeped in history, and there are hours of fun to be had for children aged two to 92, exploring the abundant and colourful life of the rock pools! With its unusual double low tide, you can spend hours pottering in the rock pools. Some of the best low tides of the year occur in the spring, usually from the middle to the end of March. This is a great time to check out the new colourful growth of seaweeds and the many animals that will have been left high and dry by the receding tide – some laying or bearing eggs. Over the summer, snorkellers and divers can marvel at the diverse range of underwater life in the often still and clear waters. Those not so keen to get wet can enjoy live pictures from beneath the waves on the marine centre's live link to the camera on the seabed. As autumn sets in, the vibrant colour of the seaweeds has all but disappeared, but there is still plenty to be found in the rock pools. Visitors to Kimmeridge Bay over the winter are likely to have the bay to themselves, and the storms usually bring in plenty of treasures for beachcombers to explore.

DID YOU KNOW?

- **Purbeck is the longest-established VMNR in Britain.**
- **Kimmeridge Bay experiences a double low tide, this means there's an extended period for rock poolers to explore.**
- **The reserve marks the most easterly known stronghold of the pink sea fan *Eunicella verrucosa*. Those unable to dive can see one on display in the marine centre.**

Alderney

About the Trust

The Alderney Wildlife Trust was launched in May 2002, in response to concerns about the lack of land management in Alderney and to combat the ensuing loss of habitat. It took over from the existing Alderney Conservation Volunteers organisation. The Trust has inherited the Longis bird hide, which continues to be very popular with residents and visitors alike.

Alderney Wildlife Trust ☎ 01481 822935
www.alderneywildlife.org

Longis

St Anne

ACCESS/CONDITIONS: Coast footpath is level but sandy. No purpose-built wheelchair access. Nearest WC is at the Nunnery car park 50 metres from the reserve.
HOW TO GET THERE: Aurigny Air Services (0871 8710717) from Southampton, Guernsey, Jersey or Le Cocqs Airlink (01481824567) from Bournemouth and Jersey, or (by arrangement) Lady Marais (01481822811) from France. Sail to Alderney's Victorian Harbour.
WALKING TIME: The full circuit takes 1 and a half hours.
30-MINUTE VISIT: Walk along the length of the reserve, starting from the Mannez Quarry Pond, follow the coast footpath and finish at the Longis Hide.
A MEMBER SAYS: 'For me, the eastern tip of Alderney, with its rugged shoreline, piping oystercatchers, varied plantlife and the view of France and other islands, is the most idyllic spot in the whole of the Channel Islands.'

Although small, Alderney is a unique place. Whether you're a birder, budding botanist or simply enjoy walking, it is unlike the rest of the British Isles. The hide gives you access to its wide range of birdlife and the coastal walk reveals the ferocity of the Alderney tidal race and richness of its coastline. Spring sees a range of calcareous grassland species in flower, with small haresear and annual restharrow spotted sporadically along the shoreline, while swathes of sand crocus and green winged orchid lie slightly further inland. Heavy bird migration is evident in spring, with large numbers of hirundines hawking insects over the pond. Summer heralds the arrival of the pyramidal orchid, which soon becomes a common sight. As summer progresses, Longis Pond becomes a haven for breeding birds, with little grebe, reed, sedge and recently fan-tailed warbler, while Alderney's endemic sea lavender closes this season with flower. During this season the leucistic hedgehog can be found throughout the reserve. Autumn sees the return of the migrants and whimbrel, bar-tailed godwit, little stint and black redstart all visit. As winter approaches, the tidal race, which flows around Alderney's coastline at an average speed of six knots, pummels the inter-tidal zone with its numbers of oystercatcher, turnstone, ringed plover, dunlin, curlew and little egret. Fort Houmet Herbé is one of the best points from which to observe Alderney's two tidal races converging.

DID YOU KNOW?

- **The reserve contains 19 Red Data Book listed species.**
- **Alderney is the only part of the British Isles to lack any form of wildlife or habitat protection legislation, with only one species protection law (1950 Bird Preservation Law). Longis provides the only protection for dozens of threatened species on the island.**

Fort Houmet, Herbé, Alderney

Isles of Scilly

About the Trust

The Isles of Scilly Wildlife Trust cares for the wildlife sites that make up 60 per cent of the landmass of Scilly and includes all of the uninhabited islands, islets and rocks and most of the coastal fringes on the inhabited islands. The Trust has an office and visitor centre on St Mary's, and nature trails on St Mary's run through wetland, woodland and meadows.

Isles of Scilly Wildlife Trust ☎ 01720 422153
www.ios-wildlifetrust.org.uk

The Isles of Scilly

St Mary's; **OS Map** SV 900114; **Map Ref** A14

OPENING TIMES: Open all year except restricted access where sea birds and seals breed – please seek advice before visiting uninhabited islands.
ACCESS/CONDITIONS: Network of permissive footpaths around the inhabited islands, with varying terrain. Wear stout footwear. The paths and boardwalks at Lower Moors and Higher Moors, St Mary's are suitable for wheelchairs.
HOW TO GET THERE: Planes fly from south-west mainland airports to St Mary's and the *Scillonian III* sails from Penzance (peak season; foot passengers only; 0845 7105555). Helicopter flies from Penzance to St Mary's or Tresco (information: 01736 363871).
WALKING TIME: Walks of varying lengths in the 4,562 acres (1,846ha) of open land and beaches leased to the Trust by the Duchy of Cornwall, spread over some 100 islands and islets, including the inhabited islands of St Mary's, St Agnes, Bryher and St Martin's.
30-MINUTE VISIT: Take one of the pleasant walks around the Garrison or from Porth Cressa around Peninnis to Old Town through the Lower Moors nature trail and back to Hugh Town.
A MEMBER SAYS: 'Scilly is an amazing place; I can't wait to come back next year! The Wildlife Trust does a fantastic job.'

Scilly is like nowhere else in the world, a microcosm of diversity; a unique way of life, a beautiful unspoilt natural environment, once visited never forgotten. Spring is full of colour and wildflowers – summer starts early here. During summer, the islands are full of life, but not crowded. The town is full of visitors and the harbour is busy with boats going between the islands and out to sea. You can easily find a quiet spot to soak in the scenery and see tame thrushes, blackbirds and flocks of sparrows after your crumbs. Summer is a great time for sea-watching with plenty of sea birds and marine life. The underwater world is rich in marine life and worth a look, too, as the water is crystal clear in Scilly. Autumn sees an influx of birdwatchers, migratory birds and the beginning of the winter storms. Winter is a quiet time but not for the farmers, busy picking the narcissus crop, the scent of which fills the air with its heady fragrance. On the island of St Agnes, you can find three different types of adder's tongue fern.

DID YOU KNOW?

- **There are no snakes, lizards or newts on the islands and few mammals, the most famous being the Scilly shrew.**
- **Bats do not hibernate here due to the mild climate so can be seen feeding all year round.**

Great Bay St Martins, Isles of Scilly

SOUTH EAST

From the iconic white cliffs and breathtaking Downs of Kent and Sussex, to the hidden glades and heathy woodland of the New Forest, the South East region is home to some real wildlife jewels, and all on the doorstep of London.

In the Thames basin of Surrey and Berkshire are some of the finest areas of lowland heathland in Europe, home to Dartford warblers, woodlarks and all of Britain's six native reptile species. During summer evenings, sleek hobbies hunt dragonflies over the heathland, followed as dusk falls by the unworldly 'churring' of the nightjar.

The rolling chalk hills of the North and South Downs are rich in wildflowers, including several species of orchid. Relatively widespread species, common in the right places, include early purple, pyramidal and fragrant orchids, while some real rarities, including military, man and monkey orchids still hang on where conditions are right. These warm, flower-rich grasslands are in their turn rich in butterflies, with chalkhill and Adonis blue, Duke of Burgundy and silver-spotted skipper the specialities of the region.

From the beech woods of the Weald to the ancient royal hunting grounds of the New Forest, the South East is the most wooded region in England. In the spring, many of these woodlands are carpeted in bluebells, greater stitchwort, wood anemone and wild garlic. Later on in the year, the woods are alive with summer migrants: the dawn chorus is a rich mix of warblers and other birds, but the real highlight is the nightingale.

These woods are also home to the most recent mammal to return to the British countryside. A small number of wild boar escaped from farms in the region during the storms of 1989, and there are now thought to be around 500 living in the wild.

To find one of the other woodland denizens, you have to cross the Solent. The Isle of Wight is one of the very few places left in England where red squirrels can still be found, protected by the surrounding sea from the larger, non-native grey squirrel which has taken its place across the rest of the country.

You don't even need to venture out into the countryside. Right in the centre of London, where grey squirrels come to take peanuts from your hand and ring-necked parakeets fly noisily overhead, you may catch sight of a peregrine hunting across the city skyline. This wonderful bird has recently moved into the city, showing that in this, Britain's most densely populated region, the opportunities for watching some spectacular wildlife really are everywhere.

Opposite: Linford, Hampshire

NOT TO BE MISSED

- **BOWDOWN WOODS**
  Mysterious hidden valleys, sunny glades and patches of heathland hold a wealth of wildlife in this 136-acre (55ha) riverside reserve in Berkshire.

- **CHOBHAM COMMON**
  The largest NNR in the South East, Chobham is best known for its population of ladybirds, butterflies and dragonflies.

- **EBERNOE COMMON**
  Over 14 of the 16 species of British bat have been recorded here, including thriving colonies of the rare barbastelle and Bechstein's bat.

- **RYE MEADS**
  Jointly managed with the RSPB, this bird-friendly reserve sees around 40 pairs of common terns travelling over 25,000 miles every year to breed here. Otters were introduced in 1991 after an absence of more than 20 years.

- **SANDWICH AND PEGWELL BAY**
  An internationally important site for its waders and wildfowl, look out for sanderling and grey plover in the winter months.

Hampshire and Isle of Wight

About the Trust

Hampshire and Isle of Wight Wildlife Trust is the leading local wildlife conservation charity in Hampshire and the Island. It looks after 57 wildlife reserves, and has 27,000 members and 1,000 volunteers.

Hampshire and Isle of Wight Wildlife Trust
☎ 01489 774400
www.hwt.org.uk

Baddesley Common and Emer Bog

Near North Baddesley
OS Map SU 395214; **Map Ref** F19

An open landscape of grassland heath. Fauna include: roe deer; white admiral and purple emperor butterflies; stonechat and tree pipit. Plantlife includes marsh gentian, heath spotted orchid and petty whin.

Blashford Lakes

Near Ringwood
OS Map SU 153075; **Map Ref** F10

Come to see over-wintering wildfowl – such as tufted duck, pochard, wigeon, shoveler and gadwall – as well as brown hawker dragonflies and red-eyed damselflies. Plants include spiked water milfoil, needle spike-rush and meadowsweet.

Eaglehead and Bloodstone Copses

Near Ashley
OS Map SZ 582877; **Map Ref** F25

This is a particularly fine chalk woodland featuring excellent spring flowers and a population of rare red squirrel. A large number of butterflies can be seen in the grassland, including brown argus and chalkhill blue.

Flexford

Near Eastleigh
OS Map SU 424215; **Map Ref** F5

A popular green haven amid urban development, where woodpecker, redpoll and siskin can be sighted. Plantlife includes ragged robin, wood club rush and wood sneezewort. A woodland walk by Monk's Brook passes through flower-rich wet meadows and woodland.

Noar Hill

Near Selborne
OS Map SU 742319; **Map Ref** F3

One of the most interesting chalk grassland and scrub sites in Britain, rich in flowers and butterflies. It is home to more than a dozen species of orchid and some 35 breeding butterfly species, including Duke of Burgundy and brown hairstreak.

Roydon Woods

Near Brockenhurst
OS Map SU 315009; **Map Ref** F6

Follow the network of paths through the home of deer, nightjars and tawny owls. Other sights include glow worms, fungi, swathes of bluebells, butterflies and dragonflies, including broad-bodied chaser.

Swanwick Lakes

Near Swanwick
OS Map SU 507099; **Map Ref** F9

This old clay works has been reclaimed by nature. Common sights include zigzag clover, orchids, butterflies and nightingales.

Winnall Moors

On the edge of Winchester
OS Map SU 490306; **Map Ref** F2

A tranquil spot featuring the rare green-flowered helleborine and southern marsh orchid. Reed and sedge warblers breed in spring, and the meadows feed snipe and redshank.

Arreton Down

Near Newport; **OS Map** SZ 538871; **Map Ref** F24

ACCESS/CONDITIONS: The footpaths across the Down are not surfaced. There are also stock tracks, or Holloways, across the site.
HOW TO GET THERE: Bus route 8 passes through Arreton from Newport and Sandown. By car, from Newport take the A3056 towards Arreton; before entering the village turn left, towards Arreton Manor (on the right bend).
WALKING TIME: The reserve covers 48 acres (19ha). It is possible to complete a circuit, with good views over the Eastern Yar valley in approximately 1 hour at a fairly steady pace.
30-MINUTE VISIT: Explore the Down.

In spring and early summer the season starts off with primroses and cowslips, then much of the Down will turn yellow with a mixture of horseshoe and kidney vetches.

Look out and listen for birds such as the yellow-hammer, white-throat, cuckoo, turtle dove and raven. As summer warms up, rare bastard toadflax and chalkhill blue butterflies can be found among flowers that include scabious, harebells, knapweed, rock-rose, musk thistles and clover. Into early autumn a member of the orchid family, autumn lady's-tresses, starts to appear and as winter approaches, the flowers set seed and migratory birds take advantage of the food and shelter. For a brief period wheatears search the grassland, warblers work the scrub edge for insects, and stonechats flit back and forth from their chosen perches.

The archaeological interest of the Down may best be observed during the winter months when vegetation is sparse. Look out for the Bronze Age round barrow and Holloways.

St Catherine's Hill SSSI

Winchester; **OS Map** SU 484276; **Map Ref** F4

ACCESS/CONDITIONS: Reserve paths are unsurfaced and uneven in places, and there are steps up the hill. A bridleway runs through the south of the site, connecting to Twyford and St Cross Road footpaths.
HOW TO GET THERE: From the centre of Winchester take the B3335 south and turn left into Garnier Road. Leave the M3 at J9 (from the north) or J10 (from the south) following signs for Alton (A31). At the next roundabout keep straight on towards Southampton (A33) and then Winchester. Car park for approximately 25 cars on Garnier Road and approximately 6 cars off Morestead Road.
WALKING TIME: The full circuit takes between 2 and 3 hours at an easy pace.
30-MINUTE VISIT: Park off Morestead Road and walk onto the Dongas for the large chalkhill population and stunning downland flowers.

Spring at this 144-acre (58ha) reserve brings carpets of cowslips, particularly on restoration areas, along with the first sightings of small blue and green hairstreak butterflies and music from willow warblers and chiffchaff.

Highlights of summer can include huge numbers of chalkhill blue butterflies, along with brown argus, marbled white and regular influxes of coloured yellow. The grassland is dotted with flowers such as rock-rose and kidney vetch along with bee, butterfly, fragrant and musk orchids. Birds include yellow hammer and skylark, while green woodpeckers feed on the anthills. Sparrowhawk and buzzard can be seen as they quarter the grassland and its resident flock of shetland sheep. Then late summer and early autumn see masses of devil's-bit scabious and delicate autumn-lady's tresses. Winter sees flocks of redwing and fieldfare, along with goldfinch and large groups of lapwing and golden plover on the nearby sewage works. In Plague Pits Valley stonechat and linnet are regular visitors.

Keyhaven and Pennington Marshes

Near Milford-on-Sea; **OS Map** SZ 310910; **Map Ref** F21

ACCESS/CONDITIONS: Easy access on level surface, but some steep slopes off the sea wall. Please keep off the marshes.
HOW TO GET THERE: By bus to Milford-on-Sea; the reserve is a 5-minute walk away. By car, head south from Lyndhurst on the A337 through Lymington and Pennington, turn left onto the B3058 and on through Milford-on-Sea to Keyhaven. Park in the public car park at Keyhaven.
WALKING TIME: Three routes take you through the reserve. The 3-mile circuit takes 1 and a half hours; the 5-mile circuit takes 2 and a half hours and the 7-mile circuit takes 3 and a half hours.
30-MINUTE VISIT: Walk along the sea wall returning along the same route.

In summer, the saltmarsh and mudflats play a vital part in the lives of breeding and migrant birds. Several thousand pairs of black-headed gulls breed here every year alongside terns and wading birds such as oystercatcher.

In autumn, wading birds and wildfowl – including dunlin, black-tailed godwit, wigeon, and brent geese – find their way here after breeding north of the Arctic Circle. Here they will spend the winter, protected from the worst of the winter storms by Hurst Spit, or use the marsh and mudflats for feeding prior to continuing their journey.

Within the mudflats the creeks provide a nursery for fish in spring, a situation exploited by the numerous little egrets and herons. At this time, small birds such as sand martins and swallows will be found feeding upon the increasing insect population.

WILDLIFE FACT: THE POWER OF NATURE

Well known as a traditional treatment for depression, St John's wort grows wild throughout the UK, in meadows, hedgerows and woodland. There are 12 closely related British species, all with similar five-petalled yellow flowers and opposite pairs of leaves.

Farlington Marshes

Near Havant; **OS Map** SU 685045; **Map Ref** F20

South East

ACCESS/CONDITIONS: The majority of the circular walk is on the sea wall. Several areas of the reserve are open access. Wellingtons or sturdy boots may be needed if conditions are wet.

HOW TO GET THERE: By bus from Havant and Portsmouth, stopping at the Hilton Hotel 0.25 miles from the reserve. The nearest railway station is Hilsea. By car, it is off the A27/A2030 roundabout. There are car parks at Broadmarsh Coastal Park and Farlington Marshes.

WALKING TIME: The 2.5-mile circular walk from the western entrance takes about 2 and a half hours if you stop to look at wildlife. The walk from Broadmarsh is 4.5 miles.

30-MINUTE VISIT: Walk to the lake viewpoint. It's especially good from July to October around high tide, when thousands of waders representing up to 20 species roost on the lake.

A MEMBER SAYS: 'This is a great place for views of Langstone Harbour and its islands. The mix of habitat is a great for seeing a variety of birds, such as brent geese and flocks of waders roosting.'

In winter the fields are grazed by up to 5,000 brent geese with other wildfowl including wigeon, pintail and shoveler. High tides can also see wader roosts running into thousands of birds on the shorter grass. Many of the birds are used to people and this allows unusually close views without the need for hides. Spring and autumn see migrant birds passing through, with waders on the pools and smaller birds in the scrub areas. Breeding birds include bearded tit, lapwing and redshank on the reserve, and out into the harbour a large gull and tern colony can be seen. Grassland butterflies are common in summer as well as many scarcer species of insect, specialists in brackish conditions. Many flowering plants have been recorded here, including unusual species such as sea barley, bulbous foxtail, slender hare's-ear, yellow-rattle, grass vetching and corky-fruited water-dropwort. Internationally important populations of migratory birds, particularly large populations of dark-bellied brent goose and black-tailed godwit, can be seen here. Thousands of waders can be seen on the lake at high tide, especially in the autumn, and the Deeps are particularly good for wildlife.

DID YOU KNOW?

- **Farlington Marshes has ongoing bird research projects carried out by the Trust in partnership with other organisations (local and international).**
- **Farlington Marshes was originally saltmarsh and mudflat, which was enclosed by a sea wall for pasture.**

Lower Test

Near Totton; **OS Map** SU 365145; **Map Ref** F8

ACCESS/CONDITIONS: Muddy in places. Boardwalks through the marsh and reedbed lead to one hide and two viewing screens. The reserve floods on high tides over about 4.4 metres.
HOW TO GET THERE: By train or bus from Totton and Southampton; by car from the M27/M271. There is on-road parking in Testwood Lane.
WALKING TIME: Walks in the 386-acre (156ha) reserve can vary from 3 to 5 miles and take between 2 and 4 hours.
WALKING TIME: A 4-mile figure-of-eight trail runs around the site. A trail leaflet is available from Hampshire Wildlife Trust.
30-MINUTE VISIT: Follow the boardwalk connecting the hide and viewing screens at the southern end of the reserve.
A MEMBER SAYS: 'It's lovely to have a special place like this where you can see so much wildlife – especially birds and insects – so close to the city.'

Much of the site is under tidal influences, during the spring and summer, saltmarsh plants such as sea aster, English scurvy grass and wild celery can be found. Further inland, there is brackish grassland with colonies of hairy buttercup, brookweed and the rare grass bulbous foxtail. The reedbeds support scarce species such as Cetti's warbler and bearded tit, as well as reed and sedge warblers. The old wet meadows have many flowering plants including water avens and green winged orchids. Over-wintering wildfowl regularly use this site. It is a particularly important winter refuge for species such as wigeon, teal and mallard. Up to 25 water pipits can be found over-wintering here. Marsh harrier and osprey are more regularly seen on passage during the spring and autumn. Waders can also be seen feeding in the scrapes, including green sandpiper, snipe and jack snipe.

DID YOU KNOW?

- *Crestrum lepidopes*, a fly new to Britain, was found here in 1999.
- After the reedbeds are cut, the reeds are used locally for thatching.

Pamber Forest

Near Tadley; **OS Map** SU 616608; **Map Ref** F1

South East

ACCESS/CONDITIONS: Circular trails lead from the marked entrance. The footpaths can be wet and muddy in winter.
HOW TO GET THERE: Bus 143 from Reading leaves hourly to Silchester and Pamber Heath; regular buses go from Basingstoke (44A, 50A, 51, 53A). By car, from Tadley, take Silchester Road and turn right into Impstone Road.
WALKING TIME: Allow at least 2 hours for a reasonable circuit, longer to cover the whole 479-acre (194ha) site.
30-MINUTE VISIT: From Impstone Road, walk across the pasture to Bowmonts Brook, follow the brook downstream and walk back up the public bridleway.
A MEMBER SAYS: 'The site is great for families and dog walkers. The open spaces allow views in several directions at once and are good places to see deer crossing.'

Traditionally used to provide timber for local crafts and industries, this remnant of the Royal Forest of Windsor is now managed for conservation and visitors. The extensive network of paths throughout the reserve ensures that you can explore the woodland, heathland and stream valleys thoroughly.

The open, sunlit rides and clearings are busy with butterflies in summer, taking nectar from the flowering plants. In spring, the stream valleys are carpeted with flowers. The heath and wood pasture on the east of the site make an interesting contrast to the woodland areas. Around the ponds in summer you can see many different dragonflies.

This area, along with Silchester Common, is grazed by cattle all year round. The woodland has coppice management and there is a programme of thinning to promote a better tree age structure. On the woodland floor, particularly in the stream valleys, flowering plants such as wild daffodil, primrose, violet, tutsan, Solomon's seal, star of Bethlehem and orpine.

DID YOU KNOW?

- The Pamber was once part of the Royal Forest and used for hunting. More recently it has been managed as high forest for the production of timber (you may notice the majority of trees appear to be of an even age) and coppice.

Berks, Bucks and Oxon

About the Trust

The Berkshire, Buckinghamshire and Oxfordshire Wildlife Trust was established in 1959 by local naturalists who could see the extent of harm being done to the wonderfully rich natural environment of the three counties. Today it owns or manages 88 nature reserves across Berkshire, Buckinghamshire and Oxfordshire.

Berkshire, Buckinghamshire and Oxfordshire Trust ☎ 01865 775476 www.bbowt.org.uk

Bernwood Meadows

Near Oxford

OS Map SP 606111; **Map Ref** G6

20 acres (8ha) of ancient ridge and furrow meadow beside Bernwood Forest. See green winged orchids in spring and brown and black hairstreak butterflies within blackthorn hedgerows. There are waymarked paths and a reserve leaflet with map is available. The reserve's flat paths can be muddy in winter.

Dry Sandford Pit

Near Abingdon

OS Map SU 467997; **Map Ref** G10

A fascinating mosaic of fossil-rich cliffs, fenland with ponds and streams, grassland, scrub and woodland set in an old quarry. Its geological wonders, nationally scarce fen and rich insect life make Dry Sandford Pit a reserve of national importance. With 18.5 acres (7.5ha), it is a top site for southern damselfly, solitary wasps, bees and marsh helleborine. There is a waymarked wildlife walk and a reserve leaflet with a map. The paths can be muddy in winter.

Foxholes

Near Milton-under-Wychwood

OS Map SP 252205; **Map Ref** G2

A beautiful woodland haven famed for its spectacular spring bluebells and abundant birdlife – but don't miss the fungi later in the year. Once part of the ancient Wychwood Forest, this tranquil woodland slopes gently down to the River Evenlode. It boasts 158 acres (64ha) of varied woodland, acid grassland and wet meadow. Visit for the fabulous display of bluebells in May, woodland birds in summer and fungi in autumn. It offers a waymarked wildlife walk (1.5 miles) and reserve leaflet with map.

Hungerford Marsh

Hungerford

OS Map SU 333687; **Map Ref** G13

This is an idyllic riverside nature reserve in west Berkshire – a refuge for a rich array of wetland birds and wildflowers. There are records of 120 bird species, including heron, kingfisher, little grebe, water rail and grasshopper warbler. River birds include mute swans, mallards, moorhens and coots. Grass snakes do well on this reserve and there are good chances to spot the threatened water vole – listen out for a tell-tale 'plop' as they launch into the river. It has waymarked paths with kissing gates. Paths can be muddy after rain and may be flooded in winter. There is street parking nearby.

Iffley Meadows

Oxford

OS Map SP 525036; **Map Ref** G8

This reserve is made up of ancient flood meadows set alongside the River Thames. It is one of the best places to see the snake's-head fritillary in spring. It features colourful meadow flowers all summer long, and hosts Cetti's and sedge warblers by the ditches. There are waymarked paths and a reserve leaflet with map is available. The flat paths can be muddy after rain and flooded in winter. Use the street parking nearby.

Inkpen Common

Near Hungerford

OS Map SU 382643; **Map Ref** G14

A remnant of rare ancient heathland below the slope of the Berkshire Downs. The 26-acre (10.5ha) reserve is a flower-filled wilderness fringed with woodland that rings with birdsong. The acid soil encourages a variety of heathland plants, including gorse, three types of heather, pale dog-violet and blue heath milkwort. Look and listen for warblers that appear in late spring and summer. There is a good range of heath plants, and fungi in autumn. Its paths are mostly flat with boardwalk over most boggy sections. There are waymarked paths and a reserve leaflet with map. The paths have kissing gates and livestock may be present. Parking on track opposite.

Little Linford Wood

Near Milton Keynes

OS Map SP 834455; **Map Ref** G1

A wonderful mix of young and mature woodland in North Bucks, this 105 acres (42.5ha) oak and ash woodland has a dense understorey of hazel and blackthorn. The thick re-growth of younger woodland is favoured by small mammals, including dormice. Mice and voles also find cover here, attracting predators including foxes and birds of prey. Stoats are also present on the site and may be seen darting across the path. The flower-rich woodland rides are a magnet for butterflies such as the scarce wood white. There is a waymarked wildlife walk and reserve leaflet with map. Its flat paths can be muddy in winter.

Moor Copse

Near Reading

OS Map SU 633738; **Map Ref** G12

Astride the River Pang, the 160-acre (65ha) Moor Copse is a diverse reserve, a wildlife treasure-trove and a haven of peace and beauty within the M4 corridor. The view of the Pang is said to have inspired Kenneth Grahame to write the children's classic *The Wind in the Willows* – and it is still home to badger and friends today. Made up of wet wood, coppice and meadow, some other reserve residents include dragonflies, scarlet tiger moth and water rail along the river fringes. The woods are carpeted with bluebells in spring. There is an ongoing project to create new wetland habitats on a newly purchased extension. Follow the waymarked wildlife walk and pick up a reserve leaflet with map. The reserve features flat paths that can be muddy in winter.

Rushbeds Wood

Near Brill

OS Map SP 672154; **Map Ref** G3

This 143-acre (58ha) reserve is made up of ancient oak-ash-maple woodland, and unimproved meadows and hedgerows near the Bucks/Oxon border. The site is notable for the abundance of butterflies, and species regularly spotted include white admiral, purple emperor and black hairstreak. The reserve has a waymarked walk and there is a reserve leaflet with map available. Its flat paths can be muddy in winter. Entrances have kissing gates and livestock may be present in the autumn.

Sydlings Copse

Near Oxford

OS Map SP 559096; **Map Ref** G5

The wonderful variety of habitats make 42-acre (17ha) Sydlings Copse in east Oxon one of the best botanical sites in the Midlands – more than 400 plant species have been recorded here. Reedbed, fen, a stream, ancient woodland, heath and limestone grassland are all packed into the steep valley. The reserve is teeming with bird and insect life. Some 30 species of butterfly have been recorded on the site, including purple emperor (below) and white admiral. Approximately 100 species of burrowing wasps and bees can also be found in the acid grassland area as well as rare plants in the fen. Mammals such as badgers, deer, foxes and bats also make their homes here. The reserve has a waymarked walk and a reserve leaflet with map is available for explorers. There are some steeply sloping paths with kissing gates and steps. The paths can be muddy in winter. There is parking a half mile from the reserve.

Chimney Meadows

Near Bampton; **OS Map** SP 360010; **Map Ref** G9

01367 870904

ACCESS/CONDITIONS: Generally flat, easy terrain but there are some bumpy areas, and bridges, gates and a boardwalk are present. Bird hides and some paths are suitable for people with limited mobility.
HOW TO GET THERE: From the A420, heading south-west from Oxford, take a right turn, signposted Tadpole Bridge and Bampton. Go right after Tadpole Bridge and the Trout Inn, towards Chimney. Free car park just outside the Chimney hamlet.
WALKING TIME: Allow at least 3 hours to walk the permissive routes around the 615-acre (249ha) reserve.
30-MINUTE VISIT: Many wildflower-rich meadows are within easy reach of the car park.

Chimney Meadows is a stunning patchwork of riverside meadows and pastures. As the restoration of these grasslands continues, wildlife is returning to the habitat that is being created. Spring and summer is the time to watch the wildflower meadows as they burst into a riot of colour.

As time progresses, the meadows pass through new colour phases, meadow butterflies flourish and birds such as the skylark, curlew and white-throat provide their unique songs. In autumn, watch birds such as finches beginning to feed on the seeds grown especially for them in a field sewn only with food plants. At this time, hay is cut and the livestock arrive to graze the meadows.

Winter is a time to enjoy the wetland birds that over-winter here, such as lapwing, redshank and snipe. The marshy grassland is perfect feeding ground for these birds. The snipe, for example, feeds on worms by plunging its long bill into the soft ground.

Dancersend

Near Tring; **OS Map** SP 904088; **Map Ref** G7

ACCESS/CONDITIONS: The unmodified paths are gently sloping and uneven. Most get muddy in winter. There are kissing gates at main entrances and livestock may be present.
HOW TO GET THERE: From Tring, head west on old A41 (not bypass) towards Aston Clinton. Take a right turn (B4009) signposted to Wendover and take an immediate left for Dancersend. After 1 mile turn right at the T-junction. There's a free car park at Dancersend Water Works.
WALKING TIME: Allow at least 2 hours to walk the permissive routes around the 116-acre (47ha) reserve.
30-MINUTE VISIT: Visitors need to park at the layby at SP903097 then walk up the track opposite to the reserve.

Nestling within a sheltered valley deep in the Chilterns in east Bucks, this wonderfully rich nature reserve is made up of mixed woodlands and chalk grassland. In spring, adder's tongue fern, Solomon's seal and fly orchid can be found among the more common cowslips and primroses. Green hairstreak, grizzled skipper and Duke of Burgundy butterflies are frequently seen along the rides and scrub.

By summer, Chiltern gentian, meadow clary, and greater butterfly orchid can be found, along with dark-green fritillary, marbled white and ringlet butterflies at the woodland edge and among the ancient anthills in the grassland.

In autumn, the ground erupts to reveal numerous fungi, including the remarkable earthstar. Look among the carpet of copper beech leaves and you may see the amethyst deceiver. All parts of this fungus, including the stem, are a vibrant violet colour. You may even spot the edible dormouse fattening up for winter.

Wildmoor Heath

Near Crowthorne; **OS Map** SU 842627; **Map Ref** G16

ACCESS/CONDITIONS: The undulating ground has unmodified but firm paths with boardwalks over the wettest sections. There are some boggy patches in winter and kissing gates around the site. Livestock may be present at any time of year.
HOW TO GET THERE: By train to Sandhurst (1 mile from reserve); regular buses run between local towns stopping close to the reserve. By car, it is on the Crowthorne Road between Sandhurst and Crowthorne.
WALKING TIME: The marked 1.5 mile circular trail takes 40 minutes at an easy pace.
30-MINUTE VISIT: Take the brief walk to Wildmoor Bottom for mires and dry heath.

Wildmoor Heath is a fine example of lowland heathland, with a mixture of both dry and wet heath, acid grassland, pine plantation and scrub. This is by no means a bleak and desolate landscape. From spring onwards, the heath is busy with songbirds and reptiles (grass snake, adder, slow worm and common lizard).

The wet heath is particularly liked by dragonflies and damselflies, including downy emerald and keeled skimmer.

During the summer, the birdsong is enhanced by the arrival of the nightjar. If you visit in the evening to see these birds, you may also see pipistrelle bats and glow-worms. The flowering heathers are at their best in August and provide nectar for many butterflies, including silver-studded blues. In autumn, fungi including the striking birch bolete can be found in the woodland fringing the heath. The rarely seen Dartford warbler remains on site throughout the year and may be spotted in thick patches of gorse.

WILDLIFE FACT: ADDERS

Brownish in colour, with a dark zigzag down its back, the adder is the only poisonous snake native to Britain. From November to February it hibernates underground, but from March to October it is frequently spotted basking in sunshine in woodland clearings or on open heathland. Naturally shy creatures, their poisonous bite is only used as a last means of defence, usually if they're caught or trodden on. Sadly, this misunderstood reptile is in danger of vanishing due to persecution and loss of habitat. They are now a protected species in the UK.

Bowdown Woods

Near Newbury; **OS Map** SU 505653 (Bomb Site car park); **Map Ref** G15

ACCESS/CONDITIONS: The flat concrete path around the heathy gravel plateau is suitable for wheelchair access. Long flights of steps lead off the plateau into the woods. Paths are bumpy and boggy in wet weather.
HOW TO GET THERE: Access to all three car parks – Bowdown Wood (SU 501656), Bomb Site (SU 505653) and Baynes Wood (SU 511651) – is from Bury's Bank Road as you head east from Greenham (near Newbury) towards Thatcham.
WALKING TIME: The three linked circular trails total 3.5 miles and take 2 and a half hours at an easy pace.
30-MINUTE VISIT: From the Bomb Site car park, follow the waymarked Wildlife Walk around the Bomb Site.
A MEMBER SAYS: 'Wonderful to see how an old army bomb site can become a wildlife haven under the Trust's care.'

Mysterious hidden valleys, sunny glades and patches of heathland hold a wealth of wildlife in this 136-acre (55ha) expanse of riverside woodland in west Berks. Stretching from the vast heathland at Greenham Common down to the River Kennet, Bowdown Woods, near Newbury, is the Trust's biggest woodland reserve in Berkshire – and for sheer variety of wildlife, it's hard to beat.

In spring, the woodland is awash with bluebells and alive with birdsong. Listen for the drumming of the great and lesser spotted woodpeckers. Sparrowhawks may be glimpsed on occasion. In summer, more than 30 species of butterfly have been seen here and in the sunny glades you may spot the spectacular silver-washed fritillary or the handsome white admiral.

The open well-drained ground is dominated by remnants of heathland with swathes of heather and bracken. Look out for dragonflies, such as the giant, four-inch long 'hawkers', which hunt for insects along the woodland edge and heathland clearings, and the smaller 'darter' dragonflies that wait on perches ready to pounce on unsuspecting victims.

Visit later in the year to experience the wonderful autumn colour and incredible fungi. Sulphur knight, inkstain bolete and porcelain fungus are just a few of the more striking species you are likely to find. Look out for the pipe club – spectacular in its strangeness, with long, thin stems like breadsticks rising up from the ground – or the rare snakeskin amanita, which has a large yellow cap with blue, felty patches sitting on a stem resembling snakeskin.

DID YOU KNOW?

- **The two swathes of ancient woodland, Bowdown and Baynes, are connected by the Bomb Site, which is a former Word War II munitions store. Don't worry, there are no bombs and nature has taken over with young woodland and heathland dominating. It's a great area for reptiles and butterflies.**
- **The toxic fly agaric fungus, which is found at the reserve has been used by Laplanders to sedate reindeer prior to herding.**

College Lake

Near Tring; **OS Map** SU 934140; **Map Ref** G4

01442 826774

OPENING TIMES: Reserve open all year (closed Monday). Visitor centre open from 10am to 5pm.
ACCESS/CONDITIONS: Surfaced, undulating path around quarry leading to many bird hides, several of which have flat concrete approach paths and are ideal for disabled access.
HOW TO GET THERE: By train to Tring, then the reserve is a 2-mile walk. Arriva buses from Aylesbury/Luton run to Bulbourne three times a day. By car, it is 2 miles from Tring on the B488. After passing the canal bridge at Bulbourne, turn left into a signed entrance.
WALKING TIME: The marked circular trail of 2 miles takes 1 and a half hours at an easy pace.
30-MINUTE VISIT: Head along the southern rim of the quarry to the Marsh Hide for views over the whole reserve.
A MEMBER SAYS: 'Remarkable – so close to urban sprawl, yet it is a remote landscape. Beautiful, peaceful, relaxing and friendly.'

A truly memorable wildlife experience for all the family. A former chalk quarry, this reserve has been transformed into a thriving centre for wildlife and supports more than 1,000 species. It boasts panoramic views of the surrounding farmland and Chiltern hills and has become a haven for many migrating birds.

After finally securing a long-term lease for the reserve in 2006, vital re-landscaping work has taken place in the marsh area to make it suitable for fluctuating water levels. Islands, dykes and scrapes have been created so there will always be some land, whatever the water level. Good trails and numerous hides give excellent views of common tern returning in spring. Lapwing and redshank breed on the marsh and hares box in the meadows. In summer, hobbies chase dragonflies and disrupt sand martins in their cliff-top colony. Around the trail, 10 species of orchid can be found and flower-rich grassland attracts butterflies such as small blue and meadow brown. Autumn provides a chance to see returning birds on passage, osprey, ring ouzel and wheatear among them. Winter visitors include large numbers of wigeon, teal and lapwing. Whooper swan, goosander and short-eared owl are scarcer, usually seen in bad weather, when it is also easier to spot snipe in the snow. Kingfisher, red kite and buzzard visit throughout the year.

DID YOU KNOW?

- Chalk from this old quarry made enough cement to rebuild 25 per cent of London after World War II.
- The reserve is excellent for fossils. As well as fossilised marine life; bones of mammoths, bears and lions have been found.
- The bee orchid flower has evolved to resemble a bee. This is to attract potential mates that inadvertently pollinate the flower.

Warburg

Near Henley-on-Thames; **OS Map** SU 720878; **Map Ref** G11

01491 642001

OPENING TIMES: Open all year; visitor centre open daily, 9am to 5pm. Groups should phone in advance.
ACCESS/CONDITIONS: The unmodified paths are flat in the valley bottom, but can be muddy in winter. Other paths are steep and uneven. There are gates and kissing gates at entrances.
HOW TO GET THERE: By train to Henley. By bus from Henley to Nettlebed, then a 1-mile walk. By car, it is 4 miles north-west of Henley-on-Thames. From the A4130, turn into Rectory Lane, signposted Bix Village. Turn sharp left again into Rectory Lane and continue down a steep hill. Take a left at the bottom of the hill signposted Bix Bottom. Continue for 1.5 miles along the narrow lane to the reserve car park.
WALKING TIME: The circular trail of 1 mile takes 30 minutes at an easy pace.
30-MINUTE VISIT: Take the marked trail around the valley bottom.
A MEMBER SAYS: 'Warburg is my sanctuary, the most beautiful peaceful bit of Oxfordshire I know.'

Warburg Nature Reserve is made up of 264 acres (107ha) of mixed woodland, coppice, chalk grassland and ponds, all set within a secluded Chiltern valley. The mixture of chalk grassland and ancient woodland makes it an ideal site for birds and butterflies. More than 2,000 species of plant, animal and fungus have been recorded here.

Green hellebore heralds the arrival of spring, followed by an abundance of wood anemone and bluebell. Red kite, buzzard, sparrowhawk and kestrel, as well as numerous songbirds, can be seen and heard preparing for the breeding season.

Silver-washed fritillary butterflies add grace to the chaotic buzz of insect activity in summer, and less conspicuous orchids like narrow-lipped, violet and broad-leaved helleborine bloom among the trees. At dusk, noctule and pipistrelle bats swoop and flutter in pursuit of their insect prey.

In autumn, numerous fungi speckle the floor beneath the reds, yellows, browns and golds of the canopy above. The conifers provide welcome shelter for goldcrest and crossbills in winter. It's a good time to look for our resident mammals, which include deer, stoat and hare.

DID YOU KNOW?

- Warburg Nature Reserve has more than 900 species of fungus, best seen in autumn.
- 15 species of orchid have been recorded here.
- You are almost certain to see red kites, which were re-introduced to the Chilterns in the 1990s.

Herts and Middlesex

About the Trust

The Trust has 43 nature reserves, covering over 1,700 acres. From woodlands to wetlands and heathland, there is a fantastic variety of wildlife to be seen. As well as many ways to get closer to wildlife there are opportunities for people to get 'stuck in' by volunteering. The Trust is also active in offering advice to landowners, planning issues, and species and habitat surveys.

Herts and Middlesex Wildlife Trust ☎ 01727 858901
www.wildlifetrust.org.uk/herts

Aldbury Nowers

Near Tring
OS Map SP 950129; **Map Ref** H9

Situated on the Chiltern escarpment and adjoining The Ridgeway National Trail, with superb views across the Tring Gap and Vale of Aylesbury, this reserve, designated an SSSI, supports splendid flora and more than 25 species of butterfly, including marbled white, green hairstreak and grizzled skipper, which come to feed on the abundant grassland plants. It is also a good reserve for solitary bees and other invertebrates. Sheep grazing helps to maintain the site. It features some steep hills with stiles and kissing gates at some points. There is limited parking.

Broad Colney Lakes

London Colney
OS Map TL 175032; **Map Ref** H19

This is a mixed habitat of wooded scrub and three lakes – all quite different from one another and providing a diversity of habitat. The lakes are the result of gravel workings in the 1920s. Now they are surrounded by trees and are a peaceful refuge for both wildlife and people. One is river-fed, one is relatively still and deep, and the smallest has partially developed into marshy woodland. A variety of land and water birds can be found here. Great crested grebes can be seen on the lake, along with tufted duck, while flocks of siskin can be seen feeding along with mixed flocks of finches and tits. In summer, dragonflies are abundant. There are firm pathways over level terrain.

Danemead

Danemead
OS Map TL 347078; **Map Ref** H17

A mix of wet grassland and pasture adjacent to Broxbourne Woods NNR. The Spital Brook supports fine hornbeams, mosses and woodland plants and sallows have been pollarded to encourage the purple emperor butterfly. Broad-leaved helleborines grace the woodland edges, while white admirals are attracted to the sunny woodland glades and lizards bask on stones and logs in the grassland. Some areas are boardwalked, but elsewhere paths may be uneven and muddy. There are stiles and kissing gates in places.

Fir and Pond Woods

Potters Bar
OS Map TL 277012; **Map Ref** H20

This is the best remaining part of the ancient Enfield Chase, with diverse woodland, meadow and wetland habitats. The woods are rich in birdlife, including woodpeckers. Grassland areas are full of insects, including grasshoppers and butterflies; the purple emperor has recently appeared here. The pond also supports large numbers of dragonflies. In autumn spectacular fungi can be found. The paths may be uneven and muddy.

Gobions Wood

Brookmans Park
OS Map TL 249038; **Map Ref** H18

About 91 acres (37ha) of varied woodland (including hornbeam) with ponds, streams and swallow holes offering a range of habitats. In spring the woodland is carpeted in bluebells and in the autumn the reserve is noted for its richness of fungi species. The woodland attracts butterflies, grass snakes, small mammals (including Daubenton's, long-eared and pipistrelle bats) during the summer and birds abound all year round. The paths may be uneven and muddy – especially during wetter months. The reserve is managed in partnership with the Gobions Woodland Trust.

Hunsdon Mead

along River Stort Navigation, from Roydon train station

OS Map TL 416105; **Map Ref** H15

The Mead has been managed on the ancient Lammas system for over 600 years, under which local farmers graze their cattle in late summer after a July hay cut. It offers a superb display of flowering plants, including cowslips, marsh marigolds, yellow-rattle, ragged robin, lady's-smock and bugle flower, and there are small colonies of green winged orchid and adder's tongue fern, quaking grass and several uncommon sedges. During the flowering period, the reserve can be viewed from the level, surfaced towpath alongside it. Please don't walk across or into the Mead between March and July.

Lemsford Springs

Lemsford Village

OS Map TL 223123; **Map Ref** H13

A small reserve that includes a mixed habitat of former cressbeds (with underground springs that keep the shallow waters at a constant temperature) a small meadow and fast-flowing river. Shallow lagoons attract wading birds, which come to feed on the freshwater shrimps in winter. Nesting kestrels can be seen most years, and water rail, little egret and kingfisher are all regularly spied. The river on the far side of the reserve attracts ducks and dragonflies. There is a circular walk, via a bridge and short boardwalk. The level paths may be muddy during wet months. Ramp to the first hide. Access is by key only.

Old Park Wood

Near Harefield

OS Map TQ 049913; **Map Ref** H24

This is an ancient woodland teeming with wildlife and abundant flowers in spring. Bluebells form a stunning carpet, along with yellow archangel, lesser celandine, wood anemone, the uncommon coralroot bittercress. Golden saxifrage and marsh marigolds grow on the stream banks and around the pond – which is important for dragonflies and amphibians. All three British species of woodpecker visit. Follow signs down slope, through gates and follow the field edge into the woods. Slopes and rough, uneven paths in places, which may be muddy.

Tewin Orchard

Tewin Village

OS Map TL 268155; **Map Ref** H10

The reserve is a small village orchard with varied and often local fruit trees (an almost extinct feature of the English countryside). Sights include the rare white-letter hairstreak butterfly. In autumn and winter windfall apples attract large numbers of redwings, fieldfares and blackbirds. Yellow-hammer, greenfinch, linnet and goldfinch also use the orchard. The Trust is restoring the orchard by planting traditional fruit varieties. For a chance to see badgers, foxes, muntjak deer, owls and small mammals, why not book the mammal-watching hide? Open from April to mid-October, the hide accommodates up to 10 people and is wheelchair friendly. Contact the Trust for more details.

Marsh Marigold

Hertford Heath and Balls Wood

Near Hertford; **OS Map** TL 351108 (Hertford Heath) TL 348106 (Balls Wood); **Map Ref** H16

ACCESS/CONDITIONS: Easy walking with no steep gradients but no surfaced paths. Wellingtons are necessary.
HOW TO GET THERE: By train to Hertford. Buses stop outside the College Arms pub, almost at the centre of the reserve. By car, the Goldington's section is north of the B1197, along Heath Lane, and the Roundings section is immediately to the north, with the adjacent Balls Wood (along Roundings Road).
WALKING TIME: The full Heath circuit of 2 miles takes 1 and a half hours. A circuit of Balls Wood is also 2 miles.
30-MINUTE VISIT: Park on Roundings Road to visit heathy clearings and pools on the Roundings section and see Balls Wood.

Hertford Heath SSSI is a rare Hertfordshire open heathland, with woodland and several heathy pools. Balls Wood varies from mature hornbeam coppice through mixed ash and maple to conifer plantations under restoration.

In spring, the rides of Balls Wood are full of birdsong and wildflowers, including wood anemone and bluebell, and woodcock and sparrowhawk breed. Little owl and lesser spotted woodpecker can also be seen on the Heath.

Late summer is the time for flowering heather and dragonflies on the heath, while Balls Wood's rides are very good for butterflies, including white admiral. Autumn, then is a good time for fungi across the reserve, while in winter flocks of tits and finches can be seen feeding.

King's Meads

Near Hertford; **OS Map** TL 353143; **Map Ref** H11

ACCESS/CONDITIONS: Some paths are suitable for disabled access and the site can be viewed from the surfaced towpath along the River Lee and the A119. Wellingtons are recommended if wet. The reserve is bisected by a railway with a level crossing, and has stiles and gates at two points.
HOW TO GET THERE: By train, there are stations at Hertford (10 minutes' walk) and Ware (5 minutes' walk). Buses from Hertford and Ware stop on the A119 immediately adjacent. By car, it is between Hertford and Ware on the A119 and close to the A414 and A10. The reserve can be accessed on foot from Hertford and Ware via the River Lee towpath.
WALKING TIME: The full circuit of the 237-acre (96ha) reserve takes 2 hours.
30-MINUTE VISIT: Walk along the towpath and stroll across the meadows to the main pool at Chadwell Springs.

King's Meads is one of the largest wetlands remaining in Hertfordshire. It consists of flood-meadows with scattered ditches, scrapes and pools, and is bordered by chalk grassland, river and canal.

In autumn and winter, the flooded areas attract visiting ducks, gulls and waders, including gadwall, shoveler, wigeon, teal and snipe. If high water levels remain into spring, many ducks stay to nest, along with lapwings and migrant yellow wagtails. Other breeding birds include stonechat, skylark, reed bunting, reed warbler and sedge warbler.

In late spring and early summer look out for the flowering spikes of the rare water violet growing in the ditches to the west of the viaduct. This plant – which is scarce and sporadic elsewhere in Hertfordshire – is making an amazing comeback to the reserve, thanks to conservation management. The chalk grassland bank on the south side of the valley is especially rich in flora, including pyramidal orchids. In July, look for a yellow haze of lady's bedstraw covering the south-west of the site. The bank attracts a variety of butterflies in the summer. The reserve supports all 19 dragonfly and damselfly species found in Hertfordshire and on summer evenings, pipistrelle, Daubenton's and noctule bats drop in to feed on insects.

Wilstone Reservoir

Between Aston Clinton and Tring; **OS Map** SP 903134; **Map Ref** H8

ACCESS/CONDITIONS: Steep steps lead from the car park to the top of the reservoir banks. For flat access use the public footpath from the east of the reserve. The high banks of the reservoir are often exposed to cold winds; wear warm clothing.
HOW TO GET THERE: By train to Tring. Buses serve Tring and Aston Clinton. By car, it is along the B489 between Aston Clinton and Marsworth (take the A489 to the reserve) or about 2 miles from Tring (from the B488, turn left onto the A489). A car park for 12 cars is on the A489.
WALKING TIME: The circuit around the reservoir takes about 2 hours.
30-MINUTE VISIT: Park at the car park on Lower Icknield Way to view the reservoir from the banks or walk along to the hide.

The 137-acre (55.6ha) Wilstone Reservoir is one of four water-bodies fed by natural springs, built around 1802 to supply water to the Wendover arm of the Grand Union Canal. It is surrounded by ancient marshes, reed swamp and willow carr.

Spring brings passage and summer migrants. Cetti's warbler has bred on the reserve. Breeding duck include gadwall and shoveler, and the reserve has one of the county's three regular heronries.

Flowering plants include celery-leaved and goldilocks buttercups. The summer moult flocks of tufted duck and pochard are of national importance.

Autumn passage again brings terns, gulls and other vagrants. In winter, waterbirds include nationally important levels of shoveler, as well as teal and wigeon. The nightly gull roost can be in excess of 20,000 birds, and corn buntings roost in the reedbed.

The reservoir was made famous by the first nesting in this country of black-necked grebes in 1918 and of little ringed plovers in 1938.

WILDLIFE FACT: BADGERS

Badgers are found all over Britain, but exist in their largest numbers in the south and south-west. They are very tidy animals – refreshing their bedding of moss, grass and leaves every couple of days and digging latrines a short distance away from their sett entrance. They prefer to build their setts in well-drained soil in woods near pasture or fields. Up to 15 badgers may live together in one sett, which is a maze of chambers and tunnels with passing places. Young are born between January and March in litters of two or three. As one of Britain's largest omnivores (they can grow up to a metre in length) the badger's diet is varied, ranging from earthworms, acorns, snails, and mice to bulbs, hedgehogs, frogs and berries. The best time to see badgers is at dusk when they emerge to forage for food. For a chance of seeing badgers, why not book the mammal watching hide at Tewin Orchard NR? (p 80)

Amwell

between Ware and Stanstead Abbotts; **OS Map** TL 376127; **Map Ref** H12

ACCESS/CONDITIONS: There are mainly level, surfaced paths and boardwalks in some sections. Ramps lead to White Hide and ground floor viewing in the James Hide. Access to the reserve from the car park is via a level railway crossing with kissing gates on either side of the track.
HOW TO GET THERE: By train, the reserve is 10 minutes' walk from St Margarets station in Stanstead Abbotts, and buses stop here from Hoddesdon and Ware. By car, the site is near the A414 and A10, and is accessed from the reserve's car park off Amwell Lane. From Stanstead Abbotts, turn off the B181 into Amwell Lane. From Ware, from the A1170 south, turn left into Lower Road and then left into Amwell Lane after about 0.5 miles.
WALKING TIME: The length of the reserve can be comfortably walked in about 2 hours.
30-MINUTE VISIT: Follow the track down to the viewpoint for a superb view of the reserve. If you have time, the James and Gladwin hides (overlooking the reedbed on the towpath side of the reserve) are two minutes walk each way from the viewpoint.
A MEMBER SAYS: 'What has been created at Amwell is rich in wildlife, a place of great beauty and hope – a place that uplifts the spirits.'

Amwell is one of the county's top wetlands and birdwatching sites, with more than 210 species recorded since 1975, and 68 species breeding since 1979. The breeding, wintering and passage communities are all of at least regional significance.

It was designated as a SSSI and forms part of the Lea Valley SPA. A flooded former gravel working, its habitats now include reedbed, marsh and carr woodland. In spring, the reserve is excellent for breeding wetland birds, with large numbers of sedge and reed warblers, redshanks, snipes, both ringed plovers and several duck species.

In summer, flowering plants include early marsh orchid, pyramidal orchid and the nationally rare marsh dock. All 19 species of dragonfly present in Hertfordshire can be seen here. Passage migrants in autumn are often spectacular, with osprey, marsh harrier and waders.

Winter is particularly good for waterbirds, with nationally significant numbers of gadwall and shoveler, plus smew and bittern. Otter tracks can occasionally be found, and grass snakes, harvest mice and bats are also present. Larger mammals include otter, polecat, stoat, weasel, badger, fox, hare and hedgehog. Daubenton's, natterer and brown long-eared bats hibernate in the railway tunnel near the car park.

DID YOU KNOW?

- Amwell was created by the removal of nearly 2 million tonnes of sand and gravel between 1973 and 1990. Much of this was used to construct the M11 and M25 motorways nearby.
- Internationally important populations of ducks come here during the winter to escape the freezing conditions in their breeding grounds in northern Europe.
- Following extinction in the 1970s, otters were re-introduced to Hertfordshire here at Amwell in 1991. Since then they have thrived.

Rye Meads

Near Hoddesdon; **OS Map** TL 389103; **Map Ref** H14

P WC i i

ACCESS/CONDITIONS: All internal paths and most hides are suitable for wheelchair and pushchair access. Guide dogs are allowed. Wellingtons often required.
HOW TO GET THERE: By train, Rye House Station is on the Liverpool Street line. By bus, go to Rye Park estate, Hoddesdon, and walk towards train station. By car, follow Rye Road in Hoddesdon, past Rye House Station and over the bridge. Follow signs to Rye Meads Visitor Centre.
WALKING TIME: There are three clearly marked walks of 550m, 750m, and 1,500m. The shortest route takes around 45 minutes, with each additional leg taking a further 45 minutes. The full circuit via all 10 hides and back takes 2 to 2 and a half hours at an easy pace.
30-MINUTE VISIT: Pop into the visitor centre for information on the latest sightings and visit the Lapwing Hide next to the car park to look over the meadows and see the grazing water buffalo (mostly in summer).
A MEMBER SAYS: 'This truly is a wetland jewel in the Lea Valley with plenty to explore and loads to discover.'

Rye Meads is jointly managed by the Trust and the RSPB. The reserve is very diverse: the Trust's land consists of ancient flood meadow, reedbed, old gravel pits and willow carr, while the RSPB manages the marshes and lagoons adjacent to the River Lee. In winter, water rail and bittern may be seen, as can roosting reed buntings and yellow-hammers. The meadows attract waders and ducks when flooded – snipe, golden plover and teal have been seen in large numbers.

In summer, the breeding birdlife includes several species of duck, kingfisher, water rail, common tern, lapwing, little ringed plover and redshank. Tits and both white-throats can be seen, and occasionally grasshopper warbler and yellow wagtail are also spotted. Meadowsweet and meadow-rue provide the pastel-coloured surroundings.

In autumn, bird passage can be spectacular with both county and national rarities occurring. Rye Meads is a good place to see snipe, teal and green sandpiper at this time of the year. Water voles, water shrews and harvest mice are abundant.

DID YOU KNOW?

- Some 40 pairs of common terns make a journey of over 25,000 miles to breed at Rye Meads.
- In the winter, the Lea Valley is an excellent place to see bitterns – one of Britain's rarest birds.
- Otters were introduced near to Rye Meads in 1991 after an absence of more than 20 years.

Stocker's Lake

Near Rickmansworth; **OS Map** TQ 042933; **Map Ref** H23

ACCESS/CONDITIONS: Routes are flat, but surfaces are uneven in places. It is suitable for pushchair and wheelchair access in parts. Walking shoes are recommended.
HOW TO GET THERE: By train, to Rickmansworth (Metropolitan Line), it's then a 10-minute walk. By bus, use the stop at Aquadrome (a 5-minute walk). By car, enter the reserve via Bury Lake Aquadrome (with parking) or, from the A412 into Rickmansworth, turn right at Mill End into Springwell Lane, go over the bridge and immediately left. Use two car parks along the reserve access lane.
WALKING TIME: The full circuit of 2 miles takes 1 and a half hours at an easy pace.
30-MINUTE VISIT: From Springwell car park, walk through the refuge area to the hides and wader scrape.
A MEMBER SAYS: 'Stocker's Lake is a great place to escape to at any time of year. There's always something to see.'

One of the oldest and largest gravel pits in the Colne Valley is now a LNR owned by Three Valleys Water. The lake and islands attract an astonishing number of waterbirds, and offer hides and a circular walk to visitors.

The site is part of a large freshwater complex at Rickmansworth, which includes the river, Grand Union Canal, two other lakes and Springwell Reedbed. Spring and autumn are good for breeding and migrating birds. The 42 regular breeding species include various duck, common terns and numerous warblers, buntings and tits.

In mid-May, see young grey herons taking flying lessons at the heronry. In summer, the surrounding meadows are in flower and dragonflies fall prey to feeding hobbies.

During winter, the lake is one of the county's foremost sites for duck and wildfowl, including shoveler and gadwall in nationally important numbers. Occasional wintering bittern have been seen in recorded years. Keep an eye out for water rail. The reserve is also important for pochard, goldeneye, smew and goosander. Flocks of fieldfares and redwings fill the meadows, while flocks of finches and tits feed in the willow and alder scrub.

DID YOU KNOW?

- **The heronry at Stocker's Lake is one of the largest in the county.**
- **The common terns nest on purpose-built rafts covered with gravel.**
- **Shoveler and gadwall are common winter visitors in nationally important numbers.**

London

About the Trust

London Wildlife Trust is a charity that works to protect London's wildlife for the future through: campaigning, community involvement and land management. It cares for more than 40 nature reserves and runs Wildlife Watch, the environmental club for junior members of the Trust.

London Wildlife Trust ☎ 020 7261 0447
www.wildlondon.org.uk

Bramley Bank

Croydon

OS Map TQ 353633; **Map Ref** H33

Common violet and enchanter's nightshade are among the interesting flowers at this 25.7-acre (10.4ha) woodland reserve, which has developed from old parkland. It supports a wide range of species, from birds including woodpeckers and nuthatch, to purple hairstreak butterfly and yellow meadow ant. Yellow flag and flote grass surround the margins of the large pond and a small clearing of acidic grassland is alive with a wealth of species, including sheep's fescue and heath bedstraw.

Crane Park Island

Twickenham

OS Map TQ 128717; **Map Ref** H30

The site of a former gunpowder factory, this is now a mosaic of woodland, scrub and reedbeds surrounded by the gently flowing River Crane. This is a special site for water vole. There is partial access for wheelchair users along a path with a tapping rail. Events are held throughout the year.

Fray's Farm Meadows SSSI

near Uxbridge

OS Map TQ 058860; **Map Ref** H25

The wildlife-rich Frays River meanders through the luxuriant Frays Farm Meadows SSSI in west London. Water vole, harvest mice and snipe are all present. The going can be very wet. For opening times call the Trust on 020 7261 0447.

Oakhill Wood

Barnet

OS Map TQ 278951; **Map Ref** H22

A woodland reserve with roosting bats on the edge of an urban park. There are ponds and meadows in the park, which is managed for wildlife. Look out for some flights of steps and steep paths. Some paths can be muddy after wet weather.

The Ripple

Near Dagenham

OS Map TQ 467826; **Map Ref** H28

An urban wasteland site that has been reclaimed by nature. Flora includes southern marsh orchids among a mosaic of meadows, birch woodland and scrub. Neighbouring Thameside City Farm offers refreshments and a WC.

Totteridge Fields

Barnet

OS Map TQ 223940; **Map Ref** H21

A bit of ancient countryside on the fringes of London that has escaped agricultural intensification. The fields have been managed since the 1700s using traditional meadow and pasture management techniques. It contains hornbeam and oak woodland with wild service tree along the southern boundary hedgerows. Summer brings wildflowers and insect activity, especially dragonflies around the pond. It is flat with a series of informal paths, none of which are surfaced.

Wilderness Island

Carshalton

OS Map TQ 282653; **Map Ref** H32

A veritable TARDIS of a reserve between two arms of the River Wandle, featuring old sedge beds, a pond and meadow. The riverside woodland attracts blackcap and chiffchaff.

Hutchinson's Bank

Croydon; **OS Map** TQ 381616; **Map Ref** H34

ACCESS/CONDITIONS: There are steep slopes in places, some with steps. The paths can be quite muddy in wet weather.
HOW TO GET THERE: Entry is from Featherbed Lane and Farleigh Dean Crescent or from the Croydon Tramlink terminus at New Addington, which is just a short walk away via a footpath leading from North Downs Road to Featherbed Lane. Very limited parking at the bottom of Farleigh Dean Crescent or in North Downs Way in New Addington.
WALKING TIME: An approximately 20-acre (8ha) reserve with a nature trail path which takes about 45 minutes to 1 hour to cover at an easy pace.
30-MINUTE VISIT: For a quick visit, the nature trail can be cut at several points along its length.

Hutchinson's Bank is one of the largest areas of chalk grassland remaining in the Greater London area. Situated on the eastern flank of a dry valley in the southern part of the London Borough of Croydon, the site has suffered from scrub invasion in recent years, but is being gradually restored under the management of the Trust.

Spring or summer visits are recommended to see rare butterflies and orchids. The nationally rare greater yellow-rattle, the scarce man orchid and the small blue butterfly are all present.

Following the chalk walk around Hutchinson's Bank brings you to Chapel Bank. This is an area of ancient woodland, scrub and chalk grassland, spiked with orchids, including common twayblade and white helleborine. Threecorner Grove is found between the two banks and is a small stand of ancient woodland of oak, wild cherry and hazel, with moschatel, wild garlic and carpets of bluebell in spring.

Sydenham Hill Wood

Near Dulwich; **OS Map** TQ 344725; **Map Ref** H31

ACCESS/CONDITIONS: It has some woodland steps and steep slopes. Muddy in some areas after rain.
HOW TO GET THERE: Entrance at Crescent Wood Road. By train, nearest stations are Sydenham Hill or Forest Hill.
WALKING TIME: The full circuit takes 1 hour at an easy pace. There's also a 45-minute nature trail.
30-MINUTE VISIT: Take a brisk walk around some of the nature trail or just find a quiet place away from the main path and simply sit and listen to the woodland sounds.

Sydenham Hill Wood is one of the remaining parts of the Great North Wood, an ancient woodland that would have been close to the medieval city of London.

Today it is a mix of more recent woodland, Victorian garden survivors, and older oak and hornbeam woodland. It escapes the effects of trampling seen in many urban woods, and spring flowers include bluebell, wood anemone, wild garlic and early dog-violet.

In summer, the woods are surprisingly full of insects and birds – this area of Southwark is a hot-spot for stag beetles (above). The infamous storm of 1987 created small-scale sunny glades and a good source of rotting and dead wood, which are important features of a healthy wood.

Camley Street Natural Park

King's Cross; **OS Map** TQ 299834; **Map Ref** H26

OPENING TIMES: Open from 10am until dusk, seven days a week.
ACCESS/CONDITIONS: The main path and visitor centre are suitable for wheelchair access. The reserve has two flights of woodland steps (not suitable for wheelchair access). Paths are bark mulched, but can be slippery in wet weather. No cycling or dogs permitted.
HOW TO GET THERE: By tube or train to King's Cross (a 10-minute walk from the reserve). By bus, 214 and 46 stop at King's Cross and in Pancras Road. Walk along the Regent's Canal towpath. By car, street parking is restricted during weekdays.
WALKING TIME: The site is under 5 acres (2ha) so a walk around it takes 20 minutes.
30-MINUTE VISIT: The setting makes a welcome change from built-up areas of the city, providing a breath of fresh air and a place to stretch your legs or just contemplate life.
A MEMBER SAYS: 'I have been volunteering at the Park for three years. I am always made to feel welcome and although I can't volunteer as much any more, it always feels like coming home.'

Camley Street is surprising and inspiring, a small oasis in the midst of the metropolis. Set against the uncompromising backdrop of King's Cross, nature rolls through its glorious seasons unhindered here. In spring, look out for frog spawn and coots building their nests on the pond, the blaze of bright yellow flag iris in the marsh and the fleshy green of leaves unfurling.

Summer brings a surge of verdant madness. Bees and butterflies flit among the grasses and flowers in the meadows, pond dippers and mini-beast hunters abound, making the most of warm days and Camley Street's summer play activities. Autumn brings a riot of berries, feasting birds and eruptions of fungi. The short days of winter offer glimpses of foraging birds and squirrels through the black scribble of winter trees, and the anglepoise grace of a heron reflected in the canal. On a midwinter's day stand at the top of the park and look out through the gentle architecture of trees to the great structures of a rich industrial heritage and you can hear the hum of a new cityscape emerging from inside its vibrant green heart.

DID YOU KNOW?

- **The site was formerly a Victorian coal drop.**
- **This LNR is a site of Metropolitan Importance for Nature Conservation.**

Centre for Wildlife Gardening

East Dulwich; **OS Map** TQ 338755; **Map Ref** H29

OPENING TIMES: Tuesday through Thursday and Sunday, 10.30am to 4.30pm. Closed over Christmas.
ACCESS/CONDITIONS: There is full wheelchair access. A 20-minute tour with a personal guide is available for visually impaired visitors by arrangement.
HOW TO GET THERE: By train, to East Dulwich (a 5-minute walk; connections to London Bridge and East Croydon) or Peckham Rye (a 15-minute walk; connections to Victoria). By buses 37, 40, 176, 185, 484 to Goose Green (a 5-minute walk) or 12, 63, 78, 312, 343 to Peckham Rye. By car, park on the surrounding streets with sensitivity to locals.
WALKING TIME: The entire area can be walked around in less than 10 minutes, but we recommend you take longer, sit and enjoy, or go round again.
30-MINUTE VISIT: The garden can easily be explored within 30 minutes.
A MEMBER SAYS: 'It's a great relaxing space to come to with the toddlers, feels calm and "away from it all" for me and is a great adventure if you're only one year old!'

A pocket of wildlife wonders that makes city living into a good thing. Wandering the smooth paths of the garden you will find wild ponds, mini-meadows, hedges and the littlest birch woodland in this handbook, all set off by some stunning art works.

Don't come looking for rarities, the delights are in seeing frogs and toads spawning in March, finding speckled wood, red admiral and other butterflies in July, and hearing swifts calling as you sit and enjoy the sheltered evening sunshine in September.

These are the urban heritage of backyard biodiversity, and at the Centre for Wildlife Gardening we aim to inspire all visitors to coax their own gardens into intense chirping, tweeting, croaking, wonderment too, making one great network for nature.

DID YOU KNOW?

- **The Information Centre is built to catch the sun, hold the heat and stay cool in summer. It has heavy insulation from recycled newspaper pulp.**
- **Last year, a cabbage the size of a truck tyre was grown by volunteers with disabilities.**

The Chase LNR

Romford, Essex; **OS Map** TQ 515830; **Map Ref** H27

OPENING TIMES: Open all year; visitor centre, 10am to 5pm (4pm in winter).
ACCESS/CONDITIONS: The visitor centre is suitable for wheelchair access, but the reserve is not and can become very muddy during the winter months.
HOW TO GET THERE: By train, District Line to Dagenham Heathway and then bus to Rush Green. On foot, it's a 15-minute walk from Dagenham East station via the footpath alongside the perimeter fence. By car, access is from Dagenham Road, which runs south from Rush Green Road (A124 Upminster-Hornchurch-Dagenham). Turn off left just before the Farmhouse Tavern.
WALKING TIME: Allow a good 2 hours to explore the 120-acre (49ha) reserve.
30-MINUTE VISIT: Look around the Slack wetland for the best chance of rarities.
A MEMBER SAYS: 'Our very own special piece of countryside within the urban sprawl of Barking and Dagenham.'

The Chase is the largest reserve cared for by the London Wildlife Trust. Spend a day exploring 120 acres (49ha) of diverse habitats, including shallow wetlands, reedbeds, horse-grazed pasture, woodland and scrub. These provide an impressive range of animals and plants throughout the year.

The Riverside Walk can reveal water voles and grass snakes. Reed warbler, lapwing, water rail, lesser white-throat and little ringed plover all breed here. During the winter months significant numbers of teal, shoveler, redwing, fieldfare and snipe dominate the scene. The site is particularly rich in birdlife during the spring and autumn migration periods, when species such as yellow wagtail, wheatear, ruff, wood sandpiper, sand martin and hobby are regularly seen. For those not especially interested in birds, it is a surprising haven of quiet within urban East London.

DID YOU KNOW?

- The Millennium Visitor Centre has a roof made of recycled tin cans and its own wind turbine.
- The reserve has evolved over pre-World War II gravel extraction pits, which after the war were filled in with bomb rubble from the blitz.
- Britain's rarest timber-producing tree, the black poplar, grows here.

Surrey

About the Trust

Surrey Wildlife Trust is a registered charity formed in 1959. It currently manages 82 nature reserves covering more than 7,000 hectares of Surrey's countryside. As well as managing its own reserves it also manages land on behalf of Surrey County Council and under access agreements with private landowners.

Surrey Wildlife Trust☎ 01483 795440
www.surreywildlifetrust.org

Bagmoor Common

Near Farnham
OS Map SU 926423; **Map Ref** J12

Woodland butterflies, notably the white admiral and purple emperor, are a feature of this reserve, which has SSSI and SPA status. Woodpeckers and tits, including willow tit, are present, along with kingfishers, and roe deer are occasionally seen. The stream on the reserve's southern boundary is inhabited by both British species of agrion dragonfly.

Brockham Hills and Lime Kilns

between Reigate and Dorking
OS Map TQ 197513; **Map Ref** J5

Yew trees, juniper, violets, primroses, orchids, and many species of butterflies – including brimstone and silver-spotted skipper – live in this former chalk quarry. The site has SSSI and SAC status. The remains of the lime kilns provide a winter roost for as many as eight species of bat. Access to the site is by foot only from the B2032. There are car parks at Betchworth station and St Andrews Church, or use the National Trust car park (a fee applies) on Box Hill.

Hackhurst and White Downs

Along the North Downs Way
OS Map TQ 096487 and TQ 112491; **Map Ref** J7

Hackhurst Downs has been designated as an SSSI and LNR, due to its abundance of chalk grassland fauna and flora. It is good for butterfly and fungi species. Hackhurst is only accessible by foot from the North Downs Way or Gomshall station. Park at White Downs car park, White Downs Lane, between Abinger and Effingham.

The Moors

Redhill
OS Map TQ 290512; **Map Ref** J8

Mallard and teal flock to feed on the floods that occasionally turn The Moors into a large lake. Moorhen, water rail, skylark, lapwing and snipe are also seen, as are banded demoiselle and bigger dragonflies like the southern hawker and emperor. Stickleback, washed in by the flood, provide food for kingfishers and grey herons. Around the pools live sedges, rushes and bur-reed – a favourite food of water voles.

Puttenham Common

between Farnham and Guildford
OS Map SU 910455; **Map Ref** J11

Puttenham Common is designated as an SSSI, and here you can see skylark and woodlark, green woodpecker and great crested grebe, as well as roe deer and many species of fungi, such as fly agaric and birch polypore.

The Sheepleas

OS Map TQ 084514; **Map Ref** J6

This reserve has SSSI and LNR status and is known for its beech woods, downland meadows, flowers and butterflies. Open glades have superb displays of spring and summer flowers.

Thundry Meadows

Near Farnham
OS Map SU 896440; **Map Ref** J13

This site has 18 species of sedge, 24 species of dragonfly and five species of bat have been recorded. Bog-bean, climbing corydalis, dyer's greenweed, golden saxifrage, heath spotted orchid, lady's-smock, marsh cinquefoil, southern marsh orchid, amphibious bistort and musk (monkey flower).

Brentmoor Heath SSSI

Near Chobham, Lightwater; **OS Map** SU 936612; **Map Ref** J2

ACCESS/CONDITIONS: There are sandy paths and tracks, which can be boggy in places, and a few steep slopes.
HOW TO GET THERE: Open access via several public footpaths running off the A322 Guildford/Bagshot Road, near West End. Bus numbers 34, 590 and 591 stop under 0.5 miles away. By car, use the two car parks off the A322 and Red Road.
WALKING TIME: It takes about 45 minutes to 1 hour to walk around the 148.7 acre (60.3ha) reserve.
30-MINUTE VISIT: From the Red Road car park follow the public footpath that takes you around New England Hill.

This is an SSSI, LNR and SPA site that offers an abundance of rare heathland flora and fauna. The site is predominantly wet and dry heath, with areas of woodland, acid grassland and ponds. Sundew, bog asphodel, Dartford warbler, stonechat, butterflies, wood ant and rare ladybirds can all be seen here.

It is a delightful reserve that is ideal for birdwatching. In spring, woodpecker can be spotted. Other residents include silver-studded blue butterfly, grayling butterfly, spiders and wood ants.

In summer, look out for adder, grass snake, common lizard, palmate newt, slow worm, ground-nesting bees, dragonflies, woodlark, nightjar, Dartford warbler, and harvest mouse. Autumn and winter bring sightings of badger, roe deer and stonechat.

Newlands Corner SSSI

Near Guildford; **OS Map** TQ 044 494; **Map Ref** J10

ACCESS/CONDITIONS: Numerous self-guided trails are available of varying lengths and terrain. All are waymarked across the site with an accompanying leaflet available from the visitor centre. Disabled parking is available on site. A self-drive buggy, designed for countryside conditions, is available for disabled visitors to Newlands Corner and Albury Downs.
HOW TO GET THERE: By train or bus to Chilworth (1.5 miles away), or drive to car park off the A25, Guildford.
WALKING TIME: The Butterfly Trail takes about 1 hour. It is waymarked with green arrows.
30-MINUTE VISIT: The Deer Trail takes about 45 minutes and can be shortened. It passes mostly through woodland.

Right: Mallard drake

Nestled in the heart of Surrey Hills AONB, Newlands has superb views, open downland covered in wildflowers and shady woodland alive with birdsong. In spring and summer, the chalk grassland is a spectacular carpet of wildflowers. The woodlands are mixed, with some deciduous trees like oak and birch, plus evergreen yew. Some of the yew trees are hundreds of years old.

The woods shelter roe deer and are home to green woodpeckers, nuthatches and tawny owls. Look for cowslip, devil's-bit scabious and several species of wild orchid. Look high in the sky to see skylarks hovering and listen for their song on a warm clear day.

The woodland areas become a mass of colour during the autumn months and are home to roe deer, woodpeckers, nuthatches and owls. Many colourful fungi can also be seen, such as the fly agaric.

In winter, marvel at the wonderful views across the Downs and watch the flocks of birds as they swoop over the hills.

Staffhurst Wood SSSI

Near Oxted; **OS Map** TQ 414 485; **Map Ref** J9

ACCESS/CONDITIONS: Ground is fairly level with some paths and boardwalks.
HOW TO GET THERE: Please refer to www.traveline.org.uk for public transport information. By car, use St Silvan's and Grants Lane car parks.
WALKING TIME: It takes about 1 and a half hours to walk around the 95-acre (38ha) reserve.
30-MINUTE VISIT: Take the self-guided trail from St Silvan's car park, Limpsfield. The walk can be made shorter by taking the bridleway back to the car park.

Thought to be a surviving fragment of ancient woodland, Staffhurst is a truly memorable and special place that is well worth a visit. With its tall beeches, oaks and areas of dense hazel and hornbeam coppice, Staffhurst is not only spectacular all year round, it also provides a haven for many species of wildlife.

The ancient woodland has SSSI and LNR status for its fine mix of oak, ash and beech. In spring, bluebells carpet the woodland floor; in summer, bird and butterfly species are abundant; while in autumn and winter, the woodland is filled with beautiful autumn colours, and deer and badgers.

WILDLIFE FACT: THE BEAUTY OF BLUEBELLS

Bluebells are one of the marvels of spring, transforming forest floors into a lush carpet of green and purple. The UK native variety has drooping flowers that grow from one side of the stem only, while the invasive Spanish variety has flowers that grow all around the stem. Visit bluebell woodlands in April and May to see the yearly spectacle (check in the listings, there are too many to list here).

Chobham Common NNR

Chobham; **OS Map** SU 971647; **Map Ref** J4

P i 🚶

ACCESS/CONDITIONS: Surfaces are soft and sandy; no stiles but some steep slopes.
HOW TO GET THERE: By train, regular trains run to Sunningdale on the Reading to Waterloo line. From Sunningdale Station turn left over the railway crossing, follow the road for 220m, turn right onto the road sign posted for Chobham and continue on until you reach the railway bridge. Cross the bridge and the first access onto the Common is across the road on the left. By bus, services run to Sunningdale from Ascot, Windsor and Bracknell during the week. There is a limited weekday bus service to Chobham from Woking and Camberley. Get off at Bowling Green Road, turn right onto the main road and walk about 220m to reach Burrowhill Green at the south-west corner of the Common. By car, use one of six car parks serving the Common.
WALKING TIME: The self-guided trail is 1 to 2 miles long and takes 1 to 1 and a half hours.
30-MINUTE VISIT: Follow the green waymarked route from Staple Hill car park, Staple Hill Road, Chobham, but cut across from point 5 back to the car park for a shorter walk.
A MEMBER SAYS: 'This vast site is just bursting with wildlife. I like to wander and explore new areas. If you tread carefully and look closely you will find a wonderful diversity of wildflowers, insects, spiders and birds. I sometimes sit by one of the pools and watch the water voles feeding by the edge – wonderful!'

The largest NNR in south-east England and one of the finest remaining examples of lowland heath. First created by prehistoric farmers, 6,000 years of management have created a patchwork of mini-habitats rich in wildlife. In spring, listen out for the distinctive calls of Dartford warblers as they hunt for insects and spiders, and for the song of skylarks and woodlark. In high summer, look for orchids, such as the southern marsh, and rare butterflies such as the silver-studded blue. Hear the eerie churr of the nightjar on a summer evening and watch dragonflies dart over heathland pools during the day. Heathland plants are then at their best, with heather, dwarf gorse and marsh gentian all flowering. In autumn, warblers stop off at the common to fuel up for their flight to Africa and watch out for the aerial displays of the hobby. Finally, with winter comes the hardier bird species escaping the Scandinavian and Arctic winter. Look for fieldfare and redwings, listen for the 'jip jip' call of crossbills, and the 'see-saw' of the great tit in January.

DID YOU KNOW?

- **Over 100 bird species have been recorded, together with most of Britain's amphibians and reptiles and 21 species of mammal.**
- **Queen Victoria reviewed her troops on Chobham Common before the Crimean War.**
- **Chobham Common is recognised as the best site in Britain for ladybirds, bees and wasps, with 29 species of butterflies and 22 species of dragonfly.**

Norbury Park SSSI

Between Bookham and Leatherhead; **OS Map** TQ 158538; **Map Ref** J3

ACCESS/CONDITIONS: Fairly level and good surfaces run from Crabtree and Fetcham car parks, but there are steep climbs from Young Street. Disabled parking and wheelchair access is available to Bocketts Farm.
HOW TO GET THERE: By car, use car parks located off the A246 between Leatherhead and Bookham.
WALKING TIME: The 2.2 mile self-guided trail from Young Street car park takes about 1 and a half hours.
30-MINUTE VISIT: Park at Fetcham car park and follow the circuit of tracks around the woodland. Visit in spring for the display of primroses.
A MEMBER SAYS: 'Norbury is so tranquil – you feel like you're the only person there.'

Norbury Park SSSI is a working landscape, with farms and a commercial sawmill. The park lies within the Surrey Hills AONB and consists of 1,300 acres (520ha). It was the first area of countryside purchased by Surrey County Council in 1931, to protect it against development. Today, Norbury Park is an attractive mixture of woodland, grassland and farmland.

During spring the woodland floors are carpeted with bluebells and primroses, and the farm fields are full of newborn lambs. Summer brings the show of orchids and chalk grassland flowers, which attract the many species of butterflies – such as silver-washed fritillary, green fritillary, marbled white and common blue.

The mixture of coniferous and deciduous trees brings an abundance of autumn colour to the landscape. Habitat management such as coppicing takes place during the winter months.

Its varied, well-managed landscape and its free-draining geology means that Norbury Park offers good walking conditions all year round. There are numerous walking trails and cycle routes that allow you to leave the beaten track, catch a glimpse of the roe deer and enjoy the hidden corners of the park.

DID YOU KNOW?

- Norbury Park Manor is mentioned in the Domesday Book.
- The rare green hound's tongue is rapidly increasing in numbers on the site.
- Some of the yew trees in Druid's Grove are said to be 2,000 years old.

Wisley Common, Ockham and Chatley Heath SSSI

Near Cobham; **OS Map** TQ 080590; **Map Ref** J1

ACCESS/CONDITIONS: Soft, sandy surfaces with no stiles, but some steep slopes. Café and countryside room are wheelchair accessible.
HOW TO GET THERE: By bus, take route 515 Kingston to Guildford via Surbiton and Wisley (National Traveline 0870 608 2608). By car, the site is off the main London to Portsmouth road (A3), south of J10 of the M25.
WALKING TIME: The self-guided trail is 1.2 mile and takes 1 hour.
30-MINUTE VISIT: Follow the blue sailor waymarkers from Boldermere car park up to the Tower and back. The route takes you through woodland and heathland so you should see many bird species.
A MEMBER SAYS: 'Wisley is a lovely mosaic of heathland, grassland and woodland. I return month after month as there is so much rich and diverse wildlife to see!'

A wonderful mix of habitats, including heathland, ancient woodland, conifer woodland, grassland, ponds and a large lake called Boldermere. This is a great reserve for exploring and birdwatching. Fantastic views towards London can be admired from the top of the 19th-century Semaphore Tower on Chatley Heath.

Spring at Ockham is often heralded by the sweet song of the woodlark. By late spring, the specialised heathland birds return from winter migration. By June, nightjars, best known for their remarkable churring song, have returned to breed. Hobbies and buzzards can be seen gliding across the heath in search of prey with which to feed their young.

High summer is spectacular, with heather in full flower and insects and reptiles abound. Large, noisy tit flocks feed in the broad-leaved woods during autumn and winter, and redwing frequent the fields on the edges of the common.

DID YOU KNOW?

- Boldermere Lake is 16 acres (6.5ha) in size and holds about 47,000 cubic metres of water.
- Chatley Heath has the only remaining Semaphore Tower in England. It is a Grade II listed building.
- The tower was once part of a chain used to pass messages between the Admiralty in Whitehall and the Royal Naval Dockyard in Portsmouth.
- Due to a positive heathland restoration programme, Wisley Common and Ockham Heath now has 250 acres (100ha) of heath, but in 1988 it had only 52 acres (21ha).

Kent

About the Trust

Founded in 1958, Kent Wildlife Trust is the leading conservation charity for Kent and Medway – protecting wildlife, educating the public, influencing decision-makers and restoring habitats. Its nature reserves include a range of habitats of extraordinary beauty. It manages over 59 reserves covering more than 7,400 acres (3,000ha), including over 55 miles of roadside reserves.

Kent Wildlife Trust
☎ 01622 662012
www.kentwildlifetrust.org.uk

Lydden Temple Ewell

Near Dover
OS Map TR 277453; **Map Ref** K9

The reserve offers 198 acres (80ha) of species-rich chalk downland. It forms part of The Road Verge Project, a unique scheme in the Lydden area, and is one of three RNRs managed under a 10-year grazing scheme, supported by Countryside Stewardship. Orchids include: early-spider, twayblade, fragrant, pyramidal, bee and autumn lady's-tresses. Butterflies spotted include marbled white, silver-spotted skipper, Adonis and chalkhill blue. Use the car park behind the George and Dragon centre in Temple Ewell.

Queendown Warren LNR

Near Stockbury
OS Map TQ 827629; **Map Ref** K5

This LNR contains 198 acres (80ha) of open downland and woodland and is managed in conjunction with Plantlife and Swale Borough Council. It is an important site for grassland orchids. The woodland is home to large beech trees, oak, ash, birch, wild cherry, and traditionally managed sweet chestnut coppice. Adders have been spotted. Use the car park in Warren Lane off Mount Lane, off Lower Hartlip Road.

Romney Marsh Visitor Centre

New Romney
OS Map TR 078261; **Map Ref** K10

☎ 01797 369487

Set in 27 acres (11ha), Romney is a nationally important site for great crested newts. Species of special interest include great diving beetles and tree sparrow, along with a number of acid grassland plants. There are also dune grassland and ponds with rare insects and plants. The visitor centre is open daily from 11am to 4pm, March to September; from Friday to Monday, 11am to 4pm, October to February. The centre is a straw bale construction with sedum roof and a wood-burning stove. It houses dramatic displays on the natural and social heritage of the Romney Marsh.

Sevenoaks

Sevenoaks
OS Map TQ 520565; **Map Ref** K7

☎ 01732 456407

The reserve covers some 136 acres (55ha), with roughly equal proportions of water and land. It includes five lakes and a mixed habitat of ponds, seasonally flooded pools, reedbed and woodland. It is a spectacular site for birds. The reserve's wetland and woodland habitats support a diverse community of plants, fungi and animals. So far, well over 2,000 species of flora and fauna have been identified. Waders and wildfowl are regular visitors, including little ringed plover, lapwing and tufted duck, plus woodpeckers and warblers.

East Blean Wood

Near Herne Bay; **OS Map** TR 194642; **Map Ref** K3

ACCESS/CONDITIONS: Waymarked paths lead from the car park and these can sometimes be muddy.
HOW TO GET THERE: By bus, Stagecoach 4 and 6 go along the A291, 0.75 miles from the reserve. By car, from the A299 Thanet Way take the A291 south at Herne Bay, then near Wealden Woods take Hicks Forstal Road to Hoath.
WALKING TIME: There is a half a mile circular walk and a 1 and a half mile figure-of-eight route through this 301-acre (122ha) reserve.
30-MINUTE VISIT: Follow the waymarked paths from the car park to area brimming with heath fritillaries, woodland birds and flowers.

The reserve covers 301 acres (122ha) of ancient semi-natural woodland situated on poorly drained London clay. In spring there are carpets of bluebells (pictured below) and other flowers, such as sanicle and yellow archangel. The lovely liquid song of nightingales may be heard in May and June.

The wood has been heavily managed in the past as wood pasture and as a source of sweet chestnut coppice. When conditions are open, after the coppice is cut, much of the ground is colonised by common cow-wheat, which is the food plant of the caterpillar of the rare heath fritillary butterfly. The high point of summer occurs when these beautiful orange and black chequered butterflies appear in June and July. Woodland birds, such as woodpeckers, nuthatches and treecreepers may be spotted throughout the year, and many toadstools can be seen in autumn.

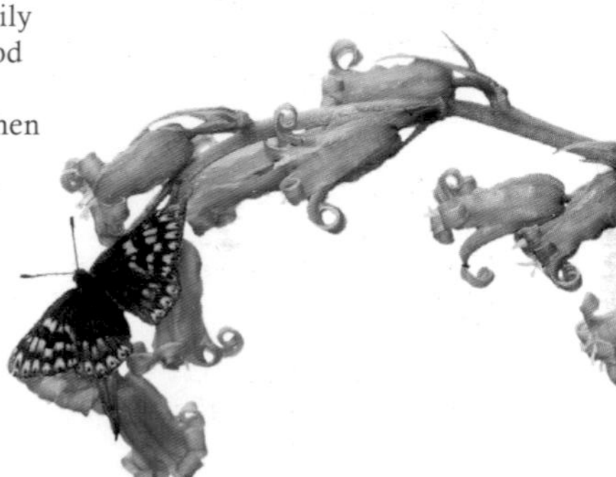

Reculver Country Park

Near Herne Bay; **OS Map** TR 225695; **Map Ref** K1

OPENING TIMES: Open all year; visitor centre, 11am to 5pm, closed Monday (Wednesday to Sunday only in September, Sunday only October to March).
ACCESS/CONDITIONS: There are firm, level paths near the car park, visitor centre and towers.
HOW TO GET THERE: By bus, take Stagecoach 7 or 7a from Canterbury/Herne Bay to Reculver. By car, follow signposts from the A299 Thanet Way.
WALKING TIME: The clifftop walk westwards to Bishopstone of 1 mile takes about 1 hour.
30-MINUTE VISIT: Explore the Roman fort and ancient towers, then take a walk along the clifftop and go down to the beach to see the fossils in the soft cliffs.

As well as immense wildlife conservation value, this coastal site also has strong historical, geological and archaeological worth. It features a visitor centre containing superb displays about the local wildlife, Reculver Towers (12th-century twin towers), the remains of a Roman fort, and of a 14th-century church.

In spring and summer, there is a colourful display of flowers and butterflies in the grassland above the cliffs, and a colony of sand martins nests in the cliffs in summer. The park is renowned for the number of migrating birds in spring and autumn.

Seashore birds and stranded marine life can be observed in winter. Meanwhile, the interesting geological features of the cliffs can be appreciated at any time of year

The reserve is managed by Kent Wildlife Trust for Canterbury City Council. The visitor centre (01227 740676) makes an excellent starting point for cliff-top walks.

Tyland Barn Visitor Centre

Near Maidstone; **OS Map** TQ 754593; **Map Ref** K6

01622 662012

OPENING TIMES: Tuesday to Sunday, February to December, 10am to 5pm (4pm on weekends). Please phone to check. Groups by arrangement.
ACCESS/CONDITIONS: Mostly compacted gravel paths. Wheelchair ramps to main barn door are available on request.
HOW TO GET THERE: By train, nearest station is Maidstone East. By bus, take Arriva 101. By car, follow 'brown badger' signs on the Maidstone to Chatham Bluebell Hill Road (A229) between M2 (J3) and M20 (J6).
WALKING TIME: Allow 2 hours to explore the barn and 2 hours for local footpaths.
30-MINUTE VISIT: You can get lots of ideas for improving your own garden for wildlife in a quick walk round the grounds. Don't miss the observation beehive.

This is Kent Wildlife Trust's headquarters and largest visitor centre, a great place to find out about the county's wildlife and the problems it faces. Although within walking distance of Westfield Wood Nature Reserve, Tyland Barn itself is more of a demonstration nature park than a reserve.

It is an ideal venue for a family outing at any time of year, especially if one of the supervised children's activities is on offer. Visit in spring for tadpoles and early flowers; see if the sparrows are nesting in the box with the video camera in May. Try your hand at pond-dipping in the summer and, in winter, find out which birds are feeding at the feeding station. The barn houses a large exhibition on wildlife and conservation, with plenty of hands-on displays for children. Outside the barn there is a nature park. This has a large pond, meadow, chalk bank and scrub habitats, as well as a birdwatching hide and displays on composting, 'green picnics' and a wide variety of different native plant species.

WILDLIFE FACT: GOING, GOING, GONE

Over time, several large mammals have become extinct in the UK. Beavers were wiped out in the 1100s, prized for their musk glands and their fur. Brown bears fell victim to the Romans, who exported them for shows back home. The last wild wolves were found in Scotland and Ireland in the 18th century, and wild boar were hunted to extinction in the 16th century. Of these, wild boar are now making a successful comeback, having escaped from captivity and now breeding successfully in the wild. There are also plans to turn back the clock and reintroduce wolves and beavers.

Pictured: Brown bear

Bough Beech

Near Tunbridge Wells; OS Map TQ 496494; **Map Ref** K8

P WC i 01732 453880

OPENING TIMES: Visitor centre; 11am to 4.30pm, Wednesday/Saturday/Sunday/ bank holidays, April to October. Group visits by arrangement.
ACCESS/CONDITIONS: View reserve from the public road/causeway south of Winkhurst Green. The trail from the visitor centre allows visits to part of the western side. Access to the main part is by permit and is for recording and study only.
HOW TO GET THERE: By train, Penshurst station is closest (2 miles). By bus, take 231 and 233 from Tunbridge Wells or Edenbridge to Bough Beech village (1.7 miles). By car, drive to the north end of Bough Beech Reservoir, 2 miles from Ide Hill, Sevenoaks. Park on the roadside or at the oast house when open.
WALKING TIME: The short walk on the causeway overlooking the reservoir takes about 1 hour. A visit to the centre plus a walk along the nature trail would take a further 2 hours.
30-MINUTE VISIT: Just park on the causeway, check the list of birds seen and scan the water from both sides of the road.
A MEMBER SAYS: 'It's the only place in west Kent where you can see water birds with such ease.'

The reserve covers the northern part of the Sutton and East Surrey Water Reservoir. The water level is high throughout the winter and early spring, falling to its lowest in autumn.

An important staging post for migrating birds during the spring and autumn, the reserve has regular appearances of ospreys and other exciting birds. The open water is important for ducks, grebes and geese, especially in winter.

In summer and autumn, areas of mud, gravel and concrete are exposed around the edges of the reservoir, providing feeding and nesting areas for waders such as lapwing and little ringed plover. Surrounding woodland and scrub attract breeding warblers, woodpeckers and finches throughout the summer. Areas of marshy grassland provide botanical interest, as well as wader feeding areas. There is a small orchard with a birdfeeding area in winter. There are some floating islands designed as resting sites for nesting terns and for other birds.

DID YOU KNOW?

- **The reservoir has a capacity of 2,400 million gallons – pumped from the River Eden and distributed to parts of Surrey and west Kent.**
- **Probably the best site for mandarin ducks in the UK.**

Oare Marshes

Near Faversham; **OS Map** TR 013647; **Map Ref** K2

ACCESS/CONDITIONS: The whole reserve may be observed from the footpath, nature trail and viewing hides. Good viewing from the road itself, especially over the East Flood.
HOW TO GET THERE: By train, go to Faversham. By bus, Arriva 333 runs from Maidstone, Sittingbourne and Faversham to Oare, 1 mile from the reserve. By car, from the A2 just west of Faversham follow the signs to Oare village and turn right to 'Harty Ferry' at the Three Mariners pub. Park at the end of the road. Continue to the bank of the Swale Estuary.
WALKING TIME: The 2-mile trail through the 166-acre (67ha) reserve takes 2 hours.
30-MINUTE VISIT: Drive slowly down to the car park, stopping at the lay-by to view birds feeding and roosting on the East Flood. View the sea or mudflats (depending on the state of the tide) from the sea wall near the car park.
A MEMBER SAYS: 'Whenever I'm in the area, I call by – it need only take a few minutes and often turns up trumps.'

Oare Marshes reserve is internationally important for water birds and other wetland wildlife. In winter you can see brent goose, dunlin, curlew, wigeon, merlin, marsh and hen harrier, short-eared owl and perhaps a bittern. In summer, the reedbeds are alive with reed buntings, warblers and just a few bearded tits. Among the breeding species found here are avocet, redshank, snipe, lapwing, water rail, bearded tit, shoveler and garganey.

Plants include sea clover, spiny restharrow, sea lavender and golden samphire. Dragonflies are abundant, and you may spot common seals on sandbanks in the estuary and little egrets or avocets on the mudflats. In spring and autumn, there is a passage of migrating birds which can include black-tailed godwit, ruff, little stint, curlew sandpiper and whimbrel.

DID YOU KNOW?

- The site was much improved when the level of the sluice which drains the fresh water from the fields into the sea was raised. Just a few centimetres created extensive shallow floods ideal for water birds.
- The numerous square concrete bases mark the foundations of huts where ammunition was stored during World War I.
- The Watch House at Oare Marshes, adjacent to the road, was originally a boat house, and the Harty ferry once ran between here and the Isle of Sheppey.

Sandwich and Pegwell Bay

Near Ramsgate; **OS Map** TR341632; **Map Ref** K4

P WC i

ACCESS/CONDITIONS: Nature trails lead to a hide with views over Pegwell Bay. Please avoid the beach at Shellness and the saltmarsh at Stonelees because of roosting and breeding birds.
HOW TO GET THERE: By bus, Stagecoach 37 runs from Ramsgate and Sandwich past the entrance. By car, the Pegwell Bay picnic site and car park is on the north side of the Stour on the A256 and is well signposted.
WALKING TIME: The circuit of 1.3 miles takes at least 1 hour to walk.
30-MINUTE VISIT: Just park and walk down to enjoy the view over the sea or mudflats (depending on the tide). Walk along the footpath to the right if you have time to spare.
A MEMBER SAYS: 'Sandwich Bay is a birdwatcher's paradise.'

This reserve offers a complex mosaic of habitats, including intertidal mudflats, saltmarsh, shingle, sand dunes, ancient dune pasture, chalk cliffs, wave cut platform and coastal scrubland. It is the best remaining complex of this type in south-east England.

Botanically, the saltmarsh holds typical plants, such as sea aster, sea lavender and the rare golden samphire. Sea holly grows here too, with yellow-horned poppy on the shingle. On the dune pastures, southern marsh orchids and pyramidal orchids can be found, while at Stonelees, marsh helleborines and bee orchids are flourishing under the management programme of scrub clearance and grazing.

Sandwich and Pegwell Bay is of international importance for its waders and wildfowl, best seen in the winter or during the spring and autumn migrations. In winter, common waders are joined by nationally important numbers of sanderling and grey plover. All these are best seen on the mudflats of Pegwell Bay. In summer, redshank, shelduck and oystercatcher stay to breed, and are joined on the shingle by ringed plovers and the rare little tern. Summer also sees the appearance of rare orchids, such as lizard, southern marsh and marsh helleborine.

DID YOU KNOW?

- Nesting birds compete with nudists on one part of the beach.
- Sandwich and Pegwell Bay gives one of the best examples of a mosaic of different coastal habitats.

Sussex

About the Trust

The Sussex Wildlife Trust was formed in 1961 and is now the largest conservation organisation dedicated to conserving the natural heritage of Sussex. With more than 25,000 members and 6,500 junior 'Wildlife Watch' members, it manages 3,500 acres (1,416ha) of land, which include some of the finest wild places in Sussex.

Sussex Wildlife Trust ☎ 01273 492630
www.sussexwt.org.uk

Amberley Wildbrooks
Amberley
OS Map TQ 030136; **Map Ref** J20

Wildfowl visiting during winter floods include Bewick's swan. Also featured are spectacular and rare wetland plants and insects, especially dragonflies. Access is restricted to the Wey South Path, which runs through the middle of the Brooks from Hog Lane in Amberley.

Burton and Chingford Ponds
Duncton
OS Map SU 979180; **Map Ref** J19

The reserve offers woodland, carr, wet and dry heath, two large ponds and bogs. Kingfisher, reed warbler and blackcap are seen, as are chaser, golden ringed and emperor dragonflies. Plants include rare cowbane, bog-bean, yellow loosestrife and cranberry.

Eridge Rocks
Eridge Green
OS Map TQ 554355; **Map Ref** J14

This 99-acre (40ha) reserve features a cretaceous sandstone outcrop, and is home to rare mosses, liverworts and ferns as well as spring bluebells and a variety of woodland birds. There is good access. The going is flat with no stiles or gates. The entrance to the private road off the A26 is next to a church. A small car park is located at the base of the rocks.

Iping and Stedham Commons
Stedham
OS Map SU 852220; **Map Ref** J18

Highlights of this site include digger wasps, field crickets, tiger beetles, as well as woodlark, Dartford warbler, nightjar, stonechat and sundew. The reserve is flat and there are no stiles, but many gates to allow entry into the grazing area of Stedham Common.

Levin Down
Charlton
OS Map SU 885133; **Map Ref** J21

This 69-acre (28ha) reserve plays host to many butterflies, including Duke of Burgundy, green and brown hairstreaks, and blues. Chalk grassland flowers abound, such as clustered bellflower, chalk heath, juniper. Warblers and finches are seen. There's an uphill climb to enter Levin Down and many steep slopes, also stiles at each entrance.

The Mens
Petworth
OS Map TQ 023236; **Map Ref** J17

P

The Mens is 395 acres (160ha) of ancient woodland in the process of reverting to a natural state. View fungi and meadow flowers as you walk the circular route. The going is flat, but often muddy, some of the tracks are bridleways.

Woods Mill
Henfield
OS Map TQ 218138; **Map Ref** J22

This flagship environmental education reserve for Sussex recently expanded to include superb downland views. Spot nightingales, woodpeckers, warblers, turtle doves and dragonflies as well as a wide range of woodland, water and meadow plants. The site is mostly suitable for wheelchair access. There is a circular nature trail and an 18th-century watermill (open for special events). Sorry, no dogs.

Filsham Reedbed

Hastings; **OS Map** TQ 775097; **Map Ref** J24

ACCESS/CONDITIONS: The boardwalks are suitable for wheelchair access with passing places and viewpoints over the reserve. Some footpaths can be muddy.
HOW TO GET THERE: Off the Bexhill Road A259 in St Leonards at Bulverhythe Recreation Ground, a public footpath runs alongside the Combe Haven, the footbridge over the river leads into the reserve.
WALKING TIME: The trails total 2 miles and take 1 to 2 hours.
30-MINUTE VISIT: Walk up from Bulverhythe Recreation Centre alongside the river to view the reserve from the bridge.

Filsham is a reedbed with ditches and lagoons, set in a river valley floodplain. Although it is the largest reedbed in Sussex, it is surprisingly hard to find, tucked away in the Combe Haven Valley (an SSSI) between Bexhill and Hastings.

The valley is an important migration route for birds, and during the autumn and winter the reedbed (a LNR) is a crucial stopping-off point for thousands of swallows and warblers, and much rarer species, such as marsh harrier and bittern. In the spring, birds including reed warbler, bearded tit and water rail breed here; rare specialist moths such as the wainscots are numerous, and unusual plants including frogbit, water violet and the insectivorous bladderwort exist wherever enough light can reach the water surface. The Trust recently completed a restoration programme to provide much better conditions for breeding birds as well as other reedbed wildlife. At the same time, improvements have been made to public access with a birdwatching screen and boardwalk.

Old Lodge

Maresfield; **OS Map** TQ 469306; **Map Ref** J15

ACCESS/CONDITIONS: Please keep to the well-marked nature trail, which leads around most of the reserve. Some stiles and steep slopes.
HOW TO GET THERE: The reserve is 4 miles north of Maresfield on the B2026 to Hartfield about 500m north of the junction with the B2188.
WALKING TIME: The circuit of 2 miles takes 1 to 2 hours.
30-MINUTE VISIT: Walk along the first section of nature trail for spectacular views over the Ashdown Forest.

Old Lodge offers open vistas of heather, with areas of pine woodland, set in the middle of the much larger Ashdown Forest. The heathlands are at their best in summer, when bees, wasps and butterflies busy themselves over the vegetation, stonechats utter their staccato call from the top of gorse bushes, and the vistas of the rolling Wealden landscape are purple-clad with bell heather.

Grazing has been restored to Old Lodge, and, in conjunction with birch and bracken control, is steadily improving the reserve for heath and acid grassland species. There are also several boggy ponds dug by volunteers, and a small stream, lightly shaded in places by young alder, all of which prove very popular with species of dragonfly that are generally uncommon in Sussex. These include the golden ringed dragonfly, black darter, and even the extremely rare small red damselfly.

Right: European honey bee

Castle Water and Rye Harbour

Rye Harbour; **OS Map** TQ 925185; **Map Ref** J25

P WC

ACCESS/CONDITIONS: The reserve is flat with easy access to many of the hides, although there are stiles where the sheep are grazing the fields.
HOW TO GET THERE: By car, it is 2.5 miles southeast of Rye along Harbour Road, near the settlement of Rye Harbour. There is a large car park with 150 spaces in Rye Harbour village.
WALKING TIME: The 5-mile circuit takes 3 to 4 hours.
30-MINUTE VISIT: Park near the industrial complex on Harbour Road to see roosting cormorants, little egret and bitterns (in winter).
A MEMBER SAYS: 'This is the perfect spot to get really close views of birds usually only seen at a distance and is a great introduction for the novice birdwatcher.'

A large coastal reserve with vegetated shingle, grassland and water features, Rye Harbour LNR, which includes Castle Water, contains a natural shingle system and tidal mudflats, saltmarsh, grazing marsh and flooded gravel workings.

It is great for birdwatching at any time of year, but especially good during winter at Castle Water – a water-filled gravel pit with islands and fringes of reeds and willows, grassy or sandy margins. The hundreds of ducks that can be viewed from the hide include pochard, tufted duck, mallard, wigeon, teal, gadwall, shelduck and occasional visitors such as smew.

Regular reserve visitors prefer to watch from the northern end of the lake. At dusk, cormorants roost in the willows, joined by little egrets and in recent years the rare and elusive bittern has begun to roost here in increasing numbers.

The grazing marsh is intersected by water-filled ditches, which are teeming during the summer months with dragonflies, beetles, molluscs and the rare and imposing medicinal leech.

During the summer rare plants are in flower on the shingle ridges. These specially adapted plants such as yellow-horned poppy, sea-kale and sea pea are able to cope with almost soil-less conditions.

DID YOU KNOW?

- **279 bird species have been recorded at Rye Harbour LNR.**
- **The endangered least lettuce is the rarest plant found here.**
- **This reserve is one of the few remaining places in Sussex where you can still see water voles.**

Ebernoe Common

Ebernoe; **OS Map** SU 976278; **Map Ref** J16

P

ACCESS/CONDITIONS: The ground is flat but can be muddy. The areas to the east and south are farmland under conversion to pasture woodland with some footpaths providing pleasant walks throughout.
HOW TO GET THERE: About 4 miles from Petworth via the A283. Take the first right for Gunters Bridge and Balls Cross onto Streel's Lane. Opposite the telephone box, turn right down the track. Small car park (approximately 15 cars) near Ebernoe Church at the bottom of the track.
WALKING TIME: Ebernoe Common is a 385-acre (156ha) reserve, and the circuit of 4 miles takes 3 to 4 hours.
30-MINUTE VISIT: Park at the church and explore some of the northern part of the reserve, taking in Furnace Pond and Furnace Meadow.
A MEMBER SAYS: 'A magical ancient woodland which has to be seen to be believed.'

A superb example of a Low Weald woodland with a history of traditional use. During spring there are carpets of flowers, such as bluebells, wild daffodils and orchids. Furnace Meadow is rich in flowers, with quaking grass, cowslip, pepper saxifrage and betony colouring the grasslands throughout the summer months.

The north part of the reserve is on clay. Here the trees are predominantly oak and ash, but there is a great variety of other species too, including field maple, hazel and wild service tree. To the south, the soils become more acidic and sandy; here beech is the more common forest tree, and in places the lemon-scented fern grows.

Autumn brings abundant fungi, including stinkhorn, chanterelle and beefsteak fungus. Bats make use of the cracks and hollows that have formed within the trees; including thriving colonies of the rare barbastelle and Bechstein's bat. On many of the trees there are communities of rare lichens that are usually not seen outside the New Forest.

The Trust has restored low-intensity grazing to the Common to maintain the flower-rich glades and rides in a more sustainable manner, and to ensure that the continued expansion of shady trees, such as holly, does not threaten the existence of other, more light-loving plants. At the same time, we need to be sure that altering the complex micro-climates within the woodland does not compromise the security of shelter-loving species, such as the bats.

DID YOU KNOW?

- **About half the reserve is ancient woodland where commoners once turned out their cattle or pigs to graze and browse. The other half is reclaimed arable, which the Trust is converting back to pasture and woodland.**
- **More than 840 species of fungus have been recorded.**
- **14 of the 16 species of British bat have been recorded here.**

Malling Down

Lewes; **OS Map** TQ 423112; **Map Ref** J23

ACCESS/CONDITIONS: There are fences and gates and some paths are very steep. The gentlest route to the top is from Mill Road.
HOW TO GET THERE: By train, go to Lewes Station, it's then a 15-minute walk (there is a small entrance in Wheatsheaf Gardens opposite the petrol station). By car, there is access from Mill Road or the layby on the Ringmer Road (B2192), where there is free parking for 10 cars.
WALKING TIME: The circuit of 5 miles takes 4 to 5 hours.
30-MINUTE VISIT: Walk up the Coombe towards the Snout, from Wheatsheaf Gardens for fabulous summer flowers and butterflies. No parking.
A MEMBER SAYS: 'One of the most wonderful wild places in Sussex.'

Superb chalk grassland and many downland flowers and butterflies, all within easy walking distance of Lewes town centre. The grassland is full of flowers. In June, parts of the Coombe are painted yellow with horseshoe vetch and later pink with centaury or creamy-white with the frothy heads of dropwort.

Orchids are a speciality of this reserve. Common spotted orchids, always found here on north-facing slopes, number in their thousands. There are pyramidal orchids too, and occasional fragrant and bee orchids, as well as common twayblade.

The summer months belong to the butterflies, and any sunny days will see thousands of these insects enjoying the nectar of the grassland flowers. The rare Adonis blue lives here, the brilliant blue male is a common sight sipping nectar from horseshoe vetch. There are also bright-blue common blues, powder-blue chalkhill blues as well as browns and many kinds of small darting skipper butterflies.

DID YOU KNOW?

- In spring 2002, over two million cowslips bloomed here.
- Round-headed rampion, locally known as the 'Pride of Sussex', is abundant here.
- In recent years, the very rare silver-spotted skipper has started breeding here.

EAST

The east of England is best known for its wetlands and coasts – the Fens, the Broads and the East Anglian coastline which together make one of the premier birdwatching areas in the country. It was on the north Norfolk coastline that the very first county Wildlife Trust came into being, back in 1929 when the-then Norfolk Naturalists Trust was established to safeguard the reedbeds and marshes to the east of Cley-next-the-Sea. Cley Marshes remains one of the jewels of the Wildlife Trusts, with its avocets, bitterns, migrant waders and wildfowl attracting a constant stream of pilgrims to this, the most famous birdwatching site in the country.

Internationally important numbers of wildfowl make the East Anglian coast their home during the winter months: tens of thousands of pink-footed geese and wigeon feed on the coastal grazing marshes, alongside Bewick's and whooper swans, teal and shoveler.

During the summer, the marshes, reedbeds and shallow lakes of the Broads are home to booming bitterns, bearded tits and marsh harriers. This is the only place in the country where two rare and spectacular insects can be found: the flamboyant swallowtail, our largest native butterfly; and the dashing Norfolk hawker, a large brown dragonfly with emerald green eyes. These wetlands and waterways are also home to a flourishing population of otters, although you will have to be very lucky (and very quiet!) to catch a glimpse of this elusive mammal.

Further inland are the Fens, once the greatest wetland in the country but now a flat landscape of rich farming. Here the Wildlife Trusts are engaged in one of the most exciting habitat restoration projects ever undertaken in Britain, to create a 3,700-hectare wetland between Huntingdon and Peterborough. The Great Fen will restore this part of the Fens to its former glory, providing homes for marsh harriers, water voles and a multitude of other species.

But there is so much more to the East than the wetlands. The Brecks, a large area of dry grassland and heath on the borders of Norfolk and Suffolk, is home to rare wild flowers, scarce insects and the stone curlew. In Bedfordshire, the chalk grasslands should be explored for their pasque flowers, orchids, and chalkhill blue and Duke of Burgundy butterflies. In north Northamptonshire, you could fill a day roaming the limestone grassland and ancient woodlands of Old Sulehay, while red kites circle overhead.

For the wildlife enthusiast, the East of England truly has something for everyone.

Opposite: Hunstanton, Norfolk

NOT TO BE MISSED

- **CLEY MARSHES**
  The very first of Britain's county nature reserves, this site has a well-deserved international reputation for birdwatching – in particular for its population of bittern.
- **GRAFHAM WATER SSSI**
  The largest reservoir in England when it opened in the 1960s, today it is one of the region's flagship reserves for its summer songbirds, winter wildfowl and migrant waders.
- **LACKFORD LAKES**
  Lackford never fails to delight thanks to its abundance of wildflowers, dragonflies and year-round birding interest. It's also one of the best places in Suffolk to see kingfisher.
- **LANGDON**
  Natural history meets social history at this enchanting reserve in Essex. It shows that countryside once threatened by intensive farming can be restored to its former native glory.
- **OLD SULEHAY**
  The largest wildlife reserve in Northamptonshire, this ancient woodland is especially prized for its wildflowers.
- **REDGRAVE AND LOPHAM FEN**
  If you want to get truly wild then this Suffolk reserve is for you. Surrounded by whispering reeds and alive with birds and dragonflies, it is the largest remaining valley fen in England.

Beds, Cambs, Northants and Peterboro (BCNP)

About the Trust

For the past 50 years, the Beds, Cambs, Northants and Peterboro (BCNP) Wildlife Trust has managed over 130 nature reserves across the three counties – together covering over nine square miles of predominantly clay woodland – and the monitoring of such species as buzzard, hairy dragonfly, oxslip, harebell and black hairstreak butterflies is managed by over 350 volunteers. To prevent the continual decline of wildlife species in the area, the Trust runs a series of training workshops to increase students' appreciation and knowledge of the local environment.

Wildlife Trust for Beds, Cambs, Northants and Peterboro (BCNP)
Bedfordshire☎ 01234 364213
Cambridgeshire☎ 01954 713500
Northamptonshire☎ 01604 405285
Peterborough☎ 01733 294543
www.wildlifebcnp.org

Beechwoods
Near Cambridge
OS Map TL 485547; **Map Ref** M23

The Beechwoods were planted on arable land in the 1840s. Today, delicate white helleborines thrive on the dry chalky soil, pushing up their flowering spikes in the spring before the budding beech leaves can cast their deep, cool shade. These orchids are usually found under beech, and this nature reserve is one of their most northerly outposts. Look out for hawthorn, wild privet and bramble.

Blow's Downs
Near Dunstable
OS Map TL 033216; **Map Ref** H7

The steep chalk hills rising from the edges of Luton and Dunstable have allowed this site to retain grassland rich in wildlife and full of colour with areas of scrub providing shelter for birds and insects. The views from the top are well worth the climb, passing through flower-rich grassland as you go. Wheatear, stonechat, whinchat and ring ouzel are among the favourites that may be seen.

Collyweston Quarries
Near Eastern-on-the-Hill
OS Map TF 004038; **Map Ref** N39

Quarried hills and hollows now covered by limestone grassland that's periodically grazed by rare breed sheep and cattle. Cowslip, rest-harrow, dyer's greenweed, rock-rose, dropwort, small scabious, wild thyme, common milkwort, tall broomrape, dodder, horseshoe vetch and kidney vetch. Five species of orchid have also been recorded – common twayblade, man, bee, and fragrant orchids of which pyramidal orchid is the more abundant.

Cooper's Hill
Near Ampthill
OS Map TL 028376; **Map Ref** H3

This reserve is on the Greensand ridge, a geological feature which stretches across the county from Leighton Buzzard in the south-west, to Gamlingay in south Cambridgeshire. It contains large areas of heather growing together with birch, oak, gorse and broom scrub. The north-western corner of the reserve supports a small area of acidic mire and ponds. Marsh violet can be found here with willow carr gently shading the water.

Felmersham Gravel Pits
Near Felmersham
OS Map SP 991584; **Map Ref** H1

Felmersham consists a rich mosaic of woodland, grassland and open water-filled gravel pits. The lakes are one of the best places for dragonflies and damselflies in Bedfordshire, with no fewer than 18 species known to have bred. Wildfowl congregate on the open water. In deep water areas rare plants such as whorled water-milfoil and bladderwort have established themselves.

Flitwick Moor

Near Flitwick

OS Map TL 046354; **Map Ref** H4

In the heart of the Flit valley, this superb wetland was left behind when peat was cut from the site as recently as the 1960s. Woodlands of oak and birch, over dense stands of bracken, reveal the acidic nature of the site. The wet fen and boggy mire provide the real treasures of the site, including fluffy seed heads of cottongrass, nine species of sphagnum moss and marsh pennywort.

Fordham Woods

Near Soham

OS Map TL 632700; **Map Ref** M21

Fordham Woods is a wet valley woodland with stands of alder trees, a habitat now rare in Cambridgeshire. It once formed part of the fen stretching past Fordham. Alder, specially adapted to waterlogged ground, dominates the wettest places. It is the only native broad-leaved tree to produce cones, and supports more than 90 insect species and many different fungi.

Glapthorn Cow Pastures

Near Oundle

OS Map TL 005903; **Map Ref** N42

Blackthorn thickets covering the site are now nesting habitat for many birds, especially warblers; three or four pairs of nightingales usually breed and can be heard singing at dusk in May and June, while roding woodcock, tawny owls, nuthatch and long-eared owls have also bred here. The larvae of black hairstreak butterflies feed on the blackthorn.

King's Wood

Near Heath

OS Map SP 929300; **Map Ref** H5

This magnificent wood is part of the largest area of deciduous woodland in Bedfordshire and its history can be traced back before the 15th century. A mixture of small-leaved lime and scattered hornbeam, as well as flower-rich woodland rides. Parts of the woodland are privately owned – please keep to the main paths.

Pegsdon Hills

Near Hitchin

OS Map TL 120295; **Map Ref** H6

Pegsdon Hills offers some of the best views in the Chilterns AONB. The steep chalk hills and quiet valleys are full of wildlife, from magnificent displays of orchids and butterflies, to nesting lapwings and circling buzzards. It's the region's best spot for squinancywort and various orchids can be found among the reserve's chalk grassland and scrub. Steep slopes and seasonally muddy can make access difficult.

Stanground Wash SSSI

Near Peterborough

OS Map TL 208975; **Map Ref** M19

Cut off from the rest of the washes by a busy railway line and enclosed by parallel floodbanks – this reserve has its own distinctive habitat. The network of deep and shallow ditches host many locally and nationally rare beetles. Along the southern margin of the reserve, the Back River contains nationally scarce plants such as fringed water-lily and grass-wrack pondweed. The site is very good for birds, and you might be lucky enough to hear snipe, redshank, and sandpipers or catch a glimpse of a peregrine.

Thorpe Wood

Near Peterborough

OS Map TL 159986; **Map Ref** M18

This beautiful ancient woodland consists of an oak-ash canopy with hazel and field maple below. The northern section is actively managed by traditional coppicing. The ground flora is diverse here, especially in spring when there are good numbers of wood anemones and a spectacular display of bluebells. Woodpeckers can be frequently heard tapping in the summer months.

Twywell Hills and Dales

Near Cranford

OS Map SP 945776; **Map Ref** N45

The gullet was formed by ironstone extraction, which exposed much limestone and unusual box formations. A large pond supports a wide range of plant and insect life. Look out for hart's-tongue fern, limestone flora with occasional knapweed broomrape and abundant wild strawberry. The Whitestones area was formed from limestone spoil and features an extensive range of limestone plants as well as occasional bee and common-spotted orchids.

Gamlingay Wood SSSI

Gamlingay; **OS Map** TL 240537; **Map Ref** H2

ACCESS/CONDITIONS: Clay soils mean conditions can be uneven and the going heavy autumn to spring.
HOW TO GET THERE: Take the B1040 from Gamlingay towards Waresley. A track on the right leads up to the wood. Park on the side of the track to the wood.
WALKING TIME: Many paths throughout the wood allow walks of various length but the full circuit takes 2 to 3 hours.
30-MINUTE VISIT: Spend your time exploring the main rides.

Gamlingay Wood is mostly ancient woodland of oak, ash and maple that has been shaped by its long history of use by man for timber and coppice products. The Wildlife Trust purchased the reserve in 1991 and its national importance is recognised by its designation as an SSSI. As well as being a rich wildlife habitat, it also has many interesting historical features, such as the original woodbank which circles the wood and a ring ditch of ancient origin. The reserve is home to good numbers of breeding birds, and in summer the rides and glades are filled with wildflowers and insects that feed on their nectar, including butterflies such as the speckled wood. In the first half of the 20th century much of the timber from the wood was harvested and large areas replanted with conifers such as Scots pine and Norway spruce, creating areas which are very different from the undisturbed broad-leaved woodland and traditional coppice plots. In spring, the woodland floor becomes a carpet of bluebells, violets and oxlips, while in summer there are thousands of common-spotted orchids on the rides. In autumn the wild service trees turn a beautiful flaming orange, and mushrooms and toadstools of all shapes and sizes can be seen.

Summer Leys LNR

Near Wellingborough; **OS Map** SP 885634; **Map Ref** N58

ACCESS/CONDITIONS: The circular walk consists of level grass and gravel paths. Tarmac paths lead from the picnic area to the hides, which are suitable for wheelchair access.
HOW TO GET THERE: South of Wellingborough on the road between Great Doddington and Wollaston. Train to Wellingborough (3 miles). No direct bus to Summer Leys, but buses run to Great Doddington and Wollaston.
WALKING TIME: 116-acre (47ha) reserve. The circular walk of around 2 miles takes about 1 hour.
30-MINUTE VISIT: Stay close to the car park to visit the marigold pond and hides overlooking the main lake and the wader scrape.

Summer Leys LNR is one of the best birding sites in the Nene Valley and its restoration following gravel extraction was designed specifically to benefit wildlife, especially birds.

During the summer, the reserve supports one of the largest breeding colonies of tree sparrows in Northamptonshire. A visit to the feeding station will reward visitors with close views of this attractive species whose numbers are in decline elsewhere in Britain.

Skylarks breed in the surrounding grassland and common tern nest on the gravel islands. Hobby are regularly seen hawking dragonflies over the water.

This is an excellent site for passage migrants and in the winter, very large flocks of lapwing and golden plover are common, sometimes over a thousand of these birds roosting on the islands and flying out to feed in nearby fields.

The reserve is also one of the best places in Northamptonshire to see the uncommon hairy dragonfly. Look for them on the edges of Marigold pond from mid-May to the end of June.

Titchmarsh LNR

Near Peterborough; **OS Map** TL 007805; **Map Ref** N44

ACCESS/CONDITIONS: The circular walk is accessed by kissing gates and is generally firm. It does get muddy, especially alongside the River Nene. The gravel path from the car park to the East Midlands Hide is suitable for wheelchair access.
HOW TO GET THERE: Off the A605 Thrapston to Peterborough Road. Turn at Thorpe Waterville towards Aldwincle, and then take the first left in Aldwincle into Lowick Lane.
WALKING TIME: A walk round the reserve takes about 2 hours. Stout footwear is recommended.
30-MINUTE VISIT: From the car park, walk to the Peter Scott Hide overlooking the pools and wader scrapes. The artificial sand martin bank can also be seen from these hides.

Titchmarsh LNR occupies a beautiful part of the Nene Valley with fantastic views over the floodplain and villages dotted along the surrounding higher ground. The main woodland, which contains an important heronry, is on the site of an old duck decoy created by Lord Lilford in the 19th century. Winter is the best time to see the large numbers of wildfowl. In particular, goosander, wigeon and gadwall reach nationally important numbers. By February, the herons are starting their breeding season with much noise and excitement coming from the 50 pairs normally occupying the heronry. They are very vulnerable to disturbance and visitors are asked not to enter the heronry at any time of the year. As spring progresses, more birds take up residence. A small colony of common terns breeds on one of the islands and in many years oystercatcher and shelduck also breed. The grasslands provide breeding sites for skylark and redshank. Kingfishers can be seen at any time of the year along the River Nene. In the grasslands look out for sneezewort, great burnet, cowslips and red bartsia. The wetter areas hold purple loosestrife, trifid-bur marigold, marsh dock and several species of speedwell.

WILDLIFE FACT: CALM WATERS ARE KINGFISHER TERRITORY

The kingfisher can be seen throughout the UK. Look out for its distinctive flash of electric-blue and listen for its shrill piping call as it flies low and fast over the water along rivers and canals. This colourful bird may be seen at many of The Wildlife Trusts' wetland reserves: try Summer Leys in Northamptonshire or Teifi Marshes near Cardigan for close up views.

Pictured: Kingfisher

Brampton Wood SSSI

Between Grafham and Brampton; **OS Map** TL 184698; **Map Ref** M20

P i

ACCESS/CONDITIONS: Wheelchair or pushchair access is possible but the wood is situated on boulder clay and wet through most of the year. Paths are often muddy and uneven.
HOW TO GET THERE: Access by car only. Nearest train station: Huntingdon.
WALKING TIME: The network of paths and rides allows you to do a short 20-minute walk or to spend all day exploring – the choice is yours!
30-MINUTE VISIT: Take a walk up the main ride, between the two large oaks and to the main cross rides. From here you will be able to see the length of the wood.
A MEMBER SAYS: 'I visit this reserve every day and there is always something new to see each time...'

Brampton Wood SSSI is the second-largest wood in Cambridgeshire and is home to a remarkable variety of plants and animals. Visitors to the wood can easily lose themselves among its paths and really feel at one with the wildlife. More than 300 plant species have been recorded here and the wood is also well known for its butterflies and birds.

Dormice were introduced into the woods in 1992 and, although they are rarely seen, they have been recorded throughout the reserve. Several nationally scarce butterflies can be seen on sunny summer days, including black hairstreaks, which take winter refuge in the blackthorn bushes, and white admirals, which collect nectar from honeysuckle.

Every season brings new attractions. In spring, you can be swept away from your cares by the heady scent of bluebells and the beautiful freshness of wood anemone and oxlip. Bluebells and violets grace the woodland floor and you may even hear the drumming of woodpeckers preparing to nest, or the melodious song of the nightingale. During the summer months, the rides are filled with wildflowers and the air hums with the buzzing of insects, including dragonflies. Meanwhile, in autumn, fascinating mushrooms and toadstools appear, and in winter the footprints of foraging animals can be seen.

Best for: 300 species of plant, including spring flowers and some rarer trees such as wild pear; singing nightingales; black hairstreak and white admiral butterflies.

DID YOU KNOW?

- Continuous woodland has occupied this site since at least 1086AD.
- Brampton used to be owned by the MoD.
- The reserve was purchased after an astounding fundraising drive. £200,000 was raised in just seven weeks.
- Brampton Wood SSSI is the only known site for dormice in Cambridgeshire.

Grafham Water SSSI

Near West Perry, Huntingdon; **OS Map** TL 143671; **Map Ref** M22

ACCESS/CONDITIONS: Parts of the paths and rides are suitable for wheelchair access.
HOW TO GET THERE: Between Huntingdon and St Neots on the A1. Leave the B661 at Buckden or the A14 at Ellington. The nearest train station is Huntingdon.
WALKING TIME: The full cycle circuit is 8 miles, but a network of shorter paths and trails takes from 30 minutes.
30-MINUTE VISIT: Take a walk through the wildlife garden and along the track to Dudney Hide where you can watch the birds on the water. If you walk through in early morning at the right time of year you may be lucky enough to hear the nightingales.
A MEMBER SAYS: 'We come back year after year to birdwatch because you never know just what you might find!'

Grafham Water was the largest reservoir in England when it opened in the 1960s. Today it is a reserve with a difference! The whole family can explore the reserve by bicycle, stopping off along the way to enjoy the wildlife and explore a number of waymarked trails.

There are wildlife spectacles to be found throughout the year, from the beauty of bluebells in the spring to the melodic song of the nightingales as summer begins to take hold. The mixture of woodland and grassland provides food and shelter for summer songbirds, including the nightingale, garden warbler and blackcap. In winter, the reservoir attracts large numbers of diving ducks, such as gadwall and shoveler, as well as nationally important populations of coot and great crested grebe. Migrant waders, such as common sandpiper and greenshank, also make use of the reservoir margins in the spring. As well as the usual species, the reservoir often attracts rarer species, including scoter and red-throated diver. The wildlife garden provides an opportunity for the less physically able to experience the reserve without having to travel large distances.

Best for: breeding and over-wintering wildfowl and waders; ancient woodland flora, including more unusual species such as wood barley and spurge laurel; black-tailed skimmer.

DID YOU KNOW?

- Until the 1960s the whole area was arable farmland with only a small stream running through it.
- Charcoal is still made by volunteers using traditional methods (for sale at the Wildlife Trust Office).

Old Sulehay

Near Peterborough; **OS Map** TL 060985; **Map Ref** M17

ACCESS/CONDITIONS: Variety of walks over mixed terrain available, including main woodland ride through Old Sulehay Forest. Site includes kissing gates suitable for wheelchair access.
HOW TO GET THERE: Located near the village of Yarwell on Old Sulehay Road, just off the Wansford junction of the A1/A47 west of Peterborough. Dispersed roadside parking around the edges of the reserve. Avoid blocking rights of way and other access points.
WALKING TIME: 212-acre (85ha) reserve. The full circuit of 2 miles takes about 5 hours.
30-MINUTE VISIT: Take one of the circular walks around the wood, quarry or grassland surrounding the lodge.
A MEMBER SAYS: 'It's a relief such a wonderful place is now protected, forever! Fantastic views and yet hidden away!'

At more than 212 acres (85ha) in size, Old Sulehay SSSI is the largest Wildlife Trust reserve in Northamptonshire. The site is large enough to allow visitors to spend the whole day looking at wildlife without leaving the reserve, and the variety of habitats provides an excellent opportunity to compare the vigour of ancient woodland with areas of relatively new habitats in which wildlife is gradually gaining the upper hand.

Old Sulehay Forest sits on a variety of soil types which results in varied flora, including bluebells, nettle-leaved bellflower, wild garlic and, in mid-May, a carpet of wood anemones that extends as far as the eye can see. Greater and lesser spotted woodpeckers live here, along with nuthatch and tree creeper.

Stonepit Quarry, a disused limestone quarry, is also very diverse in its composition, with heaps of spoil littering the area and creating a hills-and-hollows effect. The picturesque mosaic of scrub, grassland and bare earth makes it an amazing habitat for insects and wildflowers such as bird's-foot trefoil, marjoram, basil thyme, viper's bugloss, lesser centaury and autumn gentian. In May, look out for the grizzled skipper butterfly in Stonepit Close.

Ring Haw is an area of ancient woodland and limestone grassland of great wildlife value, and is especially prized for its wildflowers. The wood is mainly composed of oak and ash and includes other species, such as field maple, hazel and spindle tree. The grassland has a great diversity of wildflowers, including small-flowered buttercup, stinking hellebore, common cudweed, lesser centaury and basil thyme. The spring carpet of cowslips is breathtaking.

The Trust is embarking on an exciting new project within the arable fields in this section of the reserve to restore the fields to species-rich wildflower meadows.

Best for: varied geology and topography, including oolitic limestone; an excellent range of flora and invertebrates.

DID YOU KNOW?

- **Currently the largest Trust-owned reserve in Northamptonshire.**
- **A key reserve for the Trust's first ever ecology group.**
- **First example of reserve expansion and linkage in the local Trust.**

Pitsford Reservoir

Near Northampton; **OS Map** SP 780708; **Map Ref** N53

P i WC ☎ 01604 781350

OPENING TIMES: Lodge: 8am to dusk daily, mid-March to end-November (weekends only during winter). Access to the reserve is by permit only from the lodge, call in advance of your visit.
ACCESS/CONDITIONS: The lodge has facilities for the disabled but the paths are almost all grass and, for much of the year, these can be soft and muddy.
HOW TO GET THERE: 5 miles from Northampton between the A43 and the A508. It is on the Holcot to Brixworth Road. Buses run from Northampton to both villages but the remaining 1 to 2 miles have no public transport.
WALKING TIME: The 6-7-mile circular walk with time to stop in hides takes 3-4 hours at an easy pace.
30-MINUTE VISIT: Head north of the fishing lodge and follow the circuit round the blocks of woodland.
A MEMBER SAYS: 'There is so much to see here that no two visits are ever the same.'

The reserve is a wonderful mixture of habitats with woodland, scrub, grasslands, carr, marginal vegetation and open water. With its broad, winding arms of water set against the low hills of the area, it is Northamptonshire's 'Lake District'. In winter, wildfowl numbers can exceed 10,000, with 14 species of duck often present alongside grebes, geese, coot and swans. A feeding station on the Old Scaldwell Road also ensures a good chance of watching tree sparrows, corn buntings and many other small birds attracted to the seeds. The wide diversity of habitats offer early food and shelter in spring for a huge range of migrant birds, some of which stay to breed. Recent surveys show a breeding population comprising 55 different species.

The wealth of plants provides food and shelter for small mammals, including harvest mice, as well as an enormous range of invertebrates. In summer, the reserve comes alive with dragonflies and damselflies. Common blue and emerald damselflies with ruddy darter dragonflies make up the bulk, each totalling many hundreds of thousands in late July and early August. Butterflies add to the colour with 23 species recorded. Since flooding the valley in the early 1950s, a wetland flora has developed with an additional, interesting plant community occupying the draw-down zone each summer and autumn as water levels drop.

DID YOU KNOW?

- **Internationally significant numbers of gadwall over-winter.**
- **Over 280 species of fungus have been recorded.**
- **Over 340 species of macromoth have been recorded.**

Norfolk

About the Trust

Established in 1926 with 40 nature reserves in its care, Norfolk Wildlife Trust is the oldest in the country. You can expect to see brown hares, adders, kingfishers, harvest mice and turtle doves inhabiting the county's broads, sandy heaths and rugged north coastline. The Trust's project work mainly centres on an advisory service for landowners, the protection of existing sites from damaging new development, and encouraging others to get involved in wildlife stewardship.

Norfolk Wildlife Trust
☎ 01603 625540
www.norfolkwildlifetrust.org.uk

Cockshoot Broad

Near Ranworth
OS Map TG 343165; **Map Ref** L6

Spring and summer highlights include swallowtail butterfly, variable and red-eyed damselfly, Norfolk hawker, migrant hawker, hairy dragonfly, as well as marsh pea, marsh valerian and yellow monkey flower. Autumn and winter bring siskin and redpoll. Watch heron, marsh harrier and Cetti's warbler year round. From B1140 turn towards and through Woodbastwick; go straight on where the road bends towards Ranworth. Park by River Bure.

Hethel Old Thorn

Near Norwich
OS Map TG 171005; **Map Ref** L9

The reserve sits at the edge of a tiny south Norfolk village, nestling beside the church and peaceful churchyard. It is one of the smallest reserves in the UK (0.062 acres/0.025ha) with the oldest hawthorn in East Anglia at 700 years old. Take B1113 to New Buckenham, turn left into Hethel. Park near the church.

Lower Wood SSSI

Near Wymondham
OS Map TM 143978; **Map Ref** L10

One of Norfolk's few remaining ancient woodlands. Summer highlights include bluebells, ramsons, wood spurge, hairy St John's wort, early purple orchid and twayblade. Look out for white admirals, too. Waymarked trail.

Narborough Railway Line

Near King's Lynn
OS Map TF 750118; **Map Ref** L8

An unusual chalk grassland which is home to 30 species of butterfly, including dingy and grizzled skipper, grayling, brown argus, purple and white-letter hairstreak. Flora to enjoy in spring and summer include small scabious, eyebright, kidney vetch, marjoram and autumn gentian. From the A47 follow signs to Marham. Car park is on left 0.6 miles south of Narborough village.

Grimston Warren (Tony Hallat Memorial Reserve)

Near King's Lynn
OS Map TF 679214; **Map Ref** L4

Heathland, fen and bog wildlife are returning as restoration continues. In spring and summer enjoy marsh cinquefoil, marsh fern, white sedge and lesser water plantain. Wildlife includes the broad-billed chaser, ruddy darter and black-tailed skimmer, as well as woodlark, turtle dove, tree pipit and breeding nightjar. Paths are often muddy.

Foxley Wood NNR

Foxley, Dereham; **OS Map** TG 049229; **Map Ref** L3

P i

ACCESS/CONDITIONS: Waymarked trails. Dogs are not permitted.
HOW TO GET THERE: Bus 56 (Norwich to Wells) stops at the Foxley War Memorial, a 15-minute walk. By car, leave Norwich on the A1067 Fakenham Road, from where the wood is signposted on the right.
WALKING TIME: 304 acres (123ha) of ancient woodland and coppice. A gentle wander around all parts of the wood takes 2 hours.
30-MINUTE VISIT: You could easily venture down one of the rides as far as you like and retrace your steps when time runs out.

This is a glorious ancient woodland, thought to be more than 6,000 years old, and the trees within it are direct descendants of the wildwood that first grew on the site as the climate became warmer after the Ice Age. It is awash with colour in spring and alive with birdsong and butterflies. Its wide rides, which were originally created to allow the movement of felled timber, make wonderful paths and take you far into the wood's interior. Its tallest oaks have a cathedral-like majesty and create an atmosphere of history and tradition that is felt all year round, but the flowers, birds and butterflies make spring and summer the most colourful times to visit. A walk in spring will reward the visitor with views of yellow primroses, wood anemones, violets, pink water avens and the striking early purple orchid. Butterflies abound on sunny days, when you may see colourful brimstones and swift-moving orange tips. Look out for purple hairstreaks and white admirals, too.

Thompson Common

Near Watton; **OS Map** TL 941966; **Map Ref** L11

P i

ACCESS/CONDITIONS: Enter from the car park via a kissing gate.
HOW TO GET THERE: Leave Watton on the A1075 to Thetford Road. Look out for the Great Eastern Pingo Trail car park located behind the lay-by as the road bends to the left just before you reach Stow Bedon. If you get to Stow Bedon you've gone too far!
WALKING TIME: 346-acre (140ha) reserve. The Great Eastern Pingo Trail, an 8-mile circular walk, takes you around the pingos in about 2 hours.
30-MINUTE VISIT: Visit the first few pingos along the Great Eastern Pingo Trail and then retrace your steps.

Thompson Common comprises 346 acres (140ha) of unimproved wet and dry grassland and heath incorporating pingos, scrub and woodland. The Common is famous for its pingos, a series of 300 or so shallow pools containing a dazzling array of water plants. The pingos were formed about 9,000 years ago during semi-frozen conditions at the end of the last Ice Age. Thompson Common is one of the best-preserved pingo sites in Britain. We care for the pingos by clearing surrounding scrub and woodland, maintain a mixture of open water, fen, grassland, woodland, heath and scrub and graze open areas with ponies and sheep. Thompson Common is also one of the most important sites in Europe for water beetles and, in the UK, for dragonflies.

In the spring and summer, notable flora include water violet, marestail, marsh pennywort, fen pondweed, bogbean, marsh orchid, marsh cinquefoil, heather, quaking grass, salad burnet and dwarf thistle. Also, look out for scarce emerald, hairy and emperor dragonfly.

Right: Emperor dragonfly

Weeting Heath NNR

Weeting, near Brandon; **OS Map** TL 756881; **Map Ref** L12

OPENING TIMES: Reserve and visitor centre: 7am to dusk, April to September.
ACCESS/CONDITIONS: Visitor centre, hides and paths are suitable for wheelchair access. No access onto the heath for the protection of the stone curlew.
HOW TO GET THERE: West of Brandon on the Norfolk/Suffolk border. Buses 143,145 and 28 from Brandon. By car, leave Brandon, going north on the A1065 to Mundford. Turn left to Weeting and left to Hockwold-cum-Wilton. Car park, 2 miles from Weeting.
WALKING TIME: 341 acres (138ha) of Breckland grass and lichen heath. You could easily spend half an hour in each of the hides.
30-MINUTE VISIT: Simply sit quietly in one of the hides and watch the birdlife.

Weeting Heath is a wonderful piece of Breck heath, and is famous for its rare Breckland flora and population of rare breeding stone curlew (resident between April and September). Stone curlews breed in only two places in the UK, Breckland and Salisbury Plain. Stone curlews are extraordinary birds, with piercing yellow eyes, long yellow legs and knobbly knees. Weeting Heath has the best stone curlew breeding success rate of anywhere in the country. When the stone curlew begins to arrive in spring, the birds start nesting immediately, sometimes very near the hides, and chicks are fledged in early summer. Post-breeding flocks can be seen in late summer, before they depart again to over-winter in North Africa in September.

Little owls, woodpeckers and hobbies also frequent the reserve, and in the spring and summer visitors can also watch woodlark, tree pipit and wheatear. Look out also for small copper, brown argus and speckled wood butterflies during those warmer seasons.

WILDLIFE FACT: SIX BRITISH REPTILES

There are six native British reptiles: three snakes (adder, grass snake and smooth snake) and three lizards (sand lizard, common or viviparous lizard and slow worm). Of these, the smooth snake and the sand lizard are both very rare, almost entirely restricted to heathland in southern England. The four commoner species of reptile are still widespread across the country, best looked for as they bask in the sun on heathland or warm sheltered hedgebanks.

Pictured: Common (viviparous) lizard

Cley Marshes

Cley-next-the-Sea, Holt; **OS Map** TG 054440; **Map Ref** L2

P WC i 01263 740008

ACCESS/CONDITIONS: There is a brand new visitor centre with excellent disabled access. The boardwalk and all the hides are suitable for wheelchair access.
HOW TO GET THERE: NWT Cley Marshes is on the north Norfolk coast, on the A149 coast road, 3.7 miles north of Holt.
The Coasthopper bus service stops just outside the nature reserve.
WALKING TIME: 371 acres (150ha) of reedbed, pools and wet grassland. You could happily spend half a day moving between hides.
30-MINUTE VISIT: Cross over the road from the visitor centre and onto the reserve. Wander along the boardwalk through the reedbed and slip into any of the hides that catch your fancy.
A MEMBER SAYS: 'Cley Marshes deserves its international reputation as a birders' paradise. And it's a fabulous place for a quiet walk too.'

Cley Marshes, the very first of Britain's county nature reserves, has a well-deserved international reputation for birdwatching. The reserve was purchased in 1926 to be held 'in perpetuity as a bird breeding sanctuary'. It was Norfolk Wildlife Trust's first reserve and provided a blue print for nature conservation which has now been replicated across the UK. The East Bank, with its views over the reserve and Arnold's Marsh, is seen by many as the best birdwatching site in the country.

Four hides (with excellent wheelchair access) provide birdwatching within metres of the pools where the birds congregate. They offer unrivalled, intimate views across the pools and scrapes. In spring, the pools fill with wading birds and the chance of passage rarities, for which the reserve is famous, should not be missed.

In summer, breeding birds arrive, including the beautiful avocet with its upcurving beak. Waders return in late summer, while autumn is a wonderful time for vagrant rarities. In winter large numbers of wildfowl gather.

For the non-birder, there are tranquil walks and views along the boardwalk. The view from the visitor centre across the Marsh to the sea is breathtaking.

DID YOU KNOW?

- **Cley Marshes supports a substantial proportion of the UK's bittern population. Listen for their distinctive 'booming' call, which sounds like the sound made when blowing over the top of a bottle.**

Hickling Broad NNR

Hickling, Norwich; **OS Map** TG 428222; **Map Ref** L5

01692 598276

ACCESS/CONDITIONS: Boardwalk has waymarked trails suitable for wheelchairs and there is partial access to one hide. Visitor centre has one bathroom with wheelchair access.
HOW TO GET THERE: South of Stalham, clearly signposted off the A149 (Stalham to Caister-on-Sea). Follow the 'brown badger' tourist signs into Stubb Road. Buses from Norwich and Cromer stop in Hickling, a 20-minute walk.
WALKING TIME: 1,483 acres (600ha) of open water, reedbed, fen, grazing marsh and woodland. The walk around the reserve and a ride on the Water Trail boat takes up to 3 hours.
30-MINUTE VISIT: Follow the Swallowtail Trail (green markers) for the best chances of seeing waders, wildfowl and bittern.
A MEMBER SAYS: 'The view from the top of the Tree Tower is really breathtaking, and the boat trip over to it is equally wonderful.'

Hickling Broad is the largest expanse of open water in the Broads system and offers a great deal to see, either on foot or by boat. Its wide-open landscape and big skies make it a fine choice for a walk in any weather.

At Hickling Broad you can explore nature trails, climb the 60ft (18m) Tree Tower to see the fantastic view, observe the beautiful swallowtail butterfly or visit the hidden and secret parts of the Broad on the Water Trail.

From October to March the raptor roost at Stubb Mill, Hickling provides excellent views of raptors as they fly in to roost. Visitors are reminded that there is no parking at the 'roost'. Please park at Hickling Broad car park and walk from there (approx 0.5 miles). Birds you are likely to see include marsh harriers, hen harriers, merlins, cranes and pink-footed geese. Visitors are advised to watch from the viewing area for their own safety.

DID YOU KNOW?

- **HRH The Prince of Wales came here in late 2001 to see the results of the restoration. During the visit, he spent a good 15 minutes enjoying the view from the top of the Tree Tower – in the rain!**
- **The Broads are hand-dug pits, created during the Middle Ages by local people excavating peat to use as fuel.**

Holme Dunes NNR

Holme-next-the-Sea, Hunstanton; **OS Map** TF 714449; **Map Ref** L1

01485 525240

ACCESS/CONDITIONS: Disabled access is available to the first birdwatching hide.
HOW TO GET THERE: Coasthopper bus service and 410 (King's Lynn to Hunstanton) from Holme or Thornham. By car, north from Hunstanton on the A149 Coast Road. Look out for the signs to the reserve just before you enter Holme-next-the-Sea.
WALKING TIME: The full circuit of the 667-acre (270ha) reserve takes approximately 3 hours.
30-MINUTE VISIT: From the car park, walk to the first hide overlooking Broadwater. Retrace your steps past the visitor centre and up the slope to the pine belt. Turn left to walk through the pines and then double back along the beach.
A MEMBER SAYS: 'Holme Dunes is one of Norfolk's best-kept secrets – a really beautiful place in a fabulous location.'

Holme Dunes NNR is one of the North Norfolk coast's most attractive landscapes, and has a tangible air of fragility and mysticism. Its location makes it an important birdwatching site and 320 species have been seen. 667 acres (270ha) of mudflats, foreshore, sand dunes, dune slacks, scrub, pines, saltmarsh, freshwater and grazing marsh and reedbeds.

At any time of year, this is a delightful place for a walk, either through the pines, around the pools or along the beach. During the spring and autumn migrations, hundreds of birds pass through. In winter the site is home to a host of wildfowl. On a spring evening you can hear natterjack toads calling in the dunes. In summer, the beach is fabulous.

DID YOU KNOW?

- **The sand dunes here are very susceptible to erosion and the Trust works hard to stabilise them.**
- **The pine trees planted here help prevent landward creep.**
- **There were once plans for a large development of holiday homes here.**

Ranworth Broad NNR

Ranworth; **OS Map** TG 360146; **Map Ref** L7

01603 270479

OPENING TIMES: The Broads Wildlife Centre is open 10am to 5pm daily, April to October.
ACCESS/CONDITIONS: The boardwalk nature trail and ramp up into the visitor centre are suitable for wheelchair access. Some of the nature trails can be muddy. The floating Broads Wildlife Centre has fabulous views over Norfolk Wildlife Trust Ranworth Broad and contains interactive displays.
HOW TO GET THERE: Buses from Norwich and Yarmouth stop in South Walsham, a 10-minute walk from the reserve. By car, it is signposted from the B1140 (Norwich to Acle) at South Walsham. At Ranworth, look out for signs to Ranworth Broad car park.
WALKING TIME: 336 acres (136ha) of open water, carr and fen. It would take about 3 hours to enjoy everything the reserve has to offer.
30-MINUTE VISIT: Walk down the boardwalk nature trail to learn about the ecology of the Broads. Then use the binoculars and telescopes available on the upper floor of the visitor centre.
A MEMBER SAYS: 'Make sure you take one of the boat trips from the visitor centre to experience the extreme quiet of the Broad from the water – it's really wonderful!'

This is one of Norfolk's most popular Broads and there is plenty to see and do for both families and naturalists. Our floating Broads visitor centre is located at the end of an informative boardwalk. The Cator family gave Ranworth Broad to Norfolk Wildlife Trust in 1949. Norfolk Wildlife Trust's Patron the Queen opened the Broads Wildlife Centre in 1976.

Today, Ranworth Broad NNR is home to a great variety of birds. During summer, common terns nest on the artificial rafts and great crested grebes can be seen diving for fish. Swallows and swifts hunt for insects over the water. In the winter, large numbers of wildfowl, such as teal, wigeon, shoveler, pochard and gadwall, come here to feed. All year round, you can visit to see Cetti's warbler and great crested grebe. The Broad is home to one of the largest inland cormorant roosts in Britain. Interpretive boardwalk explains the succession from open water to dry land and the many habitats you pass through.

DID YOU KNOW?

- You can see several sunken wherries, which were sunk during World War II to prevent enemy hydroplanes from landing.
- Common terns nest at Ranworth Broad NNR on artificial nesting rafts.

Suffolk

About the Trust

From its beginnings over 40 years ago, Suffolk Wildlife Trust has grown to encompass more than 50 nature reserves covering an area of over 5,680 acres (2,300 ha), each with a featured 'star species'. The county is home to an enormous variety of wildlife, from adders and glow-worms to barbastelle bats and nightingales. The Suffolk community is engaged in a barn owl project – a joint venture with the Suffolk Ornithologists' Group to protect barn owl families.

Suffolk Wildlife Trust
☎ 01473 890089
www.suffolkwildlifetrust.org

Dingle Marshes NNR

Dunwich
OS Map TM 479707; **Map Ref** L16

Dingle Marshes is one of the few places in Suffolk that is accessible by road, and yet where you can have a near-wilderness experience. There's something exciting to see every day, but May is particularly wonderful with bittern booming and marsh harrier displaying. The reserve is a magnet for breeding and wintering wildfowl and wading birds, including the elegant avocet, white-fronted goose, lapwing and redshank. The reedbed holds a significant proportion of the UK's marsh harrier and bittern – a shy bird of which there are only 13 males left in Britain. Good walking conditions all year, but the shingle can be hard going! There is a pub/café adjacent to the car park at Dunwich Beach.

Captain's Wood

Sudbourne
OS Map TM 417417; **Map Ref** L19

An ancient woodland pasture, open all year, with impressive veteran oaks. Noted for its variety of fungi, including the oak polypore, and seven species of bat including the barbastelle, a nationally rare species. It is carpeted with bluebells in spring and there are good populations of fallow deer. A circular waymarked walk leads visitors around the wood.

The Mere

Framlingham
OS Map TM 282635; **Map Ref** L17

The Mere is best known for its sedge beds and a stream of migrating birds. It offers spectacular shows of marsh flowers in spring. Conditions are often wet and boggy and the best time to visit is from April to July.

Newbourne Springs SSSI

Newbourne
OS Map TM 274432; **Map Ref** L20

This small wooded valley with its spring-fed stream used to be a source of water for Felixstowe. Together with its small area of marsh, fen and adjacent heathland, this reserve is good for flowering plants and a variety of birds including nuthatch, treecreeper, goldcrest and all three kinds of woodpecker. Nightingale song can be heard in spring. Butterfly include the speckled wood and green hairstreak, while the dancing lights of glow worm are sometimes spotted during balmy summer nights. A marked trail takes you around the reserve and a leaflet is available from the visitor centre. There is a spectacular variety of habitats and associated wildlife. The going can be wet, uneven and steep in places.

Bradfield Woods

Bury St Edmunds; **OS Map** TL 935580; **Map Ref** L18

 01449 737996

ACCESS/CONDITIONS: The wood can be very muddy during wet weather, but the main rides are always passable. The main ride is suitable for wheelchair access, but can be a little bumpy.
HOW TO GET THERE: Turn off the A134 (Sudbury to Bury St Edmunds) towards Little Welnetham and skirting Bradfield St George. Bradfield Woods is between Bradfield St George and Felsham.
Bus information: Traveline East Anglia 0871 2002233.
WALKING TIME: A walk around the wood with time for quiet reflection takes about 2 hours. Follow the waymarked trails.
30-MINUTE VISIT: Stay on the main wide ride. Linger on a bench to enjoy the nightingales or butterflies before you head back.

One of Britain's finest ancient woodlands, Bradfield Woods is a glorious haven for wildlife, best visited between April and October. Look out for colourful flushes of spring flowers in the newly coppiced areas.

April is the best time to visit to see early purple orchid and wood anemone growing alongside nationally rare oxlip. The dense, bushy growth of young coppice provides cover for migrant songbirds, including nightingale. Visit in June to enjoy their song. On sunny summer days, the sheltered rides harbour breathtaking clouds of butterflies. If you visit the reserve in the early morning, keep quiet and you may see deer picking their way daintily along the rides. Medium sized roe deer are the most common, but the larger red deer (pictured below) and spotted fallow deer also occur. The tiny dog-sized muntjak deer is also spotted regularly in the woods.

Carlton Marshes

Near Lowestoft; **OS Map** TM 508920; **Map Ref** L13

01502 564250

ACCESS/CONDITIONS: The reserve can be wet, but the all-weather path is suitable for pedestrian and wheelchair access. The visitor centre is accessible for all users.
HOW TO GET THERE: Heading out of Lowestoft on the A146 Beccles Road, Burnt Hill Lane is on the right, with the reserve signposted with a brown sign. Train to Oulton Broad South. Bus information: Traveline East Anglia 0871 2002233.
WALKING TIME: The trail around the reserve, with stops for dragonfly spotting along the way, takes 1 hour 30 minutes.
30-MINUTE VISIT: The circular, all-weather path around the first marsh gives you the highlights of the reserve with marsh and dyke species easily visible.

Carlton Marshes lies in the Waveney Valley at the southern tip of the Norfolk and Suffolk Broads. It is the Broads in miniature. Flower studded marshes, drained by a system of dykes and grazed by cattle in summer, create a paradise for wintering wading birds and birds of prey including the hobby. Water vole may be seen in and around the dykes along with special plants including the rare and protected water soldier. In the early summer, the wet fen meadows are bursting with ragged robin, southern marsh orchid, lesser and greater spearwort and bogbean. Later in the summer, dragonflies abound. Fifteen species have been recorded here, including the Norfolk hawker. A visit at dusk during summer may be rewarded with sightings of glow-worms. The open water is heaving with life, including the insectivorous bladderwort, which traps and digests water fleas in bladder-like sacs under water. The best time to visit is May to July (the marshes are open all year, the education centre from spring to autumn).

Hen Reedbed

Adjacent to A1095 Southwold Road; **OS Map** TM 471768; **Map Ref** L14

ACCESS/CONDITIONS: Take care crossing the A1095 to reach the viewing platform over Wolsey Creek Marshes. The viewing platform adjacent to the car park is suitable for wheelchair access.
HOW TO GET THERE: From the A12 (Ipswich to Lowestoft) turn onto the A1095, the main road to Southwold. The reserve and car park are signposted on the left just before the sharp right-hand bend.
WALKING TIME: Allow at least 1 hour to reach the viewing platform at Wolsey Creek Marshes and to enjoy the mudflats.
30-MINUTE VISIT: Follow the short path to the viewing platform close to the car park. Immerse yourself there in the whispering reeds, dragonflies and birdlife.

Hen Reedbed is a blend of reedbeds, fens, dykes and pools created in 1999 to provide new breeding habitat for bittern and other wildlife. In summer, look out for marsh harrier, heron, bearded tit and even hobby hunting over the reeds and dykes. Reed and sedge warblers sing to their hearts' content alongside clouds of iridescent damselfly and nimble dragonfly.

For the best views of the largest mere, follow the waymarked trail through the reedbed to the viewing platform at Wolsey Creek Marshes. Here the pools are good places to spot wildfowl such as gadwall, tufted duck and teal. At low tide, scan the mudflats behind you for feeding waders – redshank, avocet and sandpiper are all regulars. April and May are the best months to visit. There is a large autumn starling roost of up to 250,000 birds.

SPOT THE DIFFERENCE: DRAGONFLIES AND DAMSELFLIES

Several indicators can help you tell the difference between dragonflies and damselflies. While damselflies' wings are all more or less equal in size, dragonflies have back wings that are shorter and broader than their front ones. Dragonflies are also stronger fliers and can be seen further from water than damselflies, which stay close to banks and water surfaces. When at rest, a dragonfly leaves its wings out perpendicular to its body, while a damselfly folds its in along its body. Neither species bite or sting humans. Look out for both around water.

Pictured: Common Blue Damselfly

Lackford Lakes

Lackford, Bury St Edmunds; **OS Map** TL 799706; **Map Ref** L15

01284 728706

ACCESS/CONDITIONS: Visitor centre and hides are suitable for wheelchair access. Disabled parking is directly outside the centre. Paths are flat with good surfaces providing wheelchair access year round.
HOW TO GET THERE: In the village of Lackford on the A1101. Bus details: Traveline East Anglia 0871 2002233.
WALKING TIME: The main circular route plus 'stopping off' time in the hides along the way takes 1 hour.
30-MINUTE VISIT: Choose from three different hides within a 10-minute walk of the centre (follow the signs). Use the upstairs viewing gallery for panoramic views over the reserve.
A MEMBER SAYS: 'The reserve can provide a magical close encounter with nature, be it the turquoise flash of a kingfisher, the splendour of a fishing osprey or the sheer charm of a brood of new ducklings.'

Lackford never fails to delight, with wildflowers and dragonflies to enjoy between the hides and year-round birding interest. It lies beside the River Lark and the lakes were created from former gravel pits. A superb site for wildfowl in both winter and summer, Lackford attracts tufted duck, pochard, gadwall, shoveler and goosander. There are large winter gull roosts and starling roosts – a real spectacle on late winter afternoons. This is one of the best places in Suffolk to watch kingfisher, while osprey pass through on migration. The autumn and spring migrations bring a buzz of excitement to the reserve – almost any migrant bird can turn up – black tern are regulars, but species like Caspian tern, spoonbill and more uncommon waders are also seen.

This reclaimed site has been quickly colonised by plants. Gipsywort, figwort, common fleabane and purple loosestrife occur by the water's edge and common centaury and common stork's-bill appear in the drier areas. Encroaching sallows need to be kept in check so that the open water, which hosts clouds of blue damselfies, is not lost. The otter has become a frequent visitor here. Suffolk Wildlife Trust's original 27-acre (11ha) reserve at Lackford was donated by Bernard Tickner in 1976. In 2000 RMC (now known as CEMEX) donated a further 90 hectares of land to form the Lackford Lakes reserve.

DID YOU KNOW?

- **One of the best places in Suffolk to see kingfisher.**
- **Orchids provide a surprise treat in early summer on the meadows and path edges.**
- **Seventeen species of dragonfly have been recorded here.**

Redgrave and Lopham Fen

Diss; **OS Map** TM 052802; **Map Ref** L9

☎ 01379 688333

ACCESS/CONDITIONS: Visitor centre and WC fully accessible, together with large picnic area outside. The viewing platform is suitable for wheelchair access throughout the year; most routes walkable all year round.
HOW TO GET THERE: Brown signs direct visitors from the A1066 (Thetford to Diss) and from the A143 (Bury St Edmunds to Diss). The fen is also accessed from the B1113. Bus information: Traveline East Anglia 0871 2002233.
WALKING TIME: Five main trails taking from 20 minutes up to 4 hours. The main trail, via the viewing platform, along the River Waveney and back past the spider pools, takes 2 hours.
30-MINUTE VISIT: Spectacular views of the fen (and its plants, dragonflies and hobbies in summer) can be gained from the viewing platform – a gentle stroll from the centre.
A MEMBER SAYS: 'Visitors new to the fen are astounded when they find out about its recent history. The open landscape gives a rare sense of space and people comment on the primeval feel to the site.'

Redgrave is one of the few places where you can get a truly wild experience, surrounded by the whispering reeds and alive with birds and dragonflies. It is the largest remaining valley fen in England. It is one of the most important wetlands in Europe and has international protection. As well as open fen the reserve includes a mixture of wet heathland, open water, scrub and woodland. The underlying acid and alkaline geology has resulted in characteristic wildlife including many species now rare in Britain. Historically, local people dug peat for fuel, harvested reed and sedge for thatching and grazed the drier margins with cattle. With the demise of these activities, together with post-war drainage and water abstraction, the fen began to dry out and degrade. The Trust has undertaken a major restoration project which has resulted in rehydration of the fen and the gradual return of its wonderful wildlife. April to September are the best time to visit to enjoy the fen plants and stunning dragonflies – with hobbies in hot pursuit. Winter starling roosts offer a dramatic spectacle on winter afternoons.

DID YOU KNOW?

- The small pools – a legacy of ancient peat diggers – are home to the elegant fen raft spider found in only two other areas in the UK.
- The reserve is the source of the River Waveney.
- The reserve is grazed by a herd of Polish Konik ponies, together with cattle and Hebridean sheep.

Essex

About the Trust

Since 1959, Essex Wildlife Trust has managed 87 reserves and a nature park that span 7,200 acres (2,914 ha) of woodland, farmland, coastline and waterways. Its seven conservation centres keep track of a variety of wildlife, including badgers, muntjak deer, hares, long-tailed ducks and red-throated divers. In order to maintain the current wildlife resource, the Essex Wildlife Sites Project aims to find and protect fundamental areas of land for habitat. The Trust educates 25,000 children and adults each year.

Essex Wildlife Trust☎ 01621 862960
www.essexwt.org.uk

Backwarden

Danbury, near Chelmsford
OS Map TL 781041; **Map Ref** L27

Located on part of Danbury Common, the Backwarden includes a variety of wildlife habitats including pools, bogs, marsh, woodland, aspen groves and blackthorn thickets. Flowers include tormentil, heath milkwort, marsh willowherb, pennywort, common and lesser skullcap. Dormouse, yellow-necked mouse and water shrew are present along with adder, grass snake, slow worm and lizard.

Blue House Farm SSSI

North Fambridge, near Chelmsford
OS Map TQ 856971; **Map Ref** L29

A working farm of mainly coastal grazing marsh. The fields between the farmhouse and the seawall are used as winter feeding grounds for large numbers of brent geese and wigeon, skylark in spring and summer, redshank, curlew and snipe on marshy fields, oystercatcher and black-tailed godwit on the inter-tidal areas. A public footpath leads along the sea wall. Access to the permissive path and hides is from April to October.

Danbury Ridge

Danbury, near Chelmsford
OS Map TL 790065; **Map Ref** L26

A mosaic of woodland, common and heathland, streams, bogs and farmland harbouring dormouse, as well as nuthatch, hawfinch, migrant warblers, nightingale, ringlet and small copper butterflies. Flora includes lily-of-the-valley, greater butterfly orchid and wood sanicle.

Great Holland Pits

Great Holland, near Clacton
OS Map TM 204190; **Map Ref** L22

On the site of a disused gravel workings, with heathy grassland, pasture, old woodland and ponds. Home to a wide variety of flowering plants including moschatel, yellow archangel, small-flowered buttercup, mousetail, carline thistle, clovers and true bulrush. Birdlife includes nightingale, kingfisher, coot, little grebe and woodcock. Waymarked trails.

Little Waltham Meadows

Little Waltham
OS Map TL 713119; **Map Ref** L24

Comprised of old flood meadows, dry meadows and alder-carr woodland, the reserve hosts meadow saxifrage, bee orchid and yellow oat-grass, as well as trees such as elm, hazel and alder. Green woodpecker, tawny owl, sparrowhawk, kingfisher and kestrel are often recorded.

West Wood

Thaxted
OS Map TL 624332; **Map Ref** L21

Ancient woodland with an abundance of plantlife including oxlips, St John's wort, early purple and butterfly orchids and wood barley, a local rarity. Nesting birds include goldcrest, redpoll, warblers and stock dove. Look out for dormice and butterflies, including speckled wood, brimstone and ringlet.

Roding Valley Meadows

Chigwell; **OS Map** TQ 430943; **Map Ref** L30

 01621 862960

ACCESS/CONDITIONS: A variety of surfaces, some can be muddy. 1-mile surfaced track for wheelchairs, all kissing gates are suitable for wheelchair and scooter access.
HOW TO GET THERE: Off Roding Lane. The entrance is close to the David Lloyd Tennis Centre. Buckhurst Hill, Loughton and Debden tube stations are nearby. Buses run to Debden and Loughton.
WALKING TIME: 158-acre (64ha) reserve with a variety of entrances and trails.
30-MINUTE VISIT: Starting from the main entrance by the tennis centre, walk past some of the remnants of the old RAF Chigwell roads to Andrew's Pond and the appropriately named Luscious Mead! In June, the orchids can be stunning before the hay is cut.

This reserve comprises the largest surviving area of traditionally managed river-valley habitat in Essex. Habitats consist of hay meadows, hedgerows, scrub, secondary woodland and tree plantation with the River Roding to the side.

In the summer, the meadows are rich with flowers like sneezewort and pepper saxifrage, while the wetter areas boast marsh orchid, ragged robin, marsh marigold and rare sedges. Sedge warblers, reed buntings, kingfishers and sand martins are frequently seen, along with small numbers of meadow pipits. In the winter, grey heron, little grebe, snipe, green and common sandpiper are regular visitors. In addition to the wonderful wildlife, this was the site of RAF Chigwell from 1938, and it formed a part of London's barrage balloon defences. Parts of the old site can still be seen, and forms an interesting contrast to the wildlife habitats.

Tollesbury Wick

Tollesbury; **OS Map** TL 970104; **Map Ref** L25

 01621 862960

ACCESS/CONDITIONS: Accessible at all times via the sea-wall footpath. Marked paths, sometimes muddy.
HOW TO GET THERE: Bus services to Tollesbury from Maldon, Colchester and Witham. By car, follow the B1023 to Tollesbury then follow Woodrolfe Road towards the marina and Woodrolfe Green.
WALKING TIME: 600-acre (243ha) reserve. Mostly long walks.
30-MINUTE VISIT: Walk along the sea wall past the marina for stunning views of saltings on the left and the reserve on the right with its variety of habitats.

Right: Grey heron

Tollesbury Wick is a rare example of an Essex freshwater grazing marsh, worked for decades by traditional methods which have been for the benefit of many species of wildlife. Variety is the key at Tollesbury, and it is a classic example of how an area can be developed and managed by people for wildlife. With 600 acres (243ha) of rough pasture, sea walls, borrowdykes (ditches dug in order to build the sea wall), wet flushes, pools and saltmarsh, this reserve is home to small mammals like pygmy shrews and field voles, which attract birds of prey including hen harriers and short-eared owls.

In spring and summer, butterflies, bush crickets and grasshoppers thrive on the banks of the sea walls, while reed warbler, reed bunting, grey heron and little grebe can be heard or seen in the borrowdykes. In winter, large numbers of brent geese can be seen along with wigeon.

Fingringhoe Wick

Colchester; **OS Map** TM 041195; **Map Ref** L23

01206 729678

OPENING TIMES: 9am to 5pm, Tuesday to Sunday. Closed Mondays (except bank holidays), Christmas Day and Boxing Day.
ACCESS/CONDITIONS: Good walking conditions all year round. There are various trails, including some suitable for wheelchair access.
HOW TO GET THERE: At Fingringhoe, 3 miles from Colchester. Follow the brown nature reserve signs.
WALKING TIME: 125-acre (51ha) reserve with a variety of waymarked trails.
30-MINUTE VISIT: Don't miss the view from Tony Shorter's Seat.
A MEMBER SAYS: 'I love this place. It is so peaceful and tranquil – time slips away when I am here.'

Although Essex Wildlife Trust has 87 nature reserves, Fingringhoe holds a special place in the hearts of many people who return here time after time, year after year. Perhaps it's the stunning estuary views, the nightingales or the wading birds in the winter. Whatever interests you, this is a magical place that everybody should experience.

This wonderful reserve on the west shore of the Colne Estuary has been created out of disused gravel workings, and supports an immense range of habitats. These include grassland, gorse heathland, reedbeds, ponds and a large lake. There is a mixed plantation of trees, including conifers, and the river frontage provides additional habitats such as saltmarsh, foreshore and inter-tidal mudflats – essential for the large number of over-wintering birds that can be seen here each winter. In the spring, Fingringhoe Wick is one of the best places in the UK in which to hear nightingales. They usually arrive in mid-April and the reserve staff organise regular nightingale walks, which are not to be missed.

The Visitor Centre – the Trust's first – was opened in 1975. With the superb Colne estuary on its doorstep, and surrounded by one of the finest nature reserves in the county, it is attractive to families, organised wildlife groups, school parties and walkers.

DID YOU KNOW?

- The reserve is the best spot in the UK for nightingales.
- Fingringhoe Wick is also noted for its geology.
- Adders are regularly seen basking.

Hanningfield Reservoir SSSI

Billericay; **OS Map** TQ 725971; **Map Ref** L28

01268 711001

OPENING TIMES: Daily; 9am to 5pm.
HOW TO GET THERE: Bus between Wickford and Chelmsford, alight at Downham village and walk down Crowsheath Lane. By car, off B1007 Billericay to Chelmsford into Downham Road and left onto Hawkswood Road. The entrance is just beyond the causeway opposite Crowsheath Lane.
WALKING TIME: 100-acre (41ha) reserve with a variety of waymarked trails.
30-MINUTE VISIT: Don't miss the view from the Lyster Hide.
A MEMBER SAYS: 'I never tire of visiting Hanningfield, because it's always different. The autumn colours are wonderful and the huge numbers of swifts, swallows and martins swooping over the reservoir is a joy to see.'

Hanningfield really does have something for everybody. Long walks, short walks, reservoir views or woodland walks, refreshments and shopping at the centre – it's all here in abundance and offers different experiences throughout the year. This major reservoir site is designated an SSSI due to its large numbers of wildfowl; gadwall, tufted duck and pochard are three particularly important species breeding at Hanningfield.

Excellent views can be had from the hides, including a raft that is provided to create a nesting site for terns in the summer. Some of the reserve is surrounded by mixed woodland, with Well Wood and Hawk's Wood being ancient in origin. In spring, the show of flowers, particularly bluebells, yellow archangel and stitchwort is not to be missed. With its superb visitor centre a beacon of sustainable development (it carries the coveted 'ECO Centre' Award), Hanningfield will provide everything you need for a great day out.

DID YOU KNOW?

- **Conifer plantations are gradually being thinned and underplanted with native species.**
- **Hanningfield was the first Trust visitor centre to win the 'ECO Centre' Award.**
- **Hanningfield Reservoir SSSI provides water for more than one million people.**

Langdon

Basildon; **OS Map** TQ 659874; **Map Ref** L31

01268 419103

OPENING TIMES: 9am to 5pm, Tuesday to Sunday; closed Monday (except bank holidays), Christmas and Boxing Day; 9.30am to 5.30pm, Sunday and bank holidays in summer.
ACCESS/CONDITIONS: Good walking conditions all year round. Some paths muddy in winter. Some steep slopes.
HOW TO GET THERE: Laindon station is on the Fenchurch St to Southend line and is 800m from the reserve. Bus services run from Basildon. By car, it is east of M25 J29 between the A127 and A13. Routes are signposted from the B148 turning off the A127/ A13.
WALKING TIME: 461 acres (187ha) of waymarked trails.
30-MINUTE VISIT: Walk around the Dunton plotlands to see the range of old gardens and to see how nature is taking it all back.
A MEMBER SAYS: 'Unique and memorable, Langdon is worth many visits because you will see different things each time.'

At Langdon, natural history meets social history. In addition to the reserve, visitors can see 'The Haven', an original plotland house that has been fully restored and is now a museum of plotland life. Wildlife to be seen at Langdon, while not necessarily rare, includes species once common in our countryside but now threatened by intensive farming and development.
The reserve consists of four sections: Dunton, Lincewood, Marks Hill and Willow Park. Dunton consists of the remains of old plotland homes. These were small dwellings built on plots sold to people, mainly from the East End of London, in the 1900s. The development soon expanded into a busy estate of around 200 homes. There remains a patchwork of old gardens with wide grassy avenues bordered by hawthorn scrub, old orchards and glades. These provide a superb habitat for butterflies in spring and summer. In spring, Lincewood is carpeted with bluebells, and look out for all three species of woodpecker among the trees. Marks Hill contains oak, ash and hornbeam, which are being brought back into coppice rotation, while Willow Park is the largest part of the reserve, and the many ponds attract a wide range of dragonflies and damselflies. Best for warblers, nightingale, green winged and common-sp otted orchids, wood anemone, purple hairstreak and grizzled skipper butterflies and cave spider.

DID YOU KNOW?

- **The best spot for plotlands.**
- **Locally rare cave spiders live in an old well.**
- **Marks Hill is known for its display of common-spotted orchids.**

EAST MIDLANDS

The East Midlands is not a region that is easily defined, which makes it all the more fun to explore. It incorporates the counties of Derbyshire, Leicestershire, Rutland, Nottinghamshire and Lincolnshire and all the wildlife and nature that they contain. To the north-west, for example, there is the Peak District National Park, further south there is Rutland Water SSSI, an artificially constructed reservoir built to include wildlife sanctuaries, while over to the east there are the flatlands of Lincolnshire.

The variety of habitats that you'll find here is huge. Open moorlands are rife with orchids and cowslips each spring, there's bogland, there's woodlands with songbirds, and there's pretty valleys with dragonflies darting across the streams in summertime – and that's before you have even left the Peak District.

Around Rutland Water SSSI you'll be treated to the spectacle of large numbers of gathering wildfowl in the winter-time, while in the summer it is a haven for butterflies and dragonflies. Other waterways host their own populations of waterbirds. Lincoln is well known for its large swan population, which dates back at least to the 12th century when Saint Hugh of Avalon was Bishop of Lincoln. It is said he was always accompanied by a white swan, and they are now an integral part of the town's heritage.

Across towards the coast from Lincoln is the stunning area of the Lincolnshire Wolds. This Area of Outstanding Natural Beauty (AONB) has woodlands and valleys and large open fields that gently roll across the countryside. As well as many nature reserves within the AONB, there are also several signposted walks that take in all sorts of habitats as well as fantastic scenery.

Once you arrive at the coast, there are some great dune systems, particularly around Donna Nook where wintering wildfowl are joined by hundreds of grey seals that return here each year to give birth to their pups in the shelter of the dunes.

Back inland, Nottinghamshire has a beautiful and varied landscape that's equally worth exploring. The countryside here ranges from the woodlands of Sherwood Forest to the rolling hills of the Vale of Belvoir, not to mention Nottinghamshire's flagship reserves, such as Attenborough with its superb birdwatching opportunities.

Opposite: Rutland Water

NOT TO BE MISSED

- **ATTENBOROUGH**

  An intricate network of flooded gravel pits and islands. Best known for its impressive birdwatching opportunities, including migrant birds, waders and breeding birds.

- **FAR INGS NNR**

  Wild reedbeds on the banks of the Humber estuary and a major draw for migrating birds, such as pink-footed geese and bittern.

- **GIBRALTAR POINT NNR**

  A dynamic stretch of unspoilt coastline along the Lincolnshire Wash. The diverse wildlife includes a population of natterjack toads.

- **PRIOR'S COPPICE SSSI**

  An ancient ash-maple and ash-wych elm woodland believed to be the last vestiges of the wildwood that covered all of Leicestershire and Rutland thousands of years ago.

- **RUTLAND WATER SSSI**

  One of the most important inland sites in the UK for passage waders – up to 19 species have been recorded in a single day.

- **WYE VALLEY RESERVES**

  Derbyshire Wildlife Trust has three flagship reserves in this spectacular wooded valley. In the summer, cliff-nesting birds, such as the kestrel, nest in the disused quarry faces.

Derbyshire

About the Trust

Derbyshire Wildlife Trust manages 42 nature reserves throughout the county, covering more than 1,400 acres (570ha) of land including woodland, wetland and meadow areas. It has more than 12,000 members, seven active local groups and seven Wildlife Watch groups (for younger members). It also produces a range of fact sheets and leaflets.

Derbyshire Wildlife Trust☎ 01773 881188
www.derbyshirewildlifetrust.org.uk

Brockholes Wood SSSI

Near Crowden
OS Map SK 072996; **Map Ref** N1

This upland oak woodland is rich in birdlife, including redstarts, tree pipits and willow warblers. There are limited paths and be wary of the steep banks and rock faces.

Carr Vale

South-west of Bolsover
OS Map SK 459701; **Map Ref** N7

Carr Vale is one of the best birdwatching sites in Derbyshire. Areas of water attract wintering wildfowl including wigeon and teal, while breeding species include gadwall, grebes and sedge warblers. Brown hares and water voles also visit the reserve.

Carvers Rocks SSSI

Near Swadlincote
OS Map SK 330227; **Map Ref** N25

Habitats here range from marsh to alder woodland and valley-side mire with sphagnum mosses. Birds include reed bunting and great crested grebe. There are some steep slopes.

Cromford Canal SSSI

Near Ambergate
OS Map SK 348519/332543; **Map Ref** N13

The canal attracts many insects, especially dragonflies and damselflies, while grass snakes and water voles are seen here. Birdlife ranges from ducks, moorhens and other waterfowl on the canal to woodland birds such as blackbirds and wrens.

Erewash Meadows

Between Ironville, Jacksdale and Aldercar
OS Map SK 452478/440516; **Map Ref** N16

These meadows attract birds include lapwing, snipe, reed bunting, sedge warbler and wildfowl in winter. There are also grass snakes, amphibians, dragonflies and water voles.

Gang Mine SSSI

Near Wirksworth
OS Map SK 285556; **Map Ref** N12

Metal-rich grassland, this is part of a former lead mining area with spring sandwort and alpine pennycress on neutral grassland. There is a dewpond with great crested newts. There are old mine shafts here, so please keep to the paths.

Hilton Gravel Pits SSSI

Near Hilton
OS Map SK 249315; **Map Ref** N21

This reserve attracts many species of dragonflies and damselflies including emperor and ruddy darter dragonflies and emerald and red-eyed damselflies. Common and great crested newts, frogs and toads breed here, while a variety of wildfowl visits for the winter.

Ladybower Wood SSSI

Near Sheffield
OS Map SK 205867; **Map Ref** N2

Upland oak woodland, this is one of the best places in the Peak District for lichens. There are pied flycatchers, redstarts, wood warblers, tree pipits, occasional red grouse and mountain hares. There is difficult terrain and cliffs here, so please stay on the bridleway and permissive path.

The Avenue Washlands

Near Chesterfield; **OS Map** SK 396670; **Map Ref** N8

ACCESS/CONDITIONS: Wheelchair friendly surfaced paths lead to a number of viewing screens.
HOW TO GET THERE: From Chesterfield follow the A61 south out of the built-up area, past the Hunloke Arms. After a further 0.3 miles Mill Lane is the next road on the left. The reserve entrance is 700 metres down Mill Lane on the right. There are regular public transport services stopping on the A61 at Mill Lane, in Tupton on Queen Victoria Road and in Grassmoor on North Wingfield Road. Limited on-road parking on Mill Lane, just past the houses.
WALKING TIME: You can explore the 41 acres (16.5ha) in 2 hours.
30-MINUTE VISIT: From the main (western) entrance on Mill Lane, take the path to the left up the ramp for 100 metres to a view point offering good overviews of this section of the reserve. Return and turn left for 200 metres to visit the viewing screen by the reedbed and brook.

This wetland reserve consists of newly created reedbed, marsh, ponds and grassland in the valley of the River Rother on part of the site of the former Avenue Coking Works. Important for its water vole and great crested newt populations, there is plenty of other wildlife to see. In spring, look for male skylarks and yellowhammers as they engage in their territorial displays – these farmland bird species are well established here. In summer, wetland birds including lapwing, tufted duck and little grebe breed here, while dragonflies and damselflies can be seen over the ponds and marshes. An autumn visit may be rewarded with the sight of goldfinches and linnets feeding on the seeds of thistles and other flowers, while snipe return to feed on the marshy edges. Winter visitors to the reserve include teal and wigeon on the water, and flocks of fieldfare and redwing can be seen feeding on the meadows and on the apple trees by the trails.

Deep Dale and Topley Pike

Near Buxton; **OS Map** SK 098716; **Map Ref** N6

ACCESS/CONDITIONS: Steep slopes and rocky paths.
HOW TO GET THERE: Public footpaths from Chelmorton, King Sterndale and the A6 at Topley Pike give access to the dale. The pay and display Wyedale car park is across the road from the Topley Pike access to the nature reserve. There is roadside parking in King Sterndale for footpath access across the plateau.
WALKING TIME: 1.4-mile circuit from King Sterndale will take about an hour and a half. The 2.8-mile route from Wyedale will take about 3 and a half hours.
30-MINUTE VISIT: Park near King Sterndale Church, walk south-east on the footpath across the plateau to descend into the dale. Turn right to walk south up the dale ascending the left bank to reach a cave known as 'the Thirst House'. Return to the dale bottom and continue south. Having crossed a stile in the wall walk towards the dale to the right to take a path, which returns up the daleside and across the plateau to King Sterndale.

Deep Dale is a superb example of a typical Peak District dry limestone dale, supporting a rich variety of wildlife. From the depths of the valley bottom to the heights of the plateau, through deep shaded sections to areas exposed to the full midday sun, the range of conditions here is reflected in the diversity of species you can expect to see. The reserve is a plant lover's delight, with the deep pink blooms of bloody cranesbill and the violet-blue of clustered bellflower creating splashes of colour on the steep upper slopes. The screes are a good place to look for the delicate limestone fern, while Nottingham catchfly grows on the shallow soils above the rocky outcrops. Among the many invertebrates found here is the cistus forester moth; the larvae of this nationally scarce species feed on rock-rose, which grows on the thin soils of the daleside.

Willington Gravel Pits

Near Derby; **OS Map** SK 285274; **Map Ref** N22

ACCESS/CONDITIONS: There is no access onto the reserve itself, but three viewing platforms with steps provide good views of the reserve and its wildlife
HOW TO GET THERE: The reserve lies on Meadow Lane, off the B5008 Willington to Repton road. There is a railway station in Willington – train services between Derby and Birmingham call here. The Trent Barton V3 bus service from Derby runs hourly to Willington. There is limited parking for a few cars along Meadow Lane.
WALKING TIME: A leisurely hour will take you to the final of the three viewing platforms, allowing plenty of time to stop and watch the wildlife.
30-MINUTE VISIT: Park on the lane and enjoy a short stroll to the first viewing platform, which provides good views.

A haven for wildlife in the Trent Valley, this wetland reserve is the perfect place to see a variety of bird species a stone's throw from the busy roads and big towns of Derby and Burton. The reserve is rich in birdlife all year round. In winter, large flocks of wildfowl gather, including wigeon, teal, pochard and shoveler. In early spring, large numbers of curlew can be seen on the wet grassland, before they head north to their breeding grounds. During spring and autumn, up to 20 species of wader pass through.

Among the birds that breed at Willington in summer are reed warblers, lapwings and common terns. Birds of prey also visit the reserve – these include peregrine, kestrel, hobby and sparrowhawk, as well as the very occasional marsh harrier. In addition to birds, Willington Gravel Pits' wetlands also attract several species of dragonfly and damselfly in summer.

WILDLIFE FACT: KNOW YOUR COMMON BUZZARD

Across much of northern and western Britain, the buzzard is a common sight, soaring over wooded hillsides on its broad, rounded wings held in a shallow 'V'. However, for much of the south and east, this beautiful bird is still uncommon, only just recovering from the effects of pesticide poisoning and decades of persecution.

Wye Valley Reserves

Near Buxton; **OS Map** SK 140731 (Miller's Dale); **Map Ref** N5

P WC i

ACCESS/CONDITIONS: A good network of paths, including the Monsal Trail. There are some steep climbs up the dale sides. When the river is high, the riverside path between Miller's Dale and Chee Dale becomes impassable at points. Please keep to the paths: the quarry and cliff faces can be hazardous.
HOW TO GET THERE: All three reserves can be accessed from the pay-and-display car park at Miller's Dale.
WALKING TIME: 297-acre (120ha) reserve. You can spend 1 hour or a whole day walking.
30-MINUTE VISIT: Enjoy the short circular route from Miller's Dale west along the Monsal Trail.
A MEMBER SAYS: 'This is such a stunning place to visit, particularly special in the summer when sunlight reflects from the majestic limestone cliffs allowing you to enjoy the colours and scents of some of the best limestone grassland in Europe.'

The Trust's three reserves, Miller's Dale, Chee Dale and Priestcliffe Lees, stretch for nearly 4 miles along the Wye Valley. Whether it's the spectacular limestone crags of Chee Dale, the lovely wooded slopes of Miller's Dale or the breathtaking views from Priestcliffe Lees, these reserves are both a naturalist's and a walker's treat. Base yourself at Miller's Dale car park, bring an OS map and spend a day exploring the reserve, the Monsal Trail and other routes.

Recognised as being internationally important for their dale-side ash woodland and calcareous grassland, the spectacular cliffs never fail to impress. In summer, the species-rich grassland is bursting with colour; delicate yellow cowslips in May, bright blue spires of the nationally rare Jacob's ladder in late June, grass of Parnassus and sheets of scabious in August. The heady scent of fragrant orchids fills the floor of Miller's Dale quarry in July, while at Priestcliffe Lees, the limestone flora is complemented by the delicate flowers of spring sandwort and alpine pennycress on the relict lead workings.

These reserves are wonderful places to see insects, including butterflies such as dark green fritillary and brown argus, and the dayflying cistus forester moth. The woodland flora includes the spring-flowering mezereon, alpine currant, lily-of-the-valley and an impressive range of ferns. All year round, the river gives the chance of seeing dipper, grey wagtail and water vole. In the summer cliff-nesting birds, such as the kestrel, take advantage of the long-disused limestone quarry faces.

DID YOU KNOW?

- Until 1930, Miller's Dale was a bustling limestone quarry.
- The Monsal Trail is part of what was the main Manchester to London railway line until the 1960s.
- Chee Dale features a spectacular 60m (200ft) limestone gorge.

Nottinghamshire

About the Trust

Nottinghamshire Wildlife Trust's mission is to protect and enhance the county's wildlife and its habitats. We are dedicated to improving people's understanding and appreciation of the natural world. We care for over 60 nature reserves, protecting threatened habitats and work hard to offer everyone the chance to experience Nottinghamshire's wildlife at close quarters.

Nottinghamshire Wildlife Trust☎ 0115 958 8242
www.nottinghamshirewildlife.org

Bentinck Banks

Kirkby-in-Ashfield
OS Map SK 562489; **Map Ref** N15

Here you'll find greater knapweed, burnet saxifrage, St John's wort, cowslip, orchid and quaking grass; there are bullfinch and yellowhammer in the scrub. Access is up steep embankments and steps. From nearby Portland Park, use the railway crossing.

Bunny Old Wood

Near Nottingham
OS Map SK 579282; **Map Ref** N24

Semi-natural woodland with lesser celandine, wood anemone, bluebell, wood avens and ragged robin, as well as fungi and mixed flocks of tits. Some paths are quite steep and muddy in wet weather. The entrance is adjacent to the A60.

Eaton Wood

Near East Retford
OS Map SK 727772; **Map Ref** N4

Eaton was recorded as pasture woodland in the Domesday Book; areas of an old ridge-and-furrow ploughing system can still be seen. There is primrose, wood anemone, bluebell, orchid and a dozen species of butterfly. Paths can be boggy when wet, and Eaton is best visited in April to June. There are a few parking spaces adjacent to the gate.

Harrison's Plantation

Wollaton
OS Map SK 532405; **Map Ref** N18

An important wildlife reservoir, Harrison's Plantation is mixed broad-leaved woodland, thought to date back to the mid-18th century, dominated by sycamore, with ash, wild cherry and oak. Damper areas support mature crack willow and alder. Wildlife includes great spotted woodpeckers, kingfishers, nuthatches, blackcaps and redpolls. There is a good footpath link to Martin's Pond.

Rainworth Heath

Rainworth
OS Map SK 594591; **Map Ref** N11

This is one of the last remaining areas of heathland in Nottinghamshire, notable for both dry and wet heath. The wettest locations are characterised by peaty pools fringed with sphagnum mosses and bulbous rush. Heather, bell heather, bracken, wavy hairgrass, sheep's sorrel and mat grass in dry heath can be found here, as can green woodpeckers, tree pipits, turtle doves and several species of warbler. There are good footpaths, but it is hilly in places. Access is through a stile. A longer walk can also be enjoyed by using paths linking the site to the Wildlife Trust's Strawberry Hill Heath NR.

Skylarks

Holme Pierrepont
OS Map SK 622389; **Map Ref** N19

Skylarks is a former commercial gravel pit with marsh marigolds, oxlips, cowslips and orchids; great crested grebes, kingfishers and fieldfares in winter; common terns, reed warblers and sedge warblers in summer; and damselflies, dragonflies, meadow browns, common blues and orange tips. There are good paths through the main sections.

Bunny Old Wood West

Near Nottingham; **OS Map** SJ 200614; **Map Ref** N23

ACCESS/CONDITIONS: Many of the paths in the wood are unsurfaced and there are also steep slopes.
HOW TO GET THERE: Bus number 99 from Loughborough or Nottingham. The wood is adjacent to the A60 Nottingham to Loughborough Road. Parking is available at the roadside.
WALKING TIME: The Nature Trail is approximately 1.5 miles long and will take around 1 hour at a leisurely pace.
30-MINUTE VISIT: A 30-minute stroll around the wood will give ample time to enjoy the birdsong and wildflowers. You will also be able to see the benefits of ongoing woodland management activity and the developing wildlife pond.

With its prominent position and wealth of wildlife, Bunny Old Wood West is a lovely spot to enjoy a relaxing stroll and a good place to study wildlife at close quarters. Bunny Wood is referred to in the Domesday Book and was probably used by Saxon settlers as a source of wood. In 1487 Henry VII and his army camped nearby on their way to the Battle of East Stoke. Evidence of the history of the wood lies in its sinuous shape, ancient ditches along the northern and southern edges and a parish boundary to the south side of the wood. The size of the old coppice stools also gives an indication of the wood's age. Great and lesser-spotted woodpeckers are amongst 50 bird species recorded. Summer visitors include spotted flycatchers, blackcaps and tree pipits. Hawfinches have also been seen. Over 20 species of butterfly have been recorded including the white letter hairstreak. Other animals include foxes, grey squirrels and grass snakes.

Farndon Willow Holt

Near Newark; **OS Map** SK 767521; **Map Ref** N14

ACCESS/CONDITIONS: The reserve is relatively flat, although some sections can be wet or even flooded when the river is high.
HOW TO GET THERE: The reserve is situated in the village of Farndon which is off the A46 close to Newark. To get there by bus, catch the number 90 from Nottingham or the number 54 from Newark – both stop in Farndon.
WALKING TIME: The full circuit around the reserve is less than 1 mile and at a leisurely pace will take about 45 minutes to 1 hour, including a tour of the willow collection.
30-MINUTE VISIT: A full circuit of the reserve doesn't take long, but it is possible to enjoy a stroll along the riverbank and visit the willow collection in about half an hour.

This fascinating site is one of the few remaining working willow holts that were once a common feature of many Trentside villages. Over the past 20 years the Wildlife Trust has worked to restore a unique collection of willows and the species can now be enjoyed in the special arboretum.

Situated alongside the River Trent in the pretty village of Farndon, this is a wonderful place to spend a couple of hours. There is much vigorous vegetation with scattered hawthorn scrub and small willows along the riverside. Nettles, rosebay willow herb, meadow cranesbill, comfrey, angelica and meadowsweet are all common. The marginal vegetation along the bank of the river is one of the few areas along the Trent where disturbance has been minimised. The water meadows include neutral grassland species such as common Yorkshire fog, brown bent and cock's foot. In the late spring and early summer the wet meadows are full of colourful flowers and in summer the reserve is alive with birdsong. In autumn the huge range of willow species ensure that the reserve is a riot of colour with bark ranging from yellow and vibrant greens to purple.

Ploughman Wood

Near Arnold, Nottingham; **OS Map** SK 640468; **Map Ref** N17

ACCESS/CONDITIONS: Accessed via a public footpath from Green Lane. This path can be wet and muddy at times and not all the paths within the wood are surfaced.
HOW TO GET THERE: The public footpath from Green Lane runs between the villages of Lambley and Woodborough. Take bus service 7/7b from Woodborough or Nottingham. Parking is available in the lay-by off Green Lane. Visitors with limited mobility can access the reserve via an alternative route by prior arrangement (please call 0115 958 8242 for details).
WALKING TIME: The reserve covers 80 acres (32ha) and a tour of the wood covers between 2 to 3 miles. With the walk across country to reach the wood, a full circuit should take approximately 2 hours.
30-MINUTE VISIT: You can reach the wood in 30 minutes, from the car park, but allow more time to look around.

The wood is situated on the east-west ridge that runs between Lambley and Woodborough. Documentary evidence of the wood dates back as far as the 13th century and Ploughman Wood once formed part of a much larger area of woodland which covered more than 300 acres (120ha).

The site is mainly an oak/ash woodland, with some hazel, holly, field maple and beech. This mix of tree species provides an excellent range of habitats for wildlife. There are many plant species typical of those found in ancient woodlands, such as yellow archangel, wood anemone and wood melick. The northern part of the wood is carpeted with bluebells in the spring, and honeysuckle occurs throughout the wood, climbing through trees and shrubs.

One of the most important features of the wood is the presence of substantial quantities of dead wood. This provides excellent habitat for a wide range of flora and fauna, including bracket fungi, beetles, bats and hole-nesting birds. Over 280 species of invertebrates have been recorded so far.

Treswell Wood SSSI

Near Retford; **OS Map** SK 762789; **Map Ref** N3

ACCESS/CONDITIONS: Paths through the wood can be muddy in wet weather.
HOW TO GET THERE: The wood is south of the minor road between Grove and Treswell, about 3 miles east of Retford. There are buses to Treswell from Retford (contact 0870 6082608). Limited car parking at the gate entrance.
WALKING TIME: The nature trail takes approximately 1 to 2 hours.
30-MINUTE VISIT: Wander along the main path through the wood, enjoying the wildflowers and birdsong. See the results of work being done to restore the ancient coppice management cycle with many newly cleared areas and other areas of hazel and oak regrowth.

This ancient woodland was purchased in 1973, becoming the first reserve to be owned by the Trust. Flowering plants include many indicative of ancient woodland, such as primrose and wood anemone in the spring. The ponds support marsh marigold, yellow iris and animals such as the great crested newt and many species of water beetle. Birds include woodcocks, jays, great spotted and spotted woodpeckers and, in summer, blackcaps, garden warblers and other summer visitors. Treswell Wood SSSI is a fascinating site, rich in wildlife and the focus of a lot of ongoing wildlife research. An extensive bird-ringing programme was started in 1972 and, in 1995, the wood was chosen as the site for the reintroduction of the dormouse in Nottinghamshire. Over the past 10 years, a number of local woodland craftsmen have been helping to restore Treswell and, during the winter, can be seen taking timber to make products such as chairs, hurdles and charcoal.

Attenborough

Attenborough; **OS Map** SK 516340; **Map Ref** N20

ACCESS/CONDITIONS: Attenborough Nature Centre is entirely on one level with all rooms wheelchair accessible. The paths around the reserve are generally level, flat and well surfaced.

HOW TO GET THERE: Walk from Beeston Rylands or Long Eaton via the River Trent towpath. It is close to Attenborough railway station, and the Rainbow 5 bus from Nottingham provides reasonable access (contact 0115 9503665).

WALKING TIME: The full circuit of about 4 miles takes approximately 2 to 2 and a half hours.

30-MINUTE VISIT: Explore the ponds around the car park area to see a wide range of water birds, or take a stroll round the wildlife area behind the Nature Centre or to the Kingfisher bird hide along the path towards the River Trent.

A MEMBER SAYS: 'Whether you come once a week or every day, you'll always see something of interest and the Nature Centre is the ideal place to find out more about the reserve or to unwind after a spot of birdwatching or a bracing walk.'

Attenborough was the Trust's first nature reserve, established in 1966, and is made up of a series of disused gravel pits excavated between 1929 and 1967. Interestingly, it still forms part of a large working gravel complex. Recolonisation over more than 50 years has created a wide range of aquatic and waterside habitats, home to a good variety of dragonflies and damselflies, as well as birds, with drier areas of scrub and grassland between the ponds. During the spring, waders and ospreys are regular, while black terns can sometimes be seen. In the summer, sedge warbler and reed warbler song is dominant around much of the reserve and a wide variety of dragonflies (including southern and migrant hawker), damselflies and butterflies can be seen. Passage migrants are a key feature in autumn and almost anything can turn up if the conditions are right. Winter sees the arrival of good numbers of wildfowl, such as goldeneyes, shovelers, pochards and goosanders. Recent habitat improvements have enhanced the range of wildlife habitats and the Nature Centre staff offer a warm and friendly welcome.

DID YOU KNOW?

- Attenborough was opened by Sir David Attenborough. He returned in 2005 to open the site's new Nature Centre.
- In the 1960s concern for the future of the area led to the formation of the Nottinghamshire Wildlife Trust.
- Spring thunderstorms are usually followed by an influx of black terns to the reserve.

Besthorpe

Near Newark; **OS Map** SK 818640; **Map Ref** N9

ACCESS/CONDITIONS: Some parts of the site are only accessible via public rights of way, some of which can become muddy in wet weather. The boardwalk to the hide closest to the main car park is suitable for wheelchair access.
HOW TO GET THERE: Central Trains operate services from Nottingham to Collingham via Newark and from Lincoln. There is a limited bus service between Collingham and Besthorpe. From the A1133 Newark to Gainsborough Road, take the southern of two turns into Besthorpe village.
WALKING TIME: The site is very spread out and accessed from a variety of different points. A walk around the main areas takes approximately 2 to 3 hours at an easy pace.
30-MINUTE VISIT: Take in the hide which overlooks Mons Pool to view the heronry on the island. In the late spring and summer, this would also give you time to view the wildflower meadows.
A MEMBER SAYS: 'I like visiting Besthorpe because I never know what I will see next. I once spotted an osprey on migration and there is always plenty of activity in the heronry on the island in Mons Pool.'

Formerly a site of gravel extraction, Besthorpe lies in the Trent floodplain to the north of Collingham on the east bank of the river. The site comprises two areas with a total of around 168 acres (68ha). Its wide range of habitats (reedbeds, bare earth and open water on the old works section, wet meadows and open water at Mons Pool) means that there is a wealth of wildlife, from pepper saxifrage to goosander. Spring sees the arrival of the regular breeding little ringed plover and is a time of great activity in the heronry and the adjacent cormorant breeding colony. Summer gives you a chance to enjoy the SSSI grasslands and to listen to songs of the season's birds. Autumn at Besthorpe is the time to look for passage waders, passerines and several rarities have turned up, including great snipes. Winter is quiet apart from wildfowl on Mons Pool and the deep water pit. All the regular ducks are to be seen with occasional smew or the odd rare grebe. The hide on Mons Pool closest to the car park is the best spot from which to view the heronry and the inland breeding colony of cormorants. At certain times of the year, Besthorpe Meadows are grazed by a flock of black Hebridean sheep.

DID YOU KNOW?

- **The reserve lies on the edge of the ancient parish of Meering which was fascinating for two reasons. Firstly it contained only one building and, secondly, Lady Godiva (of naked horse riding fame) once owned it.**
- **The cormorants here are river birds, believed to be the continental subspecies *sinensis*.**
- **Mons Pool at Besthorpe is home to one of the UK's few inland cormorant breeding colonies.**

Duke's Wood

Near Kirklington; **OS Map** SK 675603; **Map Ref** N10

ACCESS/CONDITIONS: It is a relatively flat site, but the main paths can be very muddy during wet weather. A number of the trails are along narrow woodland paths. There is a flat viewing/pond-dipping platform over the pond close to the entrance.
HOW TO GET THERE: Off the minor road to Eakring, which leaves the A617 near Kirklington. The entrance is approximately 400 metres from the main road down a RUPP. Bus to Eakring or Kirklington.
WALKING TIME: 18-acre (8ha) reserve. The Duke's Wood Trail of about 1.2 miles takes approximately 1 to 1 and a half hours.
30-MINUTE VISIT: In 30 minutes it is possible to enjoy much of the site's wildlife and to learn about its unique social and industrial heritage. Walk along the main path taking in the 'nodding donkey' oil pumps to the wonderful 'Oil Patch Warrior' statue.
A MEMBER SAYS: 'Duke's Wood really is one of the hidden gems of the Nottinghamshire countryside. I enjoy visiting at any time of year as there is always something to see or hear.'

Duke's Wood really is a bit of a hidden gem. There is a wealth of wildlife to enjoy but the added dimension of its industrial heritage makes it a special place. Most people are surprised to find that the wood was the site of the UK's first major onshore oil field and they really enjoy hearing the story behind the site's oil history. To be able to enjoy wildlife in such a beautiful and interesting setting is an absolute joy.

This 18-acre (8ha) reserve is a mixed deciduous woodland, including oak, ash and hazel. The site is part of the large Redgate Wood SSSI and is linked to Mansey Common, another of the Trust's reserves. Carpets of wood anemone and cowslip provide wonderful colour, while stoats roam the woods. Spring flowers and arriving summer bird visitors are what Duke's Wood is all about – look out for tadpoles, too, at the Bernard Harling Memorial Pond. Summer is a quiet time but one to enjoy the wildflowers, birdsong and the dragonflies around the ponds. Autumn can be very good for fungi. Winter brings the chance to stumble across a woodcock probing in the wet earth, or to seek out the winter tit flocks.

DID YOU KNOW?

- Duke's Wood and its surrounding area was the location of the UK's first onshore oilfield. It produced 280,000 tonnes of oil between 1939 and 1966.
- The pumps used to bring the oil to the surface are known as 'nodding donkeys' – many of these have been restored and are sited along the nature trail.

Leicestershire & Rutland

About the Trust

We care for 36 nature reserves covering more than 2,600 acres. From woodland to meadows, wetland to heaths, our nature reserves comprise some of the most important wildlife and geological sites in the counties with 20 being SSSIs and two designated as NNRs.

Leicestershire and Rutland Wildlife Trust
☎ 0116 2720444 www.lrwt.org.uk

Charley Woods
Near Copt Oak
OS Map SK 476148; **Map Ref** N29

Charley Woods are divided into the ancient woodlands of Burrow and Cat Hill, and are dominated by pedunculate oak, rowan and holly, sycamore, larch and pine. There are bluebells in spring, and nuthatches, treecreepers and woodpeckers can be seen.

Cribbs Meadow SSSI
Near Wymondham
OS Map SK 899188; **Map Ref** N30

These meadows are SSSI grassland, containing adder's-tongue fern, cowslip, green winged and common spotted orchids, winter avens, agrimony, great burnet and yellow rattle. They are divided by an old railway embankment.

Dimminsdale
Calke Abbey
OS Map SK 376219; **Map Ref** N26

A mixture of open water, streams, damp woodland, scrub and bracken-covered glades. Limestone and lead mining took place up to the end of the 19th century, and now Dimminsdale is home to varied flora and insect fauna, occasional deer and birdlife typical of broad-leaved woodland.

Great Merrible Wood
Near Uppingham
OS Map SP 834962; **Map Ref** N41

Part of the East Leicestershire ancient woodland, with layers of ash and pedunculate oak, hazel and field maple, and broad-leaved and violet helleborine. Here, you will find the most varied fungus flora of any Leicestershire wood.

Holwell Reserves
Near Melton Mowbray
OS Map SK 742234; **Map Ref** N28

These are three linked nature reserves previously connected to the mining of ironstone. Brown's Hill Quarry and North Quarry are RIGS with excellent exposures of Upper Lias clays, shales and limestone. The reserves support interesting flora, butterflies, dragonflies, birds, bats and mammals.

Kelham Bridge
Near Ibstock
OS Map SK 407120; **Map Ref** N33

A channel of the River Sence has been diverted to form pools, managed specifically for wintering and migrant birds. Raptors are a speciality and 132 species of birds, 15 species of dragonfly and 19 species of butterfly have been recorded.

Loughborough Big Meadow SSSI
Alongside the River Soar
OS Map SK 538218; **Map Ref** N27

Part of an SSSI and one of the few Lammas meadows left in England. Great burnet, pepper saxifrage and narrow-leaved water dropwort can be seen, and fauna includes sedge warblers, whitethroats and reed buntings.

Narborough Bog SSSI
Near Leicester
OS Map SP 549979; **Map Ref** N40

A varied landscape of alder, willow, reedbed, dense scrub and damp, herb-rich meadows. Over 130 species of bird have been recorded, and common blue, meadow brown and small heath butterflies can be seen.

Wanlip Meadows
Near Wanlip village
OS Map SK 603104; **Map Ref** N34

Shallow pools form when the river floods, and when these dry up, areas of mud provide a good habitat for many birds. Waders such as snipe, green sandpiper and redshank are regularly seen, with large flocks of golden plover often present in winter.

Launde Big Wood SSSI

Between Launde and Loddington; **OS Map** SK 785037; **Map Ref** N37

OPENING TIMES: Open all year except on some Saturdays in winter when shooting takes place.
ACCESS/CONDITIONS: A 10-minute walk from the road over rough, undulating ground, but well worth the effort once you reach the wood. No dogs.
HOW TO GET THERE: No public transport. From the Tilton to Oakham road, take any of several roads signposted to Launde. Continue through Launde Park with the abbey on your left, stopping at the top of the hill. Please park on the roadside verge. Be careful not to block any gateways. Walk along the public footpath to the entrance.
WALKING TIME: This is a 100-acre (40ha) reserve – a good circuit takes about 2 hours at an easy pace.

Launde Big Wood SSSI is an ancient woodland covering 100 acres (40ha) with massive boundary earthworks, huge coppice stools (clearly centuries old) and many plants known to be confined, or nearly so, to ancient woodland sites. It is one of the largest and most important semi-natural ancient woodlands in the East Midlands. The reserve is dominated by stands of pedunculate oak, ash, hazel and field maple. The wood is situated on a hill top, with superb views of the surrounding countryside. Its soils are mainly heavy and calcareous, being derived from various clays, but there are also better drained areas resulting from deposits of glacial sand and gravel. The ground flora is very rich, providing magnificent displays in the spring of plants such as wood anemone. Badgers have excavated at least two setts here, and other mammals include stoats and weasels, while nightingales and nuthatches have been noted among the wood's birds.

Lea Meadows SSSI

Near Newtown Linford; **OS Map** SK 506115; **Map Ref** N30

ACCESS/CONDITIONS: There is a stile entrance to the reserve, and another stile leads to the meadows.
HOW TO GET THERE: Lea Meadows can be walked to from Newtown Linford. From Leicester, drive through Newtown Linford village and take the left-hand fork down Ulverscroft Lane. Carry on for 1.3 miles. The entrance is on the left by a public footpath sign.
WALKING TIME: Lea Meadows is a 30-acre (12ha) reserve. The full circuit of about 1 mile takes approximately 1 hour at an easy pace.
30-MINUTE VISIT: Walk along the stream separating the two meadows to get a feel for the reserve.

Lea Meadows SSSI, covering 30 acres (12ha), is part of a medieval assart (area of private farmland) protected against incursion by a bank and ditch. The medieval farmstead can be identified by a number of shallow depressions and mounds, most noticeable during early spring when sedges line the water-filled depressions. The soil of the meadows is neutral to slightly acidic, with marshy conditions in the valley bottom and dry grassland on the higher slopes. During the summer, wetter areas provide amazing displays of hundreds of common and heath spotted orchids, as well as marsh speedwell, the rare bog pimpernel and 15 species of sedge. In the dry grassland, harebell, great burnet and devil's-bit scabious predominate. Moths recorded include the forester, ruby tiger and chimney sweeper. Butterflies seen on the reserve include painted lady and small copper. Ulverscroft Brook meanders through the reserve with alders, willows and oaks along its bank. In winter, siskin and redpoll can be seen feeding on alder cones. The brook supports native crayfish and brook lamprey, both of which are rare in Leicestershire.

Cossington Meadows

Between Leicester and Loughborough; **OS Map** SK 597134; **Map Ref** N31

ACCESS/CONDITIONS: Plenty of paths, but it can be muddy in wet weather so good footwear is strongly recommended.
HOW TO GET THERE: The reserve is west of Cossington village, between Leicester and Loughborough. There are several access points where public footpaths enter the reserve. Park off the road outside the main entrance, near Cossington Mill.
WALKING TIME: A leisurely circuit will take 1 and a half to 2 hours.
30-MINUTE VISIT: A brisk circular walk could result in seeing little grebes, lapwings and reed buntings.
A MEMBER SAYS: 'Cossington Meadows is a brilliant place to escape the noise and bustle of the city that is just a few miles away, and enjoy a walk with a close-up view of nature.'

This new wetland reserve on the River Soar floodplain is a great place to see wildlife, whatever the season. It has a wide range of rapidly establishing wetland habitat – rivers, deep lakes with shallow margins, areas of young reedbed, shallow scrapes, wet grassland and wet woodland. During spring everything bursts into life with spring migrants and passage birds, oystercatchers and little ringed plovers to be found. In the summer gadwalls, tufted ducks and great crested grebes breed on the reserve. Grasshopper warblers can be heard and, with a little luck, seen.

Autumn sees the arrival of snipes, green sandpipers and little egrets, and ducks can include garganey. In winter parties of wildfowl such as wigeons, teals and shovelers are common. Grass snakes, toads and frogs all breed on the reserve. Migrant hawkers and black-tailed skimmers are among the dragonflies commonly recorded and butterflies such as small coppers and common blues are regularly seen. Notable wetland plants colonising the reserve include flowering-rush and blue water speedwell. Birds such as kingfishers, grey wagtails and water rails are a joy to see; birds of prey include hobbies while short-eared owls regularly winter on the reserve. Rare breed Exmoor ponies and Shetland cattle graze part of the site.

DID YOU KNOW?

- Cossington Meadows is the largest of Leicestershire and Rutland Wildlife Trust's five nature reserves in the Soar Valley .
- The area was quarried for gravel during the 1980s and 1990s.
- The land was purchased by the Trust in 2004.

Prior's Coppice SSSI

South of Braunston; **OS Map** SK 832049; **Map Ref** N36

ACCESS/CONDITIONS: Open all year except some Saturdays in winter when shooting takes place.
HOW TO GET THERE: The nearest approach by public transport is Oakham, 3.5 miles away. From Braunston, take the road towards Leighfield and follow signs for Leighfield Lodge. After 800 metres you will see the reserve car park on the right.
WALKING TIME: Prior's Coppice is a 72-acre (29ha) reserve. The full circuit around the edge of the wood takes approximately 1 hour at an easy pace.
30-MINUTE VISIT: A short walk along the woodland rides and paths can reveal a surprising variety of wildlife and various woodland habitats.
A MEMBER SAYS: 'Entering this ancient woodland is like stepping back in time. I can spend hours wandering along the rides in spring, looking for wildflowers and listening to the birdsong.'

Prior's Coppice is an ancient ash-maple and ash-wych elm woodland believed to be a relic of the wildwood that covered all of Leicestershire and Rutland before prehistoric peoples started to clear it. This beautiful woodland is home to a wealth of fauna and flora, with 230 species of flowering plant and fern recorded so far.

In spring, newly coppiced areas, where light can reach the woodland floor, are carpeted with wood anemone, wood forget-me-not and primrose. Herb Paris is a particular rarity. Areas with dense coppice regrowth are perfect places to listen for warblers such as blackcaps and chiffchaffs. Rare visitors have included pied flycatchers, redstarts and red kites.

The wood is criss-crossed by grassy rides supporting a mass of wildflowers including ragged-robin, cuckoo flower and common spotted orchids. These sustain butterflies and countless other insects. The damp and shady conditions created by stands of tall mature trees support plants such as broad-leaved helleborine and many ferns. Numerous old trees with plentiful deadwood are packed with life in the form of various types of fungi, insects and hole-nesting birds such as nuthatches and lesser spotted and great spotted woodpeckers.

DID YOU KNOW?

- There have been 71 species of bird noted at Prior's Coppice to date, and 42 of these have bred.
- More than 200 species of moth are known to inhabit the wood.
- 230 species of flowering plant and fern have been recorded.

Rutland Water SSSI

Near Oakham; **OS Map** SK 878075 and SK 894058; **Map Ref** N35

Egleton: Lyndon:

OPENING TIMES: Egleton is open all year round except Christmas; Lyndon is open on weekends, bank holidays and Tuesday to Thursday from May to October.

ACCESS/CONDITIONS: Permits are required and can be purchased from the centres. Both visitor centres and some hides are suitable for wheelchair access. A motorised buggy can be pre-booked by contacting the Anglian Water Bird Watching Centre at Egleton. Dogs not allowed at Egleton, and at Lyndon dogs are allowed on short leads only.

HOW TO GET THERE: Egleton village lies 1.3 miles south-east of Oakham. Take the A606 Oakham to Stamford road or the A6003 Oakham to Uppingham road. There is at track from the village to the reserve car park. The entrance track to Lyndon lies off a minor road between Manton and Edith Weston.

WALKING TIME: The reserve covers 600 acres (242ha) and there are more than 20 hides and over 1.9 miles of self-guided trails.

30-MINUTE VISIT: Call into the visitor centres to discover the best places to visit on the day.

A MEMBER SAYS: 'You always get a warm welcome, and plenty of information on the latest sightings, in the visitor centres.'

If you are passionate about birds, Rutland Water nature reserve is the place to visit regardless of the season. In spring the reserve resounds to the songs of many resident and migrant birds, including nightingale. In summer the reserve reflects the charm of the English countryside with an abundance of breeding birds and their young. The autumn concentration of wildfowl provides one of the finest bird spectacles in the country and, as winter sets in, huge numbers of waterfowl make Rutland Water their home. You can also take the chance to see one of Britain's rarest breeding birds – following a successful translocation programme of osprey chicks from Scotland, ospreys are now breeding here. Adult birds can be seen from April to September. A camera overlooks an artificial nest and beams pictures back to both visitor centres. The reserve is also one of the most important sites in Europe for tufted duck and pochard with flocks reaching 5,000 and in excess of 1,000 respectively.

DID YOU KNOW?

- **During a recent survey, over 23,000 birds were recorded on the reservoir at one time.**
- **The reserve is recognised as one of the most important inland sites in Great Britain for passage waders.**
- **Rutland Water is unusual in that the site was declared a nature reserve before it came into existence.**

Lincolnshire

East Midlands

About the Trust

Lincolnshire Wildlife Trust manages around 8,500 acres of nature reserve, which protects all the county's differing habitat types from saltmarsh and mudflat to woodland, heathland and meadow. Many reserves are fragile environments, often being the last haven for rare plants and animals. On the larger reserves, guided walks and children's activities are held.

Lincolnshire Wildlife Trust☎ 01507 526667
www.lincstrust.org.uk

Baston Fen

Near Market Deeping
OS Map TF 145176; **Map Ref** M15

This is the only remaining Lincolnshire washland on peat soils that is managed for wildlife by winter flooding and summer grazing. Wintering wildfowl include wigeon, mallard and teal. Over 300 species of flowering plants, grasses and sedges have been recorded including purple loosestrife, marsh marigold, greater spearwort, water-plantain, water violet, frogbit, greater bladderwort and flowering rush.

Crowle Moor

Near Crowle, west of Scunthorpe
OS Map SE 759145 and SE 756137; **Map Ref** M2

This reserve is one of the richest lowland peat vegetation areas in the north of England. The drier areas carry heather, bracken and birch scrub; the wetter parts have reedbeds, cottongrass and sphagnum bog, and these habitats support a rich variety of wildlife. More than 30 breeding birds have been recorded, including woodcocks, nightjars and tree pipits.

Epworth Turbary

Near Epworth
OS Map SE 758036; **Map Ref** M3

Epworth Turbary is one of the few relicts of raised bog in the county with areas of sphagnum bog, common cottongrass and cross-leaved heath, reed swamp, fen sedge and birch woodland. Breeding birds include tree pipits, and green and great spotted woodpeckers. It is also a good dragonfly site.

Fiskerton Fen

Near Lincoln
OS Map TF 084718; **Map Ref** M10

Fiskerton Fen is a new wetland reserve created following the completion of flood defence works on the River Witham. The reserve is already home to kingfishers and other waterbirds, and a variety dragonflies and damselflies. Scrub provides shelter and song posts for birds such as yellowhammers, corn buntings, linnets and tree sparrows.

Hoplands Wood

Near Alford
OS Map TF 459718; **Map Ref** M9

This ancient oak and ash woodland supports birds such as tawny owls, treecreepers, great and lesser spotted woodpeckers and nuthatches, and warblers. The rides are rich in wildflowers including bugle, marsh thistle, lady's mantle, meadowsweet and twayblade.

Legbourne Wood

Near Louth
OS Map TF 369832; **Map Ref** M6

Legbourne Wood is one of the few remaining ancient woodlands in eastern Lincolnshire and the largest of the Trust's woodland nature reserves. Spring flowers include primroses, early-purple orchids, bluebells (below) and lesser celandine. There is a varied bird population, including one of the largest heronries in the county.

Little Scrubbs Meadow

Near Wragby

OS Map TF 145744; **Map Ref** M8

The meadow is situated in the heart of the limewoods of the Chambers Farm Wood complex. Meadow plants such as great burnet, saw-wort and devil's-bit scabious are abundant. Butterflies include purple hairstreak, white admiral and speckled wood.

Moor Farm and Kirkby Moor

Near Woodhall Spa

OS Map TF 226635/TF 225629; **Map Ref** M13

These two adjacent reserves are mosaics of heath, pastures and woodland. The diversity of habitat supports a wide range of plants and animals, some of them now rare or localised in the area; over 240 species of plant, 100 of bird, 24 of butterfly and 250 of moth have been recorded at Moor Farm. Specialities include adder and woodlark. The grassland is grazed or mown in a traditional manner in order to retain its existing characteristics.

Red Hill

Between Louth and Horncastle

OS Map TF 264806; **Map Ref** M7

Red Hill includes flower-rich chalk grassland, a disused quarry with a famous exposure of red chalk and a 60-acre (24ha) downland restoration scheme. There is a rich assemblage of chalk plants including localised species such as felwort, basil thyme, kidney vetch and pyramidal and bee orchids. The meadow pipit, a localised breeding species inland in Lincolnshire, nests in the reserve.

Scotton Common

Between Gainsborough and Scunthorpe

OS Map SK 873985; **Map Ref** M4

This reserve is the largest remaining fragment of the once extensive heathlands of Scotton Common with ling, wavy hairgrass, purple moorgrass and cross-leaved heath. The list of butterflies and moths is impressive, and the common's sandy banks attract solitary mining bees. Adders and common lizards are present.

WILDLIFE FACT: TOAD CROSSINGS

Like most amphibians, toads are creatures of habit. Every spring, they will return to the pond where they started life as tadpoles to breed, and in many cases this means crossing roads. Toads are slow, lumbering creatures and many of them are killed each year by cars, so in 1994, the Department of Transport created a road sign to warn drivers of toads crossing.

Deeping Lakes

Near Peterborough; **OS Map** TF 187083; **Map Ref** M16

ACCESS/CONDITIONS: There is an easy-access path to the bird hide overlooking the lake; the circular waymarked route may be muddy in places.
HOW TO GET THERE: The reserve is located south of the manned level-crossing in Deeping St James, on the B1166. Access is by an unmade road off the B1166, approximately 0.6 miles south of the level crossing (at the sharp bend near the banks of the River Welland).
WALKING TIME: Deeping Lakes is a 176-acre (71ha) site. A 2-hour stroll would allow plenty of time to observe its wide variety of birdlife.
30-MINUTE VISIT: Walk down the easy access path to the bird hide overlooking the main lake.

Deeping Lakes is a major new nature reserve with exciting opportunities for fenland wildlife and for the public. The main lake, known as 'the Lake', was excavated in the late 1800s and has largely developed naturally since then. The two areas of smaller lakes and pools (formerly known as Welland Bank Quarry) were excavated in the 1990s. Being of relatively recent origin they contrast markedly with the older lake. In summer, the lakes and surrounding habitats provide nesting sites for birds such as great crested grebes, mute swans and warblers. The margins of the newer lakes are home to breeding oystercatchers, common terns and lapwings. A good range of dragonflies and damselflies can be seen including four-spotted chasers and black-tailed skimmers. During spring and autumn, numbers of passage migrants pass through. It is the kind of reserve where almost anything could turn up. In winter, redwings and fieldfares feed on the berry-bearing shrubs and wildfowl and waders are attracted in large numbers.

Donna Nook NNR

Off the A1031; **OS Map** TF 422998 (Stonebridge entrance); **Map Ref** M5

OPENING TIMES: The site is open all year; the information hut is open November to December.
ACCESS/CONDITIONS: Part of the reserve is a MoD bombing target range – never enter the bombing area when the red flags are flying. All organised group visits must be booked in advance, and visitors are requested to keep out of the sanctuary areas. Dogs are not permitted in the seal viewing area; elsewhere dogs must be kept under close control.
HOW TO GET THERE: There are several access point off the main A10131 coast road. Park at Stonebridge, Howden's Pullover or Sea Lane, Saltfleet.
WALKING TIME: The site is 2,841 acres (1,150ha) and there are no formal paths.
30-MINUTE VISIT: Head for the Stonebridge car park for views over the saltmarsh and mudflats.

Sometimes bleak and often bracing, Donna Nook is one of the few truly wild landscapes left in Lincolnshire. Coastal processes alter the natural features from year to year, as sand from the beach and offshore sandbanks is blown inland by easterly winds to form dune ridges. Here, wildlife has learnt to co-exist with the practice bombing activities of the RAF. The reserve is famous for uncommon passage migrants and rarities that turn up in spring and autumn. In the summer months the flowering plants include yellow-wort, bee, marsh and pyramidal orchids. The reserve is rich in birdlife: ringed plovers and oystercatchers nest on the sandflats, and lagoons provide a breeding area for coots, little grebes, moorhens and a substantial population of reed bunting and meadow pipit. Sandwich terns are a feature of late summer. In November and December, Donna Nook is the host to a large breeding colony of grey seals. In winter the mudflats attract a wealth of birds: substantial numbers of brent geese, shelducks, twites, lapland buntings, shore larks and linnets gather, together with large flocks of knot and dunlin, accompanied by a wide variety of other waders in smaller numbers.

Snipe Dales

Near Spilsby; **OS Map** TF 330682 (Country Park)/TF 319683 (Nature Reserve); **Map Ref** M12

P WC 01507 588401

ACCESS/CONDITIONS: A metal footpath leads from the country park car park to the central ponds (disabled visitors should note there are steep slopes). Wheelchair users may gain access by car by prior arrangement with the warden. Dogs are permitted in the country park, but not in the reserve.
HOW TO GET THERE: Buses from Spilsby or Horncastle can make a diversion to stop at Snipe Dales Country Park. The service must be booked at least two (and a maximum of seven) days in advance by calling Inter-Connect on 0845 2343344. Well signposted from the A158 (Skegness to Lincoln) and from the B1195 (Horncastle to Spilsby).
WALKING TIME: There are three trails of 30 minutes, 45 minutes and 2 hours.
30-MINUTE VISIT: The There and Back Trail takes you on a short walk of about 1 mile in the Country Park.

The attractive valleys of Snipe Dales, fretted by streams, which have cut through the soft Spilsby sandstone into the Kimmeridge clay below, offer wonderful views of the southern Lincolnshire Wolds, challenging the common perception that Lincolnshire is flat. Snipe Dales is one of few semi-natural wet valley systems still surviving in Lincolnshire. It is an area of two halves with wet valleys and scrub in the nature reserve and mixed woodland forming the Country Park. This diversity of habitats supports a wide range of birds and other wildlife. The area is also rich in insect life and a great place to see butterflies and dragonflies.

Walking through the varied landscape is pleasant at any time of year. In autumn and winter, treecreepers and goldcrests forage in the woodlands, along with siskin and bramblings. In the spring, with the return of migrating warblers and breeding season getting underway, the valleys and woods of Snipe Dales are filled with birdsong. Visit in spring and summer for wildflowers including common spotted orchids and ragged robin, as well as a variety of butterflies and dragonflies.

WILDLIFE FACT: GOLDCREST

Britain's smallest bird isn't, as many think, the wren – it's the goldcrest, a tiny, mainly matt green bird with a beady black eye and a distinctive orange or yellow stripe on its crown. Its favourite habitat is coniferous woodland, particularly where there are spruce or silver fir. If you're lucky, you might see them at Snipe Dales or Gibraltar Point.

Far Ings NNR

Barton-upon-Humber; **OS Map** TA 018234; **Map Ref** M1

01652 637055

OPENING TIMES: The site is open all year; the visitor centre is open weekends (usually 11am to 5pm).
ACCESS/CONDITIONS: The paths are level except for the access to the Humber bank. Paths can become muddy after rain.
HOW TO GET THERE: It's a 10-15 minute walk along the Humber bank from Barton-on-Humber and the bus and train stations. By car, leave the A15 at the A1077 turn-off (last exit before Humber Bridge). Take the first exit from the roundabout, then the first right (look for the brown tourist signs). At the bottom the hill, turn right. The entrance to the reserve is on the left.
WALKING TIME: There is a range of walks, from many miles along the Humber bank to a short circuit from the centre of about 1 hour, with stops at the hides.
30-MINUTE VISIT: From the visitor centre walk along the Humber bank to the hide overlooking the Pursuits Pit.
A MEMBER SAYS: 'You know they are here, but when you hear your first bittern booming, it is a truly magical experience.'

There's always something to see or hear when looking out over the reedbeds of Far Ings, whether it's the sound of the reeds as they sway in a gentle breeze, the song of hidden warblers or bearded tits, the eerie boom of a bittern, or a marsh harrier drifting over then disappearing into the reedbed.

Far Ings is situated on the banks of the Humber estuary, a major east-west flyway for migrating birds. The sight and sound of skeins of geese flying over is spectacular. The pits and reedbeds at Far Ings and along the south Humber bank are a legacy of the tile and cement industry which flourished between 1850 and 1959. Thanks to pioneering management by the Trust, the reserve is now rich in wildlife and one of the UK strongholds for bittern. In spring and autumn you may see migration in action. Look for pipits, finches, swallows, martins, swifts, larks, starlings, waders and wildfowl as they move along the estuary. In late summer the reedbeds are important for hirundine roosts. Autumn and winter reward the observer on the Humber bank with sightings of redshanks, wigeons, black-tailed godwits, skeins of pink-footed geese and many more species. Among the wildfowl which spend the winter months on the pits within the reserve, look for the diminutive teal.

DID YOU KNOW?

- Far Ings has one of the best colonies of the very rare bryozoan *Lophopus crystallinus* in the UK.
- Next to Far Ings is the Chowder Ness Managed Realignment scheme.
- Far Ings is the base for the Lincolnshire Wildlife Trust's flock of Hebridean sheep.
- In the late 1800s, hundreds of men were employed to dig the clay found locally by hand.
- Nine species of wainscot moth have been recorded at Far Ings.

Gibraltar Point NNR

Skegness; **OS Map** TF 556581; **Map Ref** M14

01754 898057

OPENING TIMES: The site is open all year; the visitor centre and shop are open April to October 10am to 5pm, November to March 11am to 4pm.

ACCESS/CONDITIONS: Most paths are level and well surfaced but can be muddy at times. Some of the hides are accessible to wheelchairs. Dogs may be taken on short leads to parts of the reserve but are not permitted on the beach from 1 April to 1 September.

HOW TO GET THERE: Skegness has the nearest bus and train stations. Gibraltar Point is about 3 miles south of Skegness – follow the brown tourist signs.

WALKING TIME: The main nature trail of 2.5 miles takes 2 to 3 hours.

30-MINUTE VISIT: From the Beach Car Park head to the Mill Hill viewpoint, the highest point on the reserve and a good place to watch the migration of birds.

A MEMBER SAYS: 'There is nowhere less comfortable to be than on the outermost dune ridges in winter when there's a north-easterly gale – but nowhere more memorable either.'

Gibraltar Point is a dynamic stretch of unspoilt coastline running southwards from the edge of Skegness to the mouth of The Wash. In spring, the first of the migrants stop off to refuel or establish their territories. Natterjack toads are vocal during April and May. In summer, you may see the courtship displays of the little tern, our rarest breeding bird, and skylarks and meadow pipits are in full song on the saltmarshes. Butterflies and dragonflies can be found on the dunes. In autumn, huge whirling flocks of waders can be seen at close range during the monthly high tides. In winter, brent geese, shorelark and snow bunting give Gibraltar Point its special character, supplemented by thrushes, finches and the occasional hen harrier. Gibraltar Point impresses by its sheer scale and diversity of wildlife but to appreciate the site fully, you need to see it in different seasons: in the spring and autumn for migrations and the vast wader flocks; and then to see the lilac haze of sea lavender across the saltmarsh in summer.

DID YOU KNOW?

- Gibraltar Point was the first nature reserve in England to be officially declared a statutory LNR (1952).
- The Wash View Point is a converted wartime gun emplacement.
- During the highest tides, the visitor centre car park floods.

Whisby Nature Park

Lincoln; **OS Map** SK 911661; **Map Ref** M11

OPENING TIMES: The park is open all year; the Natural World Centre (tel: 01522 688868) is open 10am to 5pm.
ACCESS/CONDITIONS: Footpaths are level, the majority hard surfaced and suitable for wheelchairs and pushchairs, though may be muddy in places. Dogs are allowed if kept on a lead, except around Thorpe Lake where they can be walked off their leads under close control.
HOW TO GET THERE: There is a bus service from Lincoln to Thorpe on the Hill, and it's 10-minute walk from the bus stop to the park (on Saturday this service has a request stop outside the gates of the park). The park is clearly marked with brown tourist signs from the A46.
WALKING TIME: There are three waymarked lake circuits each of just over a mile – allow about 45 minutes to 1 hour. There are longer routes on the far side of the railway line, up to 3 miles in length – allow 2 to 3 hours.
30-MINUTE VISIT: First stop at the bird feeding station, with the chance of sighting tits, finches and tree sparrows, then visit one or two of the hides overlooking Grebe Lake.
A MEMBER SAYS: 'Whisby is so well laid out for visitors: it's perfect for some serious birdwatching, or I can bring the family for a Sunday afternoon stroll.'

This landscape, once barren and lifeless, now abounds with life. Whisby Nature Park was created by quarrying for sand and gravel, but nature has reclaimed the lifeless landscape of pits and bare sands. Once you are within the Nature Park it's hard to believe you're so close to Lincoln. The lakes are surrounded by grassland, marsh, scrub and willow carr. Elements of the original landscape also remain with fragments of heathland, old hedgerows and a small oak woodland. In spring and summer, the park is rich in flora and fauna. In early spring, flocks of tits and finches are joined by warblers. The lakes attract feeding sand martins and swallows, and nesting terns. Chiffchaffs, reed and sedge warblers and whitethroats can all be heard, and hopefully seen. Whisby Nature Park has also become famous for nightingales. Autumn brings the first sight of winter birds such as goldcrests, redpolls, grey wagtails and migrating warblers. In winter, the water levels are at their highest and wildfowl can be numerous.

DID YOU KNOW?

- **Thorpe Lake is up to 11 metres deep. There is reputed to be a crane abandoned at the bottom.**
- **Up to 40,000,000 gallons of water can be held in the lakes at Whisby Nature Park.**

WEST MIDLANDS

The West Midlands is more often associated with industrial development and traffic jams than wildlife, but you don't have to travel far to escape from the concrete sprawl into the natural world. The canal network in this part of England is one of the most developed, but whereas its banks were once teeming with labourers and the water full of barges laden with coal, they are now home to water voles, shrews, wildflowers, kingfishers and heron. Reservoirs that were created to supply the canals with water are now wonderful wetland habitats with large bird populations, especially in the winter time.

Conservation work is slowly undoing the damage caused by previous heavy industrialisation of the area and the very rare polecat has now repopulated the lower reaches of the Wye Valley, where otter numbers are also increasing. Before mining took over this area of Britain, much of the land was covered in forest, and pockets of ancient woodland still remain today. The dark and damp conditions are perfect for fungi and an autumn visit can reveal many different species including some of the rarer, and sometimes poisonous, ones.

To the south of the Black Country, farming took the place of mining as the area's main way of breadwinning, and Herefordshire is often described as England's most rural county, with a rich mosaic landscape of small fields, ancient hedgerows and wooded hills. From the Black Mountains in the west to the Malvern Hills in the east and down to the sweeping Wye Valley, the county embodies the finer characteristics of a traditional landscape.

The hedges, a haven for songbirds and dormice, often enclose examples of unimproved hay meadows – a habitat found less and less frequently in Britain – with great examples of colourful wildflowers such as knapwort, green winged orchid and St John's wort.

Staffordshire, to the north of the Black Country, is a heavily wooded area again with many fine examples of ancient woodland, old oaks and beeches. The sandy soils are popular with many reptiles and amphibians, such as grass snakes and lizards, as well as badgers, hedgehogs, stoats, weasels and hares.

West Midlands residents are proud of the rich diversity of wildlife that can be found here, and visitors can't fail to be delighted with the secret gems of wildlife reserves.

Opposite: The Roaches & Hen Cloud, Staffordshire

NOT TO BE MISSED

- **THE DEVIL'S SPITTLEFUL AND RIFLE RANGE**

Named after a large sandstone rock crowned with Scots pine, this fascinating reserve boasts some a diverse range of habitats. One of the few reserves in the county with a population of common lizard.

- **DOXEY MARSHES**

Designated as an SSSI for its wet grassland habitat and its breeding wading birds and wildfowl, this reserve is particularly noted for its populations of breeding snipe.

- **THE ERCALL**

An ancient oak woodland with spectacular views and more than 500 million years of geological history, The Ercall is also a great venue for spotting wildflowers and butterflies.

- **THE KNAPP AND PAPERMILL**

A pretty woodland reserve particularly noted for its riparian value: kingfisher, grey wagtail and otter are just some of the species to be found on the brook.

- **LUGG MEADOW SSSI & LOWER HOUSE FARM**

One of the largest surviving examples of Lammas meadows in the country, this reserve boasts great views across Herefordshire to the Black Mountains, as well as plenty of birdlife in the skies.

- **WOOD LANE**

A wetland site with several lagoons and rough grassland. Huge banks of sand provide a home for a large colony of sand martins, and nest platforms on telegraph poles have been erected to tempt ospreys to stay and breed.

Shropshire

About the Trust

Shropshire has landscapes of great beauty and diversity. From the hills and valleys to the south to the ancient watery wilderness of the meres and mosses to the north; from the old pitmounds of Telford to the flower-rich Oswestry uplands, there is much to discover. Shropshire Wildlife Trust looks after 37 nature reserves including woods, meadows, wetland bird havens and heathland. The Trust is exploring ways of linking up wild areas to give wildlife a better chance to move beyond the boundaries of nature reserves.

Shropshire Wildlife Trust☎ 01743 284280
www.shropshirewildlifetrust.org.uk

Brook Vessons

The Stiperstones
OS Map SJ 382008; **Map Ref** P23

An extraordinarily atmospheric place with a wonderful feeling of antiquity: gnarled ancient trees, tangled woodland, tiny meadows and boggy grazing pastures.

Bushmoor Coppice

Craven Arms
OS Map SO 430880; **Map Ref** P29

A wonderful bluebell wood in spring; also good for birds, with pied flycatchers taking advantage of the numerous nest boxes; dormice also present. Paths can be muddy; log bridges cross the streams.

Granville

Telford
OS Map SJ 719125; **Map Ref** P19

Nature has reclaimed 86 acres (35ha) of land here after centuries of mining and other industrial activity. The woodland now sings with birds and the pitmounds are dotted with orchids and ox-eye daisies. Good footpath network. Steep slopes may be avoided, but muddy paths probably can't.

Harton Hollow

Near Wenlock Edge
OS Map SO 481878; **Map Ref** P30

Walk in these woods and you tread on an ancient barrier reef. Plants such as herb Paris and sweet woodruff grow here because they thrive on the limestone that formed from the fossilised remains of ancient shelled creatures.

Llynclys Common

Near Llynclys
OS Map SJ 273238; **Map Ref** P15

A 128-acre (52ha) reserve. Good for limestone plants, especially orchids (spotted, early-purple, pyramidal, greater butterfly and twayblade), quaking grass, rock-rose, occasional adder's tongue fern and moonwort; white-throat, blackcap and chiffchaff; newts and dragonflies in Oliver's Pool. Paths can be muddy.

Melverley Farm

Whitchurch
OS Map SJ 581405; **Map Ref** P9

This 147-acre (59ha) reserve of old flower-rich hay meadows is surrounded by rambling hedgerows and mature trees. Fairly level fields crossed by a network of public footpaths. This is a working farm with livestock, so please shut all gates behind you.

Prees Branch Canal

Wem
OS Map SJ 497332; **Map Ref** P11

A short stretch of disused canal, this is a quiet backwater for all kinds of water creatures, including water voles and birds such as mallards, moorhens, swans and kingfishers.

Hope Valley

Near Hope; **OS Map** SJ 350017 (car park); **Map Ref** P22

ACCESS/CONDITIONS: Good network of tracks but can be muddy. Steep slopes and stepped paths make the site unsuitable for disabled access.
HOW TO GET THERE: Minsterley Motors (01743 791208) buses run through the valley from Bishop's Castle to Shrewsbury. The valley is within walking distance via The Stiperstones NNR's network of public footpaths.
WALKING TIME: The walk up the hill, along the western edge to the viewpoint and back to the car park, takes around 45 minutes.
30-MINUTE VISIT: Walk up through the woodland as far as you can.

This ancient woodland is recovering from a drastic attempt to transform it into a conifer forest in the 1960s. Luckily, the old oaks clung on despite the shady firs, sending out new shoots, which grew back into sturdy branches when the Wildlife Trust felled the conifers 20 years later. There is a loop walk through the woodland from the car park to the top, with fine views over The Stiperstones.

Hope Valley is an exhilarating walk at any time of year, with banks of primroses and bluebells in spring, breeding buzzards and pied flycatchers in summer, and marauding siskins in the streamside alders in winter. There are dormice in the woods but they are very secretive. They cross the road via the treetops, using touching branches. You may be lucky enough to find the small group of broad-leaved helleborine orchids by the top path in June and July.

Rhos Fiddle

Near Clun; **OS Map** SO 206857; **Map Ref** P31

ACCESS/CONDITIONS: Some rough terrain. Can be boggy in wet weather.
HOW TO GET THERE: From Clun, take the B4368 towards Newtown through the village of Newcastle-on-Clun and then right just before the bridge. Fork left at Caldy Bank. On the right-hand side, the roadside verge widens and the reserve fencing starts on the left. Park on the wide roadside verge. Be careful in wet weather and sympathetic to the needs of local farmers and other road users.
WALKING TIME: The full circuit takes about 1 hour at an easy pace.
30-MINUTE VISIT: Walk from the information board along the track running towards the centre of the reserve and back to get a real feeling of wilderness.

A wonderful upland reserve in the higher reaches of the Clun Forest on the border between England and Wales, with the ancient cattle drove road, the Ceri Ridgeway, nearby. It is a relatively extensive remnant of the heathland habitat that was formerly more widespread on the surrounding hilltops. The site was acquired by the Trust for its varied moorland vegetation, which includes wet heath, dry heath and old, agriculturally unimproved acidic grassland. In spring and summer, the calling of curlews and the ascending song of the skylark add to the atmosphere. In autumn the heather and cotton grass are at their best, while winter is the time to appreciate the colours and textures of the mosses and lichens. Don't miss the yellow mountain pansies growing in the unimproved grassland areas on the south-western slopes of the reserve. They flower from May to July and can sometimes be found as late as September.

Earl's Hill

Near Shrewsbury; **OS Map** SJ 409048; **Map Ref** P21

P i (audio)

ACCESS/CONDITIONS: Good network of paths all around the reserve.
HOW TO GET THERE: Minsterley Motors (01743 791208) runs a regular bus service from Shrewsbury to Bishop's Castle. The reserve is 8 miles south-west of Shrewsbury on the A488. If travelling by car, turn left at Pontesford (brown sign on roadside) and park in the Forestry Commission car park.
WALKING TIME: The circuit of 2 miles around the base of the hills takes approximately 1 hour. The guided walk is on audio.
30-MINUTE VISIT: Walk up to the Lower Camp on Pontesford Hill. A short circular walk is possible on the west side of the hill along the forestry track and back along the road.
A MEMBER SAYS: 'I like looking at the anthills in the field above Habberley brook. In spring they're covered in tiny plants, such as changing forget-me-not.'

Earl's Hill is renowned for its variety of habitats: grazed acid grassland on the Iron Age hill-fort summit, rocky outcrops and scree on its eastern flanks, ash woodland on the valley sides, and a clear babbling brook winding its way through a gorge created by meltwater during the last Ice Age. In spring, bluebells, wood anemones and primroses carpet the woodland floor and moschatel, ramsons and the rare upland enchanter's nightshade clothe the banks of the brook. In early summer, the grassland is speckled with the white of shepherd's cress, followed by the russet of sheep's sorrel and white of heath bedstraw. Pied flycatchers, redstarts and tree pipits nest in the wood, while buzzards and ravens wheel overhead. Grayling butterflies rest on the rocks, perfectly camouflaged and virtually invisible. Yellow stonecrop flourishes on the screes, its succulent leaves enabling it to survive in these exposed, dry areas. Autumn colours are spectacular, with views across the valley to Oaks Wood. Bracken turns a russet colour and mosses regain their bright green colour after the summer.

DID YOU KNOW?

- Mary Webb's book *Gone to Earth* was partly filmed at Earl's Hill in the 1950s.
- From the trig point on the summit there's a panoramic view of the Shropshire Hills and on a clear day, as far as Cader Idris in Wales.
- Earl's Hill was Shropshire Wildlife Trust's first nature reserve.

The Ercall

Telford; **OS Map** SJ 640096; **Map Ref** P20

ACCESS/CONDITIONS: Footpaths in reasonably good condition but steep in places. Short strolls can be carried out in flat areas, but longer walks are bound to encounter a slope or two.
HOW TO GET THERE: Bus to Wellington then walk down Ercall Lane. By car, from the M54, leave at J7 onto the B5061. Follow signs to The Wrekin and then the Buckatree Hotel. Turn left at The Wrekin towards the entrance and brown signs on the right.
WALKING TIME: 131-acre (53ha) reserve linked to the council-owned Limekiln Woods and The Wrekin. Walks can vary from 1 hour to a full day.
30-MINUTE VISIT: From the entrance head up the main footpath to the quarry, where you can see ripples in the rockface formed by waves that lapped the shores of an ancient ocean 500 million years ago.
A MEMBER SAYS: 'Not only do you have a wealth of wildlife in the rich, ancient oak woodland, but you can see millions of years of the Earth's history in the rocks.'

The Ercall is less well known than The Wrekin, but it has its own grandeur. Ancient oak woodland, spectacular views and more than 500 million years of geological history can be enjoyed here. Picture volcanoes spewing thick, sticky lava all over the barren landscape, clouds of ash pouring into the atmosphere and earthquakes shaking the land violently. That is how The Ercall was formed in its first stage some 566 million years ago. Almost 20 million years later, the sea came sweeping across this volcanic desert, leaving behind beautiful white sands marked with ripples that you still see today. This reserve is internationally famous for its geology. It visibly marks the boundary between a time of very little life, the Precambrian, and an explosion in the variety of life during the Cambrian. The geology is a year-round attraction, but most clearly seen in the winter, when vegetation is at its lowest. It's not just the old rocks that make The Ercall a wonderful place to visit. In spring, the woods are awash with bluebells and the singing of birds just returned from Africa, and in the summer, plentiful bird's-foot trefoil makes this a favoured stronghold for many butterflies, including the dingy skipper. It is also an excellent place to look for fungi in the autumn.

DID YOU KNOW?

- **The stone quarried here was used to build the M54.**
- **There is a fossilised beach at the Ercall.**

Wood Lane

Near Ellesmere; **OS Map** SJ 421331 (lagoon); **Map Ref** P10

OPENING TIMES: Open all year. Permits are required for hide access.
ACCESS/CONDITIONS: Access paths are mostly gravel but can be wet in places. An all-ability trail leads from the lower car park to the small hide. Both hides are suitable for wheelchair access. Some pools have deep water and small children should be supervised. Dogs are not allowed in the interests of birdlife.
HOW TO GET THERE: Take the A528 south from Ellesmere (towards Shrewsbury). Turn left at the Spunhill crossroads, signposted to Colemere and follow this narrow road (with care) to the car park entrance on the right-hand side of the road.
WALKING TIME: A slow stroll takes about 30 minutes, excluding times spent in the hides. Both hides are within a short walk (30 metres and 250 metres) of the lower car park.
30-MINUTE VISIT: Pop into one or both of the hides and check the log book to see what's about.
A MEMBER SAYS: 'We loved collecting bugs. I liked the hide best as we saw some ducks.'

A wetland site developed from disused sand and gravel workings, there are several large lagoons with islands and rough grassland. In spring, passage waders like greenshank, redshank, whimbrel, dunlin and green sandpiper pass through. At the same time lapwing, little ringed plover, shelduck and mallard move in to breed. Huge banks of sand provide a home for a large colony of sand martins, while tree sparrows occupy nest boxes provided especially for them. Reed warblers nest in the reedbeds. In the autumn, the waders pass through, travelling south this time, and ruff, pectoral sandpiper and little stint are occasional visitors. Buzzards, sparrowhawks and kestrels are regulars. During the summer, hobbies occasionally harass the sand martins, and ospreys pass through on migration. Gulls are always present, using the site for roosting and general loafing. In the autumn and winter, numbers increase as thousands pass through the site to the main roosts at Ellesmere and Colemere. Black-headed, herring and lesser black-backed gulls are regular. In addition, numerous wildfowl with flocks of teal overwinter in the area.

DID YOU KNOW?

- **Nest platforms on telegraph poles have been erected to tempt ospreys to stay and breed.**
- **Over 170 different species of bird have been recorded at the reserve.**

Staffordshire

About the Trust

Staffordshire's location, at the northern or southern extremes of the ranges of many species, is one of the reasons for its rich and diverse flora and fauna. There are good examples of most wildlife habitats and even an area of inland saltmarsh. Of particular importance are the lowland heathlands, the Staffordshire moorlands and the limestone valleys. The extensive network of rivers, inland waterways and meres and mosses add a further important dimension. The more than 2,100 acres (850ha) of land we manage reflect this varied wildlife habitat.

Staffordshire Wildlife Trust ☎ 01889 880100
www.staffs-wildlife.org.uk

Black Brook

Near Leek
OS Map SK 021650; **Map Ref** P1

The moorland and moorland fringe habitats at Black Brook and the surrounding Leek Moors provide important habitats for a variety of breeding birds. Key species include curlew and lapwing. Dippers can occasionally be seen along the brook, while other moorland birds include whinchat and twite. The cotton grass flowers in April, while a small area within Brund Hill is home to the locally rare globeflower.

Brankley Pasture

Near Yoxall
OS Map SK 163216; **Map Ref** P16

Mature and veteran trees. Oak, holly, crabapple, solitary wasps and bees, harebell, tormentil, fairy parasol, fly agaric, buzzard, little and tawny owl, pied flycatcher, brown hare, fox and stoat.

George's Hayes

Near Longdon
OS Map SK 067133; **Map Ref** P18

Wild daffodil, bluebell, yellow archangel, bugle, greater bellflower, fallow deer, stoat, fox, badger, water shrew, chiffchaff and woodpecker.

Hem Heath

Near Longdon
OS Map SJ 885411; **Map Ref** P8

Bluebell, wood sorrel, chiffchaff, willow warbler, nuthatch and treecreeper in summer and a huge range of fungi in autumn.

Jackson's Coppice and Marsh

Near Eccleshall
OS Map SJ 786301; **Map Ref** P12

Bog-bean, greater tussock sedge, bluebells, sedge warbler, kingfisher, pied flycatcher, badger and banded agrion damselfly.

Parrot's Drumble

Near Newcastle-under-Lyme
OS Map SJ 821519; **Map Ref** P4

Birch, rowan, alder, hazel, bluebell, stitchwort, moschatel, golden saxifrage, spearwort, marsh tit, spotted flycatcher, willow warbler and water vole.

Rod Wood

Near Leek
OS Map SJ 997531; **Map Ref** P3

Hay, rattle, ox-eye daisy, eyebright, orchids, dyer's greenweed, common and marsh valerian, creeping jenny, bilberry and green woodpecker.

Weag's Barn

Near Grindon
OS Map SK 099542; **Map Ref** P2

Mountain currant, maidenhair fern, hart's tongue fern, toothwort, lousewort, eyebright, self-heal, harebell and long-tailed tit.

Bateswood

Near Newcastle-under-Lyme; **OS Map** SJ 796471; **Map Ref** P5

ACCESS/CONDITIONS: The terrain is relatively even, although the circular walk involves some steep slopes and steps.
HOW TO GET THERE: Travelling west on the A525, take the minor road on the right just before Madeley Heath (signposted Leycett and Alsagers Bank). After just over a mile, as you take a right-hand bend, you will see a house perched above a small track on the left. Follow the track to a gate on the right-hand side. This is padlocked, but the combination is available by phoning the Trust. The Trust's parking area is through this gate and approximately a quarter of a mile along the road on the left.
WALKING TIME: A full circuit can be done in 1 and a half hours.
30-MINUTE VISIT: Simply visit the plateau, hear the skylarks, observe the dragonflies and see the swoop of a lapwing.

Bateswood represents one of the Trust's 'newest' reserves. Ten years ago the site did not exist – it was part of extensive opencast mining operations which took place throughout the area. The site has since been restored and continues to develop as a valuable area for wildlife. Today, the 61 acres (25ha) of Bateswood are best known for their population of skylarks. Visit from mid-March onwards and you are unlikely to miss their continuous song. The reserve has a range of habitats including scrub, mature woodland, plantation, wet grassland, meadows and open water. Look out for lapwing, linnet and grey partridge, along with summer flowering plants such as ox-eye daisy and bird's-foot trefoil. On warm sunny days you will also be aware of the abundance of dragon and damselflies flitting across the ponds and scrapes.

Croxall Lakes

Near Alrewas; **OS Map** SK 188139; **Map Ref** P17

ACCESS/CONDITIONS: All-ability access to the main track leading through the nature reserve. Two bird hides provide excellent views across the two lakes.
HOW TO GET THERE: From Rugeley, follow the A513, passing through Kings Bromley and Alrewas. Continue along this road, passing over the A38. After approximately a mile you will pass over the River Tame, which forms the western boundary of the reserve. The entrance to the reserve is the second track on your left.
WALKING TIME: 30-minute walk there and back, but you'll want to stop and look at the birds.
30-MINUTE VISIT: A very quick visit to the first hide.

The nature reserve is situated at the confluence of three rivers, the Tame to the west, the Trent to the north and the Mease to the east. The site is part of a complex of restored wetlands in the Trent Valley. As you walk along the access track with the main lake to your left, look out for green woodpeckers flying along the railway corridor. If you don't see them listen for their distinctive call, which sounds like they are laughing at you. You may also see kestrels hovering over the track or buzzards high in the sky.

The reserve's two lakes attract large numbers of wildfowl and wading birds during migration and in the winter. Look out for wigeon and teal. If you visit during the winter months you may well see short-eared owls flying low above the areas of tall grasses. This large bird is not commonly seen in Staffordshire. During the spring and early summer months look out for lapwing tumbling through the air as they prepare to make their nests on the ground. Otter signs, such as footprints and spraint, are commonly found on the reserve's riverbanks; however, this shy animal is very difficult to spot.

Thorswood

Near Ashbourne; **OS Map** SK 115470; **Map Ref** P6

ACCESS/CONDITIONS: The terrain at Thorswood varies considerably. The hilltop location of some of the fields means that it can be an arduous walk to get to certain areas. To do a full circuit of the reserve you will need to cross a small stream, which can become muddy at any time of the year. There is a surfaced access track from the car park to the interpretation barn.
HOW TO GET THERE: From Ashbourne, take the A52 west towards Leek. Keep following the A52, turning left just past Swinscoe. After approximately 0.75 miles turn left, heading towards Stanton village. Thorswood is approximately 0.25 miles along this road on the right-hand side.
WALKING TIME: Allow 2 hours to explore the entire reserve.
30-MINUTE VISIT: The waymarked trail can be covered in 45 minutes, but it's nicer to take longer.

Thorswood is an ideal family day out. Enjoy a picnic in the barn or follow the family quiz trail that guides you around the reserve. Whether you're interested in wildflowers or landscape history, or just want to enjoy a quiet walk, then Thorswood is the place to visit. Among the 150 acres (61ha) of Thorswood nature reserve you will find rare plants, flower-rich meadows, heathland, Iron Age barrows, evidence of historic mining activity and spectacular landscapes. Walk to the top of the hill to see our unique circular seat and enjoy the spectacular views across the surrounding landscape.

To see the site's unique flora at its best visit during the summer – although if you want to catch one of the county's finest displays of mountain pansies you'll need to drop by in late spring, too. Hares are frequently seen around the reserve – if you walk quietly around the trail you may disturb one lying in the grass. Look out for the characteristic black tips on the ears.

If you're interested in history and industrial archaeology then the various 'lumps-and-hollows' at Thorswood provide evidence of how man has influenced this landscape.

WILDLIFE FACT: RABBITS AND HARES – KNOW THE DIFFERENCE

Seen from a distance, hares are much larger than rabbits and tend to move more quickly across the ground, with a loping gait. If you see them more closely, their ears, which are about the same length as their heads – proportionately much bigger than rabbits – are black at the tips. Usually seen in grassland and fields, they hide out and rest in hedgerows and woodland throughout the UK, except north-western Scotland. Mad March hares are actually unreceptive females fending off males during the mating season. Hares can be seen at Thorswood and Brankley Pasture.

Cotton Dell

Near Oakamoor; **OS Map** SK 055451; **Map Ref** P7

ACCESS/CONDITIONS: The paths are often wet and muddy and can be very steep in places. Stout footwear essential.
HOW TO GET THERE: From Cheadle take the B5417 east to Oakamoor. As you descend into the village turn right before the bridge. After approximately 75m turn left onto the parking and picnic area owned by Staffordshire County Council. From here, head back to the main road and continue east over the bridge. Take the second turning on the left up an unadopted road. Park in Staffordshire County Council free car park.
WALKING TIME: To see and enjoy all the reserve will take at least 3 hours.
30-MINUTE VISIT: You need at least an hour.
A MEMBER SAYS: 'It's the loveliest morning's walk for miles around – such a variety of habitat, scenery and wildlife.'

Cotton Dell is a very varied reserve and is home to a wide diversity of wildlife. The woodland contains a variety of trees and shrubs, including bird cherry, alder, rowan and guelder rose. The oldest trees may be up to 200 years old. Some wooded areas are dominated by ash, oak and birch, while other areas are dominated by dense, dark conifers. Look out for the poor ground layer beneath the conifers compared to the broadleaf woodland areas, where you will find patches of bluebells, wood anemone and sorrel in the spring. The most common plant found beneath the trees is greater woodrush – perhaps not as visually appealing as blankets of bluebells, but this is an unusual plant in Staffordshire. The Cotton Brook winds its way through the centre of the reserve from Cotton to the village of Oakamoor, where it joins the River Churnet. The grasslands start coming to life in spring when cowslips appear in abundance. In summer these fields are buzzing with life, as bees, butterflies and other insects feed on the wide diversity of plants, including scabious, knapweeds, orchids and betony, while you may be lucky enough to see dippers flying up and downstream, collecting food for their young. In autumn it will be the superb colours of the trees, particularly the beech, which will grab your attention.

DID YOU KNOW?

- **The site was previously owned by the Roman Catholic Church.**
- **It is less than 3 miles from Alton Towers.**

Doxey Marshes

In Stafford; **OS Map** SJ 903250; **Map Ref** P14

ACCESS/CONDITIONS: The site is basically flat and all-ability paths have been installed, running from the disused railway line. Assisted wheelchair access is available to the main hide. The site does flood on occasion, mainly during the winter.
HOW TO GET THERE: Walk from Sainsbury's car park in Stafford.
WALKING TIME: A gentle stroll and birdwatch will easily lose 2 hours.
30-MINUTE VISIT: Walk down to Boundary Flash and the viewing platform there.
A MEMBER SAYS: 'It's a delight to have such a large nature reserve almost on my doorstep and within 5 minutes of the centre of town. The bustle of Sainsbury's one minute, the haven of Doxey Marshes the next.'

Located in the centre of Stafford, Doxey Marshes is regionally important for breeding and wintering birds. It is designated as an SSSI for its wet grassland habitat and its breeding wading birds and wildfowl. It is particularly noted for its populations of breeding snipe. Lying in the floodplain of the River Sow it has a long cultural association with the town. The reserve contains a wonderful mosaic of habitats, including reedbeds, pools, hedgerows and the largest area of reed sweet-grass in the Midlands. The Marshes contains an extensive flora of over 250 flowering plants, including species such as common meadow-rue, yellow iris, purple loosestrife, marsh valerian and flowering rush.

But Doxey Marshes is best known for its impressive diversity of birds, with over 80 species recorded. Most significant are the populations of breeding waders, such as snipe, lapwing, redshank and little ringed plover, which can all be seen in the spring and summer. Large flocks of waders, including golden plovers, are regular winter visitors, while in spring and autumn look out for green and common sandpipers, greenshanks and black-tailed godwits.

DID YOU KNOW?

- Subsidence from brine pumping caused the creation of the large pools and shallow swamp.
- Over 1,200 snipes were recorded in 1998.
- The reserve is surrounded by the M6, West Coast Mainline railway and Stafford.

Loynton Moss

Near Woodseaves; **OS Map** SJ 789243; **Map Ref** P13

ACCESS/CONDITIONS: There are a number of paths throughout the reserve, which may become boggy during the winter.
HOW TO GET THERE: Go through Woodseaves on the A519 between Eccleshall and Newport. A mile towards Newport you will cross the Shropshire Union Canal, which forms the eastern boundary of the reserve. Approximately 200 metres past the canal on the right is the entrance to the car park of the reserve.
WALKING TIME: The site deserves two hours of exploration.
30-MINUTE VISIT: You can just about do the circular walk in 45 minutes.
A MEMBER SAYS: 'Take a stroll to the top of Rue Hill for an amazing view. Rest a while and think how lucky we are that places like Loynton Moss exist.'

With 35 acres (14ha) of Loynton Moss having SSSI status, this varied reserve is recognised nationally for its conservation value and importance. Visit Loynton Moss at any time of the year and discover a unique landscape formed as a result of retreating ice sheets at the end of the last Ice Age, 10,000 years ago.

The reserve is a rich, diverse wetland teeming with life. Numerous insect species utilise this distinctive habitat, attracting many bird species, such as reed bunting. Look out across the area of fen, which is literally a thin floating raft of vegetation over water dominated by tall reed species. In the spring the drier wooded areas are vibrant with the colour of bluebells and stitchwort. Listen out for skylarks and look up to see buzzards high in the sky.

The area of SSSI consists of a range of successional habitats, including reedbed fen, scrub, alder/willow carr (wet woodland) and dry oak and birch woodland. Plants found throughout the reedbed include marsh cinquefoil, cowbane, branched bur-reed and lesser pond-sedge. The surviving areas of wet woodland contain the largest stand of alder buckthorn in the county and other unusual species, such as bog myrtle, royal fern and elongated sedge.

DID YOU KNOW?

- **Loynton Moss was Staffordshire Wildlife Trust's first nature reserve.**
- **The Territorial Army used explosives to blow a hole in the reedbed in an attempt to create open water.**
- **Three years after it was arable, there are now orchids in the grassland around the Moss.**

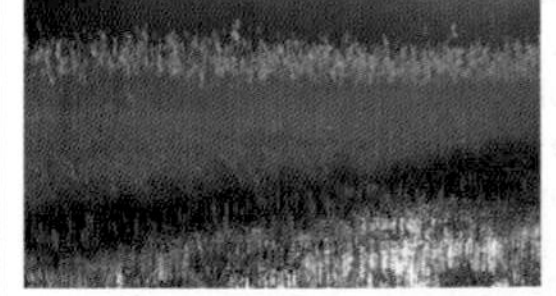

Birmingham and Black Country

About the Trust

Our aim is to ensure the diversity and richness of wildlife in the urban area, and to help people understand, protect and celebrate their environment. We have nature conservation, community and education projects. Research, surveys and monitoring inform our lobbying and campaigning for wildlife and the environment. We are committed to protect and promote biodiversity, promote sustainable development and celebrate the urban environment.

Birmingham and Black Country
☎ 0121 4541199 www.bbcwildlife.org.uk

Centre of the Earth

Birmingham
OS Map SP 045880; **Map Ref** P27

The Centre of the Earth is the Wildlife Trust's – and Britain's – first purpose-built environmental education centre, specialising in teaching and learning about sustainable development. In 1987 the Trust located the Norman Street site, which is next to the Soho Loop of the Birmingham canal. Originally a corporation yard, this once derelict 1-acre (0.5ha) site has been transformed with the help of the local community into an attractive and exciting natural landscape used as a learning resource and for play. It took four years to build. Today it is surrounded by new wildlife habitats and environmental sculptures. The centre building, officially opened in 1993, was designed by architect David Lea, renowned for his ecologically sensitive building designs, and built by Keith Hall, a founder member of the Association for Environment Conscious Building. The building is a unique timber-framed structure, built to demonstrate the sustainable use of natural resources. Open by appointment only.

Richmond Nature Garden

Birmingham
OS Map SP 047888; **Map Ref** P25

Environmental art, wildlife garden and 'World Garden', a small urban nature garden for education and community use – green oak shelter. Good access. Open by appointment only. Ring the Trust to confirm.

Hill Hook LNR

Birmingham
OS Map SK 105003; **Map Ref** P24

Hill Hook LNR is situated on the outskirts of Birmingham. The old mill pool at the centre of the site is surrounded by a mosaic of habitats, from wet woodland to the south, through the bluebell woods to the north and onwards to the wildflower meadows. A small stream runs through the site, which has good access along the dam wall running alongside the pool. Here, you can view a good range of water birds such as heron, kingfisher and swans, as well as all the usual waterfowl. For those of a more adventurous nature, muddy paths run through the rest of the site. It is managed by the Hill Hook Advisory Group, the Trust and Birmingham City Council.

Moorcroft Wood LNR

Walsall; **OS Map** SO 968953; **Map Ref** P26

ACCESS/CONDITIONS: Good access to much of the reserve on hard-surfaced path with gentle gradients.
HOW TO GET THERE: The reserve is within easy walking distance of Bradley Lane Metro station. Bus numbers 78, 263 and 680 (full details from the Centro Hotline 0121 200 2700). The reserve is close to the Black Country Route and within 10 minutes of the M6.
WALKING TIME: Allow an hour or two to walk around the whole reserve, especially if you decide to investigate the neighbouring canals.
30-MINUTE VISIT: Take a brisk walk down to the lake and see what waterfowl are visiting the site, while enjoying any woodland flowers, insects or birds on your way.

Moorcroft Wood was planted around the turn of the 19th century by the Midlands Afforestation Association, transforming a former colliery site into a recreational resource for patients at the adjacent hospital. Their far-sightedness created one of the most fascinating of urban nature reserves, now owned and managed by Walsall Council, whose local partners are the Friends of Moorcroft Wood and the Wildlife Trust. At its heart is a large lake, which attracts many waterfowl, as well as supporting a thriving population of amphibians.

The woodland is rich and fascinating, partly because of the strange, undulating terrain and poor soils. Moorcroft Wood was the sight of the first blast furnace trials, and you can discover the twisted columns of furnace slag, like strange standing stones. Their rugged surfaces support polypody fern and other unusual plants. Despite its urban location, you are more likely to see wood pigeons than feral pigeons here. Or you could discover a heron, a buzzard or all sorts of waterfowl. Expect the unexpected.

Moseley Bog

Moseley; **OS Map** SP 093820; **Map Ref** P32

ACCESS/CONDITIONS: Muddy paths. Access is difficult down to the wet woodland, but there are some sections of boardwalk around this area.
HOW TO GET THERE: About 5 miles south-east of Birmingham city centre. Take bus 11A/C from any point on the Outer Circle route to Cole Bank Road. From Moor Street, take the train to Hall Green station, then a 15-minute walk. by car, follow the brown signs to Sarehole Mill from the Stratford Road (A34).
WALKING TIME: The full circuit takes 1 hour.
30-MINUTE VISIT: From the Yardley Wood Road entrance, head into Joys Wood, following signs for Moseley Bog. Continue along the brook to emerge back into Joys Wood.

A magical mosaic of habitats, including wet woodland, wet meadows, a small bog, pond and woodland plantation. The site not only has a great mix of habitats and wildlife, but also has an amazing history, from Bronze Age burnt mounds to mill pools, and was also the playground of JRR Tolkien for part of his childhood.

Every spring there are fine displays of bluebells. Spring is the best time to see and hear the abundant birdlife, such as woodpeckers, willow warblers and nuthatches. In summer the site is alive with insects. Butterflies abound and after nightfall, moths take their place and may fall prey to foraging bats. In autumn, colourful fungi can be found, mostly in the woodland areas. The winter transforms the site into a scene from a film, sometimes spooky, but always amazing.

The reserve is jointly managed by the Wildlife Trust for Birmingham and the Black Country and Birmingham City Council.

Park Hall

Birmingham; **OS Map** SP 155908; **Map Ref** P28

OPENING TIMES: Visits by prior arrangement only.
ACCESS/CONDITIONS: The access track to Park Hall is quite steep in parts and is currently unsurfaced, creating difficult conditions for those with limited mobility. Once on the site there are no surfaced paths, however much of the site is relatively flat and easily accessible on foot in fair weather.
HOW TO GET THERE: The reserve is situated in the east of Birmingham between Castle Bromwich and Water Orton. Bus numbers 590a (from Coleshill) and 590c (from Birmingham city centre) stop outside Park Hall School, close to the site entrance. There are regular train services to Water Orton station from Birmingham New Street and Tamworth Monday to Saturday. If travelling by car, the site entrance is located on the Water Orton road (B4118).
WALKING TIME: The full circuit is approximately 2 miles and can be comfortably walked in around 2 and a half hours.
30-MINUTE VISIT: A walk through the bottom of Parkhall Wood and back along the river to Meanders Pool will take in many of the best wildlife sightings and views the reserve has to offer.
A MEMBER SAYS: 'I'd seen Park Hall on many occasions as the train often came to a stop there and wondered about the place. When I heard the Wildlife Trust were to open the site as a nature reserve I took the opportunity to visit and was amazed by the abundance of wildlife and the feeling of tranquillity.'

Park Hall is an area of remnant farmland and estate grounds on the eastern edge of Birmingham. The reserve supports a diverse range of habitats, including three ancient woodlands, grassland, wetland and a stretch of the River Tame. During spring impressive displays of bluebells, ramsons, yellow archangels and numerous other plants can be seen in the woodlands, while in the farm ponds amphibians including great crested newt, common toad and frog begin to breed. As the seasons move along the grasslands and wetlands come into their own, with colourful floral displays and abundant butterflies and dragonflies. Summer breeding birds include reed bunting, teal, swan and buzzard, while in the evenings bats forage on moths and other insects. The woodlands take on a different character in autumn, with fungi taking the place of the flowers among the changing colours of the canopy.

DID YOU KNOW?

- **Park Hall is the only site in the Vice County of Warwickshire that the scavenger water beetle *Helophorus longitarsis* has been recorded.**
- **William Shakespeare was a descendant of the Arden family of Park Hall and is said to have visited here.**
- **Otters have been sighted on the River Tame at Park Hall. We have created otter holts at the site to encourage them to stay.**

Herefordshire

About the Trust

Herefordshire Nature Trust is the largest membership-based wildlife organisation in the area, dedicated to inspiring people about wildlife, acting as a wildlife champion, creating wildlife havens and encouraging sustainable living. The Trust covers the county of Herefordshire and works closely with neighbouring Wildlife Trusts in England and Wales. The Trust is supported by over 3,000 local members and manages 54 nature reserves.

Herefordshire Nature Trust☎ 01432 356872
www.herefordshirewt.org

Brilley Green Dingle

Near Hay-on-Wye
OS Map SO 271488; **Map Ref** 017

Ancient semi-natural woodland and small stream in steep-sided valley. Stream has native crayfish and otters. Lower path can be muddy in wet weather. Sections of boardwalk and steps up steep slopes.

Common Hill SSSI

Near Fownhope
OS Map SO 591347; **Map Ref** 023

Unimproved limestone grassland, mature hedgerows and derelict orchard. Notable for its range of lime-loving plants, including rock-rose; its invertebrates, including many species of butterfly; and its old fruit trees. Steep slopes.

Holywell Dingle

Near Eardisley
OS Map SO 312512; **Map Ref** 016

Plants such as yellow archangel and anemones indicate this wood's ancient origins. Spring brings carpets of golden saxifrage and sanicle, and many types of mosses and ferns. Look out for great spotted woodpeckers, nuthatches, treecreepers and warblers.

Lea and Pagets Wood SSSI

Near Fownhope
OS Map SO 598342; **Map Ref** 024

Ancient wood overlooking the Wye Valley. Mainly forest with small areas of old coppice, which support dormice; bluebells, wood anemones and wild daffodils in spring; silver-washed fritillary in summer; array of fungi in autumn. Paths are not surfaced and can become muddy in wet weather. Some stairs where the paths climb the valley side. Park in the lay-by off the B4224.

Merrivale Wood

Near Ross-on-Wye
OS Map SO 603229; **Map Ref** 025

Ancient and secondary woodland on a steep rocky hill. The wood has a range of trees and flowers. Steep slopes. May be boggy in wet weather.

Nupend Wood SSSI

Near Fownhope
OS Map SO 580354; **Map Ref** 022

Ancient semi-natural woodland noted for its fungi and invertebrates, including grizzled skipper and silver-washed fritillary. Some steep slopes and steps. Reserve leaflet available.

Quebb Corner Meadow SSSI

Near Eardisley
OS Map SO 302520; **Map Ref** 015

Unimproved neutral grassland, marshy grassland, mature hedges and streams. A good range of common meadow flowers and butterflies.

Romers Wood

Near Tenbury Wells
OS Map SO 602629; **Map Ref** 07

Ancient semi-natural woodland. Important breeding site for pied flycatcher and dormouse; noted for its rich invertebrate fauna, including ancient woodland molluscs. May be boggy in wet weather. Open all year.

The Sturts SSSI

Near Eardisley; **OS Map** SO 336475; **Map Ref** O18

ACCESS/CONDITIONS: There are no surfaced paths. The site can flood during wet weather.
HOW TO GET THERE: Bus information: 01432 260211. By car, follow the A438 from Hereford for about 14 miles. At Letton, take a right-hand turn to Kinnersley. The reserve is on the left.
WALKING TIME: The full circuit can be completed in about 1 hour.
30-MINUTE VISIT: Step back in time in the traditionally managed hay meadows.

The Sturts SSSI is one of the largest expanses of species-rich unimproved neutral grassland in Herefordshire. The reserve is a complex mosaic of grassland types bounded by mature hedgerows and veteran trees, drainage ditches and streams. The entire site regularly floods during the winter when the nearby River Wye breaks its banks. Visit the reserve throughout the spring, summer and autumn to see a wide range of typical meadow and wetland plants; great burnet, common knapweed, dyer's greenweed, skullcap, ragged robin (below) and devil's-bit scabious. Winter floods attract waterfowl. The reserve's small ponds are an important habitat for dragonflies and other freshwater invertebrates.

Titley Pool SSSI

Near Kington; **OS Map** SO 325594; **Map Ref** O10

ACCESS/CONDITIONS: The paths at Titley Pool are all unsurfaced and may be muddy in wet weather.
HOW TO GET THERE: Bus information: 01432 260211. Titley Pool is approximately 2 miles north-west of Kington, off the B4355. After entering Titley village, but before the Stag Inn, turn left down the former driveway of Eywood House.
WALKING TIME: The full circuit can be completed in about 1 hour.
30-MINUTE VISIT: Walk down to the hide near the car park for views over the lake. The unimproved pasture is about a 5-minute walk from the car park.

Titley Pool SSSI is one of the largest areas of open water in Herefordshire and one of a number of naturally formed lakes around Kington and Mortimer's Cross. The pool is surrounded by ancient woodland and unimproved pasture. The mosaic of habitats on this reserve attracts a great range of birds. In winter, the pool is home to a wide variety of waterfowl, including teal, wigeon, tufted duck and pochard. At other times of the year, this peaceful reserve is an ideal breeding site for great crested grebes, mute swans and little grebes. Another regular visitor which often breeds here is the pied flycatcher. Green Wood has fine displays of bluebells in the spring, and the unimproved pasture has a wide range of summer flowers. The reserve is particularly good for dragonflies, including common and ruddy darters and southern hawkers.

The Doward Reserves

Near Ross-on-Wye; **OS Map** SO 549161; **Map Ref** O26

01432 356872

ACCESS/CONDITIONS: At present there are no surfaced paths on the Doward Reserves. During wet weather, they may become very muddy.
HOW TO GET THERE: Bus information: 01432 260211. The reserve is 9 miles south of Ross-on-Wye. Take the A40 from Ross, exit at Whitchurch and follow signs to the Doward Reserves. Park at Leeping Stocks, White Rocks or Forestry Authority car park between King Arthur's Cave and White Rocks.
WALKING TIME: The full circuit of about 3 miles takes approximately 2 hours.
30-MINUTE VISIT: Park at White Rocks and walk through the reserve.
A MEMBER SAYS: 'If I ever want to escape to a place where I can guarantee to be on my own, the Doward Reserves are where I head every time.'

The Doward Reserves include King Arthur's Cave, White Rocks, Leeping Stocks, Miners Rest, Woodside and Lords Wood Quarry. All of the reserves are within easy walking distance of each other. The Doward is a massive rocky outcrop in a bend of the River Wye. The reserves here are predominantly woodland but with patches of unimproved and restored grassland. There are fine displays of spring and summer woodland flowers, including wild columbine, several species of orchid, and meadow saffron. Peregrines have been seen. White Rocks, Woodside and Miners Rest are noted for their summer butterflies. During autumn, the Doward is the place to be for fungi; over 100 species have been recorded, including rare devil's bolete. The small field at Woodside is a fine example of unimproved limestone grassland and has something of interest throughout the year.

DID YOU KNOW?

- King Arthur's Cave gets its name from a series of natural caves near the reserve.
- The reserves are criss-crossed by old stone walls, topped with curiously twisted and contorted beech hedges.
- Over 90 species of fungus have been recorded in Leeping Stocks alone.

Lugg Meadow SSSI & Lower House Farm

Tupsley; **OS Map** SO 531410; **Map Ref** O21

OPENING TIMES: Open all year. Lower House Farm: 10am to 4pm, Monday to Friday.
ACCESS/CONDITIONS: Largely flat reserve with unsurfaced paths. Baynton Wood is on a steep slope. Frequent winter flooding.
HOW TO GET THERE: Bus information: 01432 260211. Off Ledbury Road (A438). Follow signs for Nature Trust.
WALKING TIME: The full circuit of 3 miles takes 2 hours at an easy pace.
30-MINUTE VISIT: Follow the permissive path down to the river (approximately 10 minutes).
A MEMBER SAYS: 'With snake's head fritillaries at your feet, otters playing in the river and curlews calling in the distance, these medieval hay meadows are the perfect place to unwind in suburban Hereford.'

Lugg Meadow SSSI and Lower House Farm are situated on the eastern edge of Hereford. The reserves consist of traditionally managed unimproved flood plain meadow, streams and ditches and a fragment of ancient woodland. The River Lugg meanders through the site. The reserves are noted for spectacular displays of snake's head fritillary, which can be seen in late spring along with a wide range of typical summer meadow flowers. Otters, kingfishers and sand martins frequent the river and curlews and lapwings can be seen during the winter. The river is particularly rich in invertebrates and is a good place to look for damselflies and dragonflies, including both banded and beautiful demoiselle. Lower House Farm, a superb early Jacobean timber-framed building, is the Trust's headquarters.

DID YOU KNOW?

- **Lugg Meadow is one of the largest surviving examples of a Lammas meadow in the country.**

Worcestershire

About the Trust

Worcestershire Wildlife Trust is the county's leading local charity working to conserve and restore wildlife and wild places. Our vision is: Worcestershire – part of a UK rich in wildlife, where everyone can appreciate, enjoy and help restore and protect wildlife for the future.

Worcestershire Wildlife Trust☎ 01905 754919
www.worcswildlifetrust.co.uk

Chaddesley Woods
Near Woodcote Green
OS Map SO 915736; **Map Ref** 01

Terrestrial caddis (common here but of national rarity); most of the woodland warblers during summer and woodcock through the year; wildflowers in the unimproved meadow, together with dyer's greenweed.

The Christopher Cadbury Wetland (Upton Warren)
Near Bromsgrove
OS Map SO 93667; **Map Ref** 03

Freshwater Moors Pool and unique inland saltmarsh Flashes Pools. Avocet, little ringed plover, lapwing, black-headed gull, finch, tit and woodpecker; dragonflies. Hides and birdfeeding stations. Non-members must purchase permit.

Droitwich Community Woods
Droitwich
OS Map SO 880624; **Map Ref** 06

A rare inland saltmarsh in the Salwarpe Valley, with salt-tolerant plants, including wild celery and dittander. Marked trails around grassland, woodland and river margins.

Feckenham Wylde Moor
Near Feckenham village
OS Map SP 012605; **Map Ref** 08

Wildlife associated with marshy, peat areas. Ragged robin, common-spotted orchid, cowslip and cuckoo flower; 16 species of dragonfly and damselfly, such as emperor dragonfly and brown hawker; reed bunting, common snipe and redwing. Park in village car park and walk up Moors Lane.

Grafton Wood
Near Grafton Flyford
OS Map SO 971558; **Map Ref** 013

Nationally rare brown hairstreak; ancient pollarded ash and oak trees, bird's-nest orchid, greater burnet saxifrage, saw-wort and violet helleborine.

Lower Smite Farm
Hindlip
OS Map SO 880590; **Map Ref** 011

Habitats include arable and pasture farmland, ponds, a new orchard, wildlife garden and historic granary building. Benches at ponds, bird food and information available at offices during opening hours (9am to 5pm, Monday to Friday). Self-guided farm trail (approximately 45 minutes) from entrance to farmhouse.

Trench Wood
Near Himbleton
OS Map SO 929588; **Map Ref** 012

Woodpecker, warblers, tit, nuthatch, woodcock, buzzard; greater butterfly orchids, herb Paris, meadow saffron and saw-wort along rides and paths; rides and glades good for butterflies. Paths can be muddy.

Windmill Hill
Near North Littleton
OS Map SP 072476; **Map Ref** 019

A limestone grassland with bee orchid, fairy flax, restharrow and wild liquorice; particularly important for butterflies and glow-worms in summer. Please observe the Countryside Code. Gates must be kept shut as there may be grazing stock. Limited roadside parking.

Monkwood

Near Grimley; **OS Map** SO 804606; **Map Ref** O9

ACCESS/CONDITIONS: A good system of hard rides throughout the wood, but Monkwood is a wet woodland and some paths can get muddy in winter. Visitors are requested to keep away from the working foresters in winter.
HOW TO GET THERE: Approximately 5 miles north-west of Worcester, reached from the A443 Worcester to Holt Heath road. From the A443, take any one of the three minor roads north of Hallow going west and signposted to Sinton Green. Take the narrow lane signposted to Monkwood, passing the side of the 'New Inn'.
WALKING TIME: The full circuit of approximately 2 miles takes 1 and three quarter hours at an easy pace.
30-MINUTE VISIT: Follow the trail through Little Monkwood.

Monkwood is an actively managed coppice and a very important reserve in the county for butterflies and moths. Thirty six species of butterfly have been recorded and over 500 species of moth. Spring sees the first butterflies; brimstone, commas and peacocks. There are many wildflowers to be seen in the spring, including early-purple orchids, lily-of-the-valley, ragged robin, and ramsons. Wood whites butterflies can be seen towards the end of May. Migrants such as blackcaps, garden and willow warblers, and white-throats also return. Dragonflies, including the emperor dragonfly, can be seen around the ponds in summer. Butterflies are in abundance, including the white admiral and silver-washed fritillary. The woodland rides are in flower, with knapweed, meadowsweet, melilot and betony. In the autumn, there is an impressive display of fungi, including many poisonous species.

Piper's Hill and Dodderhill Common

Near Bromsgrove; **OS Map** SO 958650; **Map Ref** O5

ACCESS/CONDITIONS: Some steep slopes on the west side of the reserve. Paths can sometimes be muddy.
HOW TO GET THERE: On the B4091 heading south-east from Bromsgrove to Hanbury, about 4 miles from Bromsgrove and 2 miles from Hanbury.
WALKING TIME: The full circuit of about 1 mile takes 45 minutes at an easy pace.
30-MINUTE VISIT: Wander at leisure using the existing paths.

A 38-acre (16ha) woodland SSSI containing some of the oldest and largest trees found in Worcestershire. Many of the trees are ancient beech and sweet-chestnut pollards, together with big oaks believed to be 300-400 years old. Uncommon species such as bird's-nest orchid and broad-leaved helleborine can be found in spring. Autumn is when the wood truly comes to life, as over 200 species of fungus have been found, including chanterelles and beefsteak fungus, and there is an array of colours as leaves turn, ready to fall.

Throughout the year, including summer and winter, woodland birds, such as all three species of woodpecker, tits and the nuthatch, are common. The site is also known as Hanbury Woods.

Tiddesley Wood

Pershore; **OS Map** SO 929462; **Map Ref** O20

ACCESS/CONDITIONS: Woodland paths can be muddy.
HOW TO GET THERE: Take the A44 from Pershore towards Worcester and turn left near the town boundary, just before the summit of the hill, into an unclassified road signposted for Besford and Croome.
WALKING TIME: 198-acre (80ha) reserve. Following the trails and paths around the wood should take about 1 and a half hours.
30-MINUTE VISIT: Follow the main central track through the wood.

Tiddesley Wood gives you the experience of an ancient woodland, with its rich diversity of plants, birds and insects. Our second largest woodland reserve contains a great variety of trees and shrubs. In spring, bluebells, wood anemones and cowslips fill the woodland floor. Summer brings large numbers of butterflies along sunny paths, including white admiral, peacocks and gatekeepers. Dragonflies also haunt the tracks, using them as a hunting ground. Later-flowering plants provide nectar into the autumn – interesting plants in the wood are devil's-bit scabious, meadow saffron and fragrant agrimony. There is, as you'd expect, a vibrant bird population in summer and in winter, when flocks of tits, goldcrests and redpolls search for food.

WILDLIFE FACT: LOWLAND HAY MEADOWS

There are around 9,884 acres (4,000ha) of lowland hay meadow left in England today – that's about two per cent of the area that existed just 50 years ago. One fifth of all of these are found in Worcestershire. The best examples can have up to 50 plant species in a square metre, including cowslips, knapweed and orchids, which in turn support myriad butterflies, beetles, grasshoppers, bugs and moths.

The Devil's Spittleful and Rifle Range

Bewdley; **OS Map** SO 796744; **Map Ref** O2

ACCESS/CONDITIONS: Apart from the Devil's Spittleful, the reserve is fairly flat and, due to its sandy nature, is not very muddy. It is especially prone to damage by fires and visitors are asked to take special care not to discard cigarettes, matches or other combustible materials. Grazing stock may be on the reserve.

HOW TO GET THERE: A footpath runs from the A456 Kidderminster to Bewdley Road via Sandy Lane, a track running south from the entrance to the West Midland Safari Park. Bus 353 from Worcester travels by the reserve (information: 0870 6082608).

WALKING TIME: The full circuit of 2 miles takes 1 and a half hours at an easy pace.

30-MINUTE VISIT: The best place to go (if you don't mind a slight challenge) is to climb to the top of the Devil's Spittleful on the west side of the main road into the reserve.

A MEMBER SAYS: 'It has a quite different feel from the other nature reserves and when the wolves in the neighbouring safari park are howling, it creates a wonderful atmosphere!'

This reserve is important because of the type and range of habitats (heathland, grassland and woodland). Light sandy soils support an interesting and unusual set of plants and animals, especially invertebrates. In spring, green tiger beetles can be seen running and flying among heather and on sandy paths, together with holly blue and orange-tip butterflies. Birds around at this time of year are woodcock, skylark, chiffchaff and willow warbler. In summer, grass snakes can be spotted and birds such as redstart, cuckoo, turtledove and lesser white-throat can be seen. Plants at this time of year include shepherd's cress, spring vetch and wild pansy. Day-flying moths can be seen flying over heather. In late summer and autumn, toads and common lizards are both frequent on the reserve. In winter, there are redpoll flocks, sparrowhawks, mistle thrush, fieldfare and redwings.

DID YOU KNOW?

- The Devil's Spittleful (sometimes called Spadeful) is the large sandstone rock crowned with Scots pine. It is said to have been thrown by the devil to block the course of the River Severn.
- The grey hair-grass which grows on the reserve is normally associated with coastal regions.
- It is one of the few reserves in Worcestershire with the common lizard.

Ipsley Alders Marsh

Near Redditch; **OS Map** SP 076677; **Map Ref** O4

ACCESS/CONDITIONS: Circular boardwalk around the central marsh. The ground can get very wet during winter so stay on boardwalk and paths. Cattle graze on the reserve so visitors are asked to shut gates and keep dogs on a lead.
HOW TO GET THERE: Take the A448 from Bromsgrove towards Warwick, then onto the A4189 signposted Warwick. Turn left onto Ipsley Alders Drive. Take the first right into Far Moor Lane. Follow the road and turn left into Furze Lane. Please park in Furze Lane, respecting local access.
WALKING TIME: The full circuit of 1 mile takes 1 hour at an easy pace.
30-MINUTE VISIT: From the entrance by Winyates Green Meeting Rooms, look at the information boards and stroll along the boardwalk to get the maximum view of the marsh.
A MEMBER SAYS: 'Ipsley is an attractive place and ideal for walks in the fields and woods, as well as learning more about the wildlife around.'

Ipsley Alders is a fen marsh, a rare habitat in the Midlands. At least 170 species of plant have been recorded on the reserve and dragonflies and other invertebrates are numerous. In spring and summer, the interesting flora includes hemp agrimony, common-spotted orchid, hoary willowherb, marsh and fen bedstraw, marsh woundwort, water forget-me-not and water mint. Worcestershire rarities include marsh stitchwort and blunt-flowered rush. Birds regularly breeding on the site include reed bunting and cuckoo. Snipe and woodcock often feed on the marsh and in the wood (of particular interest in the autumn) and all three species of woodpecker breed. Mallard, coot, teal, moorhen and Canada goose are frequently seen on the pools. The alder trees attract flocks of redpoll and siskin during the winter.

DID YOU KNOW?

- Ipsley Alders is a sedge peat marsh – a rare habitat in the West Midlands and the only one in Worcestershire.
- It's the only known site in Worcestershire for the black darter dragonfly.

The Knapp and Papermill

Alfrick; **OS Map** SO 751522; **Map Ref** O14

ACCESS/CONDITIONS: The reserve can be very muddy and there are very steep slopes in the woodlands. Stout footwear is essential.
HOW TO GET THERE: From Worcester, follow the A4103 Hereford Road to Bransford. At the Bransford roundabout, turn right for Alfrick/Suckley and then left along the Bransford/Smith End Green/Alfrick Pound Road. The entrance is on the left after about 3miles and just beyond the bridge crossing the Leigh Brook.
WALKING TIME: 67-acre (27ha) reserve. The full circuit of about 2 miles takes 1 and a half hours at an easy pace.
30-MINUTE VISIT: Walk through the orchard to the weir and up to Big Meadow.
A MEMBER SAYS: 'Whatever time of year you visit there is something to enjoy – I particularly love the carpets of bluebells in the woods in May.'

The Knapp and Papermill's special quality is the variety of wildlife habitats all on one site – meadows, woodland, the Leigh Brook and old orchards. It is certainly one of the prettiest of our nature reserves, in a beautiful setting, where a walk is full of places to stop and enjoy the natural scenery. In spring, violets and primroses bloom in the woodlands and marsh marigolds flower by the pond. Summer migrants such as chiffchaffs, willow warblers and blackcaps arrive. By late-April anemones carpet the woodland floors and toothwort, a rare parasitic plant, blooms by the hazel trees. False oxlips, a hybrid of cowslip and primrose, occur in the orchard, heavy with the scent of damson, apple and pear blossom. By May, the anemones give way to bluebells and the wild service trees are in full flower. With summer, kingfishers are feeding their young on the Leigh Brook. Big Meadow is first yellow with buttercups, yellow-rattle and bird's-foot trefoil, interspersed by ox-eye daisy, pink clover, green winged and common-spotted orchids. The yellows fade away by July to the purple haze of knapweed, on which butterflies and insects feed. With the onset of autumn, the orchard and woodlands bear fruit. In October, the woodlands put on a spectacular array of colour as the leaves turn, and myriad fungi can be found on the woodland floor.

DID YOU KNOW?

- This is an important site for wild service trees, which are a good indicator of ancient woodland.
- There are at least four species of earthstar, including one nationally rare species.
- The Leigh Brook is an SSSI for its riparian value: kingfisher, grey wagtail and otter are some of the species found on the brook.

Warwickshire

About the Trust

Warwickshire Wildlife Trust is the leading local environmental charity, protecting wildlife and natural places, throughout Warwickshire, Coventry and Solihull.

Warwickshire Wildlife Trust ☎ 02476 302912
www.warwickshire-wildlife-trust.org.uk

Ashlawn Cutting
Rugby
OS Map SP 516732; **Map Ref** N50

Grass vetchling, fairy flax, agrimony; 22 butterfly species, including marbled white and brown argus; forester moth, dragonflies; redwing, fieldfare, chiffchaff, willow warbler and reed bunting.

Claybrookes Marsh SSSI
Coventry
OS Map SP 380769; **Map Ref** N47

Insects include bees, wasps, beetles, hoverflies, dragonflies and marbled white and small heath butterflies. Plants include bird's-foot trefoil, hare's-foot clover, common-spotted orchid, southern marsh-orchid, yellow loosestrife and tutsan.

Draycote Meadows SSSI
Near Rugby
OS Map SP 448706; **Map Ref** N52

Green winged orchid, moonwort, twayblade, adder's tongue, buttercup, cowslip, meadow vetchling, yellow-rattle, common-spotted and bee orchids; butterflies; fungi, including waxcaps, meadow coral, smokey spindles and white spindles.

Hampton Wood and Meadow
Near Sherbourne
OS Map SP 254600; **Map Ref** N60

Primrose, bluebell, wood anemone, lesser celandine, yellow archangel and barren strawberry; butterflies, including brimstone, comma, holly blue and white admiral; birds, including kingfisher and great spotted woodpecker.

Leam Valley
Leamington Spa
OS Map SP 330658; **Map Ref** N54

Dragonflies and damselflies, including banded demoiselle, darters, chasers, hawkers and the emperor dragonfly; an abundance of butterflies, including brimstone, peacock, comma and red admiral; birds, including skylark, barn owl, little ringed plover.

Rough Hill Wood SSSI
Near Redditch
OS Map SP 052637; **Map Ref** N55

Small-leaved and large-leaved lime, bluebell, wood anemone, bilberry, heather, broad-leaved helleborine and betony. Fungi, including horn-of-plenty; an abundance of birds.

Swift Valley
Rugby
OS Map SP 505775; **Map Ref** N46

Meadow cranesbill, musk mallow, goat's-beard, meadowsweet, yellow water-lily, wild angelica, gipsywort, water figwort and skullcap; small copper and holly blue butterflies, small red-eyed damselfly, southern hawker and other dragonflies.

Ufton Fields SSSI
Southam
OS Map SP 378615; **Map Ref** N57

Man and bee orchids, greater butterfly orchid, common-spotted orchid, twayblade, lesser celandine and cowslip; invertebrates, including 41 species that are nationally scarce, 28 butterfly species and 14 species of dragonflies and damselflies.

Welcombe Hills
Stratford upon Avon
OS Map SP 205565; **Map Ref** N59

Adder's tongue, woolly thistle, quaking-grass; raven, buzzard, sparrowhawk, little owl, treecreeper, greater spotted and green woodpecker; comma butterfly.

Clowes Wood and New Fallings Coppice SSSI

Near Solihull; **OS Map** SP 101743; **Map Ref** N51

P i

ACCESS/CONDITIONS: Gently sloping, extensive path network; some areas prone to becoming muddy; narrow bridges and steps.
HOW TO GET THERE: Train to Earlswood then walk or cycle half a mile. From Junction 3 of M42, turn onto A435 towards Birmingham. Take third exit at roundabout into Station Road, then take the first right into Forshaw Heath Road, then left into Wood Lane.
WALKING TIME: 110 acres (44.5ha). It takes 1 and a half to 2 hours.
30-MINUTE VISIT: Walk around the perimeter of New Fallings Coppice and Clowes Wood, up to the railway line, then turn back towards the car park.

Broad-leaved woodland on acid soils, bisected by railway line. Diverse habitat includes heathland and wet meadow. Bluebell, wood sorrel and wood anemone herald the arrival of spring, along with less common ramsons and other woodland flowers, such as wood spurge and lily-of-the-valley. Once nearly overwhelmed by aspen and scrub, the wet meadow is now species-rich grassland once again, and flowers including heath-spotted orchid, marsh violet and lemon-scented fern can be seen in summer. In autumn, a wealth of fungi appears both under and on the varied trees, from red cracking bolete and blusher, to shaggy scaly cap. Slime moulds add an intriguing feature and perhaps may even tempt a new interest for some. In winter species of interest include scarlet elfcup and woodcock.

Snitterfield Bushes SSSI

Near Stratford upon Avon; **OS Map** SP 200603; **Map Ref** N56

ACCESS/CONDITIONS: Relatively flat, concrete access paths, some of which are suitable for wheelchairs and buggies.
HOW TO GET THERE: Train to Bearley Halt and walk or cycle three quarters of a mile. Follow signs to Snitterfield from the A46 Stratford bypass. Go through the village on the road to Bearley. The reserve lies on both sides of the road after 1 mile.
WALKING TIME: 124 acres (50ha). The circular walk takes approximately 1 and a half hours.
30-MINUTE VISIT: Head into the northern part of the wood to see coppiced areas and rides rich in wildflowers.

Surrendering to an exquisite carpet of bluebell, primroses and early-purple orchid during springtime, the woodland supports an impressive 250 species of plant, including herb Paris, meadow saffron and bird's-nest orchid, with fragrant agrimony and columbine to be found in summer. Autumn brings a splendid selection of fungi, including boletes, milkcaps, bonnets and puffballs galore, under a kaleidoscopic canopy. Sixty species of bird have been recorded here, with woodcock warranting a winter visit and turtledove and many warblers in the spring. Colourful jay can be seen burying acorns in the autumn, the forgotten seeds giving rise to many oak saplings in the coming warmer months.

Whitacre Heath SSSI

Near Coleshill; **OS Map** SP 209931; **Map Ref** N43

ACCESS/CONDITIONS: Fairly flat, one steep slope, informal paths to five bird hides. Prone to flooding and muddy in winter.
HOW TO GET THERE: Train to Water Orton and bus to Lea Marston and walk or cycle a quarter of a mile. From J9 of M42, take A4097 towards Marston, then turn right into Haunch Lane, picking up the Birmingham Road through Lea Marston. The reserve lies on the right, 0.3 miles outside the village.
WALKING TIME: 109 acres (44ha). Allow 1 to 1 and a half hours for a leisurely walk.
30-MINUTE VISIT: Walk circular route, taking in detour to bird hide overlooking the main pool to view wetland birds.

Nestled in the Tame Valley and lying in the floodplain of the adjoining River Tame, Whitacre Heath is a complex medley of shallow pools, wetland, woodland and grassland. Designated an SSSI, the site is of immense value to an abundance of wildlife, particularly birds. More than 140 species have been recorded since the early 1980s, with 40 species choosing to breed at the reserve. A springtime visit provides opportunity to spot around 40 species of breeding birds, including kingfishers, redshanks, little grebe finches, tits, thrushes and lesser spotted woodpeckers. The woodland, dominated by alder, hides plenty of mosses and liverworts, which thrive in its damp, shaded parts. Guelder rose makes a showing with pink purslane and common-spotted orchid in summer. Twenty five butterflies are registered, including brown argus and white-letter hairstreak. The reserve attracts many delightful dragon and damselflies, such as the impressive emperor dragonfly and the small but startling emerald damselfly. Lapwing can be seen in autumn and, finally, winter may bring sightings of tufted duck, snipe or even the occasional stoat.

WILDLIFE FACT: WOODPECKERS

The best time of year for woodpecker spotting is springtime, when they are out in force drumming on the tree trunks, and the leaf cover is thin enough to see up to the tops of the trees. There are three woodpecker species in the UK: the great spotted woodpecker, the lesser spotted woodpecker and the green woodpecker. All three of them have a tendency to move around a tree to the side, away from any observer, which makes them frustrating to spot, but the green woodpecker does come out of the tree to feed on ants and insects in heath and grassland. Places where you might manage to creep up on them include Ryton Wood and Whitacre Heath.

Pictured: Great spotted woodpecker

Brandon Marsh SSSI

Coventry; **OS Map** SP 386761; **Map Ref** N48

OPENING TIMES: Open all year. Visitor centre: 9am to 5pm, Monday to Friday; 10am to 4pm, Saturday and Sunday.
ACCESS/CONDITIONS: There are a number of well-surfaced, waymarked paths, which intersect the site. Relatively flat, wheelchair friendly. Stretched prone to flooding and mud in winter.
HOW TO GET THERE: Train to Rugby and Coventry then bus links to Brandon Village and walk/cycle, or take the bus to Willenhall or Wolston and walk/cycle to the reserve. 3 miles south-east of Coventry. The reserve is situated on Brandon Lane, which can be accessed off the A45 or through Brandon Village.
WALKING TIME: 225-acre (91ha) reserve with over 2 miles of paths. Walks can take anything from 1 hour to a full afternoon.
30-MINUTE VISIT: Explore the visitor centre and mouse maze and check out the birds from the Wright Hide.
A MEMBER SAYS: 'It's a wonderful place to relax and watch birds.'

This magnificent wetland SSSI, with its patchwork of pools, marsh, reedbed, grassland and woodland, is one of the jewels in the crown of the Trust's nature reserves. In spring, amphibians flourish, including great crested, palmate and smooth newts. Pond-dipping opportunities allow you to probe the aquatic world of the water boatman, whirligig beetle and pond snails. In summer, areas of undisturbed grassland support a mass of butterflies, with a dozen or so species expected on a visit. The squeaks and disputes of common shrew and field vole can easily be heard among the long grass, and fox, stoat and wily weasel hunt the prolific rabbit population. Autumn sees extensive fungi, with up to 600 species identified from field bird's-nest in the sensory garden, through to waxcaps in the short grass and jelly babies hiding in the woods. In winter birds abound, with teal, pochard, shoveler, geese, grebes, kingfisher, bittern and siskin.

DID YOU KNOW?

- Brandon Marsh is home to the largest reedbed in Warwickshire.
- 230 species of bird have been recorded.
- Brandon has a reputation for attracting rare birds on migration, and the sightings board often boasts osprey and long-eared owl.

Pooley Fields SSSI

Near Tamworth; **OS Map** SK 244048; **Map Ref** N38

ACCESS/CONDITIONS: Flat, wheelchair access adjacent to canal; kissing gates; muddy in winter.
HOW TO GET THERE: Train to Tamworth, then bus 785 to Alvecote and walk or cycle. Between Polesworth and Tamworth in north Warwickshire. Access to the site off Robeys Lane. Car park at nearby Pooley Heritage Centre (charge applies).
WALKING TIME: 65-acre (26ha) reserve. Walks can take up to 2 hours.
30-MINUTE VISIT: Head up the spoil heap to see the amazing views over Warwickshire and Staffordshire.
A MEMBER SAYS: 'Pooley Fields is an oasis for wetland birds and makes an excellent day out.'

Pooley Fields SSSI and Alvecote Meadows SSSI, another Trust nature reserve, make up part of Alvecote Pools, Warwickshire's largest SSSI, totalling 318 acres (129ha), but a substantial part of it actually crosses the border into Staffordshire. This impressive mosaic of pools, wetland, marsh, woodland and grassland makes this scenic reserve a patchwork oasis for numerous marsh-loving plants, amphibians and wetland birds. Common frogs and toads, along with smooth and great crested newts, all relish these damp spots, which also provide excellent hunting grounds for grass snakes in spring. In summer rare insectivorous wavy bladderwort looms below the surface, its only location in Warwickshire. Swamp with greater pond-sedge grades into marsh, permitting flowers, such as hemlock, water-dropwort and a colony of southern marsh-orchid. Bracken also thrives here, giving rise to rich colour later in the year. A substantial range of fungi appears in autumn, including earthball, brittlegills and fly agaric (pictured above). This is a great location for birdwatching, especially in winter. Birds are countless, and include great crested grebe, reed bunting, sedge warbler, pied wagtail and flocks of linnet and finches.

Pictured right: Elephant hawk-moth

DID YOU KNOW?

- **Once the location for Pooley Hall Colliery, coal was mined at the site between 1848 and 1965. Subsidence and flooding later created today's complex of habitats, with their considerable diversity.**
- **28 species of nationally rare invertebrates have been recorded here.**

Ryton Wood SSSI

Near Ryton-on-Dunsmore; **OS Map** SP 386728; **Map Ref** N49

ACCESS/CONDITIONS: There is an extensive network of paths and rides and visitors are advised to keep to waymarked walks to avoid becoming lost. Relatively flat, some wet and muddy stretches.
HOW TO GET THERE: Take the train to Coventry, then bus X17 or 539 to Bubbenhall and walk. One mile south of Ryton-on-Dunsmore.
WALKING TIME: 210-acre (84.8ha) reserve. A full circuit of the wood takes 1 to 2 hours.
30-MINUTE VISIT: Wander around the waymarked trails.
A MEMBER SAYS: 'This woodland is a magical place all year round.'

This ancient wood is one of eight large woods, which together form the Princethorpe Woodlands. These vital woods are the largest surviving area of semi-natural woodlands left in Warwickshire today. Joyfully celebrating spring, primrose, wood anemone and yellow pimpernel carpet the woodland floor. Some of the large, clear glades give rise to fabulous bluebell displays and dense bracken. Smooth newt, common frog and toad breed here, all providing veritable banquets for the grass snakes regularly observed at the site. In summer, Ryton Wood is significant to substantial lists of insects. Butterflies are particularly splendid, with white admiral and purple hairstreak plentiful. The woodland ponds offer concentrations of both dragon and damselflies. In autumn, fungi and lichens are plentiful, with forays producing long lists, with occasional specials, including collared earthstar and silky piggyback. In winter points of interest include ancient small-leaved lime, field maple and guilder rose.

DID YOU KNOW?

- Although part of Ryton Wood was lost to sand and gravel extraction in the 1960s, the wood has been returned to its present excellence though traditional management practices.
- These vital woods are the largest surviving area of semi-natural woodlands left in Warwickshire today.
- Colonising after the last Ice Age, small-leaved lime was once the most common tree species in much of lowland England.

NORTH

By far the most best-known landscape of the north of England is the Lake District, with its towering purple hills and sparkling blue lakes. The mountains' height cuts the area off from the rest of England and, as a result, some areas are a veritable wildlife sanctuary, harbouring species that are endangered elsewhere in the UK, such as red squirrels and white-clawed crayfish.

Up in the hills, the exposed nature of the terrain limits fauna to the hardy, such as peregrine falcons, golden eagles, ospreys and some red deer, while the lakes are home to Arctic char fish and vendace fish, and the surrounding areas are popular with many species of owls as well as natterjack toads.

But the area isn't all about the Lake District. When it comes to wildlife spotting, there are many other places the enthusiast should head to. For example, large numbers of wildfowl over-winter on the flats and marshes along the Cumbrian coast that lead down to the wide expanse of Morecambe Bay – also a popular spot for moths and butterflies. Further south still, Ribble Estuary is one of Britain's most important sites for over-wintering wildfowl with more than 150,000 arriving each year.

Over in the north-east, you'll find the bleak, wind-ravaged heathland of Northumberland National Park. The scenery here is nothing if not spectacular. Rivers wind their way through wooded valleys, old quarries dot the landscape and acres and acres of fields broken by hedgerows and meadows provide sanctuary for many a weary bird as it arrives for winter.

The many rivers in the area such as the Wear, the Tyne and the Tees attract water voles, butterflies and dragonflies and wildfowl in large numbers, while at Kielder Water – the largest man-made reservoir in Europe – visitors can again spot red squirrel, deer and a number of rare birds.

Inland in Lancashire, the Forest of Bowland is an area of upland fells and heather-clad moors that descend into steep-sided wooded valleys. One of Britain's most endangered birds of prey, the hen harrier, nests in the uplands here in greater numbers than elsewhere in the country. It offers one of nature's most fantastic aerial shows as it impresses its mate in the spring with rollercoaster moves and tumbling acrobatics. Many other upland birds also nest here – it's the sort of place where you want to double-check you have your binoculars on you, as there will always be something for you to see.

Opposite: Roseberry Topping, North Yorkshire

NOT TO BE MISSED

- **BLACKA MOOR SSSI**
  A natural woodland that forms part of the Peak District Natural Park and yet is within easy reach of Sheffield.
- **CLOSE SARTFIELD**
  One of the Isle of Man's most exciting nature reserves, Close Sartfield has one of the densest and most accessible winter hen harrier roosts in western Europe.
- **FOULSHAW MOSS**
  One of the most exciting and biggest bog restorations in the region, wildlife is flourishing at Foulshaw Moss, particularly bog plants such as sundew and cranberry.
- **GOWY MEADOWS**
  Cheshire's flagship reserve, Gowy Meadows is a lowland grazing marsh that is thought to have been drained in the Middle Ages. A great site for snipe.
- **POTTERIC CARR**
  One of the busiest nature reserves in the country, with over 21,000 people visiting visiting on foot and over a million passing through by rail. Look out for bittern, water rail and kingfisher.
- **WIGAN FLASHES**
  An important reserve for its reedbeds and open-water habitats, Wigan Flashes is alive with rich and exciting wildlife, including bittern, tern and wildflowers.

Northumberland

About the Trust

Established as a registered charity in 1971, the Trust has strong local influence and authority as the only organisation uniquely concerned with wildlife in Northumberland, Newcastle and North Tyneside. The Trust employs around 30 skilled staff, most of whom are based at its offices in St Nicholas Park, Newcastle, and many hundreds of volunteers get involved in all aspects of its work.

Northumberland Wildlife Trust☎ 0191 284 6884
www.nwt.org.uk

Annstead Dunes

Near Seahouses
OS Map NU 227305; **Map Ref** S1

This strip of dunes sits between North Sunderland Point and Dell Point. The beach down as far as the lower water mark provides an important feeding site for many waders, including redshank, ringed plover, curlew and sanderling. The inland pastures are also owned by the Trust, although access is restricted to the public right of way over the south field. Harebell and other dune flora are present in these fields.

Beltingham River Gravels

Near Haydon Bridge
OS Map NY 785640; **Map Ref** S7

The reserve contains a small area of grassland containing metal-loving species uncommon to the region, such as alpine pennycress and spring sandwort. There is also an area of mixed woodland and scrub, with spikes of narrow-lipped helleborine. Enter from road that runs through Beltingham. Please keep to the footpaths.

Big Waters

Near Newcastle-upon-Tyne
OS Map NZ 227734; **Map Ref** S5

This is the largest subsidence pond in the region and good for waterfowl and woodland birds. Other habitat includes furrow grassland, emergent and fen vegetation, carr and plantation. Visit the bird-feeding stations and pond-dipping platform. To find it head west through Brunswick village off B1318 in Wideopen. Turn right at Big Waters pub, the car park is at the entrance. Turn right at the sign for the Country Park.

Ford Moss

Near Belford
OS Map NT 970375; **Map Ref** S2

A lowland raised bog and extensive woodland dominated by heather, cotton grass, hare's tail and cross-leaved heath, with patches of sphagnum, sundew, cranberry and bog myrtle. Residents include red squirrel, fox and adders, along with curlew, red grouse and snipe. Public bridleways run along the northern and southern boundaries. A notice is posted on gate when shooting is taking place – do not enter the reserve at these times.

Juliet's Wood

Near Hexham
OS Map NY 977587; **Map Ref** S10

An area of ancient, semi-natural woodland with oak, rowan, birch, cherry, holly and hazel. Woodland plants such as dog's mercury and wood anemone are seen, along with a range of woodland birds and mammals. From Slaley Village, take the public footpath to Marley Cote Walls. The entrance is on the left after about a third of a mile.

Priestclose Wood

Near Prudhoe
OS Map NZ 107627; **Map Ref** S9

This ancient woodland with a pond offers good ground flora and a variety of birds. There are patches of wood anemone and lesser celandine in early spring, followed by greater and wood stitchwort, wood sorrel and bluebells. A footpath network leads visitors through the wood.

Briarwood Banks SSSI

Near Bardon Mill; **OS Map** NY 791620; **Map Ref** S8

ACCESS/CONDITIONS: Enter via the footpath on the west bank of the River Allen. Paths are generally steep with strenuous walking. The marked circular trail is impassable at the Kingswood Burn after heavy rain.
HOW TO GET THERE: By bus, 685 to Bardon Mill (2 miles). By car, from the A69, east of Haydon Bridge, take the road left signposted to Alston, then the minor road to the right signposted Plankey Mill.
WALKING TIME: The circular trail takes 1 hour at an easy pace.
30-MINUTE VISIT: Head over the suspension bridge, turn right into the reserve, go over the second bridge and head uphill towards Woodland Waterfall. Watch out for red squirrels along the way.

One of the best areas of ancient semi-natural woodland in the county, Briarwood Banks SSSI is a mixed deciduous wood with a diverse field layer. Woodland fauna includes pied flycatcher, the great spotted woodpecker and a wide range of mammals including red squirrel, roe deer and dormouse.

Ash dominates some of the site, although oak and birch are most common in the acidic areas, while beech is invading some areas. Standing dead wych-elm trees, the victims of Dutch elm disease, play host to a variety of invertebrates. Yew and alder are among other tree species found here. The field layer contains many species typical of ancient woodland, such as ramsons, woodruff and dog's mercury, although bluebells are curiously absent. The rare grass *Festuca altissima* can also be found.

Whitelee Moor NNR

Near Carter Bar; **OS Map** NT 700040; **Map Ref** S3

ACCESS/CONDITIONS: The reserve is remote and wild, and weather can change quickly. Visitors should have hill-walking experience if attempting long walks.
HOW TO GET THERE: By car, it is on the A68 (Newcastle to Jedburgh) at the crossing of the Scottish border. Park at the tourist car park on the border at Carter Bar, or on the track at the reserve's southeastern corner.
WALKING TIME: A leisurely visit to the 3,734-acre (1,511ha) reserve takes 2 hours.
30-MINUTE VISIT: Enter at Carter Bar and walk along the footpath to admire the wonderful views.

Whitelee Moor (SSSI, NNR, SAC) is a site of European conservation importance due to its active blanket bog and heather heaths. It also contains other habitats and species of national and international importance.

Notable breeding birds include merlin and stonechat. Black grouse, skylark, meadow pipit, dunlin, curlew, golden plover, grey wagtail, dipper and ring ouzel regularly visit the reserve.

Otters often hunt along the Rede. A herd of feral goats based at neighbouring Kielderhead Moor is now constrained by a goat fence to an area including Whitelee Moor. The Northumberland Wildlife Trust planted 86 acres (35ha) of new native woodland in the winter of 2002/3.

Hauxley

Near Amble; **OS Map** NU 285023; **Map Ref** S4

ACCESS/CONDITIONS: The Reception Hide and one other are suitable for wheelchair access. Some paths are suitable for wheelchair and other disabled access.
HOW TO GET THERE: By bus, Arriva Northumbria 518 to Amble (2 miles from the reserve). By car, from the main coastal route (A1068) just south of Amble, follow directions to Hauxley. After High Hauxley village, turn right onto a track (shared access with Mountgate Caravans) from where the reserve is signposted.
WALKING TIME: A visit takes 2 hours at an easy pace.
30-MINUTE VISIT: Visit the main Reception Hide to see some of the birds on the ponds.
A MEMBER SAYS: 'Hauxley is just one of many fantastic sites for wildlife watching on offer along the beautiful coastal stretch of Druridge Bay.'

Hauxley reserve is not only a unique location for watching wildlife, but also is an area of archeological and historical conservation importance. In 1983 erosion at the site revealed a Bronze Age cist in sand cliffs, which is now on display at the reserve. At the coast edge near Low Hauxley visitors can also see the remains of a Bronze Age cemetery.

The reserve is part of the former Radcliffe opencast coal working, which was landscaped to produce a lake with islands. It was bought by the Trust in 1983 to be developed as a public reserve. Tree and shrub planting has been carried out around the reserve boundary and near the hides. The body of water, islands, reedbeds and trees attracts large numbers of birds, including waders and many migrants. Birds include Bewick's swan, shoveler, lapwing and purple sandpiper. Small ponds created around the car park are suitable for pond-dipping.

There is a diverse flora, including kidney vetch, yellow-wort, ragged robin and bloody cranesbill, and the site is particularly attractive in summer. An interesting and spectacular, though non-native plant, is the cut-leaved teasel. The site is also home to a variety of invertebrates, including butterflies and dragonflies. Great crested newts are also present.

DID YOU KNOW?

- **Hauxley is on the migration route for birds flying from the Arctic and Scandinavian to Africa.**
- **Hauxley is an over-wintering location for birds from northern Europe and Russia.**
- **Hauxley is home to an Bronze Age cist.**

Cumbria

About the Trust

Cumbria Wildlife Trust is the only voluntary organisation devoted solely to the conservation of the wildlife and wild places of Cumbria. Supported by over 15,000 members, the Trust cares for over 40 nature reserves, campaigns for the protection of endangered habitats and species such as limestone pavements and red squirrels, and works with adults and children to discover the importance of the natural world.

Cumbria Wildlife Trust☎ 01539 816300
www.cumbriawildlifetrust.org.uk

Brown Robin

Grange over Sands
OS Map SD 411791; **Map Ref** S30

Brown Robin is approximately half woodland and half grassland, and was once part of a traditional working farm. A trail around the reserve is clearly marked and provides superb views of Whitbarrow Scar and across Morecambe bay to Arnside and, on a good day, even as far as Ingleborough. In spring, before the trees are in full leaf, the woodland floor has a magnificent display of bluebells, wood anemone, ramsons and primroses. Historically, the woodland would have been coppiced on a regular basis and recently coppicing has been reintroduced to a small enclosure within the wood.

Dorothy Farrer's Spring Wood

Staveley, Kendal
OS Map SD 482984; **Map Ref** S11

The three separate woodland enclosures that make up Dorothy Farrer's Spring Wood are fine examples of oak woodland typical of the area. Dorothy Farrer's Spring Wood itself was given to Cumbria Wildlife Trust in 1969. High Wood was purchased in 1993, and in 2000 Beddards Wood was given to the Trust. The wood was managed as coppice woodland in the past with timber from the coppicing used for bobbing, swill baskets and charcoal. Bluebells are abundant in much of the wood, with patches of wild garlic, early-purple orchids and the scarcer herb Paris.

Drumburgh Moss

Near Kirkbride
OS Map NY 255586; **Map Ref** S26

Drumburgh Moss is one of the four peat bogs on the south side of the Solway estuary, which together are considered the best in England. While peat bogs, or raised mires, used to be extensive in Cumbria, less than 11,600 acres (4,700ha) of this habitat type remain today. Drumburgh accounts for roughly two per cent of this. Mire habitats make up the bulk of the reserve, but wet woodland and grassland is also present. Sphagnum moss is highly absorbent, so it can extract nutrients from the rain. Sundews have adapted by trapping and digesting flies on sticky filaments on their leaves.

Humphrey Head

Near Grange over Sands
OS Map SD 388746; **Map Ref** S31

Humphrey Head is a limestone promontory, which is important both for its flora and fauna and for its geological exposures. The main botanical interest is the flora of the western cliffs. The combination of geographical position, proximity to the sea and the underlying limestone rock has resulted in an unusual combination of plants being present. On the cliff top, plants such as common and hoary rock-rose, blue moor-grass, limestone bedstraw, green-winged orchid and wild thyme occur. Sheep have access to these areas and maintain a relatively short turf. Further down, out of the reach of the sheep, taller herbs grow, such as bloody cranesbill and spiked speedwell. Yew, hazel and Lancastrian whitebeam cling on by sending their roots into cracks in the rock. Ivy is also frequent here.

Clints Quarry

Near Egremont; **OS Map** NY 008124; **Map Ref** S24

ACCESS/CONDITIONS: The circular path around the quarry has some steep sections with steps and can be muddy in places.
HOW TO GET THERE: Buses run from Whitehaven to Egremont, which is 1 mile from the reserve. By car, from Egremont take the A5086 towards Cleator, then the first left signed for Moor Row. Parking is in a layby on the right just after the junction or 100m further on, opposite the reserve entrance.
WALKING TIME: A leisurely walk around takes 1 to 1 and a half hours.
30-MINUTE VISIT: Walk into the quarry to experience the grassland, woodland and quarry face and return by same path.

Hidden from view, Clints Quarry is a real haven for wildlife, which has developed since 1930 when limestone extraction ceased. Six species of orchid are found here, including the uncommon pyramidal and bee orchid, with high summer the best time to enjoy them.

The quarry face is of interest to geologists, being one of the best exposures of this limestone in west Cumbria, but it is also used by nesting birds, including raven and kestrel. The ponds are home to palmate newts and sticklebacks and occasionally kingfishers can be seen. On sunny days in summer, the quarry provides a sheltered spot for gatekeeper and common blue butterflies, and five spot burnet moths. In spring, kestrels and ravens make their nests on the quarry face.

In autumn and winter, the quarry's industrial archaeology becomes more visible as the leaves fall from the trees.

Hutton Roof Crags

Near Kendal; **OS Map** SD 548776; **Map Ref** S29

ACCESS/CONDITIONS: The paths are on rocky terrain, some are quite steep. The public footpath onto Burton Fell can be very muddy.
HOW TO GET THERE: Bus 555 leaves hourly from Kendal to Burton in Kendal. By car, from M6 J36, take A65 then A6070 towards Burton. At the Clawthorpe Hall hotel turn left at road signed for Clawthorpe. Park on the roadside where the bridleway leaves for Burton, or at the top of the hill where Hutton Roof Common is accessed directly from the road.
WALKING TIME: Allow 1 and a half hours for the trail marked by red posts and 3 hours to walk from Clawthorpe Road to Hutton Roof village.
30-MINUTE VISIT: Park in Hutton Roof village and follow the public footpath onto the common. The Rakes, a very steeply angled limestone pavement, can be seen from here.

Hutton Roof Crags contains some of the best areas of limestone pavement in Britain, which harbours a wealth of rare and unusual plants and animals. Pavement occurs as part of a mosaic of other habitats that include woodland, scrub, grassland and heath. The reserve is made up of two 19th-century 'enclosures'. Lancelot Clark Storth was purchased in 1978, with help from the World Wildlife Fund. Burton Fell, which is a common, was given to Cumbria Wildlife Trust in 1992 by the New Zealand descendants of William Atkinson.

In April and May, the woodlands turn colourful as the bluebells flower. This time also sees the emergence of the first butterflies, including brimstone, speckled wood and pearl-bordered fritillary. As high summer approaches, high brown, dark green and small pearl-bordered fritillary all appear. On the limestone pavement, graylings bask in the sun, almost camouflaged against lichened rock.

In the pavement grykes, look for rigid buckler and hart's tongue ferns, together with dark red helleborine, angular Solomon's seal and lily-of-the-valley. All year, there are excellent views across to the Pennines, the Lakeland fells and across Morecambe Bay.

Foulshaw Moss

Near Witherslack; **OS Map** SD 458837; **Map Ref** S28

P i

ACCESS/CONDITIONS: The circular boardwalk/path from the car park has no steep slopes and is dry (not muddy); less formal paths onto other areas may be rough/wet and wellies are advised.
HOW TO GET THERE: Buses run from Kendal, Grange, Ulverston and Barrow to Witherslack. By car, from Kendal take A590 towards Barrow-in-Furness. At the end of the dual carriageway section at Gilpin Bridge, continue for 0.6 miles. Immediately before a signed parking layby, a track leaves road on left-hand side. Go through gate and follow track to car park.
WALKING TIME: Forty minutes.
30-MINUTE VISIT: From the car park follow the wood chip/boardwalk path onto the edge of the bog. Return via the gravel track.
A MEMBER SAYS: 'I didn't know what they meant by "It's amazing just how quickly wildlife has come back here". What used to be a dense forestry plantation, is now a really interesting place to visit and is getting better every year!'

This is the most exciting and biggest bog restoration in Cumbria, and the site is changing all the time. Since trees were removed in 2003 and ditches blocked, the wildlife is really flourishing – bog plants like sphagnum moss, sundews and cranberry are all expanding and birds and dragonflies are making use of the new habitats.

A new viewing platform will give a better feel for the huge scale of the site. Red deer, adders and common lizards, all live here too, although may be more elusive. Summer is the best time to see large red damselflies, dragonflies, butterflies and other insects. Look out for emperor dragonflies on the pond and large heath butterflies flying over the bog. Common lizards and adders are also more likely to be seen at this time.

In autumn, the eerie bellowing of red deer stags signifies that the rut is in full swing and swallows and other migrant birds use the reserve as a roost on their way south. While most plants die back in winter, this is a great time to have a close look at colourful sphagnum moss. There are many species ranging from pink, through deep wine red, orange and yellow, to various shades of green.

DID YOU KNOW?

- **During World War II, Foulshaw was home to a large colony of lesser black-backed gulls. Local people collected the eggs as a valuable food source.**

Smardale Gill

Near Kirkby Stephen; **OS Map** NY 727070; **Map Ref** S25

ACCESS/CONDITIONS: The reserve provides 3.5 miles of level walking. The railway line does not have a consistent surface, being grass on some sections and railway ballast/cinder on others. There are ramps at the Smardale Hall and Newbiggin end.
HOW TO GET THERE: The nearest railway station is Kirkby Stephen West. Buses run from Kendal, Sedbergh and Brough.
By car, from the A685, approximately 2.5 miles north-east of Ravenstonedale or 1 mile south-west of Kirkby Stephen West train station, take the turning signposted Smardale. Ignore the turning to Waitby. Cross over the railway and turn left at the junction. Ignore the sign for Smardale hamlet and cross the disused railway. Turn immediately left and then left again for the car park.
WALKING TIME: The 3.5-mile length takes 2 hours. The circular trail leaving the reserve just beyond the cottages, crossing County Bridge and returning to the reserve at the viaduct, takes 2 and a half hours from Smardale Hall.
30-MINUTE VISIT: Walk from the Smardale Hall car park as far as the Settle-Carlisle viaduct and back.
A MEMBER SAYS: 'Sitting near the viaduct on an early summer's day, a refreshing light breeze blowing up from the valley, carrying with it the song of willow warbler, redstart and wren, you can't get nearer to paradise than that!'

In spring, banks are yellow with primroses. Look closely among the dog's mercury for the four-leaved herb Paris, a plant usually indicating very old woodland, but here happily invading the old railway track! Ravens nest early and can be seen displaying over the reserve in winter and early spring. Summer migrants such as pied flycatcher and redstart arrive in late April. The railway line is alive with butterflies in summer, the speciality of the reserve being Scotch argus, but northern brown argus and dark-green fritillary are also present. Flowers to look out for include fragrant orchid and bird's-eye primrose. Autumn colours are at their best in October and November, with stunning views down the valley. Look for the bright red leaves of bloody cranesbill on the line sides. Red squirrels can also be seen at this time stocking up for winter. With the leaves off the trees, winter is a good time to look out for birds such as long-tailed tit, treecreeper and great spotted woodpecker.

DID YOU KNOW?

- **The Tebay-Darlington railway was opened in 1862 and closed almost exactly 100 years later.**
- **The Scotch argus butterfly occurs at just one other site in England (Arnside Knott).**

North

South Walney

Near Barrow in Furness; **OS Map** SD 225620; **Map Ref** S32

P WC

ACCESS/CONDITIONS: The Bank, Pier and Sea hides are all suitable for wheelchair access. Orange Badge holders may drive cars as far as Pier Hide. Other hides have steps or uneven terrain.
HOW TO GET THERE: Buses run from Barrow in Furness to Biggar, and then it is an hour to a 1 and a half hour walk to the reserve entrance. By car, from Barrow in Furness, follow signs for Walney Island. Cross Jubilee Bridge onto the Island and follow the brown signs, turning left at the traffic lights. Follow this road for about 0.6 miles then turn left down Carr Lane. Pass Biggar village and follow the road for a further 0.6 miles.
WALKING TIME: Choose from the 3-mile red trail and 2-mile blue trail.
30-MINUTE VISIT: Head to the Observation Hide in summer for a flavour of the gullery. It has information boards explaining gull behaviour. In winter, you may see wigeon, teal and eider from the Bank Hide overlooking Gatemarsh and Gate Pool.
A MEMBER SAYS: 'South Walney is the gateway to Morecambe Bay and Cumbria's prime birdwatching site. There's no finer place in the county to see high tide roosts of thousands of waders.'

Almost 25 species of bird are known to breed on the reserve. In spring, the gulls return to take up territory, and male eider – resplendent in breeding plumage – court females, often at a ratio of at least 5:1. Meanwhile, migrants, such as wheatear, pass through. Some 28,000 pairs of gulls breed, lay eggs and rear young over the reserve in summer. Walking through the colony is an experience not to be forgotten. Nesting eiders are difficult to spot as the camouflaged females sit tight on nests. At this time, shingle flora comes into its own, with henbane, viper's bugloss, hound's-tongue and yellow-horned poppy flowering. In small areas of dune, pyramidal orchid and heartsease pansy can be found. In autumn, the gulls depart (while herring gulls stay local, lesser black-backed gulls over-winter in the Mediterranean). Migrants pass through on their way back south, and others arrive to stay for the winter. In winter, redshank, greenshank, oystercatcher, and curlew enjoy the central pools, together with teal, wigeon and goldeneye.

DID YOU KNOW?

- South Walney has the largest colony of lesser black-backed and herring gull in Europe.
- It is the only place in Cumbria where grey seals can be hauled out on the beach.
- Eider ducks have bred here only since 1949.

Durham

About the Trust

Durham Wildlife Trust's purpose is to protect wildlife and promote nature conservation in County Durham, the City of Sunderland and the boroughs of Gateshead, South Tyneside and Darlington. It is one of the most active environmental organisations in the region, managing 25 nature reserves, a variety of species and habitat recovery projects and four visitor centres.

Durham Wildlife Trust ☎ 0191 584 3112
www.durhamwt.co.uk

Baal Hill Wood

Wolsingham
OS Map NZ 074386; **Map Ref** S17

This large, ancient, semi-natural oak and birch woodland enjoys a covering of bluebells in spring and a large woodland bird population. The reserve includes Bishops Oak, one of the county's largest trees. Its footpath is uneven, muddy with steep slopes and steps.

Blackhall Rocks

Easington
OS Map NZ 474389/463400;
Map Ref S18

This coastal site is rich in flora including quaking grass, salad burnet and bloody cranesbill. Butterwort, broad-leaved wintergrass, grass of Parnassus, brookweed, bird's-eye primrose, and four species of sea anemone are seen. Spy its 15 species of butterfly, including northern brown argus, and cistus forester, a rare green moth.

Edmondsley Wood

Edmondsley
OS Map: NZ 228494; **Map Ref:** S12

A mixed deciduous woodland on an ancient woodland site comprising ash, oak, hazel, holly and honeysuckle. Ground flora includes bluebells, wood sorrel, broad-leaved helleborine and cow wheat.

Joe's Pond SSSI

Near Houghton-le-Spring
OS Map NZ 328487; **Map Ref** S13

Over 140 bird species have been recorded on this 10-acre (4ha) wetland SSSI, including wintering teal and pochard, breeding great crested grebe and mute swan. All five species of owl are frequently seen, along with water vole, roe deer and fox. A short circular route traverses the pond, some of which is wheelchair accessible.

Malton

Near Lanchester
OS Map NZ 180460; **Map Ref** S16

A former colliery site, the reserve has a variety of habitats including ponds, woodland, grassland and heath. It's home to all five species of newt, butterflies and dragonflies. Tawny owls breed on site, and green and great spotted woodpeckers are frequently seen too.

Raisby Hill Grassland

Near Coxhoe
OS Map NZ 333354; **Map Ref** S19

This is a superb example of primary magnesian limestone grassland with an area of fen and open water containing typical plant species, such as blue moor-grass, rock-rose, burnet saxifrage and milkwort. The small disused quarry contains an important population of dark red helleborine and a colony of northern brown argus butterflies; brown hare and fox are frequently seen.

Shibdon Pond SSSI

Near Gateshead
OS Map NZ 192628; **Map Ref** S6

Shibdon is one of the best wetland SSSI sites in the region, comprising extensive reedbeds, open water and species-rich grasslands. Come to spot kingfisher, cormorant, breeding shoveller, water rail and good numbers of waders, as well as 16 species of butterfly and eight species of dragonfly. Otter signs are frequently recorded. It has a good footpath network including boardwalks partly suitable for wheelchair access.

Bishop Middleham Quarry SSSI

Sedgefield; **OS Map** NZ 331326; **Map Ref** S20

ACCESS/CONDITIONS: The waymarked route that provides access to the reserve has some steep slopes and a series of steps. Please keep to the paths, there are many dangerous cliff faces.
HOW TO GET THERE: North of Bishop Middleham village to the west of the A177.
WALKING TIME: The footpath circuit of about 1 mile takes approximately 1 hour depending on how often you stop to look at the wildflowers.
30-MINUTE VISIT: Visit the quarry floor to see the limestone flora.

This reserve is considered to be one of the country's most important disused quarry habitats for wildlife and has been designated as an SSSI since 1968. The magnesian limestone quarry was abandoned in the 1930s and since that time has been re-colonised by a variety of limestone flora representative of magnesian limestone grassland.

This is an internationally rare habitat type particularly rich in orchid species such as pyramidal, common spotted, fragrant and bee orchid and, most importantly, large numbers of dark red helleborines. Among the many other plants that flourish on the thin limestone soils are blue moor-grass, moonwort, autumn gentian and fairy flax.

Extensive areas of common rock-rose in the quarry support one of the country's largest colonies of northern brown argus butterfly, which can be seen on the wing in June and July. Other butterflies seen throughout the year include dingy skipper, common blue, small heath, ringlet and small and large skippers.

Hawthorn Dene

Near Easington; **OS Map** NZ 427458; **Map Ref** S15

ACCESS/CONDITIONS: There are hard-surfaced footpath in parts. The many steep slopes and steps can make access difficult to the woodland in winter when it gets muddy. The main path to the grassland is entirely surfaced.
HOW TO GET THERE: Between Easington and Seaham on the Durham Coast. Leave the A19 at either Easington or Seaham joining the B1432 and turning off into Hawthorn by the road north of the village. This road leads to the reserve.
WALKING TIME: The full circuit of approximately 3 miles takes 2 hours at an easy pace.
30-MINUTE VISIT: Take the shorter walk missing out the eastern grassland.

This is the second-largest coastal dene in the county. It comprises a steep-sided ravine woodland cutting through the magnesian limestone. It is therefore characterised by lime-loving species, with ash, elm and sycamore dominant in the canopy and a significant number of mature native yew on the steep northern slopes.

The woodland floor is covered with wild garlic, bluebells and snowdrops in the spring, with uncommon species such as early-purple orchid, bird's-nest orchid and herb Paris occurring locally in the dene.

The reserve provides suitable conditions for a wide range of woodland birds including jay, treecreeper, green and great spotted woodpeckers, and summer passerines. Mammals on the reserve include roe deer, fox and badger.

The eastern end contains an area of species-rich calcareous grassland, including fairy flax, quaking grass, bloody cranesbill and dyer's greenweed. This attracts large numbers of butterflies and is best seen in July and August.

Hannah's Meadow SSSI

Baldersdale; **OS Map** NY 937186; **Map Ref** S23

OPENING TIMES: Open all year, but there is access onto the meadows in June and July only.
ACCESS/CONDITIONS: The footpaths are surfaced but steep in places. Access to the visitor centre is via a boardwalk, which can be slippery in winter. Please close gates behind you when visiting the meadow.
HOW TO GET THERE: From Barnard Castle follow the B6277 to Romaldkirk and then the Balderhead Road via Hunderthwaite. The reserve is adjacent to the public road east of the Balderhead Reservoir car park.
WALKING TIME: The full circuit takes approximately 40 minutes.
A MEMBER SAYS: '... sitting among the wildflowers at Hannah's Meadow on a sunny summer afternoon gives one a real sense of being in a wild place. It is so important that these rare meadows are maintained where so many have been lost in the past.'

The meadows and pasture at Hannah's Meadow have evolved as a result of traditional farming practices over several centuries. They are considered some of the least improved and most species-rich in upland Durham and have been designated as an SSSI.

The grass sward is dominated by meadow fox tail, sweet vernal grass and crested dog's-tail with an abundance of wildflowers, including ragged robin, wood cranesbill, marsh marigold, yellow-rattle, adder's tongue fern and globeflower. The pasture has a more acidic character with rushes and sedges dominating and this supports breeding birds such as lapwing, skylark, redshank, curlew and meadow pipit.

In order to maintain this special wildlife resource, the Trust continues to manage the reserve by traditional methods. Sheep lamb in the spring in the hay meadows, an event that is followed by some muck spreading. Stock are removed until late July when the haycrop is cut. The grass is then allowed to grow and cows graze the fog (late grass) in September and October. Sheep are brought back into the meadows to run with the tup in November, before the winter rest period. The cycle then begins again in the spring. The drystone walls require regular maintenance and the barn has been restored using local stone.

DID YOU KNOW?

- **The meadows were previously owned and farmed by Hannah Hauxwell for over 50 years. Living alone at Low Birk Hat Farm without the luxury of electricity or running water, Hannah managed the land using traditional methods and avoiding artificial fertilisers or re-seeding. The reserve was bought on Hannah's retirement in 1988.**

Low Barns SSSI

Near Bishop Auckland; **OS Map** NZ 160315; **Map Ref** S21

OPENING TIMES: Open all year. Visitor centre is open from 11am to 4pm on weekends only throughout the year.
ACCESS/CONDITIONS: There is a well surfaced and even-graded circular walk suitable for wheelchair access. Hides are ramped and accessible to wheelchairs.
HOW TO GET THERE: West of Bishop Auckland close to the A68. From the A68 follow the brown reserve signposts through Witton-le-Wear village turning right at the Victoria Public House. Once over the level crossing, the centre is again signposted in brown.
WALKING TIME: The nature trail circuit of approximately 1 mile takes 45 minutes at an easy pace.
A MEMBER SAYS: 'The circular nature trail at Low Barns allows me to access a wonderful wildlife haven where I can hope to glimpse an otter or roe deer and sit in comfort in the hides viewing the wildfowl on the lakes.'

Primarily a wetland reserve developed following gravel extraction along the banks of the River Wear, this 124-acre (50ha) site comprises a series of interconnected lakes along with extensive alder woodland and species-rich grasslands.

The reserve is designated as an SSSI mainly for its ornithological interest and three modern hides provide visitors with good views over the lakes. In spring and summer, the resident bird populations are swollen by large numbers of migrants, including redstart, pied flycatcher and several warbler species. In winter, large numbers of wildfowl can be seen, including tufted duck, mallard, goldeneye and goosander. Rare visitors in recent years include bittern, hoopoe and wryneck.

The small ponds and scrapes provide habitat for dragonflies, such as southern hawker, and the grasslands support many butterfly species. Mammals such as stoat, fox and roe deer are frequently seen and the lakes are also visited by otters.

DID YOU KNOW?

- **The site includes the only extensive and biologically important open water body in Western Durham.**
- **The locally famous Great Flood of 1771 altered the course of the River Wear to its current position some 500m to the south.**

Rainton Meadows

Near Houghton-le-Spring; **OS Map** NZ 323485; **Map Ref** S14

ACCESS/CONDITIONS: Visitor centre, WC, lake shore and hide are suitable for wheelchair access via surfaced level footpaths.

HOW TO GET THERE: Midway between Durham and Sunderland just off the A690. Follow the brown signs for Rainton Meadows just south of Houghton-le-Spring or leave the A1(M) at Chesterle-Street and head west on the A183/A1052.

WALKING TIME: The 2 miles of surfaced footpaths provide a variety of routes, which can take up to 2 hours to complete, and take in the adjacent Joe's Pond SSSI.

30-MINUTE VISIT: A shorter route is available along the lower slopes and lake shores.

A MEMBER SAYS: 'Visiting Rainton Meadows at dusk in the late summer is a very rewarding experience with the opportunity to see long-eared owls swooping over the grasslands hunting for small mammals, and flocks of geese coming in to land on the lakes.'

The reserve occupies the site of a former opencast coal site, which is being restored to a nature reserve by the creation of an interlinked series of lakes, scrapes and marshy grassland, large areas of broad-leaved woodland hedgerows and newly created grasslands. While restoration is still at a relatively early stage, the reserve is already attracting large numbers of wildfowl and waders.

During spring and summer, the grasslands provide an ideal breeding habitat for large numbers of skylark and meadow pipit, with lapwing also breeding in numbers. Late summer and autumn attract good numbers of passage waders such as redshank, little ringed plover, snipe and oystercatcher and large numbers of mute swan visit each winter. Long-eared and short-eared owls hunt over the grasslands in winter and all five species of owl have been recorded on the reserve. Water vole and brown hare are frequently recorded.

DID YOU KNOW?

- Rainton Meadows is situated in the heart of what was once the Durham Coalfield, which had eight coal mines within 2 miles of the current reserve.
- Up to 50 mute swans have been recorded on the reserve at any one time during the winter.

Tees Valley

About the Trust

These reserves provide a taster of the area's diverse habitats and range from well established woodlands and grasslands to newly recreated habitats. The Trust works to protect and enhance the wildlife of the area. It believes in demonstrating the value of nature in enhancing the quality of life for local people, and many of the reserves are havens in urban situations.

Tees Valley Wildlife Trust ☎ **01287 636382**
www.teeswildlife.org

Brewsdale

Near Cleveland
OS Map NZ 467107; **Map Ref** R10

Brewsdale is a narrow lowland valley situated in farmland with a tributary of the River Leven flowing through it. The valley has fairly steep slopes, made up of scrub woodland with hazel, hawthorn and ash well distributed along with several large specimens of field maple. Spring and summer bring early-purple orchid, primrose, hairy St John's wort and sanicle. Summer is the time to see ringlet butterfly. Yellow-hammer and tree sparrow populate the hedgerows. Footpaths can be muddy after heavy rain and steps on the reserve can be slippery.

Cattersty Gill

Near Cleveland
OS Map NZ 705204; **Map Ref** R5

The reserve is comprised of large tracts of scrub and areas of lime-rich grassland, which are an important refuge and refuelling stop for migrants. Rarities in the past have included dusky warbler and red-flanked bluetail. Summer brings pyramidal and common-spotted orchid in the grassland and common centaury, yellow-wort, wild marjoram and harefoot clover. Access to site can be difficult. There is a kissing gate entrance.

Gravel Hole

Near Stockton-on-Tees
OS Map NZ 447231; **Map Ref** R2

Gravel Hole is a small disused sand and gravel pit with a mixture of herb-rich grassland and scrub on the north-western edge of Billingham. It features cowslips in spring, and common-spotted and fragrant orchid, fairy flax, ox-eye daisy, and quaking grass in summer. Butterfly residents include wall brown, common blue and tortoiseshell.

The Howls

Near Cleveland
OS Map NZ 466315; **Map Ref** S22

The Howls is a woodland nature reserve situated near the village of Dalton Piercy following the valley of Char Beck. It features an ash and sycamore canopy and an understorey of hawthorn, elder and in parts, gooseberry. Flora includes early-purple orchid, violet, lesser celandine, the locally uncommon twayblade, marsh marigold, meadowsweet – and the foreign invader himalayan balsam in damper spots. Fifty-three bird species have been recorded. Summer is good for warblers and the odd spotted flycatcher. The paths can be muddy after rain. Take care on the steps near the entrance. From Dalton Piercy, take the first left after crossing the river. Park on the hard-standing next to the gates. A path leads to the reserve.

Margrove Ponds

OS Map NZ 654162; **Map Ref** R9

Margrove Ponds is made up of a large shallow lake fringed by reedbeds, reed swamp and small patches of scrub. Summer sees the arrival of sedge warblers, swifts, swallows and sometimes lesser white-throat. Water birds such as tufted duck, coot, mute swan and little grebe can be seen throughout the year. Great crested newt breed in the small pond. The track along the south-west edge of the lake gives good views.

Bowesfield

Near Stockton; **OS Map** NZ 440160; **Map Ref** R8

ACCESS/CONDITIONS: Major footpaths are surfaced and suitable for wheelchair and pushchair access. Minor paths can be muddy during winter.
HOW TO GET THERE: Follow the A135 south to Ingleby Barwick, from the A66, immediately to the west of the River Tees crossing in Stockton. At the second roundabout, turn left onto the Bowesfield development. Paths lead onto the reserve.
WALKING TIME: The 37-acre (15ha) reserve has a network of surfaced pathways. A route of the Teesdale Way follows the bank of the River Tees around the perimeter of the reserve. A full circuit takes 1 hour.
30-MINUTE VISIT: Take a brisk walk around the surfaced paths, which connect a series of pools and reedbeds, for views of the ducks and wading birds.

The reserve has restored some of the natural features to a piece of riverside land that has stood vacant since it was abandoned by faring in 1994. New features include ditches, pools, ponds and wet woodland, all connected by surfaced paths and bridges.

At any time of the year an early walk may reward you with views of otter, just returning to the area. Within days of the first ditch excavations, the distinctive five-toed footprints recorded the return of this elusive mammal. This is also a good time to see fox and roe deer, both present on the site.

In spring and early summer smaller numbers of birds remain at Bowesfield to nest and raise young. Breeding species include reed warbler, reed bunting, lapwing and little ringed plover.

During autumn, numbers of duck and wading birds begin to increase as they return to the River Tees to pass the winter months. In winter more than 2,000 birds have been counted on the reserve, and flocks include lapwing, golden plover, shoveler, teal, curlew and redshank.

Portrack Marsh

Stockton-on-Tees; **OS Map** NZ 465194; **Map Ref** R6

ACCESS/CONDITIONS: Major footpaths are surfaced and suitable for wheelchair and pushchair access. The pathway on the north edge, leading onto the disused railway, is unsurfaced and has some steps. The reserve can be muddy during winter.
HOW TO GET THERE: From the A66, follow signs for the Tees Barrage, head straight over the roundabout, across the barrage and right into Whitewater Way. Follow the road around to Talpore. Portrack Marsh is a short walk from Stockton and Middlesbrough.
WALKING TIME: The full circuit takes approximately 2 hours.
30-MINUTE VISIT: Walk along the riverside footpath to the information board, then follow the footpaths to the riverside and pond-dipping platform.

Portrack Marsh is situated on the north bank of the River Tees just below the Tees Barrage and is the last remaining wetland area on the lower River Tees. The reserve's main lake (West Water) provides good opportunities to see over-wintering duck and summer visitors such as the grasshopper warbler.

The lake is fringe by common reed and reedmace and the fluctuating water levels dictate what birds can be seen. Its large water bodies are a magnet for local and migrating birds during the winter and spring months, the ditches are home to water vole and kingfisher best seen in the summer, and the scrub attracts large numbers of heron to roost. In the autumn, look out for the nests of harvest mice in the reedbeds, and witness the annual salmon run along the River Tees. Different birds can be seen at all times of the year, but particularly in the winter when the vegetation is low and they can be seen feeding in the hawthorn scrub.

Coatham Marsh

Near Redcar; **OS Map** NZ 586248; **Map Ref** R1

ACCESS/CONDITIONS: The paths are mostly surfaced. The section along the Fleet towards Kirkleatham Lane is prone to flooding in the winter. The path between the car park and the footbridge is suitable for wheelchair access.
HOW TO GET THERE: Off the A1085 (Redcar to Middlesbrough). At the crossroads with Kirkleatham Lane, turn left and head up to the next mini-roundabout. Turn left onto Tod Point Road and continue over the railway bridge. The reserve is on the left.
WALKING TIME: The full circuit with stops at the hides takes about 1 and a half hours.
30-MINUTE VISIT: Follow the footpath through the meadow and head towards the hide on Middle Marsh.
A MEMBER SAYS: 'Coatham Marsh is one of those places where you always find something to see no matter what time of year you go. In spring and summer you can expect good views of orchids and dragonflies, and in the winter it's the birds.'

Coatham Marsh is a 134-acre (54ha) reserve with wetland features that attract a diverse and important number of birds. These features include two large lakes fringed with phragmites and low-lying marsh areas which are prone to flooding but are also useful areas of exposed mud on which waders can feed.

Spring is often heralded by the return of the shelduck that come to the Tees Estuary to breed, but Coatham is also a good place for spring migrants on passage and anything can turn up. In the past this has included wood sandpiper, Temminck's stint, black redstart and even a stone curlew.

Summer sees the return of the sedge warblers as well as grasshopper warblers in some years. But summer is when the grasslands come into their own with swathes of marsh orchids and small groups of bee orchids appearing, as well as eyebright and knapweeds.

Autumn is again a time for the birds, with migrants returning to their wintering grounds. Species to look out for are the odd ruff, black-tailed godwit, and curlew sandpiper. Winter is the time for wildfowl, with large numbers of wigeon and teal over-wintering on the flooded grasslands, as well as shoveler, gadwall, tufted duck and pochard.

DID YOU KNOW?

- Coatham Marsh is the site of a battle between the Saxons and the Normans during William the Conqueror's 'Harrying of the North'.
- Some of the smaller mounds on Middle Marsh are remnants of medieval salt workings.

Maze Park

Stockton-on-Tees; **OS Map** NZ 464191; **Map Ref** R7

ACCESS/CONDITIONS: Major footpaths are surfaced and suitable for wheelchair and pushchair access. Damper areas have boardwalks.
HOW TO GET THERE: From the A66, follow signs for the Tees Barrage; the right at the first roundabout leads to the entrance. Maze Park is a short walk from Stockton and Middlesbrough.
WALKING TIME: The full circular circuit of the 42-acre (17ha) reserve takes 40 minutes.
30-MINUTE VISIT: Head along the riverbank using the cycleway.
A MEMBER SAYS: 'I remember when the site was just railway yards and coal wharfs – to see it now with so much wildlife in just a few years is great!'

Maze Park is an urban nature reserve situated on the south bank of the Tees on former railway marshalling yards, the resulting landscaped mounds have been planted up with a variety of broad-leaved species. The other major habitat found on the site is rough grassland, which is managed for butterflies – of which more than 12 species have been recorded. The reserve has an extensive network of footpaths leading around all areas of the site and forms part of the National Cycle Network.

The site has two riverside viewing points, seating, and if you follow the spiral footpath to the artwork feature on top of the largest of the mounds, gives excellent views across the Teesside area. In winter, many birds can be seen on the site and riverside, with species including stonechat, lapwing, redshank, and finches. In spring, see the different vegetation communities on the mounds at their best. Along with a great variety of butterflies found on the site, the grayling can be found in summer. In autumn, see the annual run of the River Tees salmon at the Tees Barrage, and the common seals that follow them.

DID YOU KNOW?

- **The mounds on Maze Park were formed during the creation of Teesside Retail Park.**
- **Maze Park is home to the grayling butterfly. The colony was identified in 2001.**

Saltburn Gill SSSI

Near Redcar; **OS Map** NZ 674208; **Map Ref** R4

ACCESS/CONDITIONS: The paths are often muddy in winter and care should be taken when climbing the steep flight of steps. The site is not really suitable for disabled access.
HOW TO GET THERE: From Redcar, take the A174 to Saltburn. Follow the road down Saltburn Bank onto the seafront, cross over the bridge, take the first right and park in the public car park. Walk towards the Northumbrian Water pumping station (the very large red-brick building) and the signposted public footpath to the entrance.
WALKING TIME: The walk along the public footpath and back takes about 1 hour.
30-MINUTE VISIT: Follow the footpath up to Lum Hole (where the bridleway and footpath cross), then retrace your steps back to the car park.
A MEMBER SAYS: 'It's a refuge, where you can lose a couple of hours just raking around the woods. I see something new every time I go and I've been coming for 25 years!'

Saltburn Gill is a 52-acre (21ha) SSSI woodland and a good example of the type of woodland that would once have covered East Cleveland with a mixture of oak and ash, and a hazel and holly understorey.

A public footpath runs through the reserve's entire length and provides good opportunities to see all it has to offer. Spring and early summer are by far the best times to visit the reserve, when the woodland wildflowers are out. The lesser celandines start it all off with their showy yellow flowers, followed shortly afterwards by carpets of strong-smelling wild garlic and bluebells. Other plants to look out for include woodruff, bugle, moschatel and wood avens, so keep your eyes peeled.

Summer sees the arrival of the migrants, with chiffchaffs often being the first to take up residence. The falling leaves of autumn make it easier to see the mixed tit flocks moving through the canopy as they search out the last insects before winter. Autumn is also the time for fungi and toadstools, as they help with the recycling process. The winter is ideal for spotting ferns.

DID YOU KNOW?

- A wooden footbridge once crossed over the top of the gill to allow the ironstone miners to get to the mines on Warsett Hill.
- There was a water mill at the entrance of the gill until 1903. Evidence of some of the walls can be seen at the reserve entrance.

Lancashire, Manchester & North Merseyside

About the Trust

The Wildlife Trust for Lancashire, Manchester and North Merseyside was formed in 1962 by a group of naturalists who wanted to help protect the wildlife of the old county Lancashire. Its vision is to be the key voice for nature conservation within the region and to help the people and organisations of Lancashire, Manchester and North Merseyside to enjoy, understand and take action to conserve wildlife and its habitats.

Lancashire Wildlife Trust
☎ 01772 324129 www.lancswt.org.uk

Aughton Woods
Near Lancaster
OS Map SD 543663; **Map Ref** Q2

Features of this area, located between Aughton and Caton, include bluebells, small-leaved lime, Douglas fir, golden saxifrage, fern and wood fescue. It is home to woodpeckers, nuthatch, pied flycatcher and common sandpiper. There is an access path for members along the bottom of the wood. A riverside public footpath runs along lower slopes of Lawson's Wood. Use the car park at Crook o'Lune.

Heysham Moss
Near Morecambe
OS Map SD 432603; **Map Ref** Q3

Heysham Moss consists of a variety of habitats including areas of woodland and scrub, wet grassland and, most importantly, the central area of raised bog. While the core area is relatively unmodified, the periphery has been affected by past peat cutting and drainage. The reserve is of considerable botanical interest with the central part of the bog still supporting a number of bog species: 215 flowering plant species; small skipper, grayling and small copper butterflies; 200 moth species; many dragonflies, and birds like the lesser white-throat, water rail and woodcock.

Longworth Clough
Near Bolton
OS Map SD 700150; **Map Ref** Q5

An outstanding mosaic of woodland, wetland and grassland, rich in wildlife, in the West Pennine Moors. Numerous woodland bird species breed on the reserve, including woodcock, tawny owl, tree pipit, wood warbler and long-tailed tit. A dipper has occasionally been seen feeding in the Eagley Brook. Recent survey work has confirmed that Longworth Clough supports a very rich invertebrate community. Butterflies found include small skipper, large white, green-veined white, red admiral, peacock, comma, gatekeeper and meadow brown. Please keep to the footpaths.

Red Scar, Tunbrook, Boilton and Nab Woods
Near Preston
OS Map SD 579314 to 590340;
Map Ref Q4

The woods run in a narrow band along a terrace above the tidal River Ribble and the valley of its tributary, the Tun Brook. They form one of the largest remaining areas of ancient, semi-natural, deciduous woodland in Lancashire, Greater Manchester and Merseyside. They support insect species unusual in Lancashire, and have a rich woodland flora. Bluebell, lesser celandine, ground ivy, sweet woodruff and woodland birds are all features of the woods.

Warton Crag

Near Carnforth; **OS Map** SD 493728; **Map Ref** Q1

i

ACCESS/CONDITIONS: A steep site. Some paths are very exposed and cross bare limestone, which can be very slippery when wet. Woodland paths can be muddy. There are stiles, squeeze stiles and kissing gates. Cattle graze throughout the year.
HOW TO GET THERE: An integrated bus and train system (Carnforth Connect, Line 1) operates in this area. Easy-access buses (with cycle racks) connect Carnforth railway station with Warton and other villages. For information call 01524 734311 or 0871 2002233 or go to www.transportforlancashire.com.
WALKING TIME: The full circuit distance of 2 miles takes about 2 hours at an easy pace.
30-MINUTE VISIT: Head uphill from the small car park to the 'Butterfly Garden' and Lower Terrace. There are good views, butterflies and flowers.

Warton Crag nature reserve is as exciting to explore as it is to look at from a distance; but be careful, visitors have been known to get lost in the woods! The reserve is home to an outstanding collection of butterflies, as well as some plants that are nationally uncommon and the best display of lichens on rocks in Lancashire.

In spring, the woodlands are carpeted with a mosaic of flowers: wood anemones, early-purple orchids, violets, pignut and wood sorrel. Warblers are an outstanding feature in summer, and in May and June the flora of the limestone pavement and terraces is at its peak. Species to look for include horseshoe vetch, rock-rose, blue moor-grass and pale St John's wort. Butterflies include pearl-bordered fritillary, small pearl-bordered fritillary and the nationally-threatened high brown fritillary. Autumn and winter are good times for berries, migrant birds and stunning views across Morecambe Bay.

WILDLIFE FACT: A SIGN OF GOOD AIR

If you're walking in an area carpeted with lichens, make sure you take a good lungful air. Lichens absorb water and minerals from rainwater and the atmosphere, making them extremely sensitive to atmospheric pollution. You are therefore only likely to see them in abundance where the air quality is very high. Since industrialisation, many of the shrubby and leafy lichens species have become confined to the parts of Britain with the purest air such as northern and western Scotland and Devon and Cornwall. Look out for them at Warton Crags in Lancashire, Knapdale in Scotland and Cabilla and Redrice Woods in Cornwall.

Wigan Flashes

Near Wigan; **OS Map** SD 585030; **Map Ref** Q7

ACCESS/CONDITIONS: Access is possible with a wheelchair, but there is a size limitation due to site security.
HOW TO GET THERE: The 610 bus (Hawkley Hall Circular) runs from Wigan Town Centre and stops near Hawkley Hall School near the entrance to the reserve. By car, leave the M6 at J25 head north on the A49, turn right on to Poolstock Lane (B5238). You can enter the site in several ways: at the end of Carr Lane near Hawkley Hall School; off Poolstock Lane; on Warington Road (A573), and it is accessible from the banks of the Leeds and Liverpool Canal.
WALKING TIME: It would take a day to walk around the 598-acre (242ha) site, but walks can range between 1 and 8 hours.
30-MINUTE VISIT: A quick walk is available around Ochre Flash with a self-guided nature trail.
A MEMBER SAYS: 'The Wigan Flashes have something for everyone; there are birds, butterflies, dragonflies and flowers. There are lovely walks and interesting views and lots of peace and tranquility, all within 10 minutes of Wigan town centre.'

A marshland landscape with areas of meadow, heath and mossland. The reedbeds and the associated open-water habitats are important nationally. The wet woodland is important for willow tit and there is an exceptional assemblage of plants, including eight species of orchid.

One of the amazing things about Wigan Flashes is that the reedbed is in the centre of such an urban landscape. At first glance, you would not imagine such a wild place could exist here. The natural environment is rich with exciting wildlife. You may be listening to the bittern booming, or watching the common terns feeding over the lakes or looking at one of the rare orchids and other wildflowers.

During spring the pools fill with waders like spotted redshank on their way to their Arctic breeding grounds. Sedge, reed and grasshopper warblers can be heard in the reedbeds. The summer brings a range of birds to breed, including warblers and common terns. Throughout autumn there is a good chance of seeing rarities including yellow-browed warbler, firecrest and green-winged teal. Winter sees tufted duck, shoveler, gadwall and other wildfowl.

DID YOU KNOW?

- **The Flashes (lakes) were formed as a result of mining subsidence, a legacy of the town's industrial past.**
- **Wigan Flashes is amongst the few places in northern Britain where bitterns can be found throughout the year, and hopes are high that they will soon breed.**

Mere Sands Wood

Rufford; **OS Map** SD 447157; **Map Ref** Q6

ACCESS/CONDITIONS: All hides will shortly be suitable for wheelchair access and a wheelchair-accessible path will link them to the car park.
HOW TO GET THERE: Train to Rufford (Preston to Ormskirk line), then a 10-minute walk to the reserve. By car, it is off the A59 in Rufford along Holmeswood Road, towards Southport. The entrance road shares access to Mere Sands Kennels and Cattery. Leave Holmeswood Road at the sign.
WALKING TIME: The reserve has 10 miles of footpaths. Walks can take from 30 minutes to a whole afternoon.
30-MINUTE VISIT: In summer, walk across the meadow to End Lake Platform. In winter, pop into the visitor centre to view the feeding stations, Lancaster Hide and head down to Marshall Hide for wildfowl, kingfisher and passerines.
A MEMBER SAYS: 'Mere Sands Wood offers a vast variety of habitats and associated wildlife. It's a very special place that I never tire of visiting.'

A wetland site with lakes, deciduous woodland, sandy meadows, reedbed and pine wood. It is nationally important for wintering water birds, breeding dragonflies and its geology. The key wildlife features are viewable from accessible hides, platforms and paths.

During spring, migrant birds shelter in the leafing woodland, hiding from the exposure of the surrounding open mossland. Grebes will be feeding young on the lakes and the reedbeds will be filled with the sound of reed warblers.

Summer is the time to enjoy butterflies and dragonflies here. The former sandpits on the reserve now host one of the largest breeding populations of dragonflies in the Northwest.

In autumn, wader passage is evidenced by snipe, green sandpiper and greenshank, late-flowering yellow bartsia will be carpeting the meadow in early season and a vast array of fungi will be seen in the woodland. Ducks dominate the lake in winter with teal and gadwall often visiting in significant numbers, while at the feeding stations, great spotted woodpeckers, bullfinches, tree sparrows and reed buntings abound.

DID YOU KNOW?

- The site is internationally renowned for its evidence of a recent geological past.
- Although inland, the plants that grow on the reserve's grasslands are those most often associated with coastal dunes.

Yorkshire

About the Trust

Yorkshire Wildlife Trust has worked for more than 60 years to safeguard nature in the region's landscape by protecting wildlife and wild places, and educating, influencing and empowering people. It manages 80 of the best sites and helps others to manage theirs. Its work is helping to secure the future of many important habitats and species, which might otherwise be lost.

Yorkshire Wildlife Trust
☎ 01904 659570
www.ywt.org.uk

Askham Bog

Near York
OS Map SE 575481; **Map Ref** R17

Askham Bog is a unique meeting place for wetland plants and animals from the south and east on one hand, and the north and west on the other. Specialities include Great fen sedge, bog myrtle, water violet and gingerbread sedge. The quality of the bog's insect life outshines even that of its plants. In the winter large flocks of redpoll and siskin join the woodcock and lesser spotted woodpeckers that breed in summer. The reserve is a good place to get a view of roe deer. It is not currently accessible to wheelchair users.

Broadhead Clough

Near Mytholmroyd
OS Map SE 001250; **Map Ref** R20

A scenic South Pennine reserve comprised of oak and birch woodland in a bowl-shaped clough surrounded by moorland. The flora and fauna of the woodland bogs are of particular conservation interest.

Brockadale

Near Kirk Smeaton
OS Map SE 513174; **Map Ref** R21

Brockadale (pictured right) is a picturesque limestone dale with ancient woodland, river, rich magnesian limestone grassland and floodplain grassland. Because there are so many different habitats, the flora of the reserve is particularly rich, more than 300 species of flowering plants are present. Watermeadows, undisturbed limestone grassland, semi-natural ancient woodland and more recent plantations, limestone crags and scree, and the River Went itself provide a wide range of conditions.

Chafer Wood

Near Pickering
OS Map SE 899832; **Map Ref** R12

This reserve comprises of a steep wooded valley with wonderful views across the Vale of York. This varied reserve includes a stream-side walk, flower-filled limestone grassland and mixed woodland, as well as considerable historical interest. Parking is available on the roadside just north of Ebberston. Ebberston is on a bus route.

Denaby Ings

Near Mexbrough
OS Map SE 498009; **Map Ref** R24

This SSSI wetland was formed by mining subsidence, with adjacent hay meadows, scrub and woodland. The reserve supports a wide range of birds, insects and wildflowers. Denaby Ings is an example of marshland that would once have been characteristic of the Dearne Valley.

Grass Wood

Near Grassington

OS Map SD 983652; **Map Ref** R15

Grass Wood mainly comprises ash and hazel, with beeches and firs also. This habitat is home to a wide variety of wildlife, including roe deer, badgers, foxes and other small mammals. The most notable birds within the wood are woodpeckers – the greater spotted and the green are seen and heard regularly. There are also a number of smaller birds that live within the wood, the most common being the nuthatch, tree creeper and warblers. There is a car park half-way along the reserve on the roadside. Alternatively, park in Grassington village and walk from there.

Semer Water

Near Bainbridge

OS Map SD 917865; **Map Ref** R11

Set in the Yorkshire Dales National Park, Semer Water combines marshland and open water. It is the second largest 'natural' lake in Yorkshire. With both acid and alkaline soils, there is a wide range of plants. The path that runs through the reserve is part of a much larger circular walk exploring this fantastic wild landscape.

Sprotbrough Flash

Near Doncaster

OS Map SE 537015; **Map Ref** R23

The reserve, located alongside the River Don in the spectacular Don Gorge, comprises a large area of open water created by mining subsidence, along with areas of broad-leaved woodland and grassland that are particularly rich in plants. Birdlife is prolific, with more than 60 regular breeding species. More than 480 plant species have been recorded here. Much of the reserve is wheelchair accessible via the Trans-Pennine Trail.

Strensall Common

Near York

OS Map SE 647615; **Map Ref** R16

Strensall Common is part of an internationally important lowland heath located within the Vale of York. The reserve is a mosaic of wet and dry heath, acid grassland and oak-birch woodland, with areas of open water. The reserve supports rare species including marsh gentian, round-leaved sundew, dark-bordered beauty moth, glow worm and woodlark.

Woodhouse Washlands

Sheffield

OS Map SK 423857; **Map Ref** R30

This reserve straddles the River Rother on the boundary of Sheffield and Rotherham. An urban site, it is a haven for wildlife, with wet grassland, marsh, ponds and ditch systems. It is an important site for breeding birds, amphibians and invertebrates. The Trans-Pennine Trail runs through the site.

North Cave Wetlands

Near Hull; **OS Map** SE 886328; **Map Ref** R19

ACCESS/CONDITIONS: A circular route with interpretation is available around the reserve, half of which is surfaced and accessible to wheelchair users. Two of the hides are wheelchair accessible.
HOW TO GET THERE: From the west leave the M62 at Junction 38 onto the north-bound B1230. Follow this to North Cave village. Take a left turn at the crossroads and follow the road round in a sharp left-hand bend at the cross-road. Soon after, take a left turn onto Dryham lane.
WALKING TIME: To cover the total circuit of approximately 1 mile takes approximately 1 and a half hours, including time to visit each hide.
30-MINUTE VISIT: Visit any of the hides and have a look out at the birds there.

This old sand and gravel quarry is now an amazing place for both beginner and expert birdwatchers, allowing wonderful close-up views of waders and wildfowl. Six lakes, restored from old sand and gravel workings, provide homes for many breeding and wintering birds. Deep water, shallow ledges, islands and reedbed all support different species. Hedgerows, grassland, scrapes, and a small arable field add to the site's interest.

In spring the reserve is a hive of activity, with breeding avocet, common tern, little ringed plover, lapwing and redshank. You might also be lucky enough to see migrants such as Temminck's stint and black-necked grebe.

In summer, orchids flower in the grasslands on the reserve and butterflies – including brimstone, holly blue and comma – can be seen.

Autumn is another good time to see migrants such as waxwing, while flocks of tree sparrow and siskin gather in the scrub and trees around the reserve. Winter sees good populations of ducks using the lakes, including pochard, shoveler, gadwall and teal.

Southerscales

Near Ingleton; **OS Map** SD 742769; **Map Ref** R13

ACCESS/CONDITIONS: There is a large layby on the road opposite to the entrance gate that can be used for parking. There are a couple of fields to cross before reaching the reserve, and there are usually cattle and sheep grazing in them.
HOW TO GET THERE: The nearest train station is Ribbleshead, about 1.5 miles from the reserve by road. The nearest bus takes you to Chapel-le-dale from Ingleton, 0.5 miles from the reserve.
WALKING TIME: At a leisurely pace, the complete circuit of the reserve takes 1.5 to 2 hours; the footpath through the middle of the reserve will take half an hour.
30-MINUTE VISIT: Walk half-way along the public footpath to visit the first level of limestone pavement.

One of the most impressive aspects of the reserve is the vast expanse of limestone pavement; very little of this habitat remains unspoiled apart from what survives at this reserve. The pavements contain a rich diversity of plants within their grikes (gullies naturally created by erosion), including many ferns, mosses and lichens. On your visit to the reserve you are likely to see a variety of birds of prey, including kestrel, buzzard and peregrine, all of which are found in the local area. Other species of interest include the blue moor-grass, found in the pastures, and the dark red helleborine that grows near the limestone pavement.

In spring, raven can be spotted pairing up and defending their territory against one another, or you can watch the smaller birds building their nests in the walls and trees of the reserve.

During summer see the blue moor-grass come out in flower, search for the elusive helleborine around pavements, or sit and watch the blue-grey cattle contentedly graze their way across the pasture land. During autumn view the heather patches with their beautiful purple bells swaying in the breeze. In winter, watch out for the winter visitors, the fieldfares and red wings as they scan the reserve for food.

Wheldrake Ings

Near York; **OS Map** SJ 200614; **Map Ref** R18

ACCESS/CONDITIONS: The footpath can be wet and hides are not suitable for wheelchair access.
HOW TO GET THERE: From the A19 York to Selby Road, take the road to Wheldrake and continue through the village towards Thorganby. Half a mile after a sharp right turn, there's a track on the left to the reserve. Bus information: 01904 621756.
WALKING TIME: The full circuit of approximately 4 miles takes about 2 hours including time in each hide.
30-MINUTE VISIT: This will provide just enough time to reach the first hide and scan the wildfowl or enjoy the flowers.

Wheldrake Ings is a seasonal wetland, flooded annually by the river Derwent, and supporting internationally important plant communities and bird numbers. With beautiful, internationally rare meadow communities, the reserve is a must for botanists and its equally impressive wintering birds and rare passage migrants are a must-see for birders. An amazing suite of invertebrates is also found here, along with many fish species located within the rivers and ditches. Mammals including otters and roe deer, and fabulous veteran willows can also be seen. Spring is a good time to see passage migrants, including the rare Whimbrel that stops to fuel up for its long journey. Curlew, snipe, lapwing and redshank are common breeding birds on the reserve.

In summer the hay meadow is at its best with the delicate white flowers of meadowsweet and the deep burgundy heads of great burnet scattered in among a huge variety of grasses. Kingfishers flash past along the River Derwent. Autumn sees the arrival of fieldfare and redwing, and barn owl hunt over the cut meadows. Winter provides an amazing spectacle of thousands of wintering wildfowl and waders, like golden plover, pintail, teal, wigeon and pochard.

WILDLIFE FACT: OTTERS

Otter numbers are on the increase in Britain, largely due to conservation work and less intensive use of pesticides in farming that destroyed their habitats in the 1960s. The species you see in Britain is the Eurasian otter and it is largely nocturnal, coming out at dusk to catch its diet of fish. It lives both in freshwater and around the coast. Still a rare animal, you are very lucky if you catch a glimpse of an otter, most likely in northern or western Britain, particularly around the coast of Scotland.

Flamborough Cliffs

North Landing; **OS Map** TA 240722; **Map Ref** R14

ACCESS/CONDITIONS: The path onto the northern half of the reserve follows a steep route in and out of Holmes Gut. Easier walking can be found by heading on to the southern part of the reserve, but paths can become wet and muddy after wet weather.

HOW TO GET THERE: North Landing (Flamborough) is served by regular buses from Bridlington, services 510 and 502 run approximately every hour. Telephone 01482 222222 for full details and times. By car, from Bridlington take the B1255, following the signs for Flamborough. Once in the village follow the signs for North Landing.

WALKING TIME: The full circuit of approximately 1.5 miles takes about 1 and a half hours to walk, allowing time for birdwatching.

30-MINUTE VISIT: If you are pushed for time, walk south-east from the car park and on to the cliff tops to the first cove, Newcombe Hope. You need go no further than this to get great views of the seabirds nesting on the opposite cliffs.

A MEMBER SAYS: 'When I visit Flamborough Cliffs I like to take a few minutes to just stand quietly and look out to sea. With the sounds of the waves and the wind in your hair you get a real feel for the wildness of our Yorkshire coastline.'

Flamborough Cliffs is a coastal reserve, ranging from cliff top grassland and spectacular chalk cliffs to rocky shore and sandy beach. It is a wonderful reserve at which to see huge numbers of breeding sea birds, species-rich grassland, farmland birds and a variety of invertebrates.

In spring and early summer thousands of sea birds make the chalk cliffs their home, allowing you to get unrivalled views of puffins, kittiwakes, guillemots and razorbills. Summer brings colour to the cliff top grasslands with salt-loving species, such as thrift and sea plantain, growing alongside limestone grassland species such as the bright pink pyramid orchid and beautiful blue harebell.

Within the hedgerows and scrub, breeding yellow-hammer and linnet can be found, and butterflies, such as the painted lady, are regularly seen. In autumn you might be lucky enough to see rare passage migrants like red backed shrike, barred warbler and wryneck throughout the reserve.

In winter flocks of fieldfare and redwing use the scrub in Holmes Gut for food and shelter, and Exmoor ponies provide an unusual sight grazing the cliff top grasslands.

DID YOU KNOW?

- Flamborough Head is the most northerly location at which you can find coastal chalk cliffs in the UK.
- Algal and lichen communities found in the cliffs' sea caves are one of the less known reasons for the site's international importance.
- 20 per cent of Flamborough Head's breeding sea bird population can be found on the relatively short stretch of coastline of the Yorkshire Wildlife Trust reserve.

Potteric Carr

Near Doncaster; **OS Map** SE 599003; **Map Ref** R25

ACCESS/CONDITIONS: The vast majority of the reserve has excellent access available for all. One footpath crosses a railway line and has steps. The footpaths are all well surfaced and are suitable all year round.
HOW TO GET THERE: Half a mile from Junction 3 of the M18, just south of Doncaster. Access into the reserve is via Sedum House, the head office of the British Trust for Conservation Volunteers .
WALKING TIME: There are approximately 7 miles of footpath. There is so much to see, it can easily take all day to visit Potteric Carr.
30-MINUTE VISIT: In 30 minutes you can see some fabulous wildlife, relax and unwind from the motorway, and grab a snack and hot drink from the shop.

Potteric Carr is a 494-acre (200ha) nature reserve located on the outskirts of Doncaster and is the largest Trust reserve. The main habitats include open water, reedbed, woodland, marsh, and small meadows, all of which create a rich diversity of wildlife. There is a fantastic on-site café (Low Ellers Junction), which serves up superb 'home-cooked' food and offers a warm and friendly welcome.

The reserve is a flurry of wildlife all year round. In spring there are migrating birds arriving in large numbers and in summer you can discover the excellent populations of dragonflies, butterflies, and flower assemblages. Autumn brings in the wintering birds and a wide-ranging colourful display of fungi. Into the winter months the reserve plays host to large numbers of birds and is an excellent spot to see bitterns, water rails and kingfishers.

DID YOU KNOW?

- **Potteric Carr's nature trails are nearly all on the routes of old railway lines.**
- **The wetlands were recreated in the 1960s by mining subsidence.**
- **It is one of the busiest nature reserves in the country, with over 21,000 people visiting on foot and over a million passing through by rail.**

Spurn

Near Hull; **OS Map** TA 410159; **Map Ref** R22

ACCESS/CONDITIONS: Wheelchair access is severely limited because of the sandy nature of the site. Bird hides are located at Canal Scrape and Chalk Bank; there is also a sea watching hide at the Warren. There are a number of waymarked footpaths. There is, however, a risk at high tides that the mid-section of the reserve will become washed over causing the point to become inaccessible. Please check with reserve officers on-site and do not ignore the barrier if it is closed.
HOW TO GET THERE: The reserve is located at the extreme south-eastern tip of the Yorkshire Coast. From Hull take the A1033 east towards Withernsea. At Patrington take the B1445 towards Easington village. At Easington follow the signs towards Spurn Point.
WALKING TIME: The full circuit is approximately 7 miles in distance and takes about 4 hours to walk around, including taking the time to bird watch.
30-MINUTE VISIT: There is a walk from the Blue Bell car park down to the seaward coast, to the Warren and then down the roadway back to the Blue Bell car park.
A MEMBER SAYS: 'The feeling of wilderness and the big horizons found here are like no other, there are always things to see, it is a place of constant change.'

This is a unique coastal reserve with a long sandy spit stretching 3.5 miles into the Humber Estuary from the Holderness Coast. Habitats found here include chalk grassland, mature grey sand dunes with sandy beaches on the seaward side and mud flats on the estuary side.

It is a popular venue for birdwatchers, with many rarities being seen, as well as many thousands of migrants and winter visitors. The site has a wilderness feel that pushes your comfort zone, whether it is the elements of the weather, sea or sky. The infrastructure is very low key and it is possible to wander freely over the site with that constant feeling of discovery. For most of the reserve the only restrictions to access are the dense vegetation.

Spurn's beaches are a fantastic place to seek out fossils, and interesting rocks and pebbles from the eroding coast to the north. Access to the beach is very easy. As the beaches are on both sides of the curving spit, it is always possible to obtain some shelter from the breeze by sitting in the lea of the dunes.

DID YOU KNOW?

- It is from Spurn point that Christianity was introduced to Holland.
- The difference from low to high water can be as much as 7 metres.
- The peninsula was formed 10,000 years ago after the retreat of the ice cap.
- Swallows fly south down the peninsula in spring.

Sheffield

About the Trust

Sheffield Wildlife Trust is the city's largest environmental charity, working to promote conservation, protection and improvement of the natural environment of Sheffield. Targeted work to protect vulnerable habitats and species is happening alongside initiatives to boost the wildlife value of parks and green spaces across Sheffield.

Sheffield Wildlife Trust ☎ 0114 2634335
www.wildsheffield.com

Carbrook Ravine

Near Sheffield Parkway
OS Map SK 395856; **Map Ref** R32

Situated next to the Parkway between the Manor and Woodthorpe, Carbrook Ravine seems an unlikely candidate as a nature reserve. But the ravine's mix of woods, scrub and grasslands supports a rich variety of plants and its proximity to residential housing makes it a vital open space for local communities. At the edge of two of the city's largest and most disadvantaged housing estates, it offers huge potential to enrich the residents' quality of life.

Carr House Meadows

Sheffield
OS Map SK 282954; **Map Ref** R26

This area of farmland dominated by a series of wildflower meadows is managed in a traditional way to maximise its biodiversity value. Yellow-rattle, lesser trefoil, red clover, meadow buttercup and ox-eye daisy appear, as do a variety of invertebrates, especially butterflies, and grassland and woodland birds.

Crabtree Ponds

Sheffield
OS Map SK 362899; **Map Ref** R27

This reserve provides a great site for bats, which feed on the insects that congregate over the two ponds. Leisler's and Daubenton's bats, as well as pipistrelle, enjoy the feast. Other inhabitants include frogs, palmate newts and other amphibians, and a variety of birds in the surrounding woodlands. There are footpaths and a boardwalk by the main pond. Parts of the reserve are unsuitable for wheelchair access.

Moss Valley Woodlands

Near Jordonthorpe
OS Map SK 376805; **Map Ref** R35

Just on the edge of city and countryside, these woods offer peaceful walks, linking a range of woodlands and farmland through the Moss Valley. May is the best time of year to visit, when the woods are carpeted in bluebells. Dowey Lumb is a remnant wood pasture that sits between Long Wood and Bridle Road Wood, and is a peaceful pasture full of wildflowers in the summer. Footpaths are muddy but dry out in summer months, however most are not suitable for wheelchairs or pushchairs.

Salmon Pastures

Sheffield
OS Map SK 371881; **Map Ref** R29

A truly urban reserve, Salmon Pastures consists of urban common, a new type of habitat that appears in sites in towns and cities after industry moves out. What arrives is a mix of opportunist plant species, an array of butterflies and dragonflies, and kingfishers visiting from the nearby River Don.

Sunnybank

Sheffield
OS Map SK 343863; **Map Ref** R31

This is the most well-used of Sheffield Wildlife Trust's nature reserves. Although small, it contains a pond, woodland and grassland areas supporting a wealth of wildlife in a thoroughly urban setting. Residents include fox, pipistrelle bat, tawny owl and 22 species of breeding bird. Enjoy the wildlife sculptures.

Blackburn Meadows

Near Rotherham; **OS Map** SK 412923; **Map Ref** R28

ACCESS/CONDITIONS: The reserve and its hides are suitable for disabled access. It is also linked to the Sheffield and Rotherham canal towpath, which has disabled access along most of its length. Parts of the site are unstable and are fenced off.
HOW TO GET THERE: Bus X78 runs between Sheffield and Rotherham every 20 minutes, stopping at Psalters Lane. The reserve can also be approached by foot along the Sheffield to Rotherham canal towpath. By car, from Sheffield, take Junction 34 off the M1 and follow the A6109 for 1 mile before turning down Psalters Lane.
WALKING TIME: A full circuit of the 52-acre (21ha) reserve takes about 45 minutes.
30-MINUTE VISIT: The hides provide a good opportunity to view a variety of birds all year round.

An urban nature reserve within an industrial setting, Blackburn Meadows was set up in the late 1980s when an area that had previously been used as a sewage works was reclaimed and turned into 'urban savannah'. The reserve consists of two artificial lakes, reedbed, marginal vegetation and shingle beach surrounded by areas of grassland and shrub. There are also pockets of young woodland, willow carr and a dipping pond.

Spring brings an influx of passage wading birds and warblers, including common white-throat and willow warbler. Summer sees resident swans, ducks, coots and moorhens with regular visits from kingfishers, wagtails and herons. At this time of year the reserve is a blaze of colour, with many species of wildflower and dragonfly.

Autumn and winter see the passage migrants (including jack snipe) returning alongside over-wintering wildfowl such as wigeon, goldeneye and teal. Blackburn Meadows is the best birdwatching site inside Sheffield's city boundary.

Wyming Brook/Fox Hagg

Near Sheffield; **OS Map** SK 269859 (Wyming Brook)/283865 (Fox Hagg); **Map Ref** R33

ACCESS/CONDITIONS: The reserves have footpaths and bridleways. Wyming Brook has a small amount of wheelchair access, with more planned for the next few years.
HOW TO GET THERE: Take bus 51 out of Sheffield or, by car, drive out of Sheffield along Redmires Road or enter via Manchester Road.
WALKING TIME: It takes 2 to 3 hours on a circular route around Wyming Brook, to include woodland and moorland. Fox Hagg can be covered in about 30 minutes.
30-MINUTE VISIT: Walk up from the car park until you come to a large outcrop of rock that serves as a look-out post over the valley at Wyming Brook, or follow the stream.

All year round, Wyming Brook and Fox Hagg offer magnificent views of Sheffield's Rivelin Valley. Green and luxuriant in summer, white and bleak in winter, the hillsides sweep down towards the reservoirs in the valley's centre. The Wyming Brook itself is a fast-flowing, boulder-strewn stream that descends into the valley through a mixture of deciduous and coniferous woodland, which is home to an astonishing number of bird species. As well as locally and nationally important woodland birds, the reserve is often used by birds of prey such as goshawk, which visit from the moorland areas that begin at its western edge.

Fox Hagg, just to the east of Wyming Brook, contains a similarly stunning mix of woodland and heathland. The heathland areas, dominated by heather and bilberry, make for excellent walking and are populated by species from viviparous lizard to meadow pipit. Fox Hagg is also a good place to see woodland birds like sparrowhawk, green woodpecker and linnet.

Blacka Moor SSSI

Near Sheffield; **OS Map** SK 287806; **Map Ref** R34

ACCESS/CONDITIONS: There are three main entrances and footpaths and bridleways. Most paths are not suitable for wheelchair use; some are suitable for pushchairs. Parts of the reserve can be wet and boggy, especially in winter.
HOW TO GET THERE: Buses 272 and 240 stop on Stony Ridge Road, near the Hathersage Road entrance. Take a Totley bus for the Strawberry Lee Lane entrance. By car, drive along the A625 towards Hathersage for the Hathersage Road entrance, or park at the layby on the A625 for the Piper Lane entrance. The Strawberry Lee Lane entrance is on the A621.
WALKING TIME: A complete circuit takes a couple of hours.
30-MINUTE VISIT: Wander through the woods off the A625 for a flavour of the reserve. Or, a walk on the moors gives you a sense of the size of this open heathland.
A MEMBER SAYS: 'To have Blacka Moor on our doorstep is wonderful. It's so rich in wildlife and so varied that every time I go there I discover something new.'

Despite being so close to England's fourth-largest city, you're within the Peak District National Park at Blacka Moor SSSI, which offers mixed woodlands and open heathland. A large number of upland birds breed here, including stonechat, tree pipit, linnet, reed bunting, wheatear, reed bunting, blackcap, willow warbler and woodcock. Archaeological remains of Iron Age and medieval settlements testify to the reserve's history as a living landscape.

The heather, bilberry and birch have given this magnificent place a truly wild feel. The heathland is grazed by Highland cattle in the warmer months. It has been designated an SSSI because of its important population of upland breeding birds, and is popular with walkers, mountain bikers, horse riders and naturalists.

Adders emerging from their hibernation may be seen by the lucky few in spring, before they disperse to their ancient feeding grounds. In summer, the reserve is carpeted in heather, with scattered birch and rowan trees, and copses providing shade and habitats. The land softens at the onset of autumn before bleakening with winter into a classic bare, open heathland.

DID YOU KNOW?

- There are 123 archaeological features on Blacka Moor.
- The pastures support a wide variety of fungi, including at least 14 species of wax cap fungi – some of the most threatened fungal species in Britain.
- It has the best display of bog asphodel in the Peak District.

Cheshire

About the Trust

Cheshire Wildlife Trust is a charity that works to protect and enhance wildlife in the Cheshire region. As part of its role to safeguard our fragile natural heritage, it manages 45 nature reserves that help to protect endangered species, rare plants and threatened habitats. It is all about people taking action for wildlife at a local level.

Cheshire Wildlife Trust
☎ 01948 820728
www.wildlifetrust.org.uk/cheshire

Black Lake SSSI
Norley
OS Map SJ 537709; **Map Ref** Q13
WC i 🍴

This SSSI pool with bog vegetation lies in a natural depression surrounded by Forestry Commission conifer plantation. The reserve shows a good example of early 'schwingmoor' or floating bog development. Visit for sundew, cranberry and cotton grass and a good variety of dragonflies on the open water. Access is via a Forestry Commission trackway.

Cleaver Heath SSSI
Heswall
OS Map SJ 256826; **Map Ref** Q9

This is an SSSI heathland dominated by heather with wavy-hair grass, mat grass, gorse and bilberry. It hosts a varied population of insects and birds, as well as common lizard, and offers spectacular views of the Dee Estuary. Access is via narrow rough tracks, so it is not suitable for disabled access.

Hunter's Wood
Kingsley
OS Map SJ 554763; **Map Ref** Q10

Two fields adjacent to Warburton's Wood were purchased to extend the existing wood using both natural regeneration and planting. Existing meadows are also being extended, and rides and glades will provide open ground. Mown pathways have been created around the site. Access is from a public footpath trackway.

Pumphouse Wood
Barnton, Northwich, Cheshire
OS Map SJ 635759; **Map Ref** Q11

This is a mixed deciduous, semi-natural woodland with a canopy of oak, ash and a few larch. The understorey comprises of hawthorn, elder and elm. There is a good show of bluebells in the spring. Access is via a grazed field. Once reached, the circular pathway is well defined and dry.

Red Rocks Marsh SSSI
Hoylake
OS Map SJ 206880; **Map Ref** Q8

An SSSI on Hoylake Beach with embryo and secondary sand dunes, reedbed and open slack pools. The reedbed is an important bird migration site and the reserve is the only site in England for Mackay's horsetail. A boardwalk runs along the landward side of the reserve. Access to the reserve is from the beach via sandy tracks.

Trentabank Reservoir
Near Macclesfield
OS Map SJ 962713; **Map Ref** Q14

This is a species rich, unimproved upland and acid grassland. There is a coniferous plantation surrounding Trentabank Reservoir with a large herony of about 22 pairs. You can view the heronry from the disabled viewing area and public lay-by. The viewing area is open to all.

Gowy Meadows

Near Chester; **OS Map** SJ 435740; **Map Ref** Q12

ACCESS/CONDITIONS: A public footpath crosses the site. This path is accessible all year but can be muddy. There are two stiles within the site and an old sluice bridge.
HOW TO GET THERE: Access from Thornton-le-Moors. From Chester, catch bus 80 from Stop K, or C33 from Stand 1. Alternatively take the bus from Chester to Ellesmere Port and then bus 36 which goes to Thornton-le-Moors every hour. By car take the A5117 from M53 J10 or M56 J14.
WALKING TIME: The walk along the public footpath takes approximately 25 minutes in one direction. If you continue across the River Gowy in the direction of the pretty village of Stoak, the walk takes approximately 1 hour, returning along the same route.
30-MINUTE VISIT: The public footpath that crosses the reserve passes through a green lane before bridging Thornton Brook and following the brook through to the River Gowy. This walk allows the visitor to view a large percentage of the site.

Covering 410 acres (166ha), it is thought that Gowy Meadows was drained during the Middle Ages. A lowland grazing marsh with numerous ditches, the site supports large numbers of snipe and teal during the winter months. The area is undergoing extensive re-wetting to enable the marshes to function as a natural flood defence for commercial sites downstream. Current management includes: ditch clearance to provide suitable water vole habitat and increase the spread of species such as water violet and bladderwort; fencing off of ditches to prevent poaching and bank damage by grazing cattle; and gapping up of hedges to provide corridors along the higher ground. During the winter months, localised sluices will be inserted to enable specific parts of the site to flood and provide feeding areas for waders and wildfowl.

The site is important for its water vole population as well as ditch flora and a number of scarce invertebrates, including lesser silver diving beetle. As the site develops bird numbers will increase. After one year of management, snipe and teal numbers have already soared. Buzzards are a common sight across the meadows and peregrine falcon can often be observed.

DID YOU KNOW?

- **The word 'snipe', also known in Cheshire as 'lady snipe', emanates from the Old English 'snite', which means a long, thin object. To snipe at a person relates back to the shape of a snipe's beak.**

Marston Fl
in winter, n
Northwi
Chesh

Manx

North

About the Trust

Founded in 1973, the Manx Wildlife Trust is the largest and most active voluntary body on the Isle of Man devoted to the conservation of wildlife and the environment. The Trust has 20 nature reserves covering over 200 acres (80ha), which range from two small urban sites in Port Erin and Onchan to 72 acres (29ha) of heather moorland on Dalby Mountain.

Manx Wildlife Trust☎ 01624 801985
www.manxwt.org.uk

Close Sartfield

Ballaugh; **OS Map** SC 358955; **Map Ref** S32

ACCESS/CONDITIONS: The boardwalk from the car park to the hide is suitable for wheelchair access, the remainder is wet and muddy for much of the year. Public access is generally confined to the path.
HOW TO GET THERE: From the TT course (A3), turn onto the B9 between Ballaugh village and the Sulby Glen. Take the third right and follow this road for nearly 1 mile. The reserve entrance and car park are located about 25m along a track on the right.
WALKING TIME: The circular walks of 1 mile can take up to 1 hour.
30-MINUTE VISIT: Follow the path through Close Mean and down to the hide.
A MEMBER SAYS: 'Close Sartfield is a beautiful site to experience at any time of the year – in autumn or winter the feel of the spooky trees and chance of seeing a hare or hen harrier is wonderful.'

Close Sartfield is one of the Manx Wildlife Trust's larger reserves and lies on the north-west edge of the Ballaugh Curragh, the island's premier wetland. The reserve is made up of damp hay meadows, marshy grassland, curragh (willow carr) and developing birch woodland. In summer, the meadows offer an abundance of wildflowers including up to six species of orchid. Corncrakes have been sighted on the meadows in the recent past. Close Sartfield is excellent for birdwatching in the spring, and the hide is well sited to observe hen harriers returning to their roost in late autumn and winter.

DID YOU KNOW?

- **Close Sartfield has one of the densest and most accessible winter hen harrier roosts in western Europe. Over 20 birds can be seen in the 2 hours before and during dusk, and the peak count for one evening's harrier watch on this site was 116 birds.**
- **Part of the site is grazed by a population of red-necked wallabies, escapees from the nearby wildlife park.**

WALES

So much of Wales is rural and relatively undisturbed by the invasion of man that wildlife thrives here, and there are many fantastic settings in which to observe it.

Rare species abound in its most rural areas, and although not all of the reserves contain rarities, each one has something special about it. Some are large, some very small; some can cope with large numbers of visitors, while others are more fragile. The Trusts' policy is to encourage visitors to come and enjoy the marvellous heritage of wildlife on as many reserves as possible.

Habitats vary considerably throughout the country. In the Brecknock reserves around the Brecon Beacons National Park, for example, there are majestic old woodlands, exposed rock faces and rare meadow wildflowers to be discovered. Down on the coast of Pembrokeshire, meanwhile, anemones, barnacles and seaweed thrive in the rockpools and seals are often sighted close to shore and even, on occasion, up on the beaches.

In between the high and low areas of the country there are mountain ranges that span all habitats from limestone grassland to heathland, woodland and river valleys. Each area has its own species of interest such as the orchids that grow in the limestone grassland and the upland birds such as stonechats and merlins that are found in the higher heathland. Not to mention the 600-700 breeding pairs of red kites, which are mostly to be found in Wales.

A night-time walk around many lowland areas of Wales will often reveal glow worms, especially in June or July. These are also the best months for seeing puffins which are found at various sites in Wales such as Skomer Island off the coast of Pembrokeshire.

Skomer Island is a little like the mini-Galapagos of Wales, as the stretch of water that separates it from the mainland means no predators such as dogs, cats, foxes or rodents live there and, as a result, it is a haven for ground-nesting birds. The island is covered with burrows of the Manx shearwater. There are thought to be around 165,000 breeding pairs on the 730-acre island.

The variety of plants in Wales is vast, and a look through the entries for this region will reveal the many interesting varieties to be found, such as the wood anemone, fungi and different types of moss in the area's many woodlands.

Opposite: Talybont Reservoir, Brecon Beacons National Park, South Wales

NOT TO BE MISSED

- **GILFACH**

Meadows crammed full of ancient grassland species, including dyer's greenwood, moonwart, adder's-tongue fern, mountain pansy, heath dog-violet and eyebright.

- **GLASLYN**

Montgomeryshire Wildlife Trust's largest reserve and its wildest. Visiting Glaslyn is a true mountain experience with breathtaking views over the Dyfi valley.

- **PWLL Y WRACH**

A fine example of an ancient Welsh broadleaved woodland growing along a steep river valley.

- **MAGOR MARSH SSSI**

The largest remnant of traditionally managed fenland on the Gwent Levels, it is believed that there has been farming here for almost all of the last 6,000 years.

- **SKOMER ISLAND**

They say that take one trip to Skomer Island and you're hooked for life. No wonder, with so much sea birdlife – including puffins – on show.

- **SPINNIES, ABEROGWEN**

One of North Wales's most popular wildlife reserves for its impressive range of bird species, including little egret, red-breasted mergansers and water rail.

North Wales

About the Trust

The North Wales Wildlife Trust manages 33 wildlife reserves and currently runs a range of projects, from conserving the habitat of the North Wales brown hare to the Clwyd Rare Woodland Mammal project. Together with other members of the Welsh Wildlife Trust it is rejuvenating arable farmland habitats and helping to conserve the skylark, lapwing and corn cockle.

North Wales Wildlife Trust ☎ 01248 351451
www.wildlifetrust.org.uk/northwales

Bryn Pydew

Near Llandudno
OS Map SH 818798; **Map Ref** V4

A mixture of calcareous grassland, limestone pavement and broad-leaved woodland. Six species of orchid, wild privet and juniper. Insects include reddish light arches and pretty chalk carpet moths, glow worms and cardinal beetles. Be careful on the steep sections of path at the start and end of the circular route, as they can be slippery when wet. The reserve is unsuitable for wheelchairs.

Caeau Tan y Bwlch

Near Caernarfon
OS Map SH 431488; **Map Ref** V11

This reserve has stunning views across Caernarfon Bay and Anglesey. It is comprised of calcareous grassland on its upper slopes, with wet flushes below. Flora includes black knapweed, lady's mantle, adder's-tongue fern and over 2,000 greater butterfly orchids. The site is uneven and not suitable for wheelchair access. Stout boots are recommended.

Cemlyn

Near Tregele
OS Map SP 991584; **Map Ref** V1

This reserve includes a large lagoon, separated from the sea by a spectacular, naturally-created shingle ridge. Four tern species breed here, including the rare roseate. Other breeding species include grasshopper warbler, redshank, whitethroat and linnet, goldeneye, shoveler, teal and golden plover in winter. Coastal plants such as sea kale, sea campion and yellow-horned poppy thrive.

Cors Bodgynydd

Near Capel Curig
OS Map SH 767597; **Map Ref** V8

This reserve is home to bog and mire communities. Flora such as rare marsh clubmoss, bog asphodel, greater and lesser bladderwort, sundew and bogbean all prosper. Dragonflies and bats are numerous. Birdlife includes tawny owl, woodcock, common sandpiper and goosander on the lake. On summer evenings snipe and nightjar can be seen.

Nantporth

Near Bangor
OS Map SH 556721; **Map Ref** V5

A reserve of ash woodland with calcareous glades. Plants include whitebeam, twayblade, wood violet, wood sanicle, soft shield fern, quaking grass and fairy flax. It is a breeding ground for many woodland birds, and waders can be seen on the foreshore of the Menai Strait. Snails abound; 23 species have been recorded. Paths can be slippery when wet. Do not approach exposed rock faces.

Rhiwledyn

Near Llandudno
OS Map SH 813821; **Map Ref** V3

A calcareous grassland with some exposed limestone cliffs. Look out for fulmar breeding on the cliffs. Plantlife such as dropwort, bloody cranesbill, carline thistle, ploughman's spikenard, yellow-wort and white horehound can all be seen. Access is via the North Wales Path to the Little Orme summit. It is steep, uneven and unsuitable for wheelchairs.

Aberduna

Near Mold; **OS Map** SJ 198613; **Map Ref** V7

ACCESS/CONDITIONS: A mix of public and permissive paths.
HOW TO GET THERE: 3 miles south-west of Mold, situated just north of Maeshafn. From the village green at Maeshafn take the public footpath north or west past the chapel. Both paths lead to the eastern part of the reserve.
WALKING TIME: About 1 hour at an easy pace.
30-MINUTE VISIT: Start from the village green and head north through the grassland, then follow the path until you come to some steps. Drop down and follow the path until you reach an information panel. Turn left and follow the path back through the woodland to the village green. This route will give a little taste of all the habitats at Aberduna.

A fantastic mixture of grassland, scrub and mixed broad-leaved woodland providing homes to a wide range of plants and animals. Look out for butterflies flitting through the grass and nesting birds such as white-throat and blackcap darting in and out of the scrub and woodland plants. In the spring, breeding birds fill the air with song.

The grassland is home to early purple orchids and cowslips that create a colourful display. Step into the wood and soak up the atmosphere created by the bluebells and other wildflowers. If you visit in summer, look out for birds frantically collecting food for their young. This is also the time to see over 28 species of butterfly and moth that have been recorded on the reserve, including many fritillaries. Look for exposed limestone and the common rock-rose, moonwort and fragrant orchids growing in the shallow soil. The changing leaves in autumn provide a mass of colour and the fruit and nuts provided by the wood attract many woodland animals. A winter walk might provide a glimpse of woodcock or a peregrine hunting for prey over the reserve.

Gors Maen Llwyd

Near Denbigh; **OS Map** SH 975580; **Map Ref** V9

ACCESS/CONDITIONS: Permissive paths run across the edge of the reserve. Wet, peaty paths are not suitable for wheelchair or pushchair access.
HOW TO GET THERE: 7 miles from Denbigh on the north shore of Llyn Brenig. Take the A543 from Denbigh to Pentrefoelas, turn left onto the road signposted to Llyn Brenig. After 1 mile, turn left again, go over the cattle grid and turn right approx 500m later.
WALKING TIME: 692-acre (280ha) reserve. From the top car park to the bottom hide takes half an hour.
30-MINUTE VISIT: In the summer, park in the top car park and walk on to the heath for great views. In the winter, park in the bottom car park and visit the hide for wildfowl viewing.

For a true flavour of the what the Welsh uplands are all about, visit Gors Maen Llwyd. This reserve is larger than the other 32 Trust reserves put together, yet it is a small part of a continuous block of upland heath, interspersed with conifer plantation and reservoirs. The reserve is a mosaic of differently-aged heather, perfect for providing all the niches wildlife would want in a heathland. It also boasts impressive vistas over Llyn Brenig. In spring, birds such as black and red grouse start to breed. Wheatear, skylark and chats also occur, as do curlew, hen harrier and merlin. As summer progresses, the wet areas of the heath support many sphagnum mosses and cotton grasses, bogbean, cranberry and more than 13 species of sedge. In drier areas, mountain pansy, field woodrush, tormentil, harebell and heath speedwell occur. Water voles live in the clear streams running through the peat. In winter, look out for wildfowl on Llyn Brenig from the vantage point of the hide.

Marford Quarry SSSI

Near Wrexham; **OS Map** SJ 357560; **Map Ref** V10

ACCESS/CONDITIONS: Mainly sandy ground with few muddy areas even after heavy rain. No steep slopes or difficult terrain. Steps have been installed where needed.
HOW TO GET THERE: Take the B5445 to Marford (between Rossett and Gresford), turn into Springfield Lane, 50m north of the Trevor Arms Hotel. The entrance is approx 400m on the left, immediately before a railway bridge.
WALKING TIME: 38-acre (15ha) reserve. Numerous trails include a 0.4 mile circular walk.
30-MINUTE VISIT: Take the circular walk around the site.

Marford Quarry, a disused sand and gravel quarry, is a fantastic example of how, if left to nature, industrial land can become not only extremely important to wildlife, but also very beautiful. Visitors can enjoy a leisurely walk through areas of calcareous grassland, gorse scrub and broad-leaved woodland and enjoy hearing and watching the many bird species that frequent the reserve.

Areas of open sand are especially important for burrowing bees and wasps, which are one of the major features of the reserve. Ramsons and wood anemones grow in the wooded areas during spring and cuckoos and green woodpeckers are a common sight and sound.

In summer, many wildflower species grow, including white mullein, pale St John's wort, wild liquorice and three orchids (common-spotted, pyramidal and bee). The site also supports more than 30 butterfly species and 39 moth species.

WILDLIFE FACT: SANDWICH TERN

The Sandwich tern is the largest breeding tern in Britain and Cemlyn Wildlife Trust Nature Reserve holds a significant part of the UK population. During the summer months Cemlyn becomes of Wales' top birdwatching sites.

Cors Goch

Near Bangor; **OS Map** SH 503817; **Map Ref** V2

P i

ACCESS/CONDITIONS: Uneven ground surface. Boardwalk through wettest areas. Most of the reserve is not suitable for wheelchair or pushchair access.
HOW TO GET THERE: Take the A5025 from Menai Bridge towards Benllech/Amlwch. Two miles out of Pentraeth, take the turning on the left signposted to Llanbedrgoch. About 0.75 miles beyond the village, on a small rise, there is a track to the left. Park at roadside. A large information board, 200 metres from the roadside, marks the entrance.
WALKING TIME: 168-acre (68ha) reserve. Mix of public and permissive paths giving a network of 5 miles. Boardwalk trail takes 1 hour at an easy pace.
30-MINUTE VISIT: Head to the heathland to enjoy tremendous views over the whole reserve before dropping down to the edge of the wetland and walking back along the foot of the slope.
A MEMBER SAYS: 'Fields like I remember from when I was a child: full of wildflowers.'

This is a diverse site centred on a long and shallow narrow valley. Areas of fen, heath and grassland blend into one another in a complex mosaic. From late spring, the site is awash with flowering orchids; early-purple and green winged orchid are followed by marsh helleborine, early marsh, northern marsh, fragrant and lesser butterfly orchids. Reed buntings and grasshopper warblers can be seen and heard in the summer. More than 20 butterfly species have been seen around the reserve and, in late summer, numerous dragonflies and damselflies can be seen around the wetland pools. But do not splash around too much, the rare medicinal leech (*hirudo medicinalis*) may be looking for a meal! As summer comes to an end, grass of Parnassus and marsh gentian provide a final splash of colour. During the autumn and winter, hen and marsh harriers hunt over the reserve. Snipe is often disturbed from the dense reedbed. In the early evening of a winter's day, the setting sun can bathe the whole valley in a wonderful, warm glow that is reflected in the pools and open water. The reserve also provides an opportunity to look at interesting and varied geology. Cors Goch is a treasure chest – the harder you look the more you find.

DID YOU KNOW?

- **Cors Goch was this Trust's first nature reserve. It was 'discovered' in the late 1950s and became a Trust reserve in 1963.**
- **It is one of only a handful of sites for the medicinal leech in Wales and one of only three sites in the UK for the dwarf stonewort.**

Gwaith Powdwr

Near Portmeirion; **OS Map** SH 619388; **Map Ref** V12

P WC i in Penrhyn

ACCESS/CONDITIONS: Some steep slopes. Steps to the hide and education room. One set of steps on the figure-of-eight trail. Part of the trail is closed during the nightjar breeding season (June to July). Wheelchair access by car.
HOW TO GET THERE: Train to Penrhyndeudraeth then walk; turn right out of the station, the entrance is 150m around the bend. By car, take the A487 through Penrhyndeudraeth to Penrhyn. Turn off to the toll bridge to Harlech (which links the A487 and A496). Just before the toll gate traffic control, turn left for the industrial park.
WALKING TIME: 48-acre (19ha) site. Figure-of-eight trail of 4 miles runs around the site.
30-MINUTE VISIT: Because of its past use, the site has a network of roads. By prior arrangement parking is available on the reserve.
A MEMBER SAYS: 'The nightjar walk was amazing; being out in the "wilds" at night; the sounds from nightjar, woodcock and the bats (via a bat detector)! This and the guide really put the site into perspective.'

The reserve is mainly comprised of oak, with younger woodland, birch, heathland and open areas There are also several small pools with wet woodland. Combined with the mix of social and historic elements, you'll have a wonderful and diverse day out.

The reserve was once home to an explosives factory, and the areas once occupied by factory buildings have now been cleared, decontaminated and are in the process (via a LIFE European grant) of being restored to heathland or woodland.

In the spring, the woods come alive as summer migrant birds arrive to boost the resident population to around 35 breeding species. Pied flycatcher, redstart, wood warbler and tree pipit all occur, as do linnet and bullfinch. As summer approaches, nightjar arrive to occupy the heath, and at night one can see roding woodcock, tawny and barn owls and six different species of bat.

Some factory buildings have been retained to use as hides or education centres. You do not have to be a wildlife watcher to enjoy a visit to this site, which has year-round appeal for all ages!

DID YOU KNOW?

- At one time up to 500 people worked here, producing over 9,000 tonnes of TNT per year.
- Rare bats and birds thrived at Gwaith Powdwr while it was a factory.

Spinnies, Aberogwen

Near Bangor; **OS Map** SH 613721; **Map Ref** V6

ACCESS/CONDITIONS: Hides linked by maintained paths. Estuarine hide is suitable for wheelchair access with a special gate to allow easy access for wheelchairs and pushchairs. Five small steps to the second smaller hide.
HOW TO GET THERE: 3 miles from Bangor towards the A55. Take the A5122 from Bangor, turn left at Penrhyn Castle towards Tal-y-bont. After passing over the river, the road becomes straight, the turning to the site is the only turning on the left.
WALKING TIME: The walk from the car park to both hides and back is approximately 1 mile.
30-MINUTE VISIT: Head to the estuary hide (the furthest from the entrance) for the best chance of seeing the reserve's many bird species. You could spend about 5 to 10 minutes here. The other hide is a short walk from the car park.
A MEMBER SAYS: 'This must be one of the best places to see a kingfisher.'

This site is one of North Wales Wildlife Trust's most popular reserves, with over 185 species of bird recorded. Walking from the car park, you have the opportunity to scan farmland, woodland, scrub and open water habitats as well as estuary and open sea, and can thus get firecrest, bullfinch, kingfisher and little egret all in the same half-mile walk. The main feature of this reserve is the brackish coastal lagoon, which provides shelter and food for wildfowl and waders during spring and autumn migrations. The surrounding woodland and scrub provide the habitat for summer breeding birds – around 45 species breed here regularly. The seaward hide is an excellent place to spend a winter's day sea-watching over the Lavan Sands LNR, and during late summer, there is a raft of several hundred red-breasted mergansers and great crested grebes on the sea. Winter specialities include kingfisher, greenshank, water rail and snipe.

While walking around the reserve, look out for broad-leaved helleborine, a locally rare orchid, along with hart's tongue and male fern growing in shady spots. Different types of brightly coloured fungus can also be seen, with the small scarlet elf cup being commonplace during the winter.

DID YOU KNOW?

- **The name 'spinnies' is derived from the small wooded areas, or spinneys, which surround the lagoon, and was first used here in 1899.**
- **The pools were meanders in the River Ogwen until it was canalised in the 19th century.**
- **193 species of bird have been recorded on the reserve.**

Montgomeryshire

About the Trust

Montgomeryshire Wildlife Trust was formed in 1982 and its mission is to 'rebuild biodiversity and engage people with their environment' in some of Montgomeryshire's most stunning countryside. On its 19 nature reserves, it undertakes several action plans for habitats and for individual species at risk, such as the pearl-bordered fritillary butterflies and lesser horseshoe bats.

Montgomeryshire Wildlife Trust ☎ 01938 555654
www.montwt.co.uk

Coed Pendugwm

Near Pont Robert
OS Map SJ 103142; **Map Ref** V13

Peek into this ancient woodland and you'll see a scene that hasn't changed for centuries. Sessile oaks and beech give centre stage to woodland plants of all colours, particularly bluebells, primroses, wood anemones and violets. In the shaded areas there are ferns, lichens and mosses. Woodland birds and mammals include dormouse, pied flycatcher and wood warbler.

Dyfnant Meadows

In Dyfnant Forest
OS Map SH 998155; **Map Ref** V26

This cluster of ancient meadows, surrounded by commercial forestry, survives to provide a fertile food store for a wide variety of plants and animals. There are wet patches with orchids, sundew and butterwort, marshy areas with lady's smock, lousewort, rushes and meadowsweet and a wooded dingle with sessile oak, mosses, lichens and ferns.

Llandinam Gravels

Near Llandinam
OS Map SO 022876; **Map Ref** V18

On the floodplain of the River Severn, the Trust is working with the river to create a harmonious balance of habitat erosion and creation. There are areas of shingle in which invertebrates thrive and wading birds such as little ringed plover and oystercatcher breed in safety. Plants on the river margins attract dragonflies and damselflies and provide cover for birds and otters.

Llanymynech Rocks

Near Llanymynech
OS Map SJ 267218; **Map Ref** V14

A spectacular outcrop of limestone straddling the border between England and Wales, this reserve has diverse flora including pyramidal, fragrant and greater butterfly orchids, and other floral species such as autumn lady's-tresses and rock-rose. The old quarry faces are home to jackdaws, and peregrine falcon breed on the site.

Llyn Mawr

Near Caersws
OS Map SO 009971; **Map Ref** V20

This 30-acre (12ha) reserve includes a mesotrophic lake in which aquatic plants and water-loving plants thrive. These include shoreweed, quillwort, yellow water lily, broad-leaved pondweed and bog-bean. Marshy areas have cinquefoil, bog asphodel, bog pimpernel and sundew. Birdlife includes curlew, sandpiper, snipe, wigeon, pochard, goldeneye and goosander.

Pwll Penarth

Near Newtown
OS Map SO 137926; **Map Ref** V22

Once part of the neighbouring sewage treatment works, this is now a wildlife haven. There is a lake with shallow margins for curlew, snipe and other wading birds and deeper water for dabbling ducks. Islands were created for nesting birds and a sand martin cliff was built. A small arable field is sown with cereals each year for the benefit of tree sparrows.

Cors Dyfi

Near Machynlleth; **OS Map** SN 701985; **Map Ref** V19

ACCESS/CONDITIONS: Almost 600m of level boardwalk is wheelchair accessible.
HOW TO GET THERE: The reserve is 3.5 miles south west of Machynlleth on the A487 Aberystwyth road and is situated next to the Morben Isaf Caravan Park.
WALKING TIME: The full circuit is approximately 700m and can easily be walked in 1 hour, but much longer should be allowed to view the wonderful flora and fauna and to spot the sometimes elusive water buffalo.
30-MINUTE VISIT: The walk around the reserve can easily be completed in 30 minutes.

This tranquil site has a variety of habitats – open water, swamp, bog, wet woodland, scrub and gorse, each supporting its own mix of flora and fauna. In spring, a herd of water buffalo graze the reserve. These big, beautiful, and very friendly animals live up to their name and are often seen swimming across the open water. In summer, reed bunting, grasshopper warbler, cuckoo and nightjar are just a small sample of the birds that can be seen and heard. There is also lots of dragonfly and damselfly activity, with species such as common and black darter dragonfly and common blue, blue-tailed and azure damselfly. Look out for two very interesting plants – royal fern and bog myrtle as well.

During the autumn and winter, marsh harrier are occasionally seen hunting over the reserve and snipe are often disturbed from the dense reedbeds. Otter signs, such as spraints and tracks, and even the occasional sighting of these elusive animals all add to the experience.

Llyn Coed y Dinas

Near Welshpool; **OS Map** SJ 223052; **Map Ref** V16

ACCESS/CONDITIONS: A short, level circular walk past the dipping pond, leading to the bird hide, all of which is wheelchair accessible.
HOW TO GET THERE: There is a bus stop next to the reserve entrance and the most frequent service is the number 75 bus to Llanidloes. By car, the reserve is clearly visible at the south end of the Welshpool by-pass, the A483. The entrance is 100m up the old main road to Welshpool town centre on the A490.
WALKING TIME: The full circuit is approximately 500m and can easily be walked in 30 minutes, but much longer should be allowed for a visit to the bird hide.
30-MINUTE VISIT: Head straight to the bird hide for good views of the birds.

Right: Black-headed gull

A beautiful lake now fills this old gravel pit, which provided material to build the Welshpool by-pass that runs past the reserve. This stunning site is a great place to see a wide variety of birdlife up close from the comfort of the large bird hide. In winter and spring visitors can observe the many birds that live here permanently, including coot, moorhen, mute swan and Canada geese. Flocks of teal and wigeon join resident mallard, tufted duck and coot. There are also occasional visits by whooper swans from the Arctic and goosanders. Summer sees the manmade cliffs by the bird hide teeming with sand martins, whether excavating new nest holes or returning with food for their young. In years where floods have removed natural nest sites, the cliffs on the reserve provide a secure site. From spring through to autumn, artificial tern rafts are put onto the lake and are used mostly by black-headed gulls. Otter are occasionally seen on the reserve throughout the year.

Severn Farm Pond

Near Welshpool; **OS Map** SJ 228068; **Map Ref** V17

ACCESS/CONDITIONS: The two bird hides, the teaching area, the sensory garden and the elevated boardwalks are all wheelchair accessible.
HOW TO GET THERE: Located on the Severn Farm Enterprise Park, a short walk from the centre of Welshpool. Welshpool railway station is approximately 500m from the reserve entrance. By car from Welshpool take the B4381 over the railway bridge, then first right into the Enterprise Park, and first right again. The reserve is straight ahead.
WALKING TIME: The full circuit is approximately 700m and can easily be walked in 1 hour, but much longer should be allowed for a visit to the bird hides, sensory garden and sculptures.
30-MINUTE VISIT: Visit the first bird hide, overlooking the lake.

Severn Farm Pond is a little oasis of just over 3 acres (1.3ha), where plants, birds and other animals live in safety, even though people and a busy industrial estate surround them. Elevated boardwalks take you on an amazing journey around the reserve and make you feel like you're walking on water. It's a different world, suspended above pools and marshy wetlands, full of buzzing insects, such as damselflies and dragonflies, frogs, newts and toads. Two bird hides give different outlooks over the reserve and its diverse range of habitats. There are sculptures based on different types of wildlife, a sensory garden and a teaching area with wonderful painted wildlife murals, as well as raised dipping ponds and a picnic area with recycled picnic benches. In summer, the reserve turns purple with the flowering of the purple loosestrife. Dragonflies and damselflies can be seen darting about. Winter and spring are good times to see the resident bird species, such as moorhen, coot, mallard, little grebe and reed bunting. The reserve is part of the flood-prevention scheme for the industrial estate, so a large part of the reserve can be under water at times, but this in itself can be spectacular sight.

WILDLIFE FACT: NEWTS

Of all the species of newts in the UK, the great crested newt is the largest, growing up to 17cm long. They live around weedy ponds and small lakes, although some have been found in dew ponds far from any larger bodies of water. They hibernate from October to February and then are nocturnal, so it's rare to see them, but they are found at Parc Slip.

Dolydd Hafren

Near Montgomery; **OS Map** SJ 206005; **Map Ref** V23

P ☐ i

ACCESS/CONDITIONS: Access via a footpath to the two bird hides. The path can be muddy after flood conditions.
HOW TO GET THERE: From Forden village drive west, turn right off the sharp left bend at the Gaer Farm and down the track to the entrance.
WALKING TIME: 104-acre (42ha) reserve. The full circuit takes 1 hour to walk, but you could spend all day in the hides.
30-MINUTE VISIT: If you only have a little time, stop at the first tower hide and scan the large pool.
A MEMBER SAYS: 'I didn't know what they meant by "mad as a March hare" until I saw their antics here on the reserve.'

This 104-acre (42ha) river flood valley reserve was acquired to let the river erode and move in its natural way across the valley floor, creating a mix of oxbow lakes, river shingle and rough grazing. The two tower hides allow you to appreciate the site's beauty to the full. To sit and watch the cattle grazing among the long grass and reed-fringed pools takes you back 1,000 years. This rural idyll is made more convincing by the endless songs of the skylarks.

In the winter, the curlew take advantage of this grassland, when perhaps 100 can be seen, and although the river can be very angry after heavy rain, good numbers of goosander are often seen.

Spring and summer bring the nesting birds. Look out for the yellow wagtail and the little ringed plover. There is even a chance of seeing redshank or oystercatcher. The pools are a haven for reed and sedge warblers and also the nationally scarce, and unfortunately named, mudwort. In early spring, brown hares can be seen boxing and chasing each other – an amazing spectacle!

The forces of nature are very obvious at Dolydd Hafren. On one side are the plants and animals trying to make a habitat for themselves. On the other is the River Severn that, at times, causes complete chaos! Erosion caused by huge surges of water after heavy rain means that habitats are frequently destroyed. The other side of the balancing act is that new habitats are created. Sand martins nest in areas of bank exposed by erosion; waders find safe nesting sites on islands of spoil and shingle and oxbow lakes provide habitats for newts and frogs.

DID YOU KNOW?

- The Trust has set aside a small area to grow winter food for the birds.
- A flooding wetland reserve like this is superb for wildlife and can help prevent flooding downstream. If only more land could be managed in this way, the world would be a better place.
- The river shingle at Dolydd Hafren holds a strange collection of insects and spiders, some of which are very rare.

Glaslyn

Near Machynlleth; **OS Map** SN 826941; **Map Ref** V21

P i

ACCESS/CONDITIONS: The footpaths are generally good but muddy and wet in places and not suitable for wheelchair access. The reserve is very exposed and the weather can change very rapidly, so visitors should be prepared for changing conditions.
HOW TO GET THERE: Glaslyn is clearly signposted from the minor mountain road between the B4518 near Staylittle and the A489 at Machynlleth.
WALKING TIME: Approximately 2 hours.
30-MINUTE VISIT: Walk from the car park to the viewpoint and back.
A MEMBER SAYS: 'Wild and windswept with stunning views.'

Not only is this the largest reserve currently managed by Montgomeryshire Wildlife Trust at 230ha (540 acres), but it is also the wildest and most regionally important site. The Trust is increasing the area of this valuable habitat at Glaslyn by returning an area of agriculturally improved grassland to heather moorland.

Visiting Glaslyn is a true mountain experience, giving a sense of wilderness and isolation. Walking through the reserve, you will appreciate the landscape of the Welsh mountains and the reserve's lake, bogs, heathland and steep ravine, all culminating in a breathtaking view of the Dyfi valley and the green patchwork of the Welsh lowlands below.

During the winter, the lake occasionally attracts diving ducks, notably goldeneye and Greenland white-fronted geese. In the spring, male red grouse can be seen displaying and setting up territories. Meadow pipits, skylarks and wheatears are also more visible. It's worth looking over the ravine, as ring ouzel and peregrine falcons are often seen there. In the summer, the bogs and wet heath are looking their best. Carnivorous plants, such as sundew and butterwort, occur on the mossy bog areas, growing among tufts of cotton grass and bog asphodel. The site is also the most southerly in the UK for the cloudberry.

In the autumn, the moor looks its best as the heather blooms with purple flowers, some years even carpeting the mountain. The more secretive spring quillwort reveals its presence as the leaves of this prehistoric underwater fern wash up on the lake shore.

DID YOU KNOW?

- The lake is poor in wildlife because of the low nutrient supply in its acidic water.
- One unusual plant, spring quillwort, grows in the lake.
- The ravine is a harsh environment for any colonising wildlife.

Roundton Hill

Near Churchstoke; **OS Map:** SO 293947; **Map Ref:** V24

P i

ACCESS/CONDITIONS: The waymarked route to the top of the hill is long and demanding with some very steep sections.
HOW TO GET THERE: Take the A489 to Churchstoke and follow signs up the lanes to Old Churchstoke and the entrance.
WALKING TIME: The walk to the top of the hill takes 2 to 3 hours.
30-MINUTE VISIT: If you only have a little time to enjoy the woodland birds and plants, follow the path along the stream, through the oak woodlands and past the bat caves.
A MEMBER SAYS: 'The blooms of foxgloves, mullein and ragwort on the rock screes were more beautiful than any garden I have seen.'

This large craggy hill of acidic grassland with a stream and oak woodland at its base is a distinctive landmark affording spectacular views. In contrast to the physical presence of the hill, the wildlife can be subtle and in many ways mysterious, with small ephemeral flowers and an odd collection of mosses, lichens and fungi. The call of the buzzards is as familiar as that of the ravens. It's also worth looking out for peregrine and visiting red kite. In the winter, the antics of the ravens can distract even the most ardent walker. At this time of year the lesser horseshoe bats are sleeping the winter away in the disused mine shafts. The spring brings a particular delight to botanists in the form of spring ephemerals, including the shepherd's cress and common whitlow grass. The redstarts, willow warblers and pied flycatchers return to the oak woodland ready for the summer. The summer and autumn bring a surprising diversity of fungi including a colourful range of waxcaps. The summit of the hill in summer is a wonderful carpet of heath bedstraw, sheep's sorrel and bird's-foot trefoil. Rock stonecrop, which conserves water in its fleshy leaves, grows on crags below the summit alongside limestone-loving plants like wild thyme and lady's bedstraw.

The craggy rocks provide ideal nesting areas for exciting raptors, such as peregrine falcons. Wheatears and meadow pipits breed in the scree and gorse and in the woodland pied flycatchers and redstarts are frequent visitors to the nestboxes provided.

DID YOU KNOW?

- Some of the acid grassland found here is closely related to that found on the Breckland heaths in Norfolk.
- The top of the hill is the site of an Iron Age hill fort. The shapes in the ground can still be seen.
- The lesser horseshoe bats roost in the mines only in the winter. No one knows where they spend the summer.

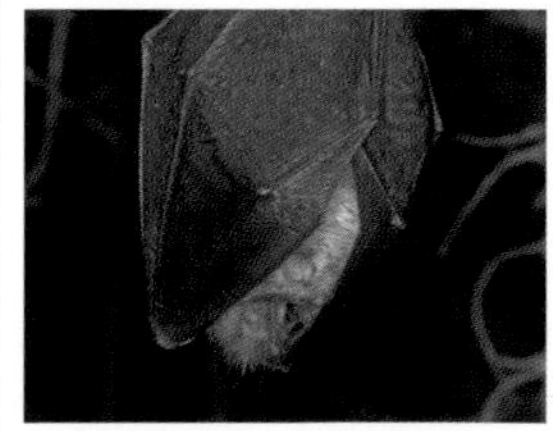

Radnorshire

About the Trust

Established in 1987, Radnorshire is one of the most recently established of the Wildlife Trusts in the UK. Considerable efforts have been made towards developing an educational network for people in the Trust's locality. There is a visitor centre at the Gilfach Farm reserve and regular talks, children's events and exhibitions held throughout the year.

Radnorshire Wildlife Trust ☎ 01597 823298
www.radnorshirewildlifetrust.org.uk

Bailey Einon

Near Llandrindod Wells
OS Map SO 083613; **Map Ref** V35

A reserve of varied woodland, managed mainly by natural processes, which shares many of the characteristics of the 'wildwood' that covered much of Wales thousands of years ago. Birds are well represented with over 40 breeding species.

Cefn Cenarth

Near Pant-y-dwr
OS Map SN 967763; **Map Ref** V27

This wood is part of a much larger block of woodland typical of the uplands of this part of mid-Wales. Sessile oak dominates the canopy. Breeding birds include wood warbler, redstart, spotted flycatcher, three species of woodpecker, tawny owl, coal tit, nuthatch, treecreeper and mistle thrush.

Llanbwchllyn SSSI

Near Painscastle
OS Map SO 116466; **Map Ref** V38

The reserve is designated a SSSI as an example of an uncommon mesotrophic lake. Mallard, teal, tufted duck, pochard and goldeneye are commonly seen. Mute swans and cormorants are often found, and common sandpipers are regular visitors.

Llandeilo Graban

Near Erwood
OS Map SO 099436; **Map Ref** V39

The reserve has a rich and varied flora that supports a large number of invertebrates and animals. The uncommon Welsh stonecrop occurs here. Butterflies include small heath, meadow brown, speckled wood and dark-green fritillary. Take great care walking along the roadside verge. There is information about Llandeilo Graban and other RWT reserves at Erwood station craft centre at SO088439.

Mynydd Ffoesidoes

Near New Radnor
OS Map SO 191652; **Map Ref** V31

At over 600m, the site is one of the most isolated and exposed reserves in mid-Wales. It is a terrain of dwarf shrub heath over thin blanket peat, hosting raven, red grouse, short-eared owls and woodcock as well as northern eggar and emperor moths. This is very difficult terrain. The key for the access gate and forestry track can be borrowed from Trust office.

Pentrosfa Mire

Near Llandrindod Wells
OS Map SO 058596; **Map Ref** V36

The reserve features a mire and an artificial lake with a large snipe roost and flocks of teal in winter. In summer look for sedge warblers, marsh cinquefoil, heath spotted orchid and bog-bean. Brown hare and otters can also be seen. There is a boardwalk to the lake, but no access from the far side. Please don't walk on the mire.

Sideland

Near Penybont
OS Map SO 103638; **Map Ref** V34

This reserve contains ash, penduculate oak, downy birch and rowan. Spring brings a wonderful display of bluebells. Birds are very conspicuous, with both green and great spotted woodpeckers breeding. This is difficult terrain. Access is via permissive path over three fields.

Rhayader Tunnel

Near Rhayader; **OS Map** SN 963673; **Map Ref** V30

ACCESS/CONDITIONS: A tarred, easy-access trail extends through the reserve. Long, steep slopes over the tunnel. Access is not advised to the railtrack bed. There is no access to the tunnel.
HOW TO GET THERE: Take the B4518 Elan Valley Road from Rhayader over the River Wye. Just before the turning onto the Aberystwyth Mountain Road, take the Elan Valley Trail on the left. Walk 300m up the trail to enter the reserve at its north east corner.
WALKING TIME: The linear walk from Elan Valley Trail of 1.5 miles takes approximately 40 minutes.
30-MINUTE VISIT: There is a linear walk of half a mile through the reserve.

The reserve contains an old railway cutting and tunnel, which is used in winter as a bat roost. The reserve also has some good areas of unimproved grassland on the embankments and above the tunnel. The Elan Valley Trail runs through the reserve linking the town of Rhayader to the Elan Valley lakes and dams. In summer, the reserve is botanically diverse with orpine, broad-leaved helleborine, wood bitter-vetch, knapweed, betony and great burnet in profusion and prickly sedge. This is the best time to see the glories of unimproved grasslands with the yellow St John's wort and purple foxglove lining the track. In the fields alongside, red kites often drift by almost at head height. On the old concrete posts, several rare lichens occur. Birds include red kite and buzzard overhead, while redstart, nuthatch, pied and spotted flycatchers breed. Passing over the tunnel, the trail descends, giving sweeping views over neat hedges to the higher hills of mid-Wales and the Elan dams. It's hard to believe that this latter section was very recently dense conifer plantation.

Withybeds and Wentes Meadow

Near Presteigne; **OS Map** SO 309651; **Map Ref** V32

ACCESS/CONDITIONS: A level site with easy access. There is a 220m boardwalk around Withybeds (accessed via a gravel path and a 15cm step). A tapping rail and Braille information boards are provided. The circular path is wheelchair accessible. Winter flooding occasionally occurs in Withybeds.
HOW TO GET THERE: Buses run to Presteigne; take a left at the bottom of Pound Lane. By car, take the B4355 Knighton Road from Presteigne. 400m before reaching the bridge over the River Lugg, turn right into the reserve car park.
WALKING TIME: The circuit of less than 0.4 mile can be easily covered in 20 minutes.
30-MINUTE VISIT: Linger awhile along the 0.6 mile circuit.

Right: Meadow cranesbill

A semi-urban reserve on the boundaries of Presteigne, which gives the opportunity to enjoy some very natural woodland habitat and, in summer, an open lush meadow with meadow cranesbill. The reserve has two distinct characters; open, unimproved mesotrophic grasslands adjoin the reserve parking area and a gravel path leads alongside the old mill leat to the wet willow woodlands (an SSSI). In winter, the woodlands look wild and disorganised, but come spring and summer the lush vegetation rises head high with a mass of meadowsweet scenting the air. The River Lugg (SSSI) borders the reserve and has brown trout, otters and damselflies. Water vole and grass snakes have been observed in the tall vegetation around the small pond and leat.

Burfa Bog SSSI

Near Presteigne; **OS Map** SO 275613; **Map Ref** V33

P i

ACCESS/CONDITIONS: Wet at times. Boardwalk access only partial across the wetter areas. Access into wet woodlands is not advised. South west meadow is very tussocky and wet. Cattle grazing May to October. Dogs are not permitted.
HOW TO GET THERE: Infrequent bus to Walton (Hereford to Llandrindod service). By car, take the A44 to Walton, then B4362 to Ditchyeld Bridge and turn left. The reserve is on the left.
WALKING TIME: 23-acre (10ha) reserve. The full circuit takes approximately 40 minutes.
30-MINUTE VISIT: Turn left from the entrance and walk to the motte and bailey castle. Climb to the top for the view, then continue to the sedgebeds and footbridge.
A MEMBER SAYS: 'One hot summer's day we were tempted by the stile and boardwalks into fields lined by alder-shaded streams. Walking around, we passed by dragonflies, orchids, and butterflies on heavily scented thistles. We loved every minute and will return.'

Burfa Bog is an island of wildlife within an agricultural landscape backed by the rolling hills of the Radnor uplands. The reserve has a very gentle feel to it and in summer the meadows fill with flowering heath spotted orchids, ragged robin and marsh valerian. In the sedgebeds, the hemlock water dropwort buzzes with hoverflies and dragonflies.

Three smaller streams bisect the reserve and in winter about half of the reserve is waterlogged. The streamside woodland dominates and has two distinct types, with open, wet, coppiced alder woodland spreading into diffuse marshy areas, and more mature alder with a closed canopy. The ground flora varies from mesotrophic marsh communities – with marsh marigold, meadowsweet, cuckoo flower, ragged robin and lesser spearwort – to fen communities dominated by lesser pond-sedge.

There are 39 species of breeding birds, including tree sparrow, white-throat, spotted and pied flycatchers, bullfinch, marsh and willow tits, linnet, kestrel, yellow-hammer, goldfinch, blackcap and garden warbler. Visiting birds include snipe, curlew, grey partridge and peregrine. Look out for buzzards overhead.

The reserve's butterfly population includes dark-green fritillary, orange tip, speckled wood, small heath and ringlet. The large wetland cranefly and hazel leaf-roller weevil are frequently seen and frogs are also common across the reserve. Mammals include otters and badgers.

DID YOU KNOW?

- **The alders have been coppiced since Norman times, judging by the size of some of the coppice stools.**
- **Alder makes very good clogs.**
- **Within living memory, clogs were made from the alders at a cottage that used to stand close to the motte.**

Gilfach

Near Rhayader; **OS Map** SN 967716; **Map Ref** V29

OPENING TIMES: Nature Discovery Centre is open from 10am to 5pm from Easter to the end of September.
ACCESS/CONDITIONS: Visitor centre and hide are suitable for wheelchair access. Access via kissing gates throughout most of the reserve. Steep slopes on some trails.
HOW TO GET THERE: Just off the A470, 2 miles north of Rhayader and 7 miles south of Llangurig. Follow the brown 'Nature Reserve' signs. Visitor centre is 1 mile across reserve.
WALKING TIME: Nature Trail is a 3-mile circuit, and the Oakwood Trail a 1-mile circuit. Allow at least 2 hours for the full Nature Trail and extra time to stop at the visitor centre and otter hide.
30-MINUTE VISIT: Follow the Nature Trail (yellow signs from both the visitor centre and the A470 car park) to the waterfall on the River Marteg.
A MEMBER SAYS: 'All the worries of everyday life seem to fade away and you're taken back in time. Facilities are good and the walks are interesting for all levels of walker.'

Gilfach captures the very essence of the wildlife, historical and cultural heritage of Wales. Escaping the ravages of modern agriculture, Gilfach shows the visitor the wonders of traditional farming and the wildlife legacy it has left us.

The meadows contain a range of ancient grassland species, including dyer's greenweed, moonwort, adder's-tongue fern, mountain pansy, parsley fern, heath dog-violet, and eyebright. A large number of waxcap fungi are found across the reserve. The reserve is rich in lower plants, with 413 species of lichen found to date. The species list for birds is currently 73, of which 55 species breed here, including dipper, grey wagtail, common sandpiper, pied flycatcher, linnet, siskin, redpoll, marsh and willow tit, wheatear, bullfinch, buzzard, kestrel, barn owl, spotted flycatcher, meadow pipit, and skylark. Other visitors include curlew, merlin, red kite, goshawk, peregrine, goosander, kingfisher, and reed bunting.

Along the river damselflies, such as the beautiful demoiselle and emerald, are found and common green grasshopper and bloody-nosed beetle are frequent in the grasslands. Keep an eye out for butterflies such as ringlet, wall brown, small heath, green hairstreak, and small pearl-bordered fritillary.

Larger mammals include otters, polecats, stoats, weasels, badgers, foxes, hares and hedgehogs. Daubenton's, Natterer's and brown long-eared bats hibernate in the railway tunnel.

DID YOU KNOW?

- There are many archaeological features at Gilfach, including a Bronze-Age tumulus.
- There are over 400 species of lichen at Gilfach, many of which are found on the rocks of Yr Wyloer.
- Gilfach is also one of the best sites in the UK for waxcaps and other grassland fungi.

South and West Wales

About the Trust

The fourth-largest in size in the UK, the Wildlife Trust of South and West Wales covers Carmarthenshire, Ceredigion, Pembrokeshire, and the old county of Glamorgan. Their reserves include four islands. Ten of their reserves are Special Areas of Conservation, seven are National Nature Reserves and 40 are Sites of Special Scientific Interest.

The Wildlife Trust of South and West Wales
☎ 01656 724 100 www.welshwildlife.org

Coed y Bwl

Castle upon Alun
OS Map SS 909751; **Map Ref** V76

 01656 724100

Famous for its spectacular wild daffodils, the reserve is best visited in spring to see the carpets of these impressive flowers, along with wood anemone and, in some areas, large expanses of bluebells. A wide range of woodland birds includes tawny owl, great spotted woodpecker, nuthatch, treecreeper, marsh tit, blackcap and chiffchaff.

Coed Maidie B Goddard

Near Llechryd
OS Map SN 210437; **Map Ref** V44

 07970 780553

The varied landscape of this reserve includes meadow, wet grassland, young ash woodland, conifers and mature mixed woodland. There is a heronry in the coniferous woodland and the strange clattering cries of the breeding herons can be heard in spring. Plants occurring include goldilocks, ragged robin, dog's mercury, bluebell, and wood sorrel. The reserve is also home to a wide range of butterflies in summer.

Ffrwd Farm Mire

Pembrey
OS Map SN 420026; **Map Ref** V63

 07989 346562

There is a transition across this site from relict sand dune and rough pasture through species-rich fen to reedbed and open water. The wetland habitats support marsh marigold, bog-bean and marsh orchids, with a variety of scarcer plants such as bird's-foot, floating club-rush and water dock. Birds include breeding Cetti's warbler, reed bunting and reed warbler.

Gelli-Hir

Fairwood Common
OS Map SS 562925; **Map Ref** V68

 07971 114306

This is a good-sized secondary broad-leaf woodland with a large lake that has recently been restored. There is active coppicing in some areas. Animals include otter, dormouse and yellow-necked mouse. Look out for silver-washed fritillaries, which can be seen along the paths in the summer months. Access is by stile, but a gate is available for wheelchair access.

Pengelli Wood

Near Felindre Farchog
OS Map SN 130393; **Map Ref** V45

 07971 114301

Pengelli Forest is part of the largest block of ancient oak woodland in west Wales. The steep slopes are dominated by sessile oak and birch with a characteristic ground flora of wavy-hair grass, common cow-wheat and bilberry. Three trees of the native wild crabapple are present. This is the only known location for the Midland hawthorn in Pembrokeshire.

Priors Wood and Meadow

Three Crosses
OS Map SS 577938; **Map Ref** V67

 07971 114306

Mixed woodland and meadow provide a wide array of habitats that are home to many species. In the meadow areas you can find whorled caraway, black knapweed, devil's-bit scabious, ragged robin, and yellow rattle. The woodlands are also very diverse, including sweet chestnut and small-leaved lime as well as many other species such as oak, ash, alder, birch and elm.

Lavernock Point

Near Penarth; **OS Map** ST 182682; **Map Ref** V77

 01656 724100

ACCESS/CONDITIONS: Public footpaths and permissive paths throughout the reserve, including several stiles. Terrain may be a little uneven. There is kissing gate access 91m beyond the gate. Some cliff-top paths susceptible to erosion. Not suitable for wheelchairs.
HOW TO GET THERE: 5 miles south of Cardiff, and 4 miles east of Barry. Bus services 88 and 94 from Cardiff, Penarth and Barry pass close to the reserve. Car access is from the B4267 via Fort Road, sign-posted Lavernock Point.
WALKING TIME: The reserve is 20 acres (8ha) in size. Allow an hour and a half to explore the network of paths at a leisurely pace and enjoy the coastal views.
30-MINUTE VISIT: Head straight through the meadow and south to the coast to get the best of the views.

Lavernock Point is a beautiful piece of limestone grassland alive with meadow plants and butterflies. There are stunning views across the Channel, taking in both Flat Holm and Steepholm. At low tide a beautiful wave-cut platform extends from the bottom of the limestone cliffs, and a good perch at the cliff edge provides fantastic views of waders below as well as opportunities for sea watching. The woodland and scrubby woodland edges are filled with birds.

In spring, flowers in the limestone grassland start to appear, such as cowslip and early orchids, and the migrant breeding birds start to reappear. By summer, many butterflies can be seen, such as meadow brown, ringlet, gatekeeper and comma, as well as beautiful flowers, including common centaury, yellow-wort, dyer's greenweed and devil's-bit scabious. In autumn, large flocks of migrating birds, such as swallows and finches, pass overhead. By winter, birds like fieldfare and redwing are abundant, feeding on the many berries in the scrubby areas.

Old Warren Hill

Near Aberystwyth; **OS Map** SN 614788; **Map Ref** V28

 07970 780553

ACCESS/CONDITIONS: The paths are very steep in places and there are short flights of steps. They can be muddy in places in the winter.
HOW TO GET THERE: The Aberystwyth circular town bus service stops in Penparcau, from where the reserve is just over a 1 mile walk.
WALKING TIME: The reserve totals 20 acres (8ha). The full circuit round the figure-of-eight path network is around a half-mile. Allow an hour and a half for a leisurely walk and plenty of stops for the wildlife and views.
30-MINUTE VISIT: A short walk up the stream gulley to the west of the site will reveal some spectacular fallen trees and the best of the bluebells.

Old Warren Hill is a beautiful mixed woodland. Its summit lies within an Iron-Age hill fort from which there are spectacular views across the valley. The woodland is full of old trees, particularly oaks, covered in mosses and with lovely, gnarled branches. Many bird species typical of old woodlands can be spotted, including great spotted woodpecker, nuthatch, pied flycatcher and treecreeper. In winter, large numbers of buzzard, red kite and raven can be seen overhead through the leafless trees, as they wheel and circle above. Spring brings migrant birds and the return of the breeding pied flycatchers. As the months pass the spectacular carpets of bluebells reach full bloom in April and May. In summer, the reserve is alive with breeding birdsong and a huge variety of invertebrates that thrive in this habitat. By autumn, woodland fungi abound and the spectacular colours of the season reach their peak. The place has a special, feel to it throughout the seasons and is a favourite with walkers, local residents and Trust members from further afield.

Parc Slip

Near Bridgend; **OS Map** SS 882843; **Map Ref** V74

P WC ☎ 01656 724100

ACCESS/CONDITIONS: 1 mile of access for all trails, with tarmac path and ramp into the main hide. Gentle slope to the south, but nothing steep.

HOW TO GET THERE: Bus number 63 from Bridgend bus station stops outside the Fountain Inn at the bottom of Fountain Road, and there is a train station at Tondu. Tourist sign posts indicate the route from junction 36 of the M4 for car drivers.

WALKING TIME: The reserve is 247 acre (100ha). The full circuit takes approximately 1 hour at an easy pace, but longer walks are available.

30-MINUTE VISIT: Park pond and the wetland areas/scrapes at the north of the site, near the visitor centre (only open occasionally during the summer), provide easy access and some good wildlife spots.

Parc Slip is a great example of how nature can re-colonise an area once dominated by heavy industry and opencast mining. Extensive, newly created woodland, grassland and wetland can be explored, created on a former opencast coalmine, after a restoration project that has been running for over 20 years. Important wildlife habitats, including wildflower meadows, ponds, marshes and broad-leaved woodland now support a wide variety of flora and fauna. This includes species such as brown hare, lapwing and butterflies and dragonflies, damselflies and great crested newts, which use the numerous ponds and scrapes for breeding.

In spring, sand martins arrive early over the northern wetlands, and lapwing display in the adjacent fields. Thousands of southern marsh orchids flower in the damp meadows in summer, and breeding teal, tufted duck and little grebe can be seen. Small blue and dingy skipper butterflies can be seen on a sunny June day. Autumn brings nationally rare fungi, and is a good time to spot the field signs that otters leave. Winter is a great time for wildfowl.

WILDLIFE FACTS: PUFFINS

With its distinctive black and white markings, upright stance and brightly-coloured bill, the puffin is an unmistakable bird. Its colourful appearance is heightened by its red and black eye markings and bright orange legs. Puffins like to breed in offshore islands and on high seacliffs and nest in burrows, under boulders or in cracks in cliffs where predators cannot easily reach them. Best looked for at a breeding colony. Try Skomer Island in Wales, or Handa Island in Scotland.

Skomer Island

Near Haverfordwest; **OS Map** SM 725095; **Map Ref** V62

OPENING TIMES: Day visits from April to October (not Monday, except Bank Holidays). Opens on Good Friday if before 1 April. Boats leave Martin's Haven at 10am, 11am, 12noon, returning from 3pm. Crossing is weather-dependent – call 01646 603110 for updates.
ACCESS/CONDITIONS: Full access to Lockley Lodge. Narrow, sloping access to landing jetty to boat. Easy walking on the reserve. Steep flight of steps from landing stage. Visitors should take precautions for changes in weather and take a hat, sunblock, waterproofs and provisions. Dogs are not permitted.
HOW TO GET THERE: Take the Dale Princess ferry from Martin's Haven. The 'Puffin Shuttle' bus serves Martin's Haven, but the timetable varies during the year. Call Richards Brothers (01239 613756) for further information.
WALKING TIME: Full circuit is approximately 4 miles and a leisurely walk should take around 3 hours.
30-MINUTE VISIT: Up to Captain Kites for views of North and South Haven, views of puffins, kittiwakes, fulmars and a good chance of seeing chough. If unable to visit Skomer, pop into Lockley Lodge on the mainland for live-feed cameras showing bird colonies and seal beaches, and even Manx shearwater chicks in their burrows (all season dependent).
A MEMBER SAYS: 'Skomer is a really special place to me. I first came here as a child, and I've been coming back ever since. It's a wildlife enthusiast and photographer's paradise.'

Skomer Island comprises 759 acres (307ha) of principally flat plateau, about 61m above sea level, intersected by a series of ridges with springs, streams, manmade ponds and prehistoric features. One trip to Skomer and you're hooked for life. It's about the best place you can go in the south of Britain for really up-close views of seabirds; you can get to within a few feet of the puffins on the cliff-top paths. The carpets of flowers in early summer are truly spectacular, and on a warm summer's day the heady scent of the bluebells and sea campion is unforgettable.

Spring brings migrants: hundreds of thousands of Manx shearwaters returning to their burrows, with kittiwakes, razorbills and guillemots coming to the island to line the cliff edges and breed. May brings carpets of bluebells, followed by red campion, thrift and, by late summer, heather, providing a colourful backdrop throughout the year. June and July is the time to see puffins feeding their young before they leave the island by August.

Stay overnight on the island to hear the cacophony of Manx shearwaters as they return to the island in the dark from April to September. Grey seals are present all year, pupping between the end of August and November. There's nothing like being on an island for really feeling you're immersed in nature, and no trip is ever long enough.

DID YOU KNOW?

- **Skomer has its own subspecies of the bank vole called the Skomer vole that is unique to the island.**
- **There are no ground predators on the island, only predatory birds.**
- **Skomer and its sister island Skokholm, to the south, are together home to over a third of the world's population of Manx shearwaters.**

South Gower Cliffs

Near Port Eynon, Gower; **OS Map** SS470844 to SS450850; **Map Ref** V75

P WC ☎ 07971 114306

ACCESS/CONDITIONS: The paths can be muddy and uneven underfoot. Please take care on the coastal cliffs. There are moderate ascents and descents.
HOW TO GET THERE: The Gower Explorer and First Cymru buses (114 and 119) run from Swansea Quadrant bus station (www.traveline-cymru.org.uk or call 0870 608 2608). By car, take the A4118 from Swansea to Port Eynon.
WALKING TIME: The walk along the cliffs is a little over 3 miles. Allow 2 hours or more to see the whole site.
30-MINUTE VISIT: Visit Port Eynon Point for spectacular views and some sea watching from the monument on the summit.
A MEMBER SAYS: 'This stretch of the Gower Coast is so special! I first came here when I was 13, shipped off on holiday from my home in London, to stay with my aunt and uncle in Swansea. I knew then that I'd get back here one day.'

Situated in the Gower Peninsula AONB, The South Gower Cliffs offer beautiful panoramic views of the Bristol Channel and South Wales coastline, with all the colours that maritime grassland has to offer.

Here you can see the tranquil and scenic beauty of South Gower, combined with the extreme coastal processes that have helped to shape the land and create the unique habitats found today. Rich maritime grassland and coastal scrub give way to sandy beaches, rock pools and cliff faces, providing something for everyone; from the most avid botanist to the young adventurer exploring the world of rockpools for the very first time.

The reserve has extensive species-rich limestone grassland, scree, maritime heath, scrub, quarries, sea cliffs, caves, rocky foreshore and relict sand dune grassland.

Spring is the season for Gower's famous yellow whitlow grass and spring cinquefoil, also Dartford warblers. During summer, enjoy bloody cranesbill, hoary rock-rose, spiked speedwell and stonechats and white-throats wherever you look. This is the premier site for the silky wave moth, on the wing in July. During August and September, goldilocks aster is in flower, and Port Eynon Point becomes the best site in south Wales for the noble art of sea-watching, with rare birds recorded every year.

Autumn brings fungi, including at least 11 species of waxcap, and during winter look for chough on the cliffs, and marine birds offshore. The reserve forms part of the Port Eynon to Rhossili coastal walk.

DID YOU KNOW?

- Yellow whitlow grass grows nowhere else in Britain.
- Some of the caves on Gower have been inhabited for at least 30,000 years.
- South Gower Cliffs are home to the famed Culver Hole, a natural fissure in the cliff face created by centuries of coastal erosion. Legend has it that Culver Hole was once used as a hideaway for smugglers' contraband.

Teifi Marshes

Near Cardigan; **OS Map** SN187450; **Map Ref** V43

OPENING TIMES: Reserve open all year. Visitor centre open Easter to December from 10.30am daily. Closing hours vary through season. Phone 01239 621600 for details.
ACCESS/CONDITIONS: The Welsh Wildlife Centre is fully accessible with lift to all floors. Gorge Trail has steep steps along one stretch of the riverbank, and the far side of the otter trail and Gorge Trail can be very muddy in winter. The Otter Trail linking the car park to the hides is good underfoot. The track is wheelchair accessible with ramped access to the hides, which also have low viewing windows.
HOW TO GET THERE: Signposted Welsh Wildlife Centre from the A487 at Cardigan. Take the old railway track from Cilgerran south of Cardigan. Alternatively, walk from Cardigan (bus stop) under the main road bridge over the Teifi, and along the Cardi Bach bike trail that runs from Cardigan to Cilgerran, through the reserve and past the visitor centre.
WALKING TIME: Full circuit of the Otter Trail is around 1.5 miles. Allow 2 hours for a leisurely walk taking in all the hides and some of the woodland trails.
30-MINUTE VISIT: Badger trail, signposted from the car park and visitor centre is a circular walk – takes in wildflower meadow, views of the river and across the reedbed and marsh.
A MEMBER SAYS: 'To see a family of otters playing in the river just in front of my eyes and hearing the haunting cries of rutting deer was a wildlife experience I shall never forget.'

Teifi Marshes borders the River Teifi and is a mixture of reedbed, marsh, open water, meadows, river and woodland. The Teifi is a spectacular river, of great importance to wildlife all the way from source to sea. Here, near the estuary, it widens to a broad, fast-flowing spectacular course, which is well used by otters that play and feed in its waters and on its banks.

In winter, see large numbers of teal, wigeon and other wildfowl, and hear water rail. At dusk, experience a large, startling roost in the reedbed. Spring brings the arrival of sand martin and chiffchaff. The woodland is a mass of bluebells, campions, wood anemones, celandines, primroses and stitchworts. It is a good place to see nuthatch and pied flycatcher, which nest in the woods. Reed and sedge warblers can be heard in the reedbed, grasshopper and Cetti's warblers too. The Otter Hide (a mini roundhouse) is the best place to observe the water buffalo grazing the marsh in spring and summer.

In summer, you may also see 16 species of dragonfly, butterflies, including brown and purple hairstreaks, and breeding birds such as peregrine. Lots of waders in autumn include greenshank, godwit and also occasional migrating osprey. Hear the rutting calls of sika and red deer. The Kingfisher Hide is the best place to see young kingfishers learning to fish in summer and autumn.

DID YOU KNOW?

- **The river gorge used to be quarried for slate, employing almost 400 people.**
- **The River Teifi was once home to the last-ever recorded beaver population in Wales, before the species' extinction in 12th century through hunting and persecution.**
- **The milk of water buffalo, which graze the reserve, is low in cholesterol compared to milk from dairy cows and is used to make mozzarella cheese.**

Brecknock

About the Trust

Brecknock Wildlife Trust has been operating for over 40 years, working for the protection of the wildlife habitats and species in the old county of Brecknock (now the southern third of Powys). The Brecknock Wildlife Trust manages over 20 nature reserves across Brecknock, covering a range of habitats including wildflower meadows, old pastures, and woodlands.

Brecknock Wildlife Trust
☎ 01874 625708
www.brecknockwildlifetrust.org.uk

Brechfa Pool

Near Llyswen
OS Map SO 118377; **Map Ref** V40

This large, shallow pool has seasonally exposed, muddy margins containing a range of characteristic plants, including mudwort and the rare pilwort. It is home to a range of wading birds and waterfowl, particularly in winter, including green sandpiper, teal and widgeon. Please try to avoid disturbing wildlife at the pool.

Cae Bryntywarch

Near Trecastle
OS Map SN 853267; **Map Ref** V50

A good example of how meadows used to be before modern farming methods changed them. Look out for betony, wood bitter-vetch, soft-leaved sedge, devil's-bit scabious, lousewort, nesting meadow pipits, basking lizards and small pearl-bordered fritillary butterflies.

Craig y Rhiwarth

Near Pen-y-Cae
OS Map SN 846159; **Map Ref** V53

A partly wooded limestone escarpment adjacent to Craig y Nos Country Park (where toilet facilities, information and food are available). It contains cliffs, screes and ash woodland and some of the best limestone grassland in the area. Enjoy rare whitebeam trees, ravens and broad-leaved helleborine. Please keep away from cliff edges and loose scree slopes.

Drostre Wood

Near Llanywern
OS Map SO 094305; **Map Ref** V49

This is a small woodland in which summer brings the aroma of bluebells and speckled wood butterflies chasing each other in sunny glades. Badgers feed here at night. Birdlife includes nuthatches, greater spotted woodpeckers and song thrushes.

Glasbury Cutting

Near Glasbury
OS Map SO 185394; **Map Ref** V41

Glasbury offers a pleasant walk along a disused railway cutting with ferns, primroses, cowslips, foxgloves, pipistrelle bats, green woodpeckers and earthstar fungus along the way. Look for signs of dormice – when feeding on hazelnuts, it gnaws a distinctive circular hole in the nut.

Llandefaelog Wood

Near Sarnau, Brecon
OS Map SO 029322; **Map Ref** V46

A small but delightful woodland with benches on which to stop and take in the sights, sounds and smells that abound. Most notable for its amazing spring show of bluebells that carpet the woodland floor. Also good for daffodils, brown long-eared bats and nuthatches.

Cae Eglwys

Near Sarnau, Brecon, **OS Map** SO 025333; **Map Ref** V42

ACCESS/CONDITIONS: There are no formal paths, just open meadow on gently sloping ground. Visitors can walk anywhere within the site. Please note the site can be muddy.
HOW TO GET THERE: From Brecon take the B4520 Brecon to Upper Chapel road. After 2.5 miles take the left turn to Sarnau. In Sarnau, take the left turn near a post box. Follow this rough track for 0.5 miles until you cross a cattle grid. Park near the grid but do not block it. The entrance is the gate immediately on your left. (Please note that there is parking space for one car only by the entrance itself.)
WALKING TIME: Loop walk takes no more than an hour. Occasional guided walks as part of the Trust's events programme and regular reserve work party (see website).
30-MINUTE VISIT: Walk through gate and round to right to the heart of the meadow and its panoramic views.

What better place to spend a relaxing sunny summer afternoon than wandering around Cae Eglwys nature reserve? Enjoy the purples of knapweed, the creamy white of sneezewort, the yellow of fleabane and delicate blues of harebells as they mingle with the golden yellows of grasses swaying in the breeze. All this is set against the panoramic back-drop of the Brecon Beacons and Black Mountains.

This lovely old meadow lies on the side of a hill overlooking Brecon town. Wood anemones and celandines herald the coming of spring when the rare adder's tongue fern is visible before the grass overtakes it.

Summer is a wonderful time at Cae Eglwys, with a range of now less common wildflowers such as burnet saxifrage, harebell, knapweed and cat's ear coming into flower.

Look out for the 15 species of butterfly that have been recorded here, including holly blue, common blue and clouded yellow. Autumn sees the meadow sward turning golden and brown, and winter brings in flocks of birds such as fieldfares and redwings, which come to feed on the meadow insects and hedgerow berries.

Coed Dyrysiog

Near Aberbran, Brecon; **OS Map** SN 980310; **Map Ref** V47

ACCESS/CONDITIONS: Visitors are advised to stay on the formal dirt path. Some steep slopes, tree roots and steps, and can be slippery when wet.
HOW TO GET THERE: From the A40, 3 miles west of Brecon, take the turning to the right signposted to 'Llanfihangel Nant Bran, Trallong, Aberbran' in to Aberbran. Turn right over bridge and through village. After 0.25 miles take left turn signposted to 'Llanfihangel Nant Bran.' Site is the woodland one mile on the left.
WALKING TIME: Loop walk takes about an hour and a half.
30-MINUTE VISIT: Via northern entrance, follow path until you can see the Nant Bran river below you. Return the same way.

This ancient woodland nestling in the Nant Bran valley is unusual in that it is a wooded common. Majestic oak trees tower over a dense understorey of hazel, with the Nant Bran winding its way past the lower edge of the reserve.

The reserve is well worth a visit at any time of year. In spring carpets of bluebells and wood anemones greet you along with early-purple orchids. The calls of chiffchaffs mark the start of summer and are joined by pied flycatchers that nest in the wood. Wood and water avens flower by the side of the path and down by the river meadow saxifrage shows off its pure white blooms. Look out for the delicate moschatel, also known as 'town hall clock' because its flowers are arranged like the four faces of a clocktower.

In autumn, the leaves of the trees turn golden and slowly drop to reveal the intricate network of branches forming the canopy. Even in winter, when the trees are bare, mosses and ferns maintain a splash of green.

Darren Fawr

Near Merthyr Tydfil, **OS Map** SO 022102; **Map Ref** V54

ACCESS/CONDITIONS: There are no paths on site, but visitors are free to wander around the upper flatter areas away from the scree slopes and cliffs. A path leads up to the reserve from the golf course car park. The site is very exposed and visitors should wear appropriate clothing.
HOW TO GET THERE: From the A470 travelling south towards Merthyr Tydfil, take the left turn (Vaynor Road) towards Cefn Coed and Pontsticill. Take the first left (Cloth Hall Lane) and follow it up to Merthyr Golf Course car park. Park here. The reserve is a further mile north north-east on foot from the golf course.
WALKING TIME: Loop walk takes about 2 hours.
30-MINUTE VISIT: It is not possible to visit Darren Fawr in 30 minutes due to a one-mile walk up to the reserve.

Darren Fawr is the largest and most spectacular of the Brecknock Wildlife Trust's reserves. Scree slopes with aromatic wildflowers, sheer cliffs with very rare trees and soaring ravens and a hill top with limestone pavement and far-reaching views. This reserve has it all!

Spring sees the gradual greening of this upland wilderness with splashes of colour from bird's-foot trefoil attracting common blue butterflies. The limestone rocks influence the range of wildflowers and plants growing here with salad burnet, the aromatic wild thyme, rock-rose, the delicate quaking grass and limestone bedstraw being good examples. Look out for peregrines hunting along the cliffs and in autumn ravens can be seen displaying up high. In winter a dusting of snow marks out the high peaks of the Brecon Beacons mountain range visible from here. Look beneath your feet and you will see ferns living within the grykes of the limestone pavement, keeping out of the elements.

WILDLIFE FACT: THE WONDERFUL WORLD OF ORCHIDS

Orchids have a glamour and an appeal all of their own. They combine an often flamboyant appearance with a 'sexy' charisma, bringing a touch of the tropics to the English countryside. The 50 or so species of native orchids include some of our most sought-after rarities, while others can be found on road verges or areas of wasteland.

Pictured: Greater butterfly orchid

Pwll y Wrach

Near Talgarth; **OS Map** SO 162328; **Map Ref** V48

ACCESS/CONDITIONS: Easy access trail from the car park to the centre of the reserve has a handrail along its length and is at a gradient suitable for wheelchair and pushchair access. Other trails leading to the waterfall and around the rest of the reserve can get very muddy after rain. Caution: some steep drops down to river. Dogs to be kept under close control.
HOW TO GET THERE: Bus 39 to Talgarth (Brecon to Hay-on-Wye). By car, from the centre of Talgarth, take the road over the river up past the Bell Hotel. Turn left up Penbont Road and left again up Hospital road. After 0.5 miles the wood begins on the right of the road, with the main entrance. The second entrance is just a bit further up the road.
WALKING TIME: The circular walk from the car park to the waterfall takes about 1 and a half hours at an easy pace. Occasional guided walks as part of the Trust's events programme and regular reserve work party (see website). Self-guided geological tour leaflet available from the Trust office.
30-MINUTE VISIT: Walk along the easy access trail into the centre of the reserve and back, looking out through the tree canopy for a bird's-eye view.
A MEMBER SAYS: 'It is always a delight to come to Pwll y Wrach. I walk there regularly and always see something different every time.'

Pwll y Wrach is a wonderfully atmospheric woodland at any time of year. It is particularly delightful to walk among the wildflowers in spring, with the River Enig babbling over rocks in the background. At the far end of the reserve, the river forms a spectacular waterfall cascading over a sandstone cliff into the Witches' Pool below.

The reserve is located in the Brecon Beacons National Park in the foothills of the Black Mountains. It is a fine example of an ancient Welsh broad-leaved woodland growing along the side of a steep valley down to the River Enig. During spring, the woodland floor becomes carpeted with celandines and bluebells. Rarer plants include early-purple orchid, bird's-nest orchid, herb Paris and the unusual toothwort. In the summer, lesser horseshoe bats, brown long-eared and pipistrelle bats flit through the trees foraging for insects, and elusive dormice commute through the network of overhanging branches during the night. Autumn reveals a beautiful display of brown and golden leaves and fungi of all shapes and colours. Winter frosts and snow give the reserve a particular beauty. Occasionally, the waterfall freezes, giving a spectacular display of frozen motion in its icicles. There is abundant birdlife in the wood all through the year, with pied flycatchers nesting in the woods and buzzards circling on thermals overhead. There are also interesting geological features and rock exposures to be found.

DID YOU KNOW?

- Pwll y Wrach is Welsh for the Witches' Pool, which lies directly below the waterfall .
- Toothwort is different from most plants, it isn't green as it has no chlorophyll and is parasitic on tree roots such as hazel.
- Pwll y Wrach is the Trust's most visited reserve.

Wern Plemys

Near Ystradgynlais; **OS Map** SN 788093; **Map Ref** V55

ACCESS/CONDITIONS: The reserve and its paths can get quite boggy at any time of year. Top reserve boundary is marked by a disused railway line, now a path, which can be used to make a circular walk. Dogs to be kept under close control at all times.
HOW TO GET THERE: From the A4067 running through Ystradgynlais, take the B4599 Trawsffordd road. At the T-junction with College Road turn left and then immediately turn right over the bridge over the River Tawe. Turn right passing the Gough Arms on the left, and go to the end of Heol Glantawe; park in the car park. On foot enter Diamond Park, crossing one bridge in front of you and then a second to your right. Follow a path that runs parallel with the stream to the main site entrance.
WALKING TIME: The full circuit from the entrance takes about 45 minutes.
30-MINUTE VISIT: From the entrance, follow the waymarkers past the old farmhouse to the meadow. Walk up to the top of the meadow, cross the stile in the right-hand corner and up onto the bed of the disused railway line.
A MEMBER SAYS: 'It's hard to believe this was a heavily mined area not too many years ago. Nature has been given a chance to re-paint its pretty picture upon the landscape and fill it with many little gems. A wonderful place to sit for a while and let the world go by.'

The reserve feels different from many other sites, it has a feeling of wilderness, with the wildflower meadows blending seamlessly into the surrounding woodland. From the old tramway above the reserve you have excellent views across the Swansea valley and on to neighbouring hills. And all this right on the edge of Ystradgynlais!

The reserve consists of a mosaic of extensive woodlands and several small wildflower meadows. The meadows were once part of a farm and the ruins of the farmhouse remain. In spring, visitors can hear the distinctive call of the chiffchaff, one of the first migrants to arrive after winter, and the opening leaves give the woodland its first touch of green.

In summer, the wildflower meadows are awash with a range of colourful hues, and buzzards can be seen soaring overhead. The late-flowering purple heads of devil's-bit scabious can be seen in the autumn attracting hoverflies and butterflies. During a walk in winter, you may be able to see flocks of tits and finches moving through the trees.

DID YOU KNOW?

- **The remains of the old farmhouse still remain – can you find them?**
- **The whole area used to be heavily mined, but has now been reclaimed by nature.**
- **Rare plants such as whorled caraway still survive in the forgotten meadows.**

Vicarage Meadows

Near Abergwesyn; **OS Map** SN 850526; **Map Ref** V37

ACCESS/CONDITIONS: The reserve can get quite boggy at any time of year. Situated in an exposed position, it can be very cold in winter. Dogs to be kept under close control at all times.
HOW TO GET THERE: From the A483 at Llanwrtyd Wells, take the minor road north west through Llanwrtyd and Cwm Irfon towards Abergwesyn. Park safely (not blocking any entrances) on the roadside only, just before the bridge over River Irfon at Abergwesyn, and then on foot take the right of the two tracks off to the left, passing by two houses to a gate.
WALKING TIME: A walk around the reserve takes up to 1 hour at an easy pace. The walk can be extended into the adjacent Nant Irfon NNR. Occasional guided walks as part of the Trust's events programme and regular reserve work party (see website).
30-MINUTE VISIT: Go straight through the first field in to the second field to admire the colourful display of wildflowers.'
A MEMBER SAYS: 'In the last 40 years, 97 per cent of hay meadows in the UK have been replaced by a monoculture of ryegrass. Vicarage Meadows is part of that rare 3 per cent that shows what a colourful and diverse landscape existed.'

Vicarage Meadows lies adjacent to the nearbt Nant Irfon NNR. It consists of two unimproved fields, separated by a line of spaced beech trees. The second field is particularly rich in wildflowers. Many years ago, the local vicarage owned Vicarage Meadows. The fields provided a hay crop and a place to graze horses and cows. The small stone barn was used as a shelter for milking cows. The Trust continues to use traditional management methods, with a hay crop being taken off one field and Exmoor ponies grazing the whole site, giving the reserve's many wildflowers the chance to flourish.

During spring, the second field shimmers with bluebells. In summer, the floral display continues with the yellow of dyer's greenweed, the pink of orchids and the dense, purple heads of devil's-bit scabious. Small pearl-bordered fritillary butterflies can be seen at close range feeding on flower heads – and watch out for common lizards scurrying away. In autumn, the trees of the valley put on a beautiful golden display, and a brisk walk in winter truly reveals the remote solitude of this lovely valley.

DID YOU KNOW?

- The reserve gets its name because, many years ago, the fields belonged to the local vicarage.
- Five species of orchid can be found here.
- Dyer's greenweed, which is abundant in the second field, is so called because of its use in the past for dying cloth.

Gwent

About the Trust

Gwent Wildlife Trust manages over 30 reserves and dormice, fritillary butterflies, orchids and other species benefit from the conservation work carried out from the lower Wye to the Rhymney river valley in South East Wales. The Trust works in the last remaining parts of fenland left on the Gwent Levels and in traditionally handled meadows and woodlands.

Gwent Wildlife Trust
☎ 01600 740600
www.gwentwildlife.org
www.welshwildlife.org

Allt-yr-Yn

Newport
OS Map ST 299888; **Map Ref** V70

This reserve has a variety of habitats, including ponds, woodlands and grasslands. Spring brings a good display of woodland flowers and in summer the unimproved meadows are home to a variety of interesting flowers including common-spotted orchid, meadow vetchling and ox-eye daisy. Other notable species on the reserve include broad-leaved helleborine and adder's tongue fern.

Branches Fork Meadows

Near Pontypool
OS Map SO 269015; **Map Ref** V61

A mixture of oak woodland, invading scrub and damp, heathy grassland. Heather and devil's-bit scabious are prominent in the drier areas, and orchids can be found in the marshy areas. The site is very good for insects, from hoverflies to grasshoppers. Butterflies such as small skipper, large skipper, meadow brown and small heath can be seen in summer. Goldcrest, long-tailed tit, bullfinch and treecreeper occur all year in the willow scrub and fringing woodland. Frogs, toads and lizards also make the most of the reserve.

Brockwells Meadow SSSI

Near Chepstow
OS Map ST 470896; **Map Ref** V71

This reserve consists of a set of species-rich limestone meadows. There is a rich variety of limestone flora and more than 70 species of plant have been recorded, including green winged orchid, autumn lady's-tresses, large thyme and yellow-wort. Many species of butterfly and moth have been recorded. The meadows are an important breeding site for the rare hornet robber-fly.

Coed Meyric Moel

Cwmbran
OS Map ST 271942; **Map Ref** V65

This is an excellent site for butterflies and other insects. The reserve comprises a small area of oak woodland and a meadow. It is part of a larger block of ancient woodland. The meadow flowers include knapweed and various species of vetch. Butterflies such as meadow brown and small skipper can be seen, along with hoverflies and a range of beetles.

Dixton Embankment

Near Monmouth
OS Map SO 527149; **Map Ref** V52

A flat, limestone terrace built to buttress an embankment of the A40, which now supports a wide range of wildlife. Plants include yellow-wort, bee orchid, ploughman's spikenard, pyramidal orchids and wild onions. There is a rich diversity of insect life including large numbers of six-spot burnet moths. Butterflies include common blue, marbled white and the dingy skipper. As the site is just above the River Wye, rare species such as the white-legged damselfly can be seen in abundance.

Henllys Bog SSSI

Near Cwmbran

OS Map ST 264927; **Map Ref** V25

Henllys Bog is small valley mire surrounded by woodland. Eighty-five plant species have been recorded on the reserve, including the insectivorous butterwort and round-leaved sundew. In the centre of the mire, purple moor-grass tussocks dominate along with purple loosestrife, meadow thistle, dyer's greenweed and fragrant orchid. The site is rich in invertebrates, including the dark bush-cricket and rare spiders. Birdlife includes tits, woodpeckers, nuthatch, siskin, redpoll, woodcock, and grey wagtails feed along the stream.

New Grove Meadows

Near Monmouth

OS Map SO 502067; **Map Ref** V59

This reserve consists of four adjacent meadows. The grassland flora in the northern two meadows is indicative of an unbroken history of traditional management. In April, the yellow flowers of cowslip burst forth across these meadows. In May, early-purple orchids appear at the field edges, followed by large numbers of green winged orchids and common-spotted orchids. Autumn sees an impressive array of grassland fungi including yellow, red, pink and green waxcaps.

Priory Wood SSSI

Near Usk

OS Map SO 353058; **Map Ref** V56

This beautiful wood supports a fine range of trees and is renowned for its cherry trees. Other species include oak, ash, birch, beech and yew. Many species of insects and fungi live on the rotten wood. The woodland flora boasts a profusion of bluebells (pictured below) in spring. Birds include spotted and pied flycatchers, sparrowhawk, woodcock and the occasional hawfinch. This rare large-billed finch favours woods like this, which offer a range of tree seeds and fruit.

Solutia Reserve at Great Traston Meadows

Near Newport

OS Map ST 346843; **Map Ref** V73

This Gwent Levels reserve is notable for its grassland, divided by reens (drainage ditches) that provide marshy habitats. The flora includes reeds, rushes and sedges in the damper areas. In the drier grassland areas, species such as meadow vetchling can be found, along with specialities such as southern marsh-orchid and the rare grass vetchling.

Strawberry Cottage Wood SSSI

Near Abergavenny

OS Map SO 312215; **Map Ref** V51

P layby only

This fine example of a sessile oak woodland lies within the Brecon Beacons National Park. Flowers include slender St John's wort, violets, yellow archangel and wood melick. Many woodland birds have been recorded, such as pied and spotted flycatcher, redstart, woodcock, sparrowhawk and all three species of British woodpecker. Grass snakes have been seen here.

Croes Robert Wood SSSI

Near Monmouth; **OS Map** SO 475060; **Map Ref** V60

ACCESS/CONDITIONS: The reserve is on a hillside and paths can be steep, wet and muddy. Care is needed.
HOW TO GET THERE: Bus 65 from Monmouth to Chepstow stops at the village of Trellech. By car from Monmouth take the B4293 south signposted to Mitchel Troy and Trellech. Continue along the B4293 until the village of Trellech. In Trellech follow signs for Cwmcarvan. The reserve entrance is 250m down the hill on the right.
WALKING TIME: The reserve is 35 acres (14ha) and a full circuit can take 2 hours.
30-MINUTE VISIT: Walk along the top path from the car park into the woods. Look out for the display of woodland flowers in the spring.

This reserve is an outstanding example of sustainable conservation in action. The ancient semi-natural woodland is being successfully managed by coppicing, providing a habitat for one of Britain's most threatened mammal species, the dormouse. The excess timber is then used to produce barbeque charcoal to sell locally.

If you visit in spring, the woodland is a carpet of bluebells, wood anemones and yellow archangel. Lesser celandine grows along the paths and wood sorrel appears in damper areas. Look out for the rare herb Paris, which flowers from June onwards.

In the summer, twayblade and common-spotted orchid are in flower. Autumn is the best time to look for the most obvious sign of dormouse presence – characteristically gnawed hazelnuts. This is also a great time to see a whole variety of fungi. As well as dormice, the reserve is home to yellow-necked mice.

Dan-y-Graig

Near Risca; **OS Map ST 235905**; **Map Ref** V69

ACCESS/CONDITIONS: Much of the reserve is on a steep slope. Bridges and steps have been built at strategic points. Paths can be wet and muddy close to streams and boggy areas. There is a boardwalk adjacent to the pond. The path is steep beyond the pond. Paths are not suitable for wheelchair access.
HOW TO GET THERE: Frequent buses from Risca. By car, turn off the A467 Risca Bypass at the Risca roundabout and drive north into Risca town centre. Turn left onto Dan-y-Graig Road and bear left uphill by Dan-y-Graig Cottages; the entrance is on the right.
WALKING TIME: 3-acre (1.2ha) reserve. The full circuit takes 40 minutes.
30-MINUTE VISIT: There is plenty to see around the pond close to the entrance.

Despite its small size, this reserve contains a variety of habitats – deciduous woodlands, limestone grassland, a pond fed by streams and springs creating boggy areas, and some industrial regeneration. The geology of the area is quite complex: underneath the reserve is a Roman lead mine and there is still visible evidence of lime kilns.

In spring, there is a good show of primroses and the sections of woodland carpeted with ramsons are readily distinguished by smell as well as sight. Hart's tongue fern is abundant, with smaller numbers of male and shield ferns. Wild strawberry grows on the limestone grassland, where the anthills support scarlet pimpernel and pearlwort. The pond is home to water shrews, minnows and sticklebacks. Look out for dragonflies in the summer.

The pond was originally built to provide water for the copper works that stood on the site of the adjacent brickyard. It is now home to water shrews, minnows and dragonflies. Kingfishers and grey wagtails have been seen. Springs feed the pond and the clear water is home to three species of horsetails.

Springdale Farm

Near Usk; **OS Map** ST 411991; **Map Ref** V64

ACCESS/CONDITIONS: This is a working farm with livestock in most fields. Please keep dogs on leads and stay on the paths. Parts of the reserve are steep and muddy with some steep flights of steps.
HOW TO GET THERE: From Usk town centre (on the A472) take the B-road towards Llanllowell, Llantrisant and Wentwood. Pass Usk Prison and continue for two miles until you pass under the A449 dual-carriageway bridge. Take the next left after the bridge and follow the narrow road for two miles. The reserve is on the left at the top of the hill.
WALKING TIME: The full circuit takes about 2 and half hours to walk.
30-MINUTE VISIT: Walk from the car park across the first field, through the gate and up to the top of the slope for some lovely views of the surrounding area.

This working farm was acquired for its grassland, in particular a superb set of hay meadows. It offers stunning views across the Usk Valley up to the Brecon Beacons National Park and down towards the Severn Estuary. The meadows are at their most spectacular during the summer, with common-spotted orchids, knapweed, tormentil and pepper saxifrage. A thin band of limestone bedrock provides the conditions for Gwent's largest population of dyer's greenweed. The reserve also includes a woodland, which has a wonderful display of woodland flowers in the spring, including violets, wood anemones, bluebells, early-purple orchids and moschatel. Listen out for blackcaps, willow warblers, chiffchaffs and marsh tits. Autumn is notable for the diversity of fungi in the wood and short-grazed areas of grassland support colourful waxcaps. In winter look out for flocks of fieldfares and redwings feeding in the species-rich hedgerows.

WILDLIFE FACT: WOOD ANEMONE

The pretty spring flower indicates an area of ancient woodland. Known to grow in abundance when the conditions are right, each stem has a single white star-shaped flower, often with a pink or purple tinge. It's sometimes called the 'windflower', as its thin stems tremble in the breeze.

Magor Marsh SSSI

Near Newport; **OS Map** ST 427869; **Map Ref** V72

ACCESS/CONDITIONS: Flat, wet and marshy terrain. Access mainly on boardwalk, but there are steps in places and sections of uneven muddy paths. Livestock may be present. Dogs are not allowed on this reserve.
HOW TO GET THERE: Bus 61 from Newport stops directly outside the reserve and buses X10, X11, X14 and 62 stop at Magor. By car, head for the village of Magor on the B4252 from either the A48 from Newport, or junction 23A off the M4. Continue through Magor and take a turning on the right, signposted Redwick. The reserve is along this road.
WALKING TIME: The butterfly trail markers take you on a full circuit (about 1 hour) of the reserve, including a visit to the hay meadows.
30-MINUTE VISIT: Follow the signs to the bird hide for good views over the pond.
A MEMBER SAYS: 'My first visit was unforgettable – the warden rushed off in great excitement as a bittern had just been sighted! This is a great place for birdwatching – expect some surprises!'

Magor Marsh SSSI is the largest remnant of traditionally managed fenland on the Gwent Levels. The site provides a glimpse of the ancient past – it is believed that there has been farming here for almost all of the last 6,000 years. It is a prime example of the succession of plant communities from open water to marsh and scrub woodland. Two hay meadows are maintained using traditional methods. They are only grazed during autumn and winter. The hay crop is mown in mid-summer to provide winter feed. Snipe and reed buntings breed in the rough pasture and the cuckoo can be heard in the summer.

In spring, marsh marigolds can be seen over the whole reserve and by late spring and early summer the hay meadows are a mass of wildflowers. These can include meadow thistle, yellow flag, yellow rattle, ragged robin and lesser spearwort. In autumn and winter, the pond provides sanctuary for resident birds and for migrants such as garganey. Over-wintering birds include large flocks of teal. The reserve is also one of the richest sites in Wales for water beetles, including the spectacular great silver water beetle, Britain's largest beetle.

DID YOU KNOW?

- **This was the Gwent Wildlife Trust's first reserve and it has been successfully managed for wildlife for over 40 years.**
- **The reserve is actually below sea level.**
- **Water levels within the reserve are controlled through a system of sluices in the drainage ditches or 'reens'. Look out for otter spraints – otters often use the sluices as sprainting sites.**

Pentwyn Farm SSSI

Near Monmouth; **OS Map** SO 523095; **Map Ref** V58

ACCESS/CONDITIONS: The reserve consists of gently sloping grassland. Paths can be muddy. Please keep to the footpaths at the field margins. Livestock may be present at certain times of the year. Full mobility kissing gates have been installed.
HOW TO GET THERE: Bus 65 runs between Monmouth and Chepstow (Monday to Saturday, every 2 hours). By car from Monmouth take the B4293 south signposted to Mitchell Troy and Trellech. Approximately one mile from Monmouth, take the left turning for Penallt, Trellech and Chepstow. About two miles up the hill, take the first left turning signposted Penallt. In Penallt turn left at the crossroads then right just before the war memorial (follow signs for the Bush Inn).
WALKING TIME: 27-acre (11ha) reserve. The full circuit takes 1 hour at an easy pace.
30-MINUTE VISIT: From the car park follow the unsurfaced green lane up to the medieval barn from where the hay meadows can be viewed.
A MEMBER SAYS: 'Pentwyn Farm SSSI is an excellent place to while away a summer's afternoon revelling in the sights, sounds and smells of the hay meadows.'

Situated 210m above the Wye Valley AONB, this farm provides outstanding views across the valley to the Forest of Dean. Its hedgerows form part of the link to the other Wye Valley woodlands and the meadows echo days gone by. The traditional small farm layout of cottage, green lanes, stone stiles and drystone walls has been maintained. No artificial fertilisers have been applied for 20 years or more, and no pesticides are used in farming. It is important for its four unimproved hay meadows (SSSI) and its hedgerows and ranks as one of the larger areas of unimproved grassland remaining in Gwent.

In spring, early purple orchids and cowslips are present, and it is a good spot for migrant birds. The floristic display continues into summer, when a range of orchids (greater butterfly, green winged, common spotted and common twayblade) are mixed into the colourful carpet of ox-eye daisy, yellow rattle and eyebright. The hedgerows provide good habitat for dormice, and in autumn, partially eaten hazelnuts betray their presence. The hedgerows also provide plentiful food supplies for over-wintering flocks of birds such as fieldfares and redwings.

DID YOU KNOW?

- Six different species of orchid can be found on the reserve – see how many you can spot.
- The name Pentwyn means 'top of the mound', 'pen top', and twyn means 'hillock' or 'mound' and is a common Welsh name.
- The restored medieval barn is a traditional Monmouthshire 'Dead Man's Barn'. The derivation of the term is unknown.

Silent Valley SSSI

Near Ebbw Vale; **OS Map** SO 187062; **Map Ref** V57

ACCESS/CONDITIONS: Care is needed on the steep, muddy paths. There are steps along most routes.
HOW TO GET THERE: Buses E3 and E4 run from Newport to Cwm. By car from Ebbw Vale, take the A4046 south. Go straight over at the roundabout. After Waunlwyd village, join the bypass (do not take the Silent Valley landfill road). Take the next left to Cwm village, then take the left turn after the Bailey's Arms – look out for the brown nature reserve sign on the right. From Newport, take the A467 towards Risca. Follow the road past Risca and continue up the valley until the turning on the left towards Cwm on the A4046.
WALKING TIME: The full circuit takes about 2 and half hours. There are often group and school visits and events – see the Trust's event programme.
30-MINUTE VISIT: A short walk throught the wood to the glade will provide a view of some of the most attractive areas of beech wood.
A MEMBER SAYS: 'There is no better place than these woods on a crisp, sunny morning, with the redwings and siskins in the trees and the ravens flying in the hills above.'

A mature, open, veteran beech woodland interspersed with alder carr, wet flushes and areas that were once meadows. There are also old mining spoil sites and an old coal tip, all now colonised by mosses, lichens, heather and grasses.

The reserve (much of which has SSSI status) takes its name from the stillness and quiet of the beech wood in the height of summer. It is an example of how the decline of heavy industry in Wales has led to a resurgence in local wildlife.

In spring, there is a display of woodland flowers, which includes bluebells, lesser celandine, wood sorrel and golden saxifrage. Redstarts nest in the woods. In summer, bats are hunting for insects in the evenings and yellow mouse-ear hawkweed flowers on the spoil tips. Small pearl-bordered fritillary can be observed.

Autumn is the best time to look for fungi in the woods. There is an added bonus of seeing the purple flowering heather on the spoil tip and the hills above the reserve. Winter brings large flocks of tits and finches passing through the woods in feeding parties and ravens can be seen overhead.

DID YOU KNOW?

- **The woodland forms one of the most westerly and highest natural beech woods in Britain.**
- **This is a wonderful site for fungi – an unusual species of toothed fungus has recently been found on the reserve.**
- **It's a good place to hear the 'yaffle' alarm call of the green woodpecker.**

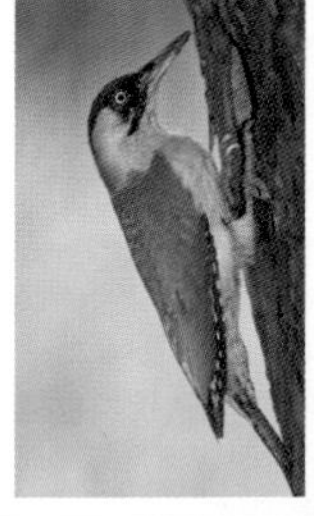

Snowdonia
National Park

SCOTLAND

Scotland offers a raw beauty unrivalled by other parts of Britain. It is a land of dramatic contrasts – from the rolling hills of the Southern Uplands to the splendour of the Highlands, breaking up in the north and west into a succession of headlands, sea lochs, islands and stacks. Its rugged charm is similar to that found in Wales and the Lake District, but on a much grander scale. The scenery is simply breathtaking and can change before your eyes as the weather suddenly turns and the light plays across the landscape.

It is easy to get distracted by the sheer beauty of the terrain, but equally fascinating is the diverse range of species that have made their home here. Scotland is a haven for more than 90,000 species, from the bottlenose dolphins of the Moray Firth to the capercaillie of the Central Highlands and the thousands of seals and puffins inhabiting the coastline.

The high mountains attract only the hardiest of species, such as the ptarmigan and mountain hare, who both don their white winter coats to aid camouflage in these gruelling habitats.

Meanwhile, the coast and offshore islands attracts thousands of bird species. Two fantastic locations are the Isle of Eigg, in the Inner Hebrides, with its red-throated divers, and Montrose Basin, Angus, excellent for pink-footed geese and whooper swans among other species. Further south the Falls of Clyde, near Lanark, is excellent for peregrines, offering the closest views of the bird in Britain.

Another iconic species to look out for is red deer. Numbers have increased dramatically in recent years and their current population stands at roughly 300,000. They can mainly be found in the Highlands and islands, although large numbers can be found in the Galloway Hills.

One of the hardest Scottish mammals to spot in the wild (primarily due to its nocturnal habits) is the pine marten. This sleek woodland predator is slowly expanding its range again throughout Scotland. Once persecuted for its highly prized fur, it is now becoming an ever-more regular visitor to gardens across the Highland mainland and Eastern Lowlands.

The spectacular coastlines also offer some great marine life. Grey seals are widespread on Scotland's rockier west coast. The Scottish population is estimated at up to 120,000. Summer is a great time to see them, when they can be found basking on the rocks, soaking up the sun. Bottlenose dolphins can be seen all around the coastline, although Moray Firth is the most renowned place for spotting them. With such a diverse range of landscapes and habitats on offer, there are endless places to explore in Scotland and once you've had a taste for it, you'll want to go back for more.

Opposite: Lochan na h-Achlaise in the Highlands

NOT TO BE MISSED

- **FALLS OF CLYDE**
One of Scotland's most popular nature spots thanks to its nest of peregrines and wildlife-rich river path.

- **KNAPDALE**
Over 11 miles of intoxicating coastline with brightly-coloured marine life, such as anemones, starfish, camouflaged spider crabs and sugar kelp.

- **LOCH ARDINNING**
Superb views of Ben Lomond, resident black grouse and some rare invertebrate life, such as the uncommon northern damselfly.

- **LOCH FLEET**
A great venue for sightings of dolphins, porpoises and common seals, with waders and shelduck feeding on invertebrates at low tide.

- **LOCH OF THE LOWES**
Loch of the Lowes is famous for its breeding osprey, and their eyrie is situated just 200 metres from the nature reserve's viewing hide.

- **MONTROSE BASIN**
This reserve is visited by over 1,000 pink-footed geese in the winter months, not to mention the 4,000 wigeon, pintail, mallard and eider that over-winter here.

Scotland

About the Trust

The Scottish Wildlife Trust (SWT) is the largest voluntary body working for all the wildlife of Scotland, representing more than 30,000 members who care for wildlife and the environment. As a registered charity, our members are vital in supporting our mission to protect Scotland's rich natural heritage. SWT seeks to raise public awareness of threatened habitats and species and manages more than 120 Scottish reserves.

Scotland Wildlife Trust☎ 0131 312 7765
www.swt.org.uk

Carlingnose Point

South Fife coast
OS Map NT 135809; **Map Ref** U13

This reserve is home to both dropwort, rare in Scotland, and the locally scarce field gentian. Other flora includes bloody cranesbill and lesser meadow-rue. The area is home to occasional breeding fulmar as well as warblers and migrant birds on passage.

Carstramon Wood

Near Gatehouse-of-Fleet
OS Map NX 592605; **Map Ref** T9

This is an ancient oak woodland with fantastic veteran beech. Summer migrant birds include pied flycatcher, redstart, wood and willow warbler. There are stunning bluebells in May, and abundant ferns and lichens. Park in layby below the wood.

Cullaloe

Near Aberdour
OS Map NT 188877; **Map Ref** U12

At Cullaloe, visitors can see rare plants such as water sedge and mudwort. Birdlife includes sedge warbler, whitethroat, great spotted woodpecker, bullfinch, black-tailed godwit and spotted redshank. There is a good path to the viewpoint.

Dumbarnie Links

Largo Bay
OS Map NO 441022; **Map Ref** U11

This reserve consists of dune grasslands and features cowslip, primrose, meadow cranesbill, common and greater knapweed, and viper's bugloss. Here, you can spot skylark, stonechat, meadow pipit, shore birds and seabirds. Common blue, small copper and meadow brown butterflies splash the links with colour.

Handa Island

Reached by ferry from Tarbet
OS Map NC 138480; **Map Ref** U2

This is an offshore island with sea cliffs. Over 200,000 seabirds gather here in summer to breed, including guillemots, great and Arctic skuas, kittiwakes and puffins. There is a 3.5-mile circular path, but note that care must be taken near the cliffs – stay on the path or boardwalk at all times. Ferries operate April to early September and crossings are weather-dependent, £10 (£5 children).

Hill of White Hamars

Orkney
OS Map ND 313885; **Map Ref** U1

This reserve consists of sea cliffs and coastal grassland. Scottish primrose, grass of Parnassus, field gentian and fairy flax can all be seen. Birdlife includes black guillemot, shag, rock dove, fulmar and gull. Care must be taken as the cliffs and cliff paths can be dangerous.

Loch of Lintrathen

Near Kirriemuir
OS Map NO 278550; **Map Ref** U7

From late autumn, birds such as greylag goose flock to this loch in their thousands. You may also see tufted duck, shoveler, great crested grebe, mallard, coot, heron and osprey. A track runs along the shoreline and through the woods. Visit in October to March for the best wildfowl-spotting opportunities.

Longhaven Cliffs

Near Peterhead

OS Map NK 116394; **Map Ref** U5

Longhaven's spectacular granite cliffs are alive with breeding seabirds and clifftop plants. Here, you can see bell heather, crowberry and devil's bit scabious. Kittiwake, guillemot, shag, puffin and fulmar can all be spotted. A footpath runs the length of the reserve, but care must be taken – cliffs and cliff paths can be dangerous. The reserve is best visited between May and September to see the greatest variety of seabirds and plants.

Red Moss of Balerno

Near Edinburgh

OS Map NT 164636; **Map Ref** T5

This is one of only 20 raised peat bogs in the Lothians. It teems with plantlife, including bog asphodel, round-leaved sundew, marsh ragwort and cuckoo flower; fauna includes common lizards, dragonflies, frogs, toads, small pearl-bordered fritillary and willow warblers. Half of the boardwalk is suitable for wheelchairs.

Seaton Cliffs

Arbroath

OS Map NO 667416; **Map Ref** U10

These spectacular red-sandstone cliffs are home to marsh orchid, primrose, violet and sea campion. Arctic tern, eider and gannet can all be seen here. The path is tarmaced in places, but the cliff path is steep and the cliffs are dangerous – take extra care when it is wet. Visit from May to July to see the widest variety of seabirds, flowers and butterflies.

Stenhouse Wood

Near Tynron

OS Map NX 795930; **Map Ref** T8

This mixed deciduous woodland is home to moss, dog's mercury, ramsons, fern, honeysuckle, bugle, bracken, bluebell, goldilocks buttercup and toothwort. A footpath circles the upper part of the reserve. Visit May to September for wildflowers.

WILDLIFE FACT: BRITAIN'S OLDEST TREE

There is a yew tree in the small village of Fortingall in Perthshire that is believed to be the oldest tree in Britain, somewhere between 3,000 and 5,000 years old. That means it has been standing since well before Julius Caesar invaded Britain in 55BC. Yew trees are famously long lived and often start to grow again after 500 years, long after most other trees have died – the yew has been called 'the tree of eternity', and it is easy to see why.

Ayr Gorge Woodlands

Near Failford; **OS Map** NS 457249; **Map Ref** T7

ACCESS/CONDITIONS: There is a network of footpaths on the west side of the river – however, these are steep in places.
HOW TO GET THERE: From Ayr town centre take the A719 north-east for about 3 miles to the junction with the A77. Continue straight over the roundabout onto the B743 Mauchline Road and continue until Failford. Park in the lay-by in the village.
WALKING TIME: The return walk to the wooden bridge takes around 1 hour. Continuing on around the southern half of the reserve will add an additional hour.
30-MINUTE VISIT: Plunge yourself deep into the woods. Stop and stand awhile – you'll be amazed by the amount of wildlife you can see and hear.

Ayr Gorge is an impressively steep ravine in the river valley. Beneath the tall broad-leaved trees, there is a sparse shrub layer of holly, hazel and rowan. In spring, the canopy comes alive with birdsong, with spotted flycatchers and great spotted woodpeckers among the species worth looking out for. The aim of the long-term management of the reserve is to improve the age range of trees so that the woodland is sustained long into the future. The summer months are the ideal time for seeing woodland plants such as foxglove, enchanter's nightshade and glossy green ferns. While mammals can be less active in autumn and winter, reduced foliage means that you have a better chance of catching sight of a roe deer, otter or badger. You also have spectacular scenery as well, with mosaics of reds, yellows and oranges as the leaves fall in colder weather.

According to local legend, it was in these woods that Robert Burns and Highland Mary met to arrange leaving Scotland for the West Indies. Sadly, Mary died before the arrangements were complete. It's also said that Alexander Peden (the renowned Covenanter) preached to his congregation gathered on the opposite side of the river from the top of the sandstone steps known as Peden's Cove.

Isle of Eigg

Inner Hebrides; **OS Map** NM 474875; **Map Ref** U6

OPENING TIMES: Eigg is accessible by ferry during the summer.
ACCESS/CONDITIONS: Some paths around the island can be steep and slippery. Tides affect activities.
HOW TO GET THERE: There is a Caledonian MacBrayne ferry (foot passengers only) from Mallaig – take the A82 north from Fort William for about 1.25 miles, then turn left onto the A830 to Mallaig. A private ferry runs daily in summer (not Thursday) from Arisaig, about 9 miles from Mallaig. Both ferry crossings take 1 hour (call 01687 482477 for more information).
WALKING TIME: Eigg has five walking routes, each from 1 to 4 hours in duration.

Set within a NSA, with three SSSI and a listing in the Geological Conservation Review, Eigg has exceptional qualities. In spring, the hazel scrub woodland becomes home to a generous carpet of bluebells, wild garlic, wood anemone, wood sorrel and primroses. Further afield, golden eagles, buzzards and ravens can be seen patrolling their high kingdoms. The summer months herald a whole new range of plant life, with honeysuckle and enchanter's nightshade taking over in the woodlands. The bird world is visited by cuckoo, whinchat, whitethroat, willow warbler and twite, while 18 species of butterfly and many dragonflies and damselflies can regularly be seen. Between July and September, minke whales are also a frequent sight from the ferry crossings over to the island. As the days start to get shorter and the temperature cooler, great northern divers and jack snipe can be spotted as well as passing redwing, fieldfare, snow bunting and brambling.

Jupiter Urban Wildlife Centre

Near Grangemouth; **OS Map** NS 920810; **Map Ref** T3

OPENING TIMES: Open all year, Monday to Friday, 10am to 5pm.
ACCESS/CONDITIONS: The reserve has a well-maintained nature trail with pathways suitable for wheelchair access.
HOW TO GET THERE: The reserve is north of the M9 between Junctions 5 and 6. From Beancross Road turn north on to Newlands Road, then left to Newhouse Road and left on to Wood Street. The route is well marked with tourist signs.
WALKING TIME: You can spend anything from 30 minutes to a whole day exploring Jupiter.
30-MINUTE VISIT: You can whizz around the nature trail, or pick up some information on the bugs and beasts of Jupiter from the centre to enjoy a self-led adventure.

Jupiter has been developed as a base for volunteers, school groups, community groups and the public. It was built as a demonstration site to show how urban greenspaces could be created from wasteland, and how green amenity areas, including gardens, can be managed to meet both human and wildlife needs.

The main task for the Jupiter Project has been the development of a wildlife garden. Two large ponds were excavated in 1991, the diggings from which were formed into two low hillocks about 3 metres above the surrounding flat area. Jupiter is also a valuable training ground for conservation workers, who are able to learn and experiment with practical techniques of habitat creation and maintenance. May and July are the best times to see the wildflowers in full bloom. Children will enjoy pond-dipping, as they search for intriguing creatures such as the water scorpion.

Pease Dean

Near Pease Bay; **OS Map** NT 790704; **Map Ref** T4

ACCESS/CONDITIONS: There are paths throughout the reserve, including the end of the Southern Upland Way. Please keep to paths wherever possible and keep dogs under close control. Do not attempt to cross the railway line. The steepest slopes of the Dean are dangerous and should be avoided. Take care crossing the narrow road bridge.
HOW TO GET THERE: Pease Dean is above Pease Bay, reached by turning off the A1 road 1 mile south of Cockburnspath. Parking is available opposite the static caravan park at Pease Bay.
WALKING TIME: The Dean is a steeply wooded 82-acre (33ha) reserve. The full circuit takes 2 hours.
30-MINUTE VISIT: If time is short, looking down the Pease Dean from on top of Pease Bridge can give you an insight into the life of the reserve.

The best areas of the reserve for wildlife have a mix of ash, oak and hazel with alders along the burnside. Beneath these trees, dog's mercury, an indicator of ancient woodland, is abundant and in early summer the air is thick with the garlic scent of ramsons. Primroses, bluebells and red campion add their colour to this thick layer of wildflowers. Great spotted woodpeckers, treecreepers, dippers and parties of long-tailed tits are regularly seen and marsh tits breed here, close to the northern limit of their range in the UK. In summer, willow warblers, blackcaps and whitethroats fly in from their southern wintering areas to join the resident tits and thrushes and fill the woodland with song. The reserve has a long history as woodland – Robert the Bruce was said to have cut timber here during his siege of Berwick in 1318 and the site once provided wood for the monks of Coldingham Priory. There is a fortified tower dating from the 15th century at the top of Tower Dean. During construction of the main Edinburgh to London railway in the 19th century, a huge embankment was created which cuts Tower Dean into two parts. At one time there was a mill at the seaward end of the reserve, and you can still see its remains.

Falls of Clyde

New Lanark; **OS Map** NS 883414; **Map Ref** T6

OPENING TIMES: Open all year; the visitor centre is open 11am to 5pm daily (noon to 4pm in January and February).
ACCESS/CONDITIONS: There are surfaced footpaths on the reserve, including part of the Clyde Walkway long-distance path, which follows the river. Visitors are asked to stay on the paths as the gorge edges can be unstable and slippery. The visitor centre is fully accessible for wheelchair users.
HOW TO GET THERE: There are two trains every hour from Glasgow. The bus from Lanark bus station to New Lanark is the 135, or it's a 25-minute walk. By car, from Glasgow, follow the M74 to Junction 7 and then take the A72, or follow the M8 to Junction 6 and then take the A73. From Edinburgh, follow the A70 or A71 and then take the A706. From the south, follow the M74 to Junction 13, then follow the A73. From Ayr and the west, take the A70.
WALKING TIME: A full walk around onto the Corehouse side and back is approximately 6 miles in length and takes 4 hours at an easy pace.
30-MINUTE VISIT: Dundaff Linn, the smallest of the waterfalls, is on the riverside path (dippers, kingfishers and maybe an otter can be seen here), and the 84ft Corra Linn fall is a brisk walk away.
A MEMBER SAYS: 'The Falls of Clyde really is my favourite place to be. I especially enjoy visiting the peregrine falcons on the reserve – the views of the birds are incredible.'

The reserve's peregrine falcons begin to nest in early spring and should have laid their clutch of eggs by April. Onlookers can watch the development of the chicks throughout the following months. This is also a great time to join the ranger on badger watches as the cubs begin to emerge from their underground setts in spring.

Early summer brings views of the young peregrines as they take their first uncertain flights. Five species of bat residing at Falls of Clyde may be observed on evening strolls throughout the summer. The river-edge trail is an excellent place to see flowers such as campions, water avens and marsh marigolds. You may also spot a dipper, or the bright colours of a kingfisher as it darts across the river. In autumn, the woodland is a mosaic of colour and a good time for fungal forays. In winter, the sightings of otters increase. Visit May to August for flowering plants, September to November for fungi, April to August for breeding birds, and any time for the spectacular scenery.

DID YOU KNOW?

- An attraction for at least two centuries, the Falls of Clyde were visited by Wordsworth, and many artists such as Turner have painted the dramatic landscapes.
- Scotland's first public hydro-electric scheme was opened here in 1927.
- The Falls are home to nesting peregrines and some of the best views of these birds in Britain.

Gight Wood

Near Methlick; **OS Map** NJ 820392; **Map Ref** U4

P i

ACCESS/CONDITIONS: The forestry road leads through Badiebath Wood and across the field to the entrance beside Gight Castle. A steep path leads down to Hagberry Pot footbridge along riverbank to Otter Bridge. From here the path climbs up the gorge and returns along the top to Gight Castle.
HOW TO GET THERE: The wood is 0.75 miles from Cottown, off the Methlick Road in a remote location on steep land sloping down to the River Ythan. It is about 28 miles from Aberdeen, 2 miles from Methlick and 3.3 miles from Fyvie. Park in the Forestry Commission car park.
WALKING TIME: The walk into the reserve takes about 30-45 minutes, and the circular path will take 2 hours.
30-MINUTE VISIT: Walk along the track through Badiebath Wood to Gight Castle for commanding views of the surrounding countryside.
A MEMBER SAYS: 'Gight Wood is my favourite reserve, from the fantastic blooms of hawthorn and cherry in spring to the beautiful autumn colours.'

Gight Wood lies on the north bank of a deep ravine of the River Ythan. It forms the easternmost part of a series of woodlands and riverine grasslands extending all along the tightly winding valley to Fyvie. Brooding over the woods, at the downstream end, is the ruin of Gight Castle, once the home of Byron's mother.

The reserve today is largely a broad-leaved woodland. Tree species native to the area include oak, ash, elm, birch, rowan, bird cherry and the wild cherry, which brightens the gorge woods with its wonderful spring blossom. Beneath the tree canopy there is hazel and blackthorn, and the ground flora includes a number of locally uncommon plants. Next to the river, woodland species give way to wet marshy grassland. Here, there are only a few scattered trees, mainly willow, alder and aspen, while reed grass and yellow flag are abundant. Many roe deer live in the wood, and there are also foxes, badger, red squirrels and hare. If you are very lucky you may see an otter or a heron. Visit from April to June for spring blossom or October to November for autumn colours.

DID YOU KNOW?

- Gight Wood was noted as a type 'rare in these places' in 1662.
- A dwelling has been on the site of Gight Castle since the 14th century.
- Red squirrels have their very own rope bridge across the River Ythan on the reserve.

Knapdale

Near Loch Sween; **OS Map** NR 766884; **Map Ref** T1

P i

ACCESS/CONDITIONS: The reserve and several of the trails are easily accessible from the car park.
HOW TO GET THERE: Knapdale is at the head of Loch Sween at the north end of the Kintyre Peninsula in Argyll, approximately 7.5 miles west of Lochgilphead, off the B8025 to Tayvallich.
WALKING TIME: The reserve is 1,730 acres (700ha), and there are walks of 1 to 3 hours and cycle trails of 1.5 to 3 hours.
30-MINUTE VISIT: Even a short wander through Knapdale's forest tracks will afford magnificent views.
A MEMBER SAYS: 'The landscape of Knapdale is like nothing else I have seen before in the UK, full of hidden glens and secret lochs.'

Swathed in both native Atlantic oak woodland and coniferous plantations, much of the reserve is carpeted with rare mosses, ferns and lichens. The woodlands support many bird species, red squirrel and notable plants such as the swordleaved helleborine. Sika, roe and red deer occur together with a variety of butterflies and moths. In summer, redstart, tree pipit, willow and wood warbler are typical of the oak woodland. You may hear the great spotted woodpecker drumming or see buzzards and ravens flying overhead. Visit any time for birds and attractive scenery, or from May to July for woodland plants. The tidal lagoons of Loch Sween are covered with soft mud, while in other parts rock faces drop into deep water. Marine life on these cliffs ranges from brightly coloured anemones and starfish to camouflaged spider crabs, large sugar kelp to carpets of small red seaweeds. The freshwater lochs support an excellent array of dragonflies. Herons and cormorants frequently fish from the rocky promontories, while other coastal birds include oystercatchers, redshank, curlew, eider and merganser. The area is marked as a potential site for the trial reintroduction of the European beaver. Indeed the area is so rich in wildlife that much of it has been designated a SAC. The area is also seen as the first kingdom of the Scots, and is rich in archaeological sites and history.

DID YOU KNOW?

- **The reserve has over 11 miles of coastline.**
- **The area was once the heartland of Dál Riata, the first kingdom of the Scots, in the 6th and 7th centuries.**
- **The reserve is the proposed site for the first reintroduction of European beaver to the UK.**

Loch Ardinning

Near Glasgow; **OS Map** NS 564779; **Map Ref** T2

ACCESS/CONDITIONS: The nature trail is suitable for wheelchair users.
HOW TO GET THERE: The reserve is 1 mile from Strathblane on the A81 (Glasgow to Aberfoyle). Park in the lay-by off the A81 – please note, fast traffic, blind bends and rises mean caution is required when parking here.
WALKING TIME: The nature trail of approx 1 mile follows a marked circuit starting at the east end of the dam and around the northern shore of the loch. Follow the numbered posts and waymarkers.
30-MINUTE VISIT: Take the footpath that follows the loch and continues up the hill to a fine viewpoint.
A MEMBER SAYS: 'The reserve is like Scotland in miniature: lochs, moorland and woods, and all just 15 miles from Glasgow.'

The northern part of the loch is densely populated with reeds, rushes and sedges, the luxuriant growth resulting from the sheltered, shallow conditions. To the west of the loch lies a wet wood, or carr, consisting of mature willows, birch and alder. The loch is also a haven for a variety of wintering and breeding wildfowl, including tufted duck. It is rich in invertebrate life, such as the uncommon azure damselfly. The water lobelia is a local speciality, flowering in the loch shallows in July. There are superb views of Ben Lomond from the high point on Muirhouse Muir, and the Muir supports a variety of resident birds, including black grouse and curlew, as well as summer visitors such as the whinchat and cuckoo. Look out for patches of bog cranberry, bog myrtle and bog asphodel on the muir.

DID YOU KNOW?

- The loch was the site of a battle in 570 AD between the kings of what later became Northumberland and part of Cumbria.
- From the highpoints of the Loch Ardinning reserve you can see the Arrochar Alps, which are over 35 miles away.
- The reserve is home to a small but important black grouse population.

Loch Fleet

Near Golspie; **OS Map** NH 794965; **Map Ref** U3

ACCESS/CONDITIONS: The pathway through Balblair Wood is suitable for wheelchair access.
HOW TO GET THERE: The reserve is east of the A9 between Dornoch and Golspie. The north is accessed via the Golf Course Road to Littleferry from Golspie; the south via the minor road around the south side of the basin, left at the crossroads and up the unsurfaced track to the car park.
WALKING TIME: There are various walks from 1 to 2 hours in length, particularly in the pinewoods, through Ferry Links and along the beach, which includes a 1.8-mile stretch at Coul Links.
30-MINUTE VISIT: Common seals and birds can be observed from the road along the south shore. Take a quick stroll to the seaward opening of the estuary for excellent views and plenty of fresh sea air.
A MEMBER SAYS: 'Loch Fleet has a beautiful pristine sandy beach which stretches for miles. I love to walk along it at any time of the year.'

The reserve at Loch Fleet contains within its boundary coastal heath, sand dunes, pine woodland and mudflats. Waders and shelduck feed on the invertebrates in the mud at low tide, and eiders on the mussels along the course of the river. In summer, Arctic and common terns fish in the shallows, and in winter, large numbers of wigeon graze the eel-grass growing on the tidal flats. Long-tailed duck and the common scoter take advantage of the estuary's sheltered water in winter. The pine woodland at Balblair Wood supports a number of rare pinewood plants and mammals such as pine martin, red squirrel and roe deer. There are also Scottish crossbills, crested tits and common species such as treecreeper, sparrowhawk, buzzard and great spotted woodpecker. In summer, osprey fish regularly on the reserve, although they do not breed there, and in winter, peregrines and hen harriers regularly visit to hunt. Both within the estuary and along the coast, common seals can be seen, particularly when they haul out on sandbanks at low tide. Visit Loch Fleet May to July for flowering plants, April to September for waders and October to March for wildfowl.

DID YOU KNOW?

- You can often see dolphins and porpoises from the beach.
- In summer ospreys hunt for fish over the estuary.
- You can see hundreds of common seals hauled out on the sandbanks at low tide.

Loch of the Lowes

Dunkeld; **OS Map** NO 050440; **Map Ref** U9

OPENING TIMES: Open all year round, 10am to 5pm.
ACCESS/CONDITIONS: The visitor centre and hide are suitable for wheelchair access.
HOW TO GET THERE: The reserve is 6 miles from Perth and 2 miles from Dunkeld, off the A923 Dunkeld to Blairgowrie Road (signposted from the A9). There are trains and buses to Dunkeld, and the 1.6 mile Fungarth Walk links Dunkeld to the reserve. There is free parking 120 metres from the centre.
WALKING TIME: This is a 235-acre (95ha) reserve. Viewing only – there is no opportunity to walk on the reserve.
30-MINUTE VISIT: Take a look around the display in the visitor centre to learn about the history of the site and the protection and conservation of osprey. You'll also have time to sit in the hide and view the wildlife – including the magnificent osprey.
A MEMBER SAYS: 'Possibly the best views of osprey in the country and not as crowded as some other visitor centres.'

The star attraction from early April to late August is a pair of breeding osprey. Their eyrie is situated within 200 metres of the observation hide, allowing osprey family life to be observed through telescopes and on a monitor in the visitor centre. Otters are present but sightings are unpredictable. Fallow and roe deer are seen regularly from the hide, while red squirrel are present in the woodland. You may also see redstart, spotted and pied flycatcher, crossbill and kingfisher. Wildfowl can be observed throughout the year. Great crested grebes, coots, mallard and mute swans are regular breeders and numbers of goldeneye, wigeon, teal, pochard and Canada goose peak in early winter. Up to 3,000 migrant greylag geese roost on the loch during winter. Wildfowl can be observed throughout the year with peak numbers of duck in early winter. Visit April to September for breeding birds and October to March for wildfowl and scenery.

DID YOU KNOW?

- **Osprey have an impressive wingspan of 1.45-1.7m. Among Scottish birds of prey, only the golden eagle and the sea eagle have a larger wingspan.**
- **Loch of the Lowes is the only British loch on which great crested, Slavonian and little grebe have bred at the same time.**
- **Osprey first appeared at the Loch of the Lowes in 1969, just a few weeks after the reserve had been established.**

Montrose Basin

Montrose, Angus; **OS Map** NO 690580; **Map Ref** U8

OPENING TIMES: The visitor centre is open daily, 10.30am to 5pm, 15 March to 15 November (Friday to Sunday, 10.30am to 4pm for the rest of the year).
ACCESS/CONDITIONS: The visitor centre is suitable for wheelchair access.
HOW TO GET THERE: The reserve is 1.5 miles outside Montrose on the Arbroath Road. Take a train to Montrose then a bus (every hour). The bus stop is 500 metres away from the visitor centre.
WALKING TIME: The full circuit is 10 miles. Pick up a reserve walks guide from the visitor centre.
30-MINUTE VISIT: Go to the visitor centre or take a leisurely stroll along the river from Old Montrose Pier.
A MEMBER SAYS: 'I like the part when we went out onto the mud. It was fun but my wellie boot almost got stuck. The other bit I liked was looking through the telescope, it was amazing how many birds I saw. The best bird I like is the swans. I like how they float nice and slow down the water.' [Schoolchild, after a visit to Montrose Basin]

Montrose Basin comprises the estuary of the River South Esk, reedbed and saltmarsh habitat and farmland.
The visitor centre offers magnificent views of wildlife on the basin through high-powered telescopes. Three television cameras bring the wildlife directly into the centre. During spring and summer, visitors can get a bird's-eye view of the family life of blue tits and swallows. From September onwards, several thousand pink-footed geese visit the reserve and in October and November, the numbers peak at over 35,000 birds. The winter is also the best time to see all the wintering wildfowl using the reserve. From the wigeon hide at the western side of the reserve it is possible to see around 4,000 wigeon, pintail, mallard and eider ducks at high tide. Winter is also the best time to see large concentrations of waders such as redshank, knot and oystercatcher. During spring and summer, it is perhaps the eider duck which is the most notable species, with around 300 pairs nesting on the reserve. In the farmland fields, waders such as lapwing, redshank and oystercatcher breed and numerous reed buntings and sedge warblers nest.

DID YOU KNOW?

- There are 390,000 hydrobia in 1 square metre of mud at Montrose, food for the likes of the shelduck.
- An oystercatcher can eat 315 cockles a day.
- Montrose Basin comprises 1,082 acres (440ha) of mud.

The mountain Buachaille Etive Mor near Glencoe, one of the best-known views in Scotland

NORTHERN IRELAND

Despite its small area, Northern Ireland has a great variety of scenic countryside, which reflects its contrasting geology and topography.

The dramatic coastal landscape of County Antrim forms one of the most spectacular stretches of coastal scenery in the world, home of the famous Giant's Causeway with its celebrated basalt columns and formations set in stunning cliff scenery. This whole stretch of coast provides habitat for a diverse range of flora and fauna, and is a great place for birdwatching. A walk along the cliffs can give you a glimpse of rare choughs. The Glens of Antrim are also a stronghold for the red squirrel.

In the south of County Down, the impressive Mourne Mountains literally rise up from the sea. The landscape here is varied, ranging from mountains to farmed hill countryside and coastline. The Mourne mountain range affords not only spectacular views, but also an opportunity to spot a huge range of wildlife.

Further west and inland takes you into County Armagh. There are a number of places to explore here, around the edge of Lough Neagh, the largest lake in the United Kingdom and home to a variety of birdlife, including thousands of tufted duck, pochard, goldeneye, and scaup in winter. Further west again takes you into County Fermanagh with its wonderful wetland habitats surrounding Lower and Upper Lough Erne. Here you can see numerous wading birds including curlew, redshank, lapwing and snipe. You could even spot the elusive pine marten in the forests of Fermanagh.

Heading north will take you into County Tyrone and County L'Derry, where the landscape changes into the sparse highlands and the lush river valleys of the Sperrin Mountains, where there are no end of beautiful places to explore. Here you still have the chance of hearing the call of the corncrake if you are very lucky.

A visit to Northern Ireland is truly a unique experience. Its rolling hills and jagged indented coastline make for varied and exciting wildlife-watching opportunities.

Opposite: Dun Bhaloir, Tory Island, Donegal
Below: Fanad Head, County Donegal

NOT TO BE MISSED

- **BOG MEADOWS**

A remnant of the River Blackstaff floodplain, Bog Meadows is a wildlife haven right in the heart of Belfast. Situated in west Belfast, it comprises a mosaic of reedbeds, meadow ponds, woodland, streams and associated wildlife.

- **SLIEVENACLOY**

Acquired by Ulster Wildlife Trust in 2000, this 310-acre (125ha) grassland nature reserve in the Belfast Hills offers spectacular views across Northern Ireland. It is home to rare orchids, butterflies, waxcap fungi and birds such as skylarks and curlew.

Ulster

About the Trust

The Ulster Wildlife Trust is a local nature conservation charity working for a healthy environment across Northern Ireland both on its land and in its seas. It works across Northern Ireland:

- **managing nature reserves for wildlife**
- **supporting community environmental action**
- **teaching people about nature**
- **campaigning for a healthy environment.**

Ulster Wildlife Trust☎ 028 4483 0282
www.ulsterwildlifetrust.org

Ballydyan

Between Crossgar and Saintfield
OS Map J 416548; **Map Ref** W15

A real wildlife corridor with many birds and mammals using the reserve to get from one place to another or to hunt. Look out for ravens, sparrowhawks, willow warblers, bull finches, foxes, rabbits, and the holly blue butterfly. Paths can be muddy and are unsuitable for wheelchair access. There is a circular walk which takes around 20 minutes at a slow pace.

Ballynahone Bog

Near Maghera
OS Map H 860980; **Map Ref** W8

The second largest area of intact raised bog in Northern Ireland. It is a designated ASSI and NNR, noted for its interesting bog flora, including nationally rare sphagnum moss, liverwort and bog rosemary. The reserve is also very rich in insects, dragonflies, and butterflies, including the large heath and green hairstreak. All of the region's amphibians and reptiles can be found here, including the common lizard and smooth newt. A vast number of raptors have also been spotted hunting over and around the reserve, including hen harriers, buzzards, kestrels, sparrow hawks, long-eared owls and merlins.

Blessingbourne

Near Fivemiletown
OS Map H 448487; **Map Ref** W14

This nature reserve is typical of many estates of its type, with an artificial lake, surrounding fen and semi natural woodland. Though originally landscaped, the lake and wood have been reclaimed by white-clawed crayfish, smooth newts, marsh marigolds, purple loosestrife, brown hawker dragonflies, reed buntings, grasshopper warblers and milkwort fungus. Paths can be muddy and are unsuitable for wheelchairs. There is a circular walk that takes about an hour. Parking for approximately 50 cars at Round Lough (opposite the entrance). Overnight accommodation is available on the estate.

Cottage Farm

Near Omagh
OS Map H 437797; **Map Ref** W9

A peaceful and secluded wood, this nature reserve is part of a fully operational farm in private ownership. The woodland flora reveals a lot about its history: the profusion of bluebells and anemones suggest the wood is long established, whilst specimen exotic trees and small larch plantations represent past human influence. The mammal list includes otters, badgers, foxes, several bat species and red squirrels. Along the river, keep your eyes peeled for kingfishers and banded demoiselle. Paths can be muddy and are unsuitable for wheelchair access. An informal path along the river makes for a pleasant 30-minute stroll. Parking is available on the side of the road for three cars. Please note, this reserve is only open to Wildlife Trust members; however, if an event is being held at these sites, non-members can attend for a small charge.

Edenderry

Near Belfast

OS Map J 318683; **Map Ref** W13

Situated 4 miles south of Belfast city centre, this nature reserve is very interesting for its fauna and flora. Divided into two areas, it has one part planted deciduous woodland and another part fen and willow. Species present include toothwort, water rail, song thrush, and the ground beetle *Carabus clatratus*. The path can be muddy and is unsuitable for wheelchair access. Limited roadside parking is available in Edenderry village.

Feystown

Near Glenarm

OS Map D 315105; **Map Ref** W5

Situated in the Glens of Antrim, this small meadow is the prime site in Ireland for wood cranesbill. Apart from Feystown, this beautiful wildflower has only been reported during the past decade at two sites, both in the Glens of Antrim. Other interesting plants include yellow rattle and the greater butterfly orchid. This is a small reserve and is best viewed from the roadside, where there is limited parking. Permission for access required from Ulster Wildlife Trust. Note, there is no walking at this reserve.

Glendun

Near Cushendall

OS Map D 201317; **Map Ref** W2

Glendun is an organic hill farm in the Antrim Glens. Great views can be enjoyed from the glen's heather-clad plateau. This upland habitat is breeding ground for the threatened red grouse. The pasture on the lower slopes is grazed by Irish moiled cattle and sheep. Other wildlife you may see includes waxcap fungi, dippers and red squirrels. The muddy and uneven terrain of the farm is not suitable for wheelchairs. The upper section of the trail is very steep and only recommended for experienced hill walkers.

Isle of Muck

Off Islandmagee

OS Map D 464024; **Map Ref** W7

This wonderful island, a designated ASSI, has the third largest colony of cliff-nesting seabirds in Northern Ireland. Kittiwakes, fulmars and razorbills all breed here and peregrines commonly hunt over the island. You can see puffins, otters seals, and cetaceans offshore. The island is accessible by boat, or can be viewed from the mainland at Portmuck. Dangerous cliffs rise to 34 metres high and there are no recognised paths on the island. Permission for access required from Ulster Wildlife Trust. Note that there is no walking at this reserve.

Milford Cutting

Near Armagh

OS Map H 859427; **Map Ref** W16

This small secluded nature reserve, outside of Armagh City, is an old railway cutting with a mix of flowery calcareous grasslands and scrubby woodland. The grassland occupies the steep railway banks and is dotted with a variety of orchids in early summer including common twayblade, fragrant and common-spotted orchids and the rare marsh helleborine. Apart from wildflowers, the site boasts Northern Ireland's largest colony of an unusual tree species, the Irish whitebeam. The nature reserve is an important wildlife corridor for mammals and birds. A circular path takes 25 minutes at an easy pace. Roadside parking in Milford village (a 5-minute walk).

Straidkilly

Midway between Carnlough and Glenarm

OS Map D 302165; **Map Ref** W3

This small nature reserve, a designated ASSI, is perched above Glenarm village on a limestone escarpment, dominated by hazel woodland with pockets of interesting grassland. Best known for its flora, the site is beautiful in spring when the woodland floor is a sea of colour. Red squirrels can be found in the woodland. Other mammals on the reserve include rabbits, wood mice, shrews and stoats. Fine views of the stunning Antrim coast and the Mull of Kintyre can be enjoyed from the picnic area. The path can be muddy and is unsuitable for wheelchair access. A circular way-marked 0.6-mile trail takes about 30 minutes at an easy pace, although some sections are steep. There is parking on the roadside verge.

Glenarm

Co Antrim; **OS Map** D 304111; **Map Ref** W4

ACCESS/CONDITIONS: Some of the paths can be steep, muddy and unsuitable for wheelchair access.
HOW TO GET THERE: Take the A2 coast road from Larne towards Carnlough, and Glenarm village is located on the A2 before Carnlough. From Glenarm take the B97 to Ballymena, and the reserve's entrance gates are on the left after approx half a mile, just after the quarry. There is a small car park for about five vehicles about 1.5 miles from the entrance.
WALKING TIME: Glenarm is a 445-acre (180ha) reserve. The full circuit takes 3 to 4 hours at an easy pace.
30-MINUTE VISIT: From the metal gate at the car park, follow the track along the river then take the track to your left. Continue uphill to a forestry track, turn right and continue to the next metal gate on your right. Go through there and back down to the river.

Glenarm is a designated ASSI, and the reserve includes semi-natural broad-leaved woodland, hazel coppice, unimproved grassland and part of the River Glenarm. During the spring and summer, the woods are alive with songbirds, including wood and garden warblers. On the river, look out for dippers and grey wagtails. Overhead, buzzards and ravens will be soaring. The woods are most colourful in the spring with an array of wildflowers. Toothwort and wood cranesbill are found on the reserve. Butterflies on the wing during the summer will include wood white and silver-washed fritillary. In the autumn, look out for the wonderful variety of fungi. Winter brings winter thrushes, together with common crossbill and siskin. Red squirrels are present throughout the year. Please note, this reserve is only open to Wildlife Trust members; however, if an event is being held at these sites, non-members can attend for a small charge.

Slievenacloy

Near Stonyford; **OS Map** J 245712; **Map Ref** W11

ACCESS/CONDITIONS: Surfaced tracks and kissing gates allow access for all. The ground can be very wet and uneven off the tracks. and some of the site is moderately steep.
HOW TO GET THERE: From Belfast take the Colin Glen Road (A501) heading towards Lisburn. Turn right just before the filling station onto the Ballycolin Road. After about half a mile, take a left onto the Flowbog Road. Cars can be parked along the Flowbog Road.
WALKING TIME: A 310-acre (125ha) reserve. There are surfaced tracks and three waypoint trails available (between 1 and 3 hours).
30-MINUTE VISIT: If pressed for time, head up the hill to Hill House and head west (left) for a panoramic view of the reserve, the earthen ring and the cattle.

Slievenacloy is a lush and secretive valley, hidden away behind the Belfast Hills and offering breath-taking views across Northern Ireland. Just a few minutes up the road from Belfast, you are instantly transported away from the bustle of the city when in this grassy wilderness. A LNR lying in the heart of a greater ASSI, Slievenacloy is a vast wildlife paradise of unimproved grassland, meadows, rush and heath – home to a multitude of protected and threatened creatures and plants. In winter, the reserve can seem very bleak as the wind rushes and whistles across the hill tops, but the site is a prime stop off point for many over-wintering birds to feed and shelter, including snipe, fieldfare and hen harrier. In the spring, the wildflowers begin to appear, primroses, cuckooflower and early purple orchids being the most easy to spot. In the summer, the wildflowers come out in full force, filled with butterflies, dragonflies and day flying moths. Traditional breeds of cattle such as highlands and belted galloways can be found roaming the hills, essential for the management of the nature reserve. Autumn is fungi season, and the grassy slopes are covered in a vast and colourful array of waxcap mushrooms, only found in undisturbed grassland habitats.

Umbra

Near Coleraine; **OS Map** C 726358; **Map Ref** W1

ACCESS/CONDITIONS: No specially built paths, but as the site is mainly duneland, it is usually dry underfoot. The site is not suitable for wheelchair access.
HOW TO GET THERE: The reserve is next to the Umbra level crossing on the A2 Coleraine to Limavady coast road, between Downhill and Benone. Roadside parking is available near the entrance.
WALKING TIME: A 113 acre (45ha) reserve. Walks can take up to 1 hour during the summer when the wildflowers are in bloom.
30-MINUTE VISIT: For a great view of the ocean and a chance to see a wide range of flowers, walk straight through the dunes to the sea. The route back offers a clear view of the magnificent cliffs.

Umbra comprises about 113 acres (45ha) of dunes, dune slacks, woodland and scrub, and is bounded by the open beach of Magilligan Strand to the north, the River Umbra and the high basalt cliffs inland, and the Benone complex to the west. In spring and summer, the dunes are full of flowering plants, many scarce in Northern Ireland. As the summer progresses, rarities such as the marsh helleborine and grass of Parnassus can be seen, and butterflies such as dark green and silver-washed fritillaries and grayling put on a show. Look out for peregrines hunting overhead. The autumn brings fungi and migrant seabirds offshore such as the red-throated diver. Porpoises are also recorded regularly offshore. Umbra is a designated ASSI and SAC, and is part of the Magilligan dune complex. Please note, this reserve is only open to Wildlife Trust members; however, if an event is being held at these sites, non-members can attend for a small charge.

WILDLIFE FACT: HARBOUR PORPOISE

The harbour porpoise is the smallest European cetacean (dolphins and whales), and also the commonest around our coasts. Despite this, porpoises can be difficult to see, especially during rough weather when the small dorsal fin will be lost amongst the waves. Your best chance of seeing one is from a clifftop on a calm, summer's day at high tide, when they feed surprisingly close in to the shore. During the winter they move further offshore, following their food. Unfortunately this makes them more vulnerable to being entangled and dying in fishing nets.

Bog Meadows

Belfast; **OS Map** J 312726; **Map Ref** W10

ACCESS/CONDITIONS: All paths are accessible for wheelchair users with the exception of the viewing mounds. They are constructed from concrete or quarry dust, but may become muddy in places during the winter months, and keeping to the footpaths provided is requested.
HOW TO GET THERE: Take bus 10 A-F and get off opposite Falls Park. Pedestrian access is available from Falls Road, St Katherine's Road and Milltown Cemetery. By car, take the M1 to Donegall Road, then follow the signs. Free parking facilities are provided at the bottom of Milltown Row on the left hand side.
WALKING TIME: There is a trail of 1.1 miles. A leisurely stroll would take about 1 hour.
30-MINUTE VISIT: From the car park, go down the path between the playing fields and the stream. Cross the footbridge and turn right. Continue along until you reach another footbridge with turrets. Don't cross; instead, follow the footpath around to the left and then take the first left. This will lead you to the pond where you can feed the ducks or contemplate a large part of the reserve from the viewing mound. To return, follow the path, turning right at the junction, then left over the first footbridge to lead back to the car park.
A MEMBER SAYS: 'I really enjoyed seeing all the different types of birds and waterfowl so close to the city centre. It's great that this green space in the heart of the city has been spared from development. It's a super resource for local communities, especially for children who can learn so much from being outdoors, take part in educational activities such as pond-dipping and have fun at the same time.'

Situated in west Belfast, beside the M1 motorway, this LNR has been awarded the Man and the Biosphere Urban Wildlife Award for Excellence by UNESCO. It is an oasis for wildlife and people in the city, comprising a mosaic of reedbeds, meadows, ponds, woodland, streams and hedgerows. During the summer months, the nature reserve hosts significant numbers of African visitors of the feathered variety, including sedge, willow and grasshopper warblers, sand martins and swallows. An array of wildflowers abounds including orchids, as well as many species of butterfly. Winter is the best period to see ducks, geese and swans that use the pond. Watch along the pond margins and in the meadows for snipe. Throughout the year, traditional breeds of hardy cattle such as Irish moiled and blue-greys graze Bog Meadows. They are well suited to the local environment and can withstand all weather conditions, come the wind, hail or shine.

DID YOU KNOW?

- Bog Meadows is a surviving remnant of the floodplain of the River Blackstaff. It was formed by melting glaciers during the last Ice Age and the floodplain once spread over 1,000 acres (400ha).
- In 1987 a concerned group of people, calling themselves Friends of the Bog Meadows, decided to do something to preserve this remaining area of wetland. In 1998 they became a local branch of the Ulster Wildlife Trust and received funding from the Peace and Reconciliation Fund to purchase the land and manage it for conservation, recreation and education.
- Bog Meadows is excellent for birds. Fifty species of breeding birds and over 100 non-breeding species have been recorded in the past. This was the last recorded breeding site in the Belfast area for the corncrake – an extremely rare bird in Northern Ireland.

Ecos

Ballymena; **OS Map** D 122037; **Map Ref** W6

ACCESS/CONDITIONS: All paths are bitmac or tarmac surfaces of between 1.5 and 3 metres wide. They are mostly flat with only some short inclines, and free motability scooters are available for badge holders.
HOW TO GET THERE: From Ballymena train and bus stations either walk through the town centre or take number 128 bus to the Fairhill shopping centre. By car, follow the M2 motorway bypassing Ballymena to Junction 11. At the exit, follow the signs for Ballymena town centre and Ecos. Turn left at the first roundabout to enter Ecos nature reserve.
WALKING TIME: The longest walk is 3 miles in length and easily explored in an hour and a half. There are also many shorter routes available.
30-MINUTE VISIT: From the visitor centre, keep the lake on your left hand side and turn left at every path junction to take a circular route around the lake. This is an excellent walk, past some mudflats on the lake shore, and through grazing and wildflower meadows.
A MEMBER SAYS: 'This used to be a boring bit of open ground with a few birds. Now it's teeming with wildlife thanks to the Ulster Wildlife Trust.'

Ecos boasts a wide variety of habitats for enthusiasts and amateurs to enjoy in all seasons. Included in the 150 acres (60ha) of parkland are a man made lake, several scrapes, a mature woodland, wet woodland, wet grassland, hay meadows, wildflower meadows, hazel coppice, willow coppice and meandering rivers. The tranquility of the lake is broken in summer months by all the ducklings, goslings and cygnets calling to their parents for reassurance. A gentle amble round some of the 4 miles of paths will bring you through the meadows that are ablaze with wildflowers in spring and summer. In winter, flocks of teal and lapwing are regular visitors to the muddy edges of the lake, where occasionally unusual visitors such as white-winged black terns can be seen. Godwits and other migrating waders are also present. Large flocks of tits flitting along the hedges and through the willow coppice are a particular treat, but there is always something interesting to see at Ecos.

DID YOU KNOW?

- There have been 108 species of bird recorded in the reserve since it opened in 2000.
- 341 small tortoiseshell butterflies were counted in one day during August 2001.
- There are over 10,000 frogs living in the reserve.

Lagan Meadows

Near Belfast; **OS Map** J 335703; **Map Ref** W12

ACCESS/CONDITIONS: A solid path runs around the meadows' perimeter, with rougher paths through the middle. Much of the area is fenced for cattle grazing with plenty of step-over stiles. The river towpath, adjacent to the site, is suitable for wheelchair access.
HOW TO GET THERE: Buses 8A, 8B or 8C stop at Stranmillis Road. By car, from Belfast city centre, take the Malone Road, and turn left down Bladon Drive, just after the Stranmillis Road junction. Lagan Meadows is immediately at the end of the road, where on-street parking is possible.
WALKING TIME: This is a 32-acre (13ha) reserve and a circuit of about 1 mile takes 1 hour.
30-MINUTE VISIT: From the entrance, turn right down the hill and then left over the track past Lester's Dam. Continue down to the towpath, turning right and continue for 10 minutes, then turn right up the steep slope by the beech trees. The path continues back to the entrance.
A MEMBER SAYS: 'I can't believe that this tranquil site is only a 10-minute drive from the centre of Belfast.'

Situated in the beautiful Lagan Valley regional park, this LNR occupies the damp grassland of the valley floor and the surrounding areas of scrub and woodland. The meadows are grazed by cattle during the summer months, but late spring is the best time to see meadow flowers such as ragged robin and common spotted orchid. Unusual species include large bittercress, whorl-grass and wood club rush. During summer evenings, the grasshopper warbler can be heard reeling its song among the tussock sedge. Sedge warbler and reed bunting also breed in these areas. Summer is the time to see butterflies, such as wood white, and dragonflies, such as banded demoiselle. During autumn and winter, fieldfares and redwings visit to feed on the hawthorn berries. Winter is also a great time to see jays in the woodland and snipe in the marshy areas.

DID YOU KNOW?

- Lester's Dam, built in the 1790s, provided Belfast with its first public water supply.
- The meadows are part of the Lagan Valley Regional Park which runs for 11 miles along the River Lagan and is 4,000 acres (1,600ha) in size.
- Tussock sedge leaves are armed with hacksaw-like jagged edges.

Glossary

Access For All Trail
Provides access for those with special needs

(Medieval) Assart
Woodland that has been given up to pasture

Coppice
Woodland where the trees are cut back to ground level about every 10 years, producing fast-growing shoots for fencing and firewood

Culm grassland
Unimproved wet pasture found in Devon and South-west Wales

Lammas meadow
Traditional hay meadows opened up as common land to grazing animals after Lammas in August

Ley
Improved grassland grown in rotation and cut for silage or grazed

Molinia
High-altitude purple moor grass

Permissive paths
Path where landowner has given permission for it to be used

Ramsar site
Site of importance for nature conservation, designated under the Ramsar Convention

Red Data Book species
Endangered species listed in various Red Data Books

Rhyne/reen
Type of drainage ditch; the name is usually used in reference to the Somerset Levels

Understorey
Shrubs or young trees in woodland

COMMON ABBREVIATIONS

AONB
Area of Outstanding Natural Beauty

ASSI
Areas of Special Scientific Interest. Only applies to reserves in Northern Ireland

CES
Constant Effort Site: a site generally used for bird ringing

CGS
County Geological Site

CNR
Community Nature Reserve

Defra
Department for Environment, Food and Rural Affairs

LDP
Long Distance Path

LNR
Local Nature Reserve

MWR
Marine Wildlife Reserve

NNR
National Nature Reserve

NR
Nature Reserve

RIGS
Regionally Important Geological/ Geomorphological Site

RNR
Roadside Nature Reserve

RUPP
Roads used as public paths

SAC/cSAC
(candidate) Special Area of Conservation under the EU Habitats Directive

SAM
Scheduled Ancient Monument

SNCI
Sites of Nature Conservation Interest – a local name for a nonstatutory site that is important for wildlife

SPA
Special Protection Area designated under the EU Birds Directive

SSSI
Site of Special Scientific Interest

VMCA
Voluntary Marine Conservation Area

VMNR
Voluntary Marine Nature Reserve

Photo credits

Many thanks to all of the Wildlife Trusts who have sent through images of their reserves for use in this book. The following photographers and photographic agencies have also kindly allowed use of their images:

Amy Lewis, Communications Manager; Henry Stanier (BCNP Wildlife Trust); Jim Asher, Nigel Philips and Helen Taylor (Berks, Bucks and Oxon Wildlife Trust); Stuart Hutchings, Victoria Whitehouse and Friends of Churchtown Farm (Cornwall Wildlife Trust); Steve Price (Derbyshire Wildlife Trust); T Bates and T Harris (Dorset Wildlife Trust); G Bode and D Brinn (Gwent Wildlife Trust); Peter Emery (Hampshire and Isle of Wight Wildlife Trust); Clare Gray (Hertfordshire and Middlesex Wildlife Trust); Ian Andrews (Kent Wildlife Trust); Chris Hill (Leicestershire and Rutland Wildlife Trust); Paul Grimshaw and Rachel Shaw (Lincolnshire Wildlife Trust); Anna Guzzo (London Wildlife Trust); Duncan Hutt (Northumberland Wildlife Trust); Neil Hoyle, Charles Langtree and Michelle Naysmith (Nottinghamshire Wildlife Trust); Niall Benvie, Michael Davidson, Mike Read and Andy Reynolds (Scottish Wildlife Trust); John Harding and Ben Osbourne (Shropshire Wildlife Trust); Lynne Newton (Somerset Wildlife Trust); Gwyn Thomas, Lizzie Wilberforce, Rob Parry, Phil Ward and Sarah Kessell (South and West Wales Wildlife Trust); Colin Hayes (Staffordshire Wildlife Trust); David Hosking (Suffolk Wildlife Trust); G Sweetnam (Surrey Wildlife Trust); Ivor Chuter and Neil Fletcher (Sussex Wildlife Trust); Dave Hall and David Kjaer (Wiltshire Wildlife Trust); Phillip Precey; Elliot Smith.

Alamy; Britainonview; FLPA; Getty Images; Nature Picture Library; Oxford Scientific.

Key to Maps
MAP U
SCOTLAND
MAP T
MAP W
NORTHERN IRELAND
MAP S
REPUBLIC OF IRELAND
MAP R
MAP Q
ENGLAND
MAP M
MAP P
MAP N
MAP L
MAP V
WALES
MAP O
MAP D
MAP H
MAP G
MAP E
MAP K
MAP C
MAP J
MAP F
MAP B
MAP A
N
100km
100miles
Key to maps
Coastline
International border
Regional border
County border
M5 Motorway
A30 Dual carriageway
A39 Main road
Urban area
Maps © JP Map Graphics Ltd, based on XYZ Digital Map Company data

A Cornwall

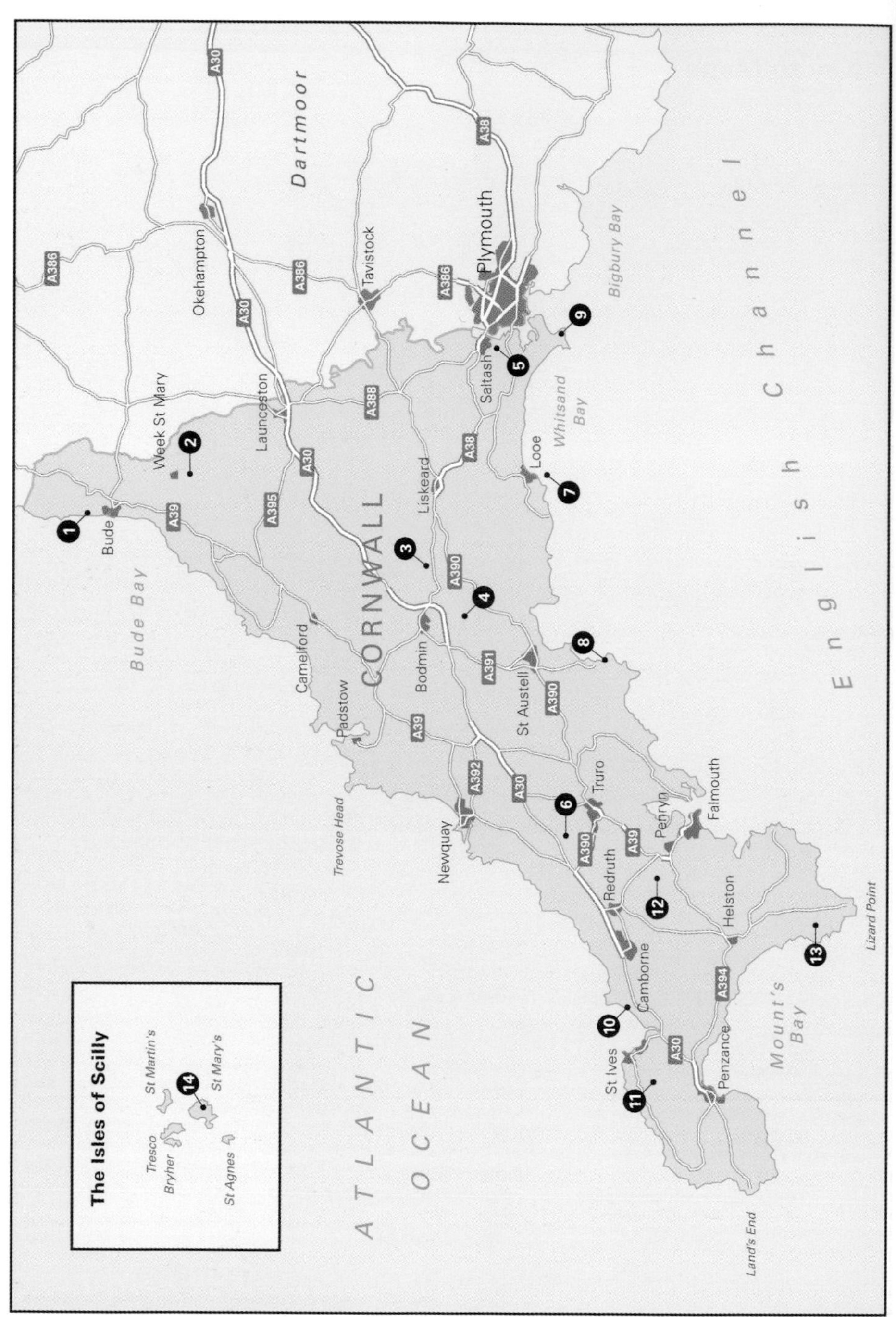
The Isles of Scilly
Tresco
Bryher
St Martin's
St Mary's
St Agnes
14
ATLANTIC
OCEAN
Land's End
St Ives
11
10
Penzance
A30
Camborne
Mount's Bay
A394
13
Lizard Point
Helston
12
Redruth
A39
A390
Penryn
Falmouth
Truro
6
A30
A392
Newquay
Trevose Head
Padstow
A39
St Austell
A390
A391
8
Bodmin
CORNWALL
Camelford
Bude Bay
4
A390
3
Liskeard
A38
7
Looe
Whitsand Bay
Saltash
5
9
Bigbury Bay
English Channel
Plymouth
A386
A38
Tavistock
A386
Dartmoor
A30
Okehampton
A386
A30
Launceston
A388
A30
A395
A39
Bude
1
Week St Mary
2

B Devon

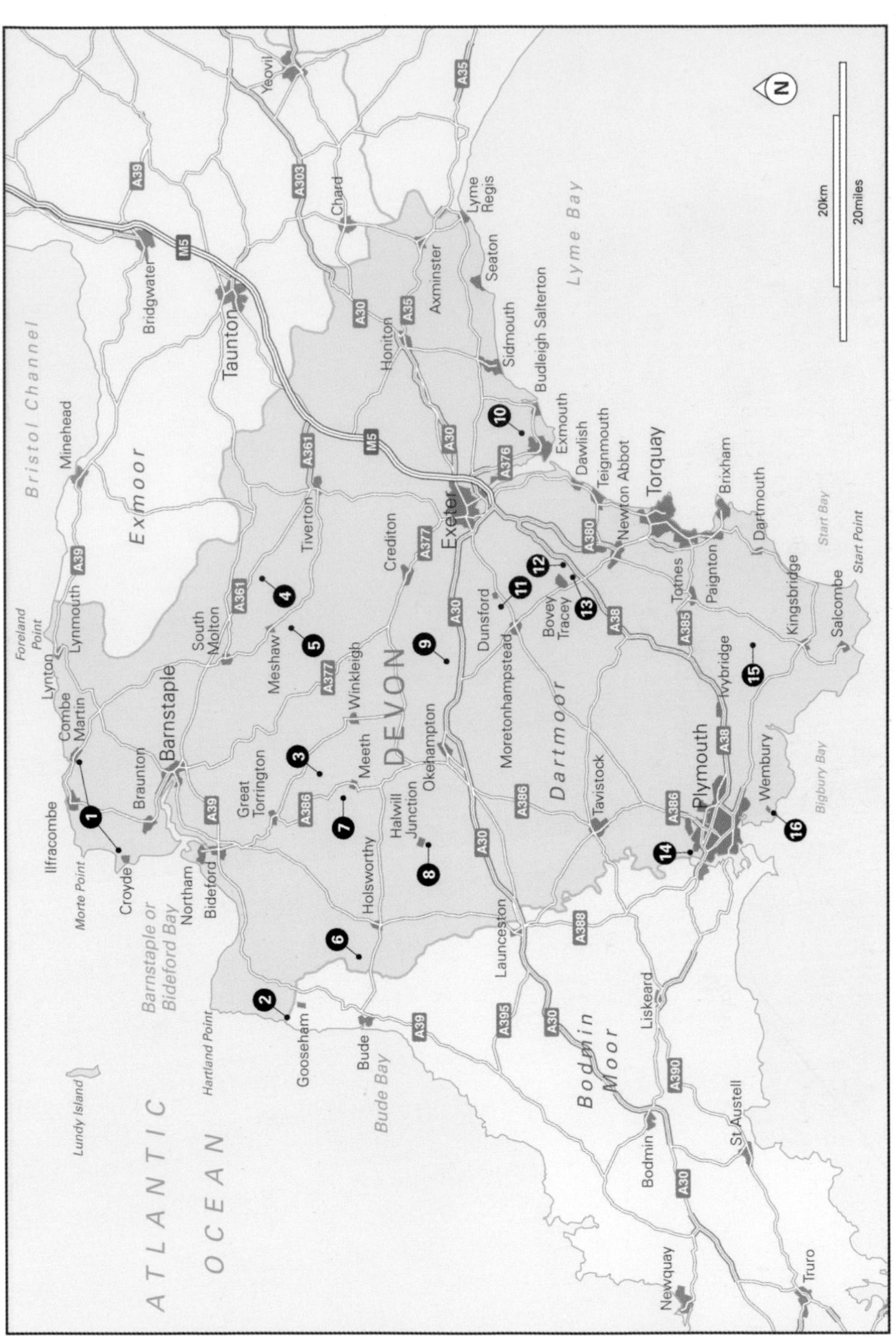
ATLANTIC
OCEAN
Bristol Channel
Exmoor
DEVON
Dartmoor
Bodmin Moor
Lyme Bay
Barnstaple or Bideford Bay
Bude Bay
Bigbury Bay
Start Bay
Start Point
Lundy Island
Hartland Point
Morte Point
Foreland Point
Ilfracombe
Croyde
Braunton
Combe Martin
Lynton
Lynmouth
Minehead
Bridgwater
Taunton
Yeovil
Chard
Lyme Regis
Seaton
Axminster
Honiton
Sidmouth
Budleigh Salterton
Exmouth
Dawlish
Teignmouth
Newton Abbot
Torquay
Brixham
Dartmouth
Paignton
Totnes
Kingsbridge
Salcombe
Ivybridge
Wembury
Plymouth
Tavistock
Bovey Tracey
Dunsford
Moretonhampstead
Exeter
Crediton
Tiverton
South Molton
Barnstaple
Meshaw
Winkleigh
Meeth
Great Torrington
Okehampton
Halwill Junction
Holsworthy
Northam
Bideford
Gooseham
Bude
Launceston
Liskeard
Bodmin
St Austell
Newquay
Truro
M5
A30
A35
A303
A39
A361
A377
A376
A380
A38
A385
A386
A388
A395
A390
20km
20miles
N
1
2
3
4
5
6
7
8
9
10
11
12
13
14
15
16

C Somerset

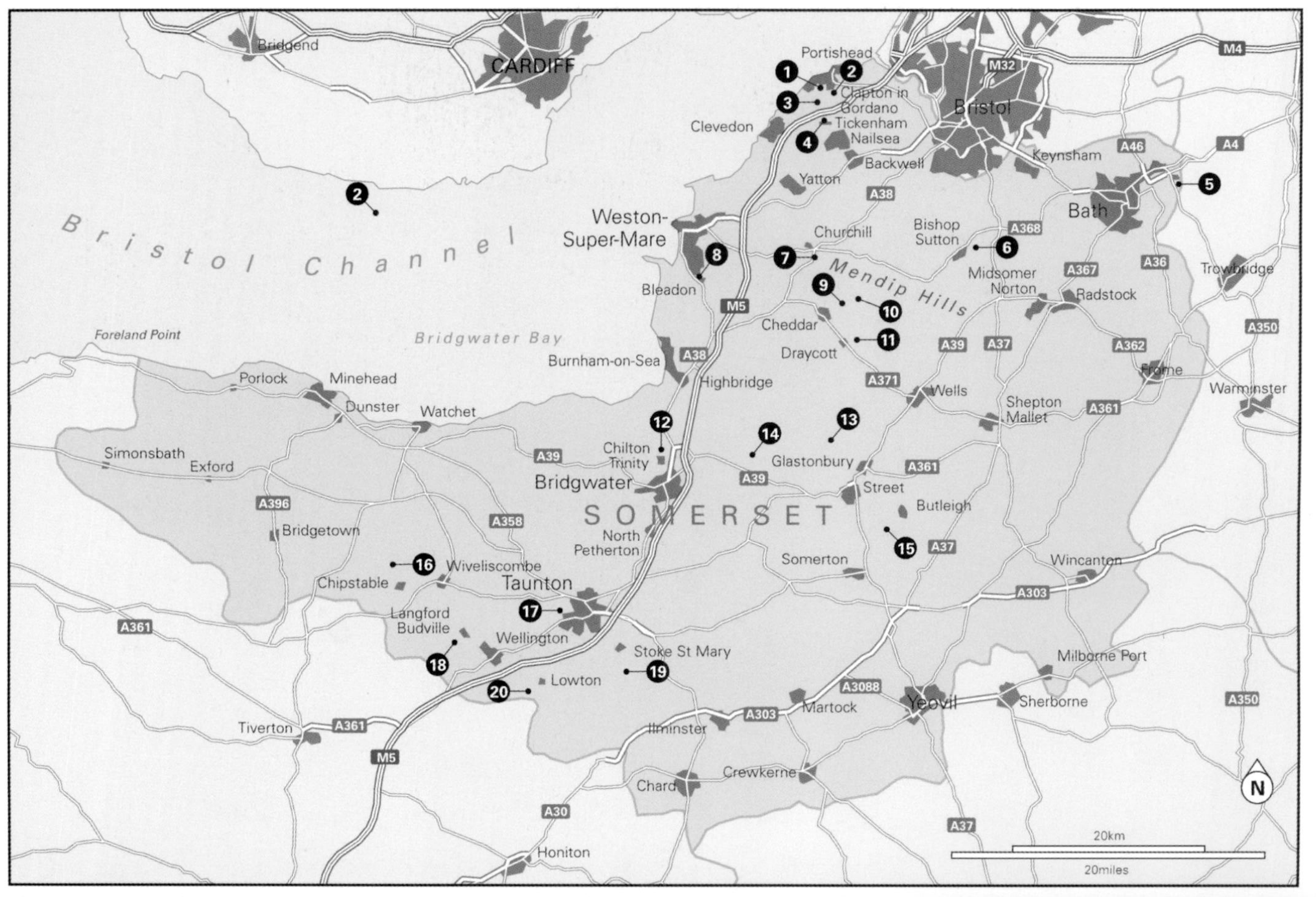
Bridgend
CARDIFF
Portishead
Clapton in Gordano
Tickenham
Nailsea
Clevedon
Backwell
Yatton
Bristol
Keynsham
Bath
Trowbridge
Bristol Channel
Weston-Super-Mare
Bleadon
Churchill
Bishop Sutton
Midsomer Norton
Radstock
Mendip Hills
Cheddar
Draycott
Foreland Point
Bridgwater Bay
Burnham-on-Sea
Highbridge
Wells
Shepton Mallet
Frome
Warminster
Porlock
Minehead
Dunster
Watchet
Chilton Trinity
Glastonbury
Street
Butleigh
Simonsbath
Exford
Bridgwater
SOMERSET
North Petherton
Bridgetown
Somerton
Wincanton
Wiveliscombe
Chipstable
Taunton
Langford Budville
Wellington
Stoke St Mary
Milborne Port
Lowton
Sherborne
Yeovil
Martock
Ilminster
Tiverton
Crewkerne
Chard
Honiton
M4
M32
M5
A4
A46
A36
A350
A38
A368
A367
A39
A37
A362
A371
A361
A358
A396
A303
A3088
A30
N
20km
20miles
1
2
3
4
5
6
7
8
9
10
11
12
13
14
15
16
17
18
19
20

D Gloucestershire

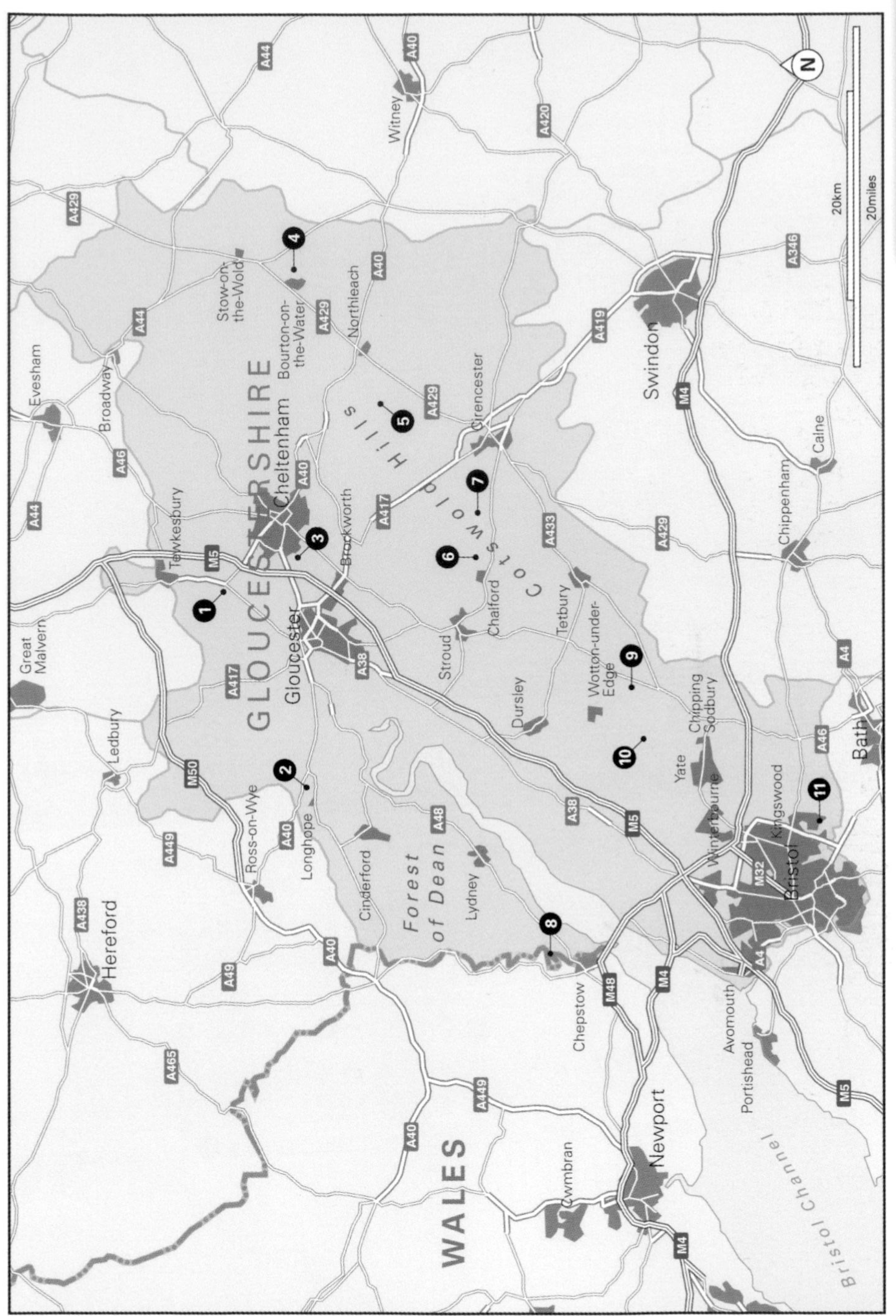

E Wiltshire

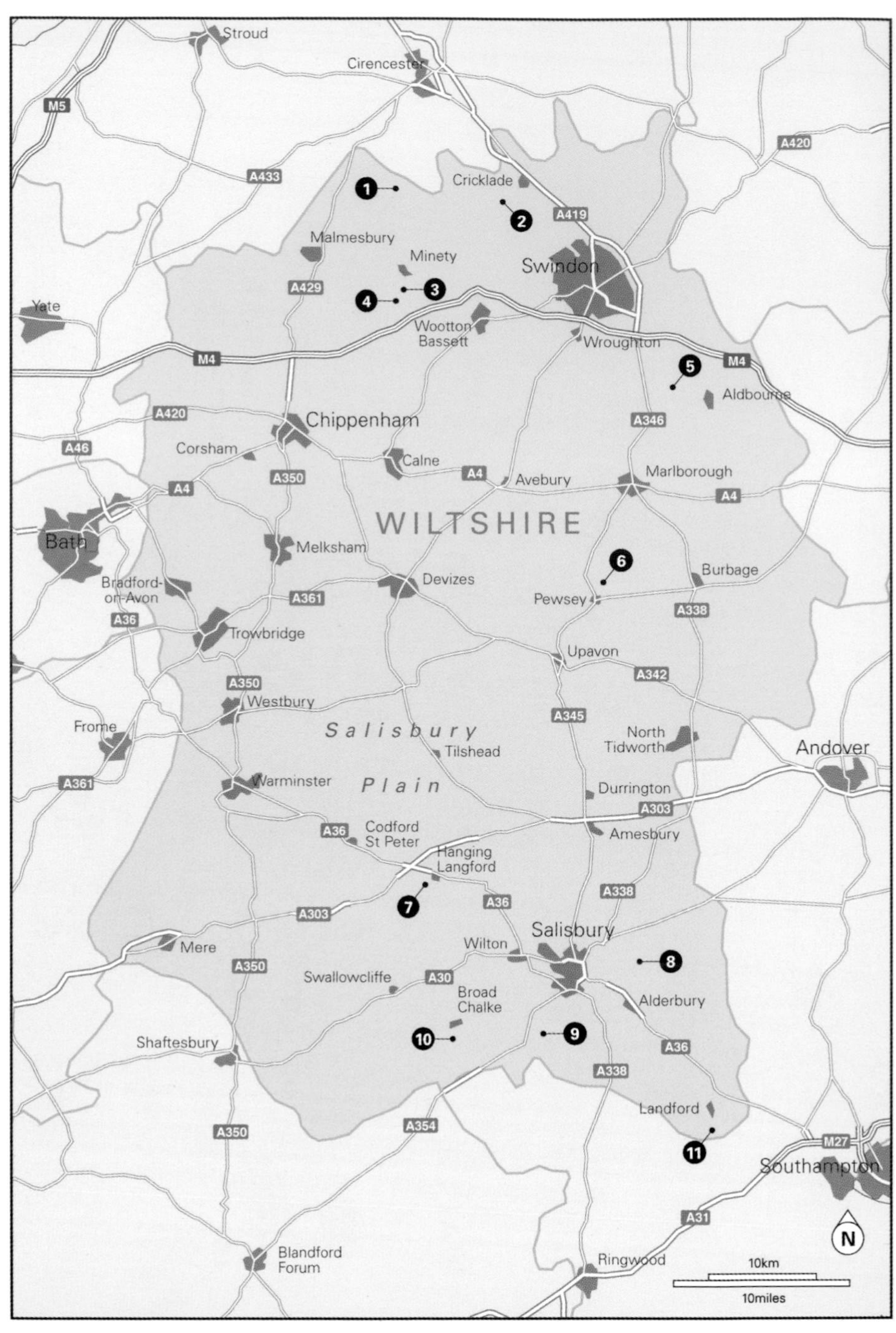

Stroud
Cirencester
M5
A420
A433
Cricklade
A419
Malmesbury
Minety
Swindon
A429
Yate
Wootton Bassett
Wroughton
M4
A420
Chippenham
A346
Aldbourne
A46
Corsham
Calne
A350
A4
Avebury
Marlborough
A4
WILTSHIRE
Bath
Melksham
Bradford-on-Avon
Devizes
Pewsey
Burbage
A361
A338
A36
Trowbridge
Upavon
A350
A342
Westbury
A345
Frome
Salisbury
Tilshead
North Tidworth
Andover
A361
Warminster
Plain
Durrington
A303
A36
Codford St Peter
Amesbury
Hanging Langford
A338
A36
A303
Salisbury
Wilton
Mere
A350
Swallowcliffe
A30
Broad Chalke
Alderbury
Shaftesbury
A36
A338
Landford
A350
A354
M27
Southampton
A31
N
Blandford Forum
Ringwood
10km
10miles

F Dorset and Hampshire

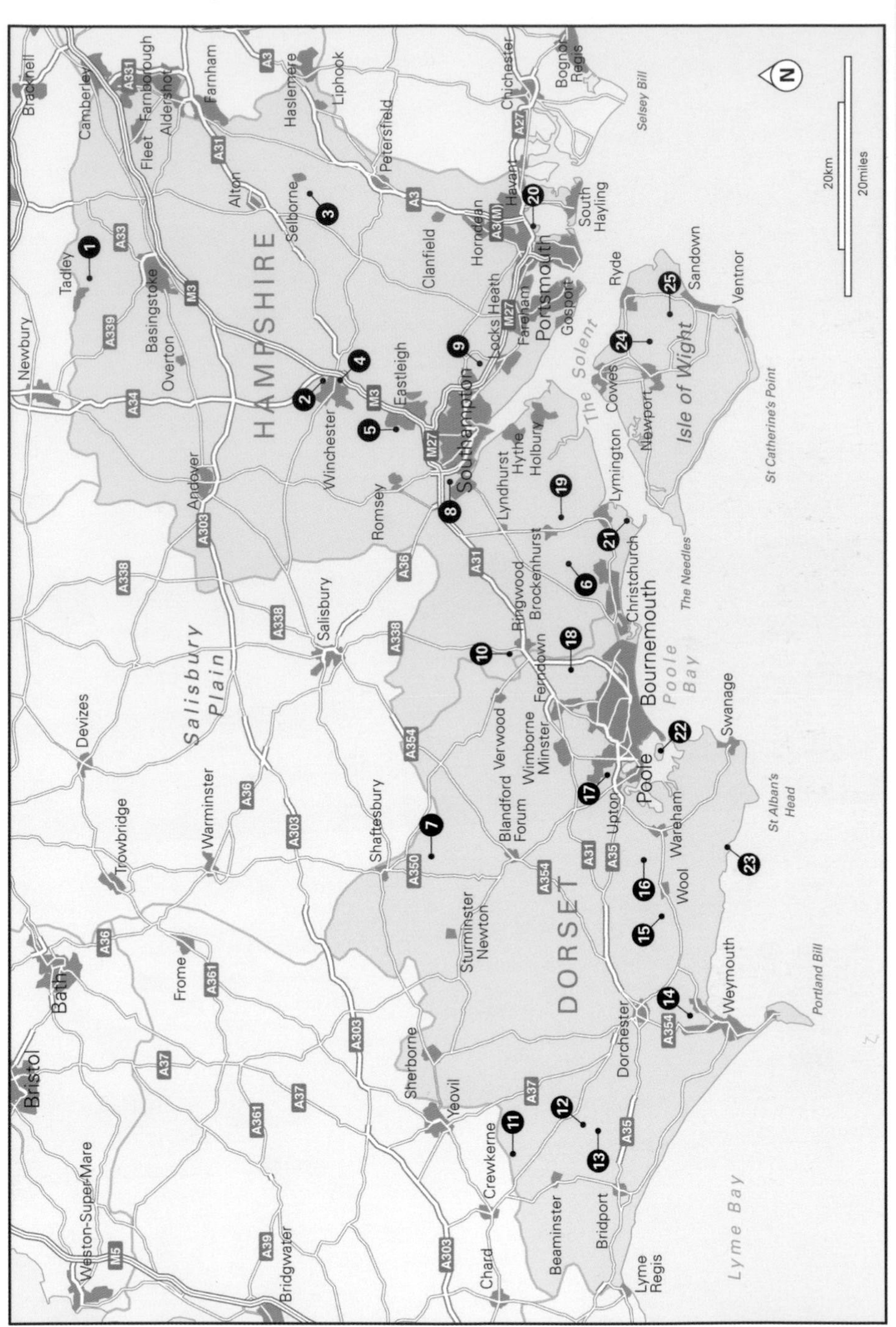

G Oxfordshire, Buckinghamshire and Berkshire

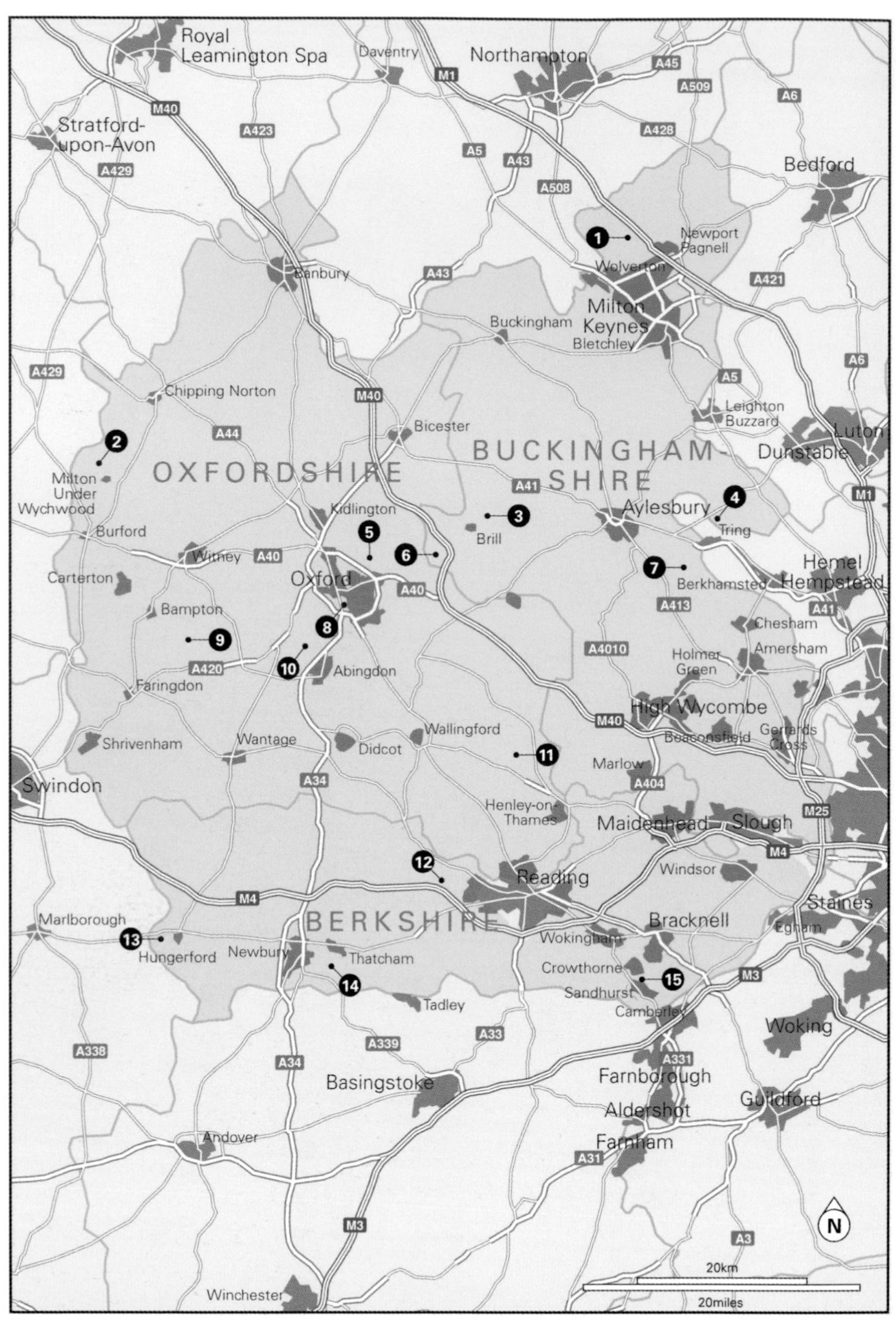

H Greater London, Hertfordshire and Bedfordshire

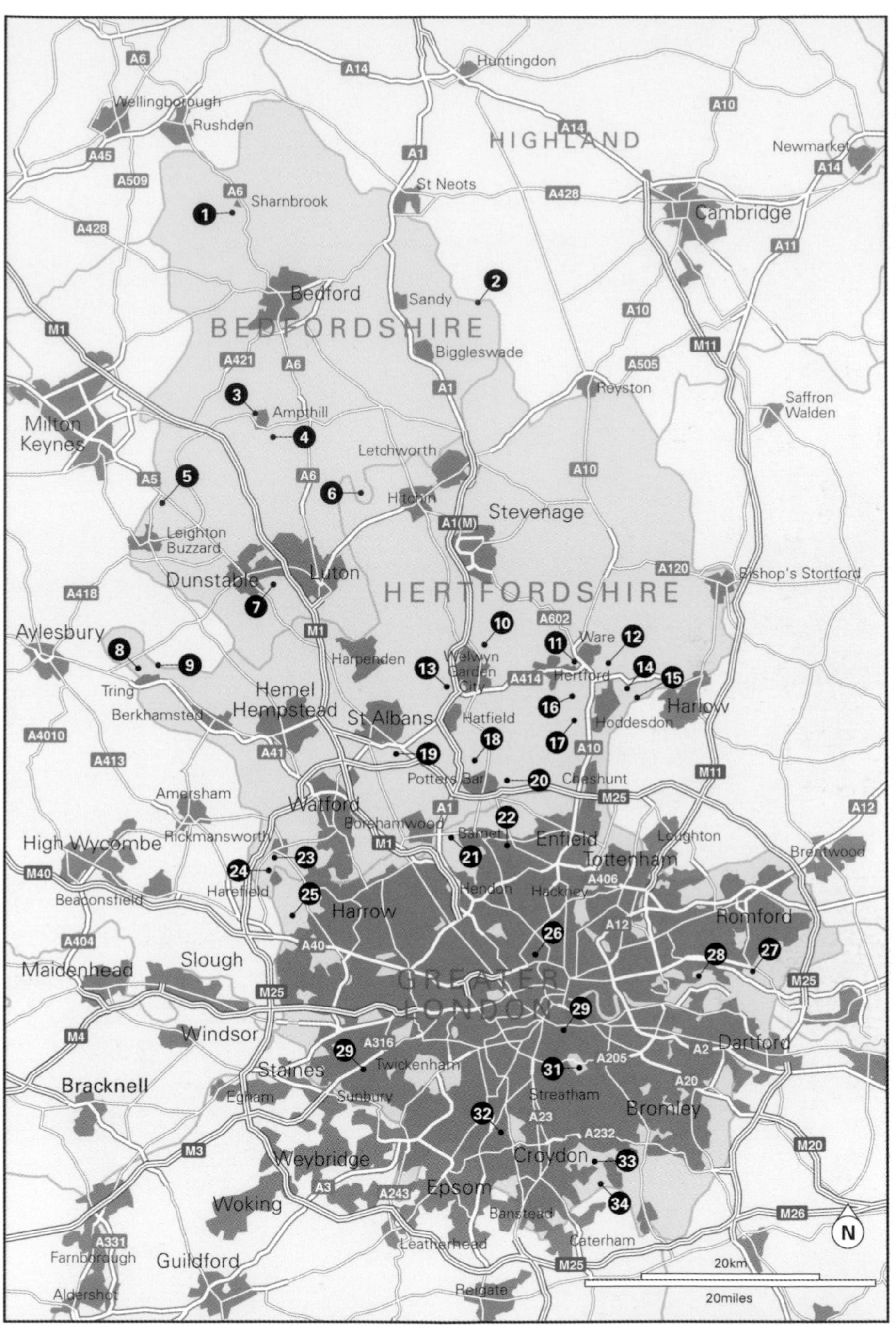

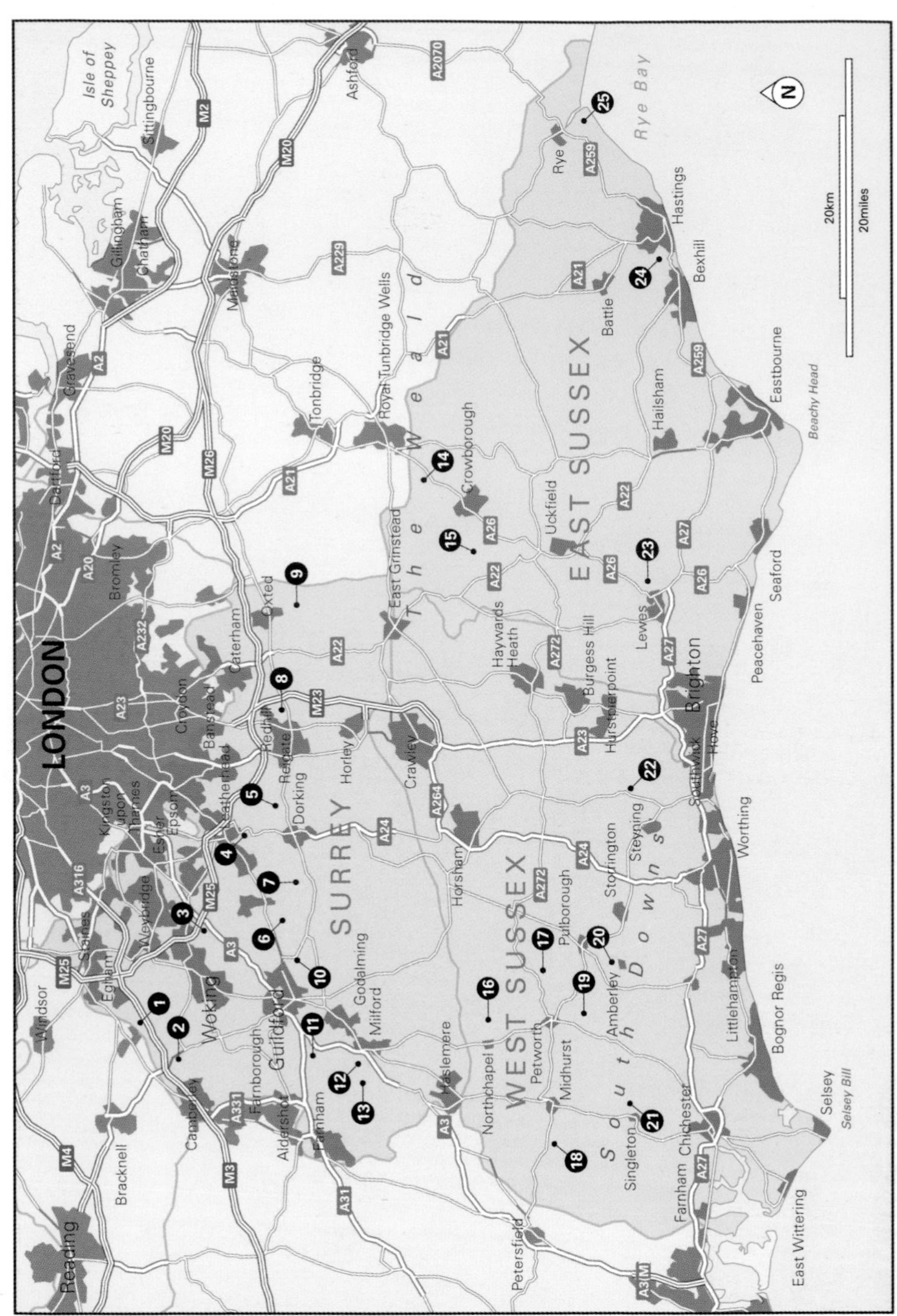
LONDON
SURREY
WEST SUSSEX
EAST SUSSEX
The Weald
South Downs
Isle of Sheppey
Rye Bay
Beachy Head
Selsey Bill
Reading
Bracknell
Windsor
Staines
Egham
Weybridge
Woking
Camberley
Farnborough
Aldershot
Farnham
Guildford
Godalming
Milford
Haslemere
Northchapel
Petworth
Midhurst
Petersfield
Singleton
Chichester
East Wittering
Selsey
Bognor Regis
Littlehampton
Amberley
Pulborough
Storrington
Steyning
Worthing
Southwick
Hove
Brighton
Hurstpierpoint
Burgess Hill
Haywards Heath
Lewes
Peacehaven
Seaford
Eastbourne
Hailsham
Bexhill
Hastings
Battle
Rye
Uckfield
Crowborough
East Grinstead
Horsham
Crawley
Horley
Dorking
Reigate
Redhill
Leatherhead
Epsom
Esher
Kingston upon Thames
Banstead
Croydon
Caterham
Oxted
Bromley
Dartford
Gravesend
Gillingham
Chatham
Sittingbourne
Maidstone
Tonbridge
Royal Tunbridge Wells
Ashford
20km
20miles
N

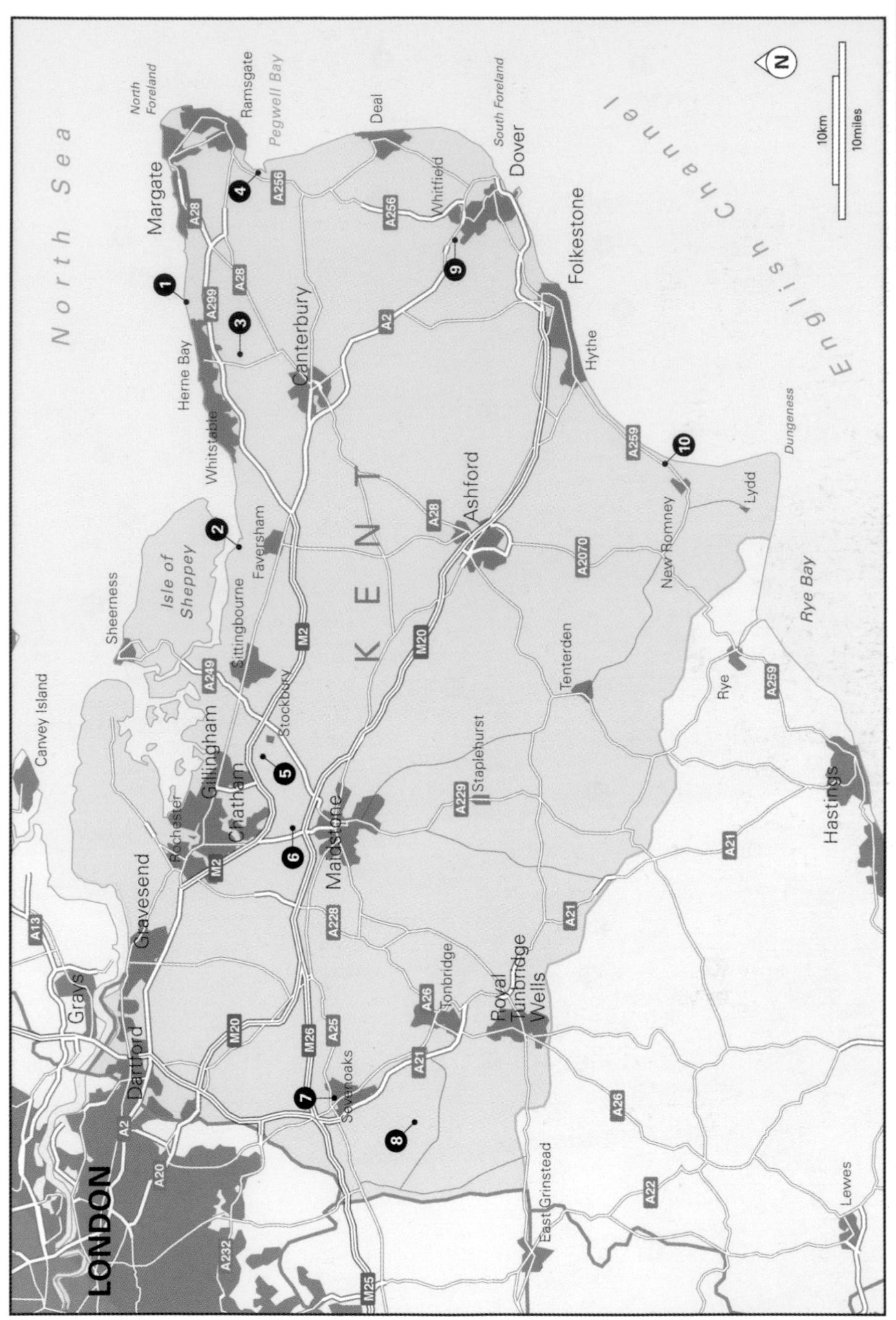
North Sea
English Channel
KENT
LONDON
Margate
Ramsgate
North Foreland
Pegwell Bay
Deal
South Foreland
Dover
Whitfield
Folkestone
Hythe
Canterbury
Herne Bay
Whitstable
Faversham
Sittingbourne
Isle of Sheppey
Sheerness
Canvey Island
Gillingham
Chatham
Rochester
Gravesend
Grays
Dartford
Stockbury
Maidstone
Staplehurst
Tenterden
Ashford
New Romney
Lydd
Dungeness
Rye Bay
Rye
Hastings
Sevenoaks
Tonbridge
Royal Tunbridge Wells
East Grinstead
Lewes
A28
A299
A256
A2
A259
A2070
M2
M20
A249
A229
A228
A21
A26
M26
A25
A13
A20
A232
M25
A22
10km
10miles
N
1
2
3
4
5
6
7
8
9
10

L Norfolk, Essex and Suffolk

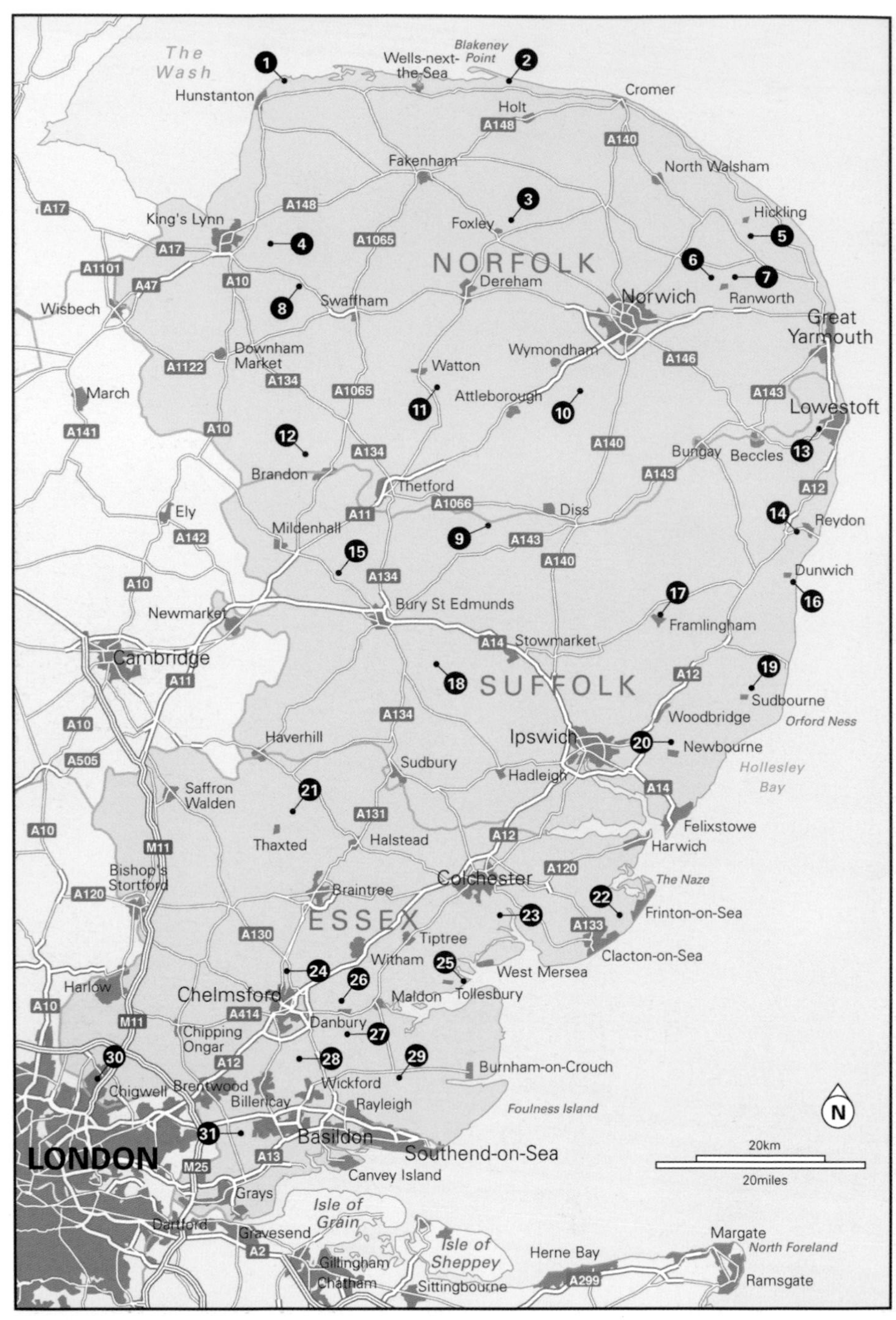

M Lincolnshire and Cambridgeshire

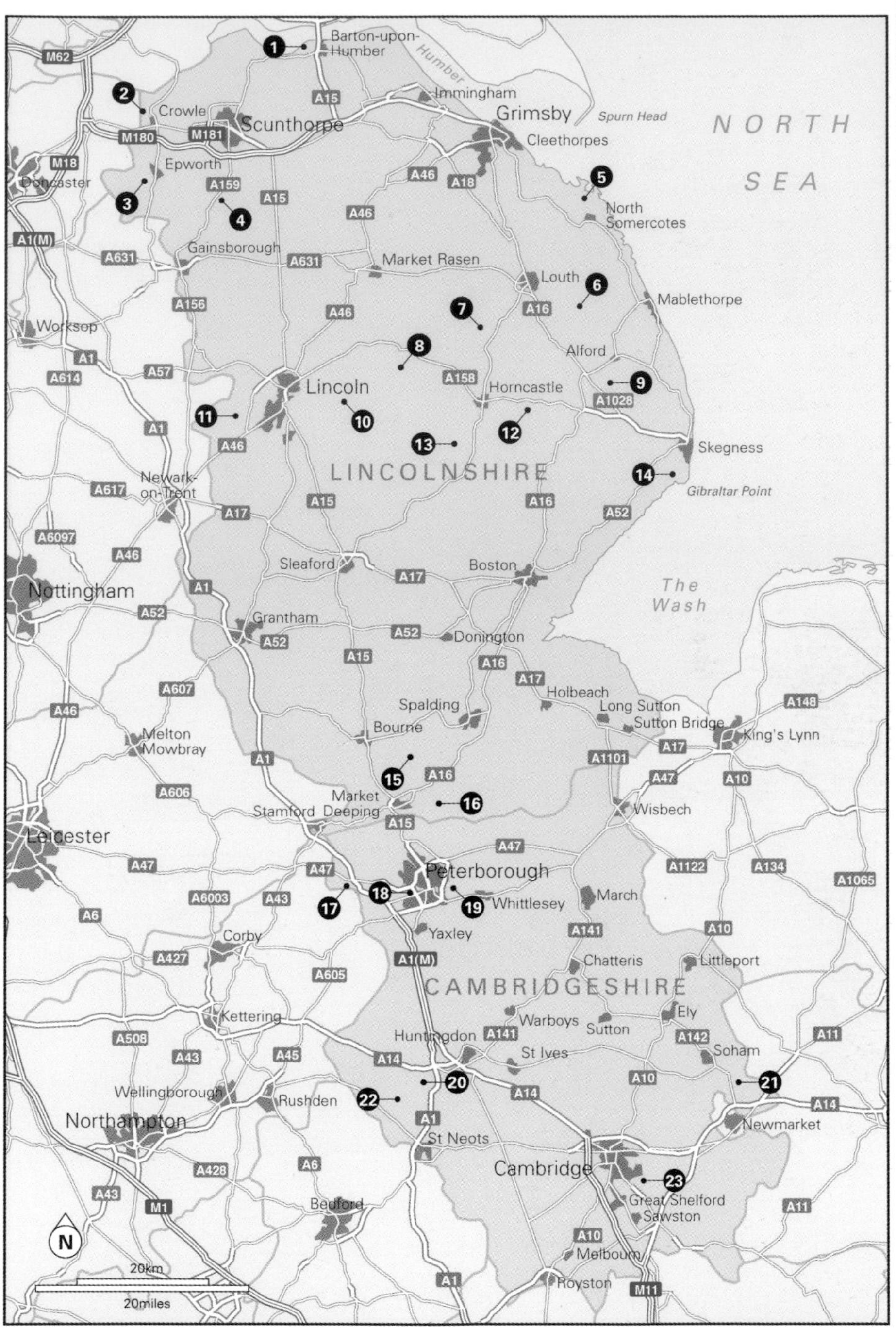

N Derbyshire, Nottinghamshire, Leicestershire, Warwickshire and Northants

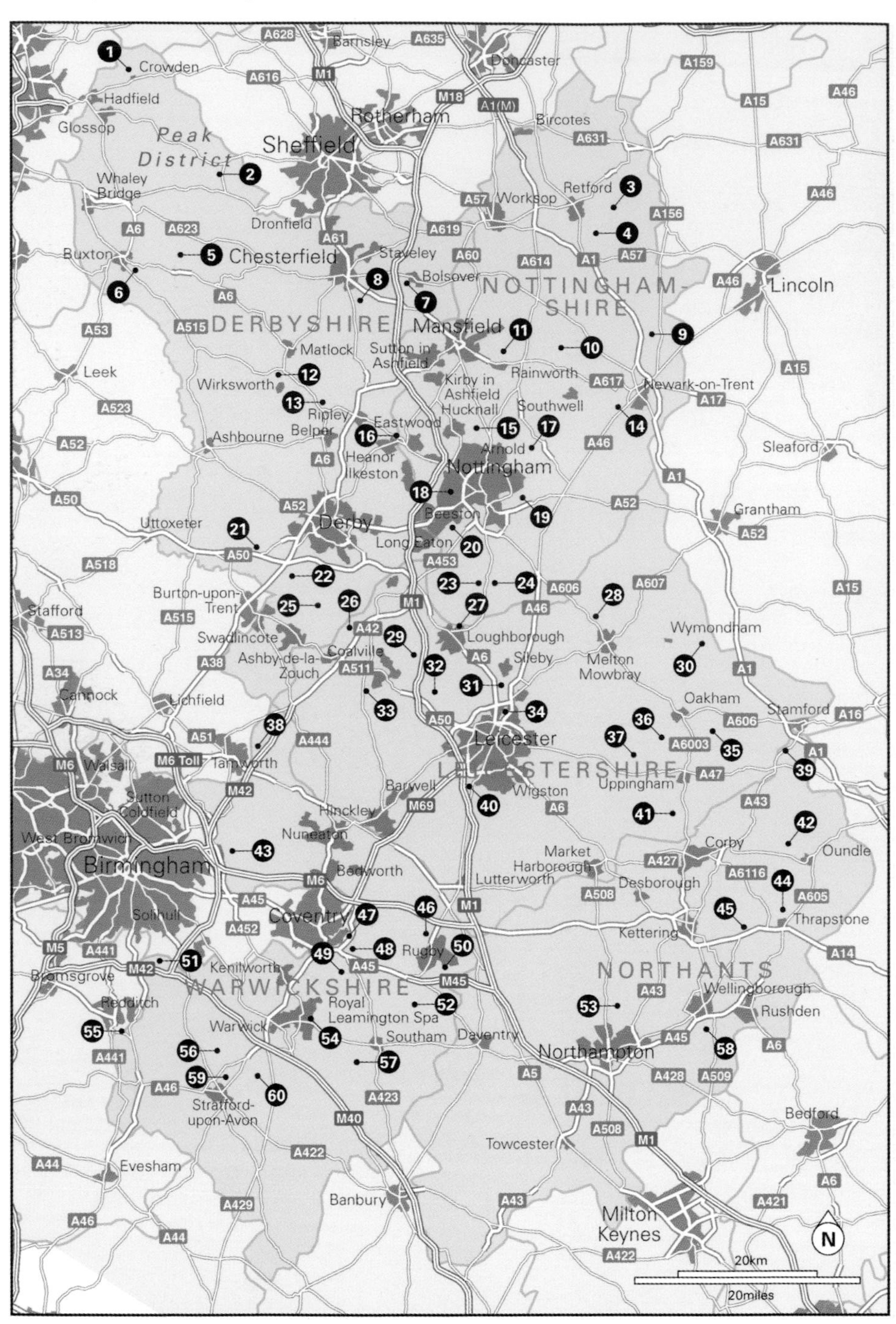

0 Herefordshire and Worcestershire

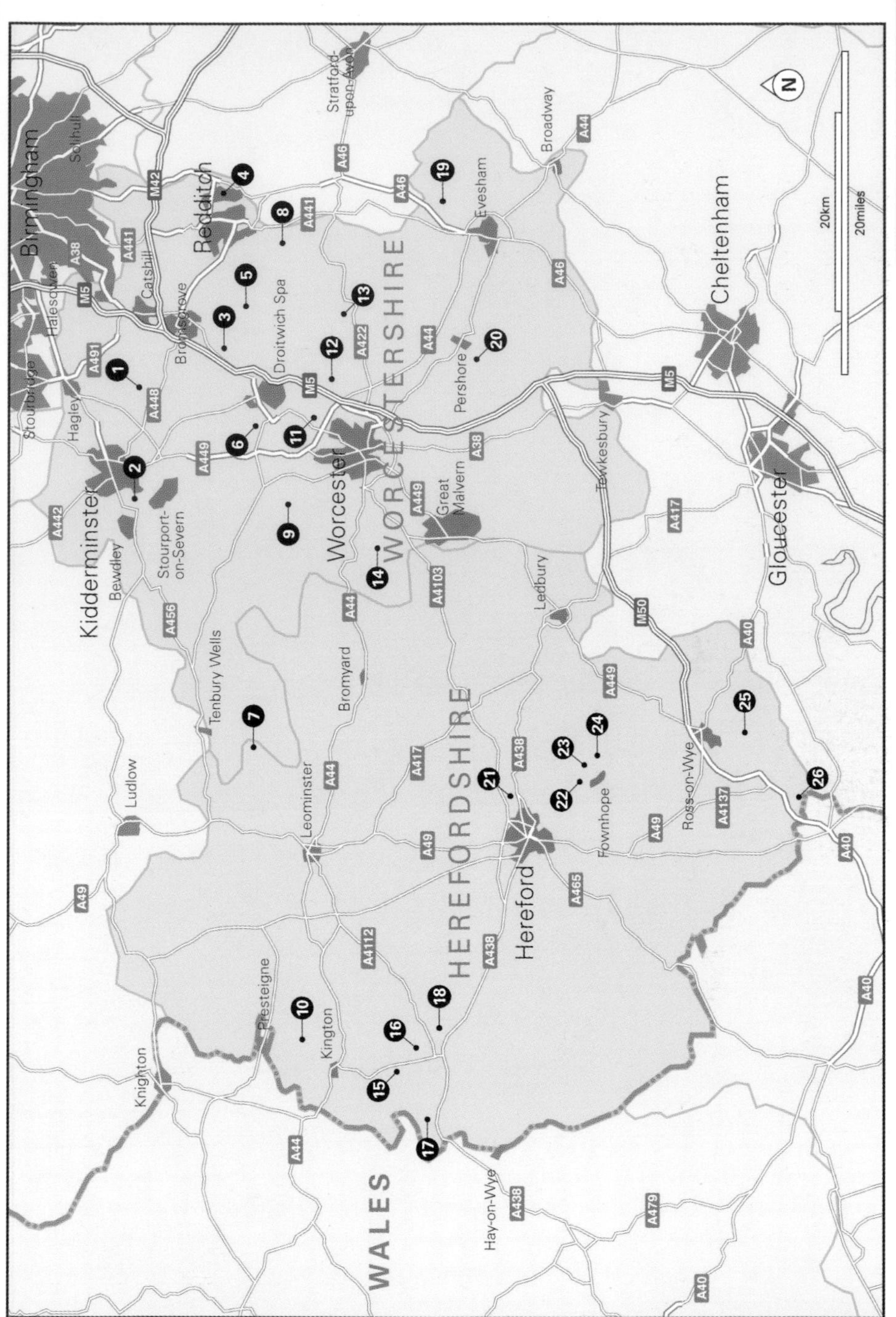

P Shropshire and Staffordshire

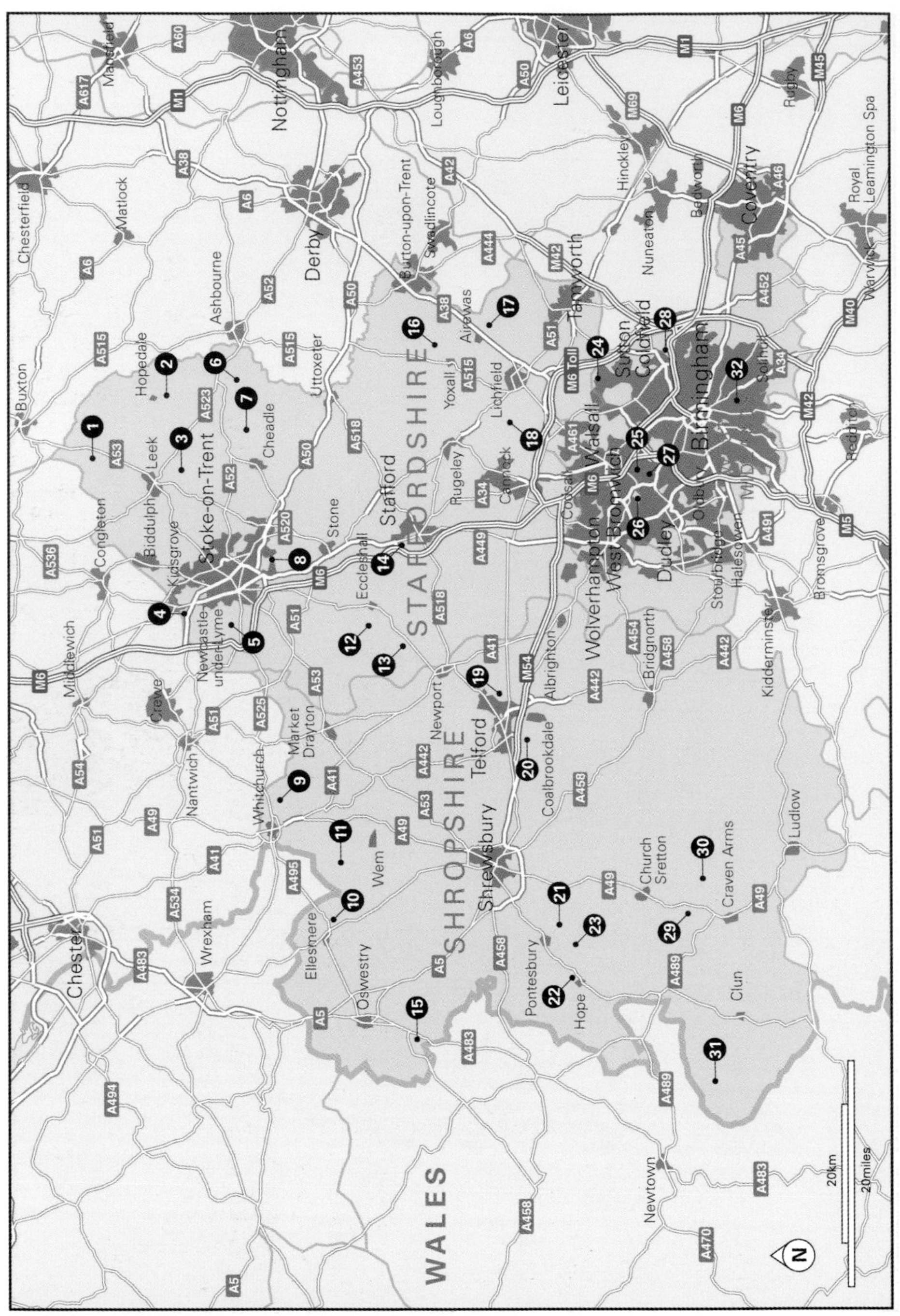

Q Lancashire and Cheshire

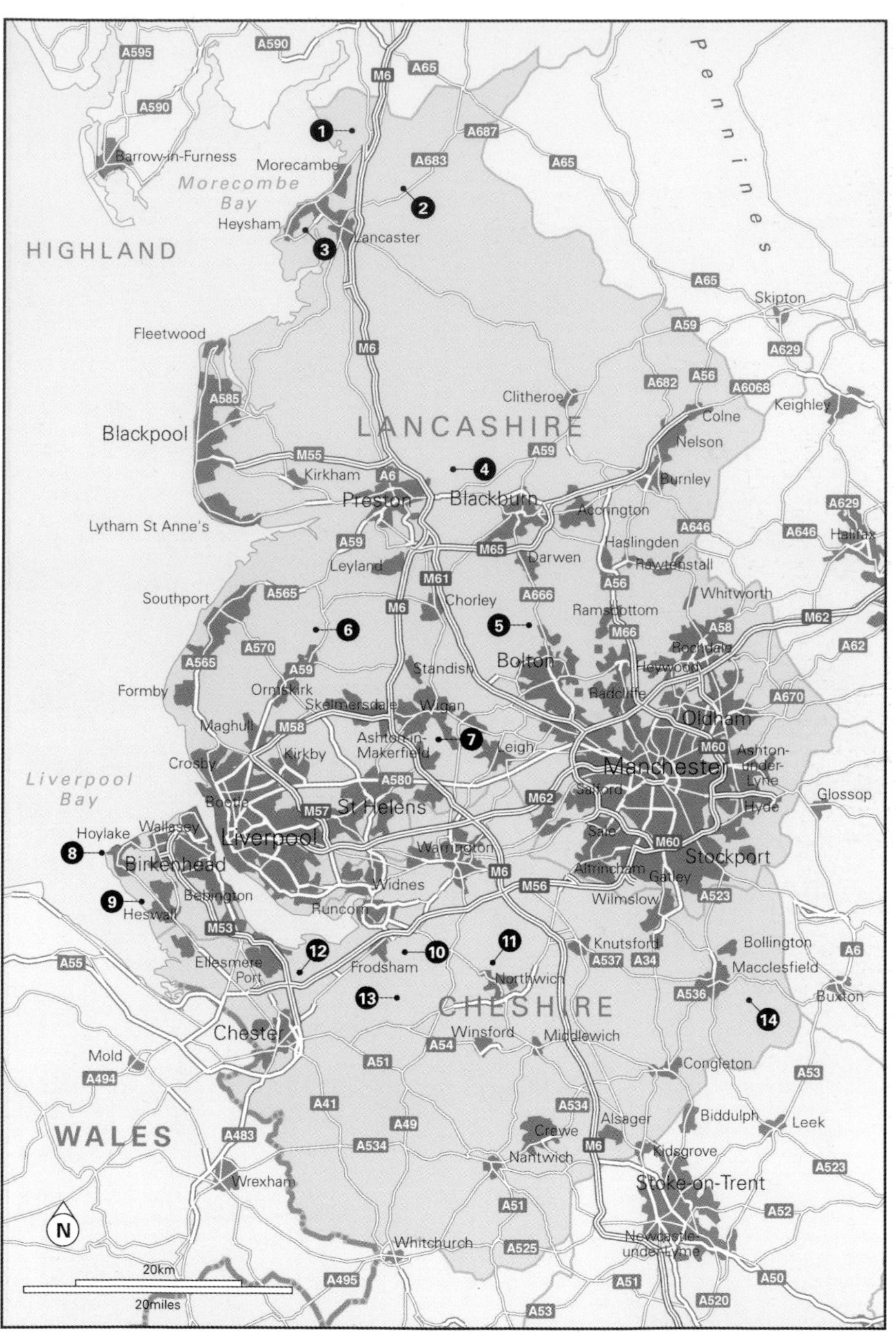

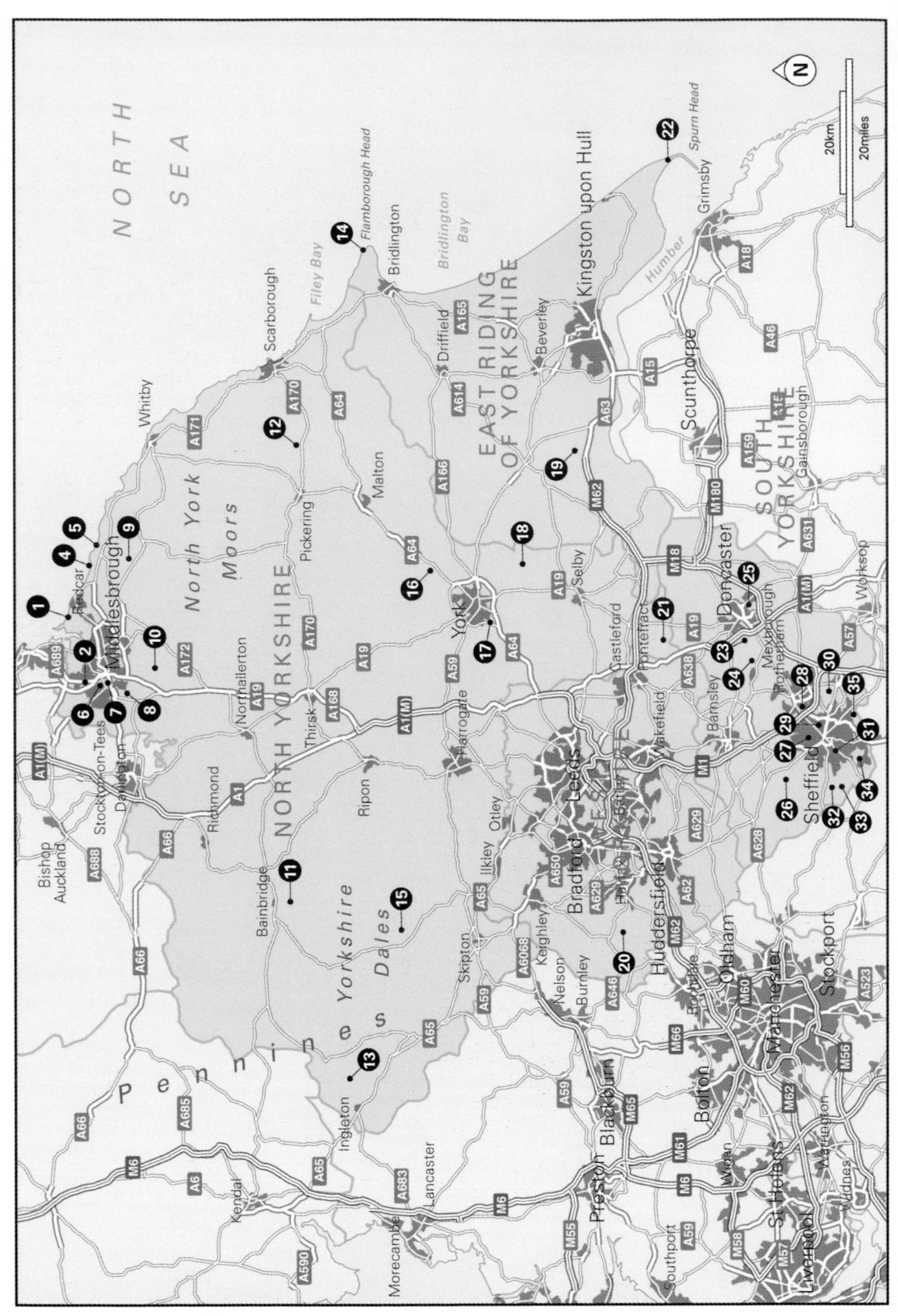
NORTH SEA
North York Moors
NORTH YORKSHIRE
EAST RIDING OF YORKSHIRE
SOUTH YORKSHIRE
Yorkshire Dales
Pennines
Whitby
Scarborough
Filey Bay
Flamborough Head
Bridlington
Bridlington Bay
Driffield
Beverley
Kingston upon Hull
Humber
Spurn Head
Grimsby
Scunthorpe
Gainsborough
Redcar
Middlesbrough
Stockton-on-Tees
Darlington
Bishop Auckland
Northallerton
Richmond
Thirsk
Pickering
Malton
York
Selby
Ripon
Harrogate
Bainbridge
Ilkley
Otley
Skipton
Ingleton
Leeds
Bradford
Keighley
Halifax
Huddersfield
Wakefield
Castleford
Pontefract
Doncaster
Barnsley
Mexborough
Rotherham
Sheffield
Worksop
Lancaster
Morecambe
Kendal
Nelson
Burnley
Blackburn
Preston
Bolton
Oldham
Manchester
Stockport
Wigan
St. Helens
Warrington
Widnes
Liverpool
Southport
20km
20miles
N

S Northumberland, Cumbria and Durham

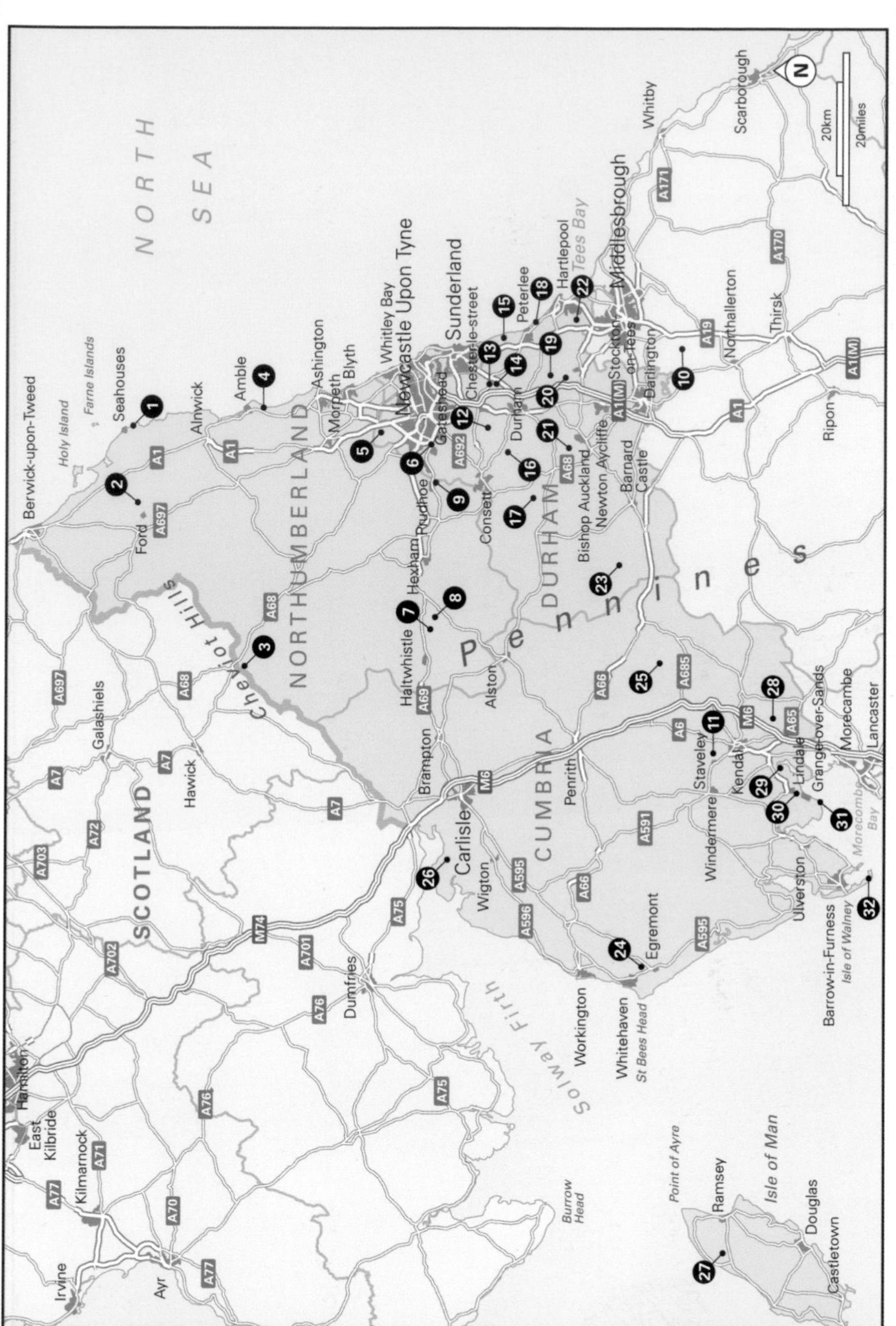

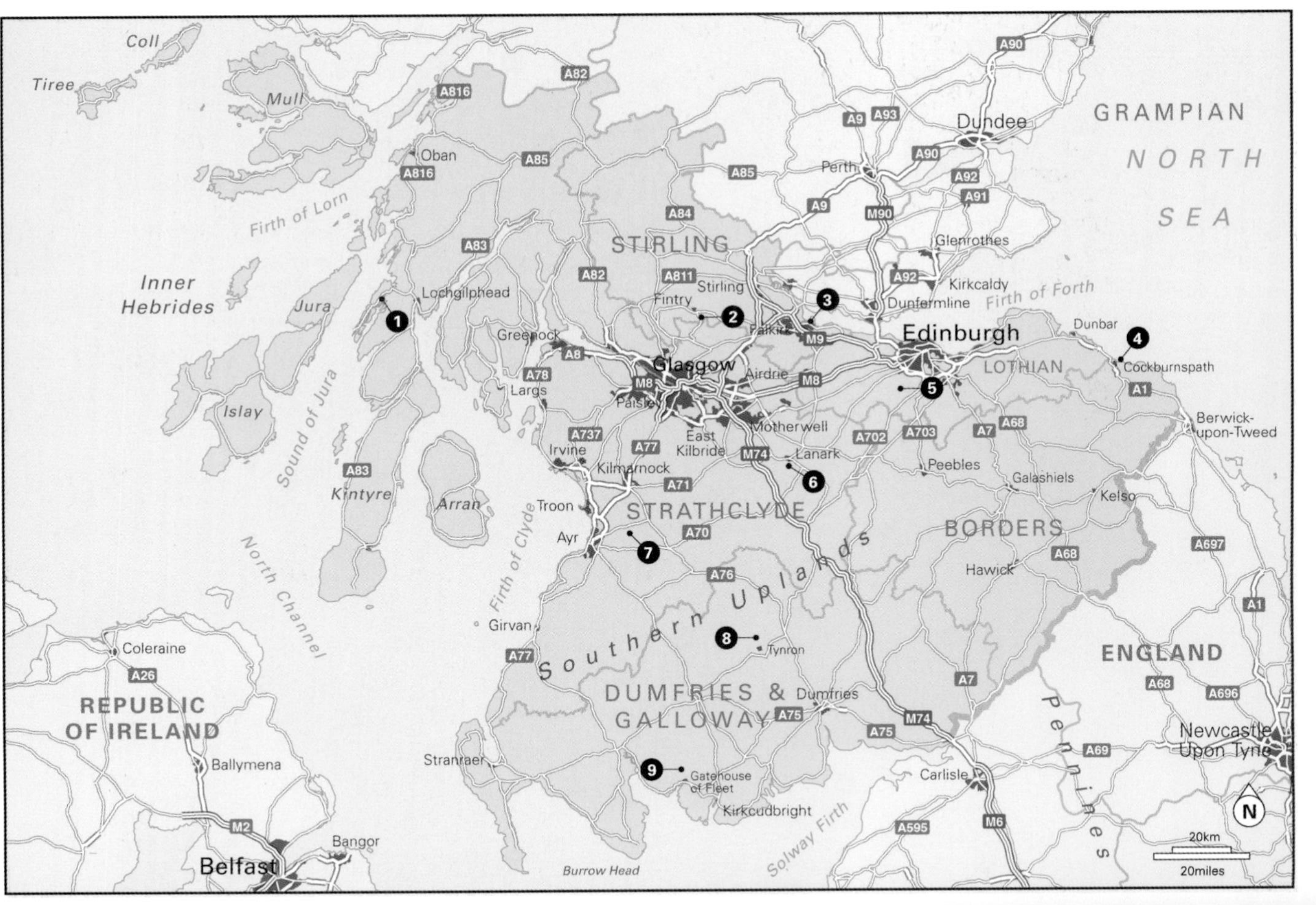
Coll
Tiree
Mull
Oban
Firth of Lorn
Inner Hebrides
Jura
Islay
Sound of Jura
Kintyre
Arran
Lochgilphead
Greenock
Largs
Glasgow
Paisley
Irvine
Kilmarnock
Troon
Ayr
Firth of Clyde
North Channel
Girvan
STIRLING
Stirling
Fintry
Falkirk
Airdrie
Motherwell
East Kilbride
Lanark
STRATHCLYDE
Southern Uplands
Tynron
DUMFRIES & GALLOWAY
Dumfries
Stranraer
Gatehouse of Fleet
Kirkcudbright
Burrow Head
Solway Firth
Perth
Dundee
Glenrothes
Kirkcaldy
Dunfermline
Firth of Forth
Edinburgh
LOTHIAN
Dunbar
Cockburnspath
Berwick-upon-Tweed
Peebles
Galashiels
Kelso
BORDERS
Hawick
GRAMPIAN
NORTH SEA
ENGLAND
Pennines
Carlisle
Newcastle Upon Tyne
Coleraine
REPUBLIC OF IRELAND
Ballymena
Belfast
Bangor
20km
20miles
N

U Northern Scotland

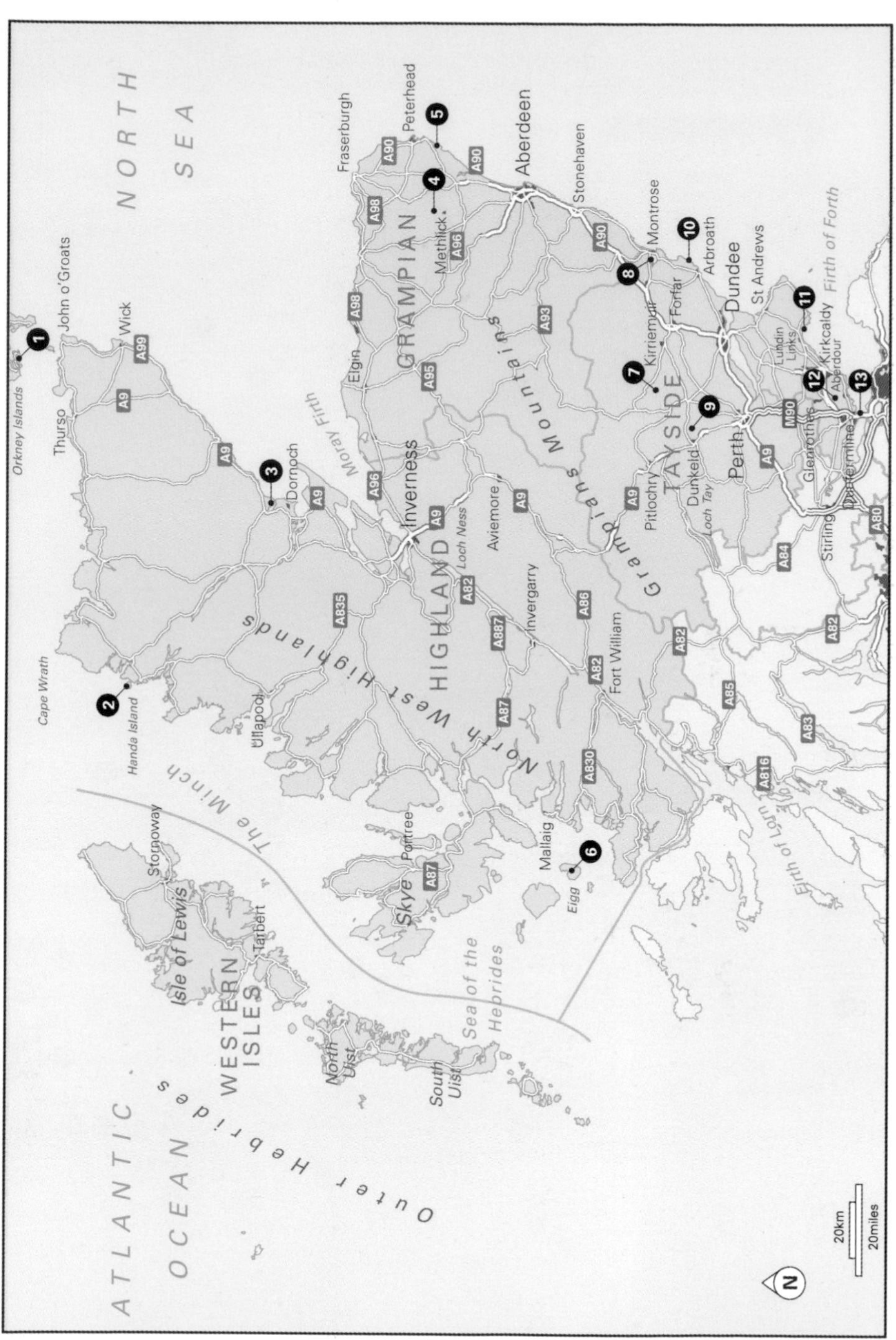

V Wales

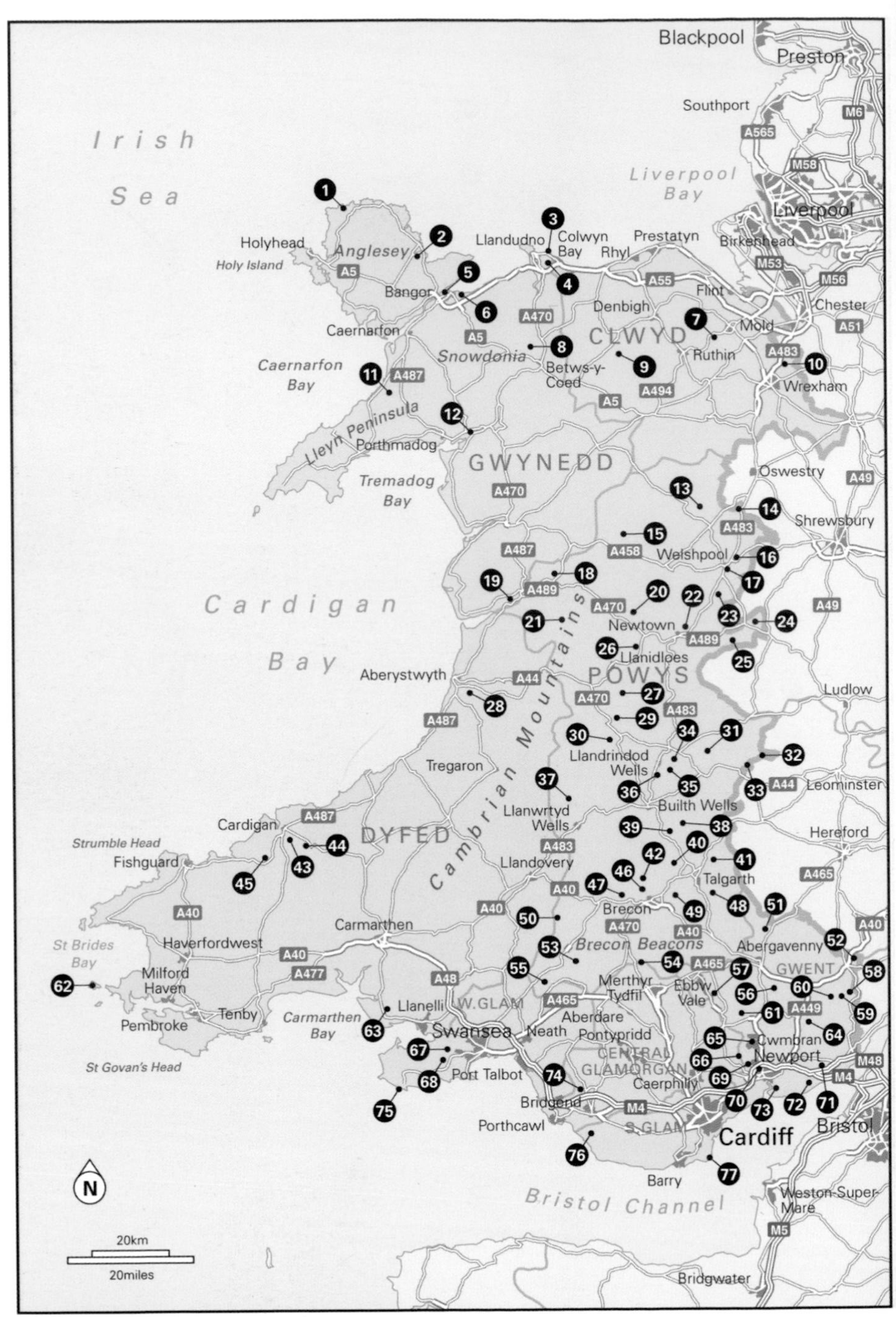

Blackpool
Preston
Southport
Irish Sea
Liverpool Bay
Liverpool
Birkenhead
Holyhead
Holy Island
Anglesey
Llandudno
Colwyn Bay
Rhyl
Prestatyn
Bangor
Flint
Chester
Denbigh
Mold
Caernarfon
CLWYD
Ruthin
Snowdonia
Betws-y-Coed
Wrexham
Caernarfon Bay
Lleyn Peninsula
Porthmadog
Tremadog Bay
GWYNEDD
Oswestry
Shrewsbury
Welshpool
Cardigan Bay
Newtown
Llanidloes
Cambrian Mountains
POWYS
Aberystwyth
Ludlow
Llandrindod Wells
Tregaron
Builth Wells
Leominster
Llanwrtyd Wells
Cardigan
DYFED
Hereford
Strumble Head
Fishguard
Llandovery
Talgarth
Brecon
Carmarthen
Brecon Beacons
Abergavenny
St Brides Bay
Haverfordwest
GWENT
Milford Haven
Merthyr Tydfil
Ebbw Vale
Llanelli
W.GLAM
Tenby
Carmarthen Bay
Aberdare
Pembroke
Swansea
Neath
Pontypridd
Cwmbran
St Govan's Head
CENTRAL GLAMORGAN
Newport
Port Talbot
Caerphilly
Bridgend
Porthcawl
S.GLAM
Cardiff
Bristol
Barry
Bristol Channel
Weston-Super-Mare
Bridgwater
N
20km
20miles

W Northern Ireland

Maps

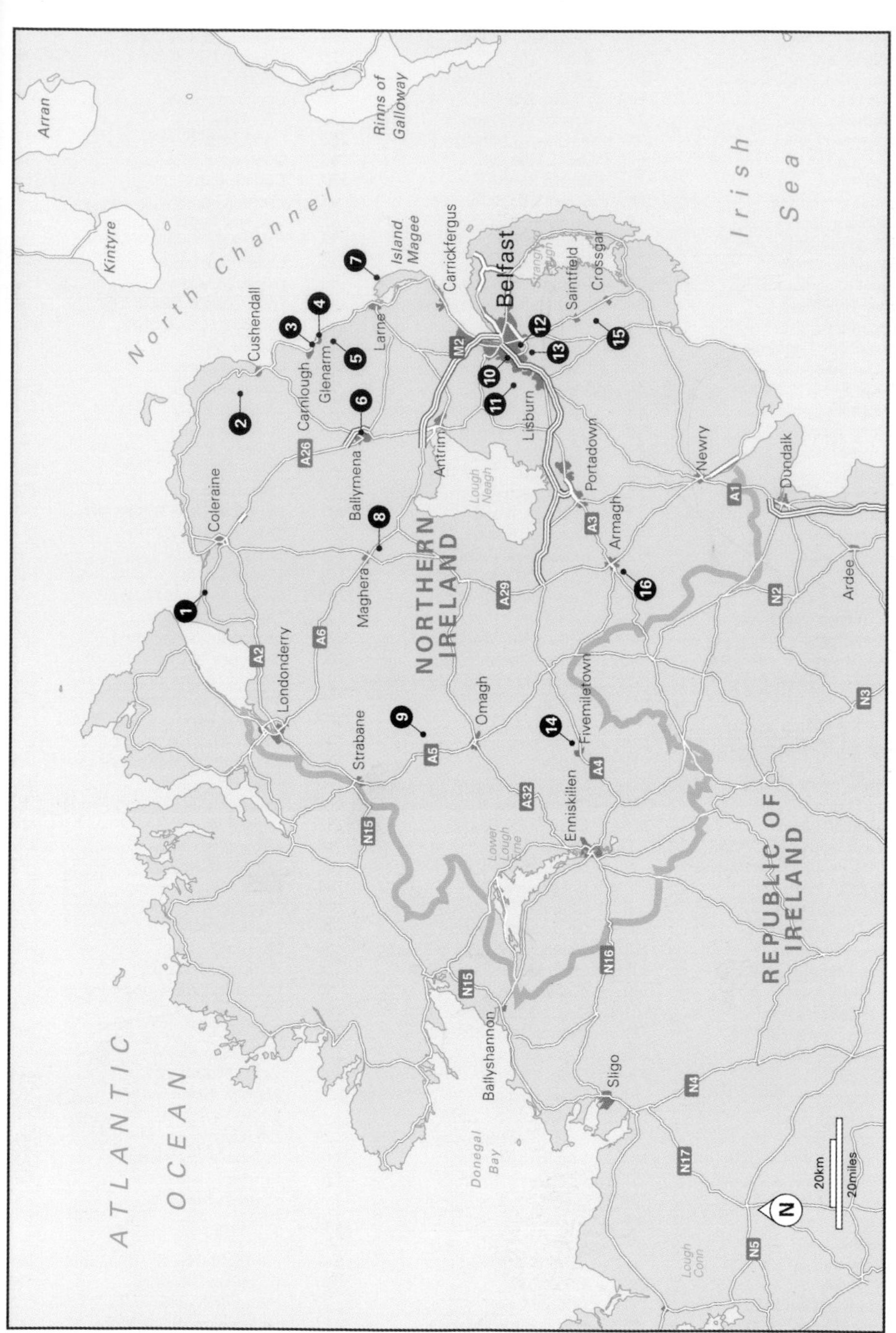

Index